with ♡
Veronica Esagui, DC

Veronica's Diary V

The Gift

1996–2003

Veronica Esagui, DC

PAPYRUS
PRESS, LLC

Oregon, USA

Copyright © 2017 by Veronica Esagui, DC

Library of Congress Control Number: 2017902347
ISBN 978-0-9826484-5-2

First Edition
Veronica Esagui, DC

Book Cover/Graphic Designer: Jean Sheldon
Illustrations: Derrick Freeland

PAPYRUS
PRESS, LLC

21860 Willamette Drive, West Linn, OR 97068

To order additional copies of this book
www.veronicaesagui.net

Printed in the United States of America

To Time
Sometimes a long haul that drags as long as infinity,
but when looking back,
we can only catch a slight glimpse of our mere existence.

To Irene Nemirovsky
An author I never met except through her enlightening writings. Thank you for showing me how to look deeper into the singularity of each thought, the transformation of each event, and the clarity of each nucleus within us.

Author's notes

The people and the stories portrayed in this book are all true as to my recollection but I have changed the names of some individuals to protect their privacy.

Contents

Illustrations

~ Chapter One ~

Patrick's Family

March 12, 1996

My plane trip to California started with a bomb scare at Amsterdam Airport Schiphol, followed by a two-hour delay. But that was not as dramatic to the senses as when halfway through the eleven-hour flight a three-year-old girl seated behind me experienced a diarrhea outbreak. I got up to look for another seat, but none was available. When I returned, I had to step over a puddle of water. The water from the bathroom closest to where I sat with five other passengers had managed to crawl under our seats like some liquefied space invader. A flight attendant holding a stack of paper towels said, "Nothing to worry about. It's just a little water." She had beautiful white teeth.

We smiled back politely as she and another attendant laid the paper towels on the outside of the bathroom door and on the floor next to our aisle. Seated in our narrow seats and buckled like a bunch of caged chickens on the way to the slaughterhouse, way, way up in the clouds with nothing to hold us but a leaky airplane; it could be worse. *Stop it,* I told myself. *All this means is the little girl lost control of her bowels and the toilet is overdue for a plumbing job. As long as the plane doesn't drop out of the sky, what's your problem?*

It was eight thirty in the evening when I sighted the beaming sparkles of the jeweled lights below. San Francisco welcomed us with open arms as we carefully landed like an eagle efficiently approaching her nest, eager to feed her wide openmouthed eaglets. When flying on a Portuguese airline, the Portuguese like to applaud enthusiastically or make the cross when landing safely, sometimes both. I was not in a Portuguese airline but being Portuguese, I didn't want to break the tradition. The young woman next to me gave me a look that said, "Are you for real?" Her lips were moving but I could not hear a word. As usual, just before landing, I temporarily lost whatever hearing I had left. I assumed she was asking me why I was clapping like a seal. I managed to put on a polite grin, but likely came across as a painful grimace, since both my eardrums felt like they were about to burst from the pressure as we descended. I remained seated after everyone disembarked. A flight attendant came over and said something while pointing to the exit. Most likely she was telling me I had to leave so that's what I did.

After going through customs, I stood facing the revolving airport door with all my traveling gear: my backpack, under my left arm a Turkish broom—my only souvenir after traveling through sixteen countries, my upright rolling luggage, and my rickety rolling cart with a stack of thick chiropractic and medical books tied onto it with a rope.

Less than two weeks ago, after our three long months abroad, Patrick had died in Austria during our honeymoon. The hacking coughing attacks I had been experiencing for over a month and gotten worse since Patrick had been taken to the hospital in Salzburg, Austria, had subsided while in the plane, but now they were back in full force. People going by gave me a cautious look and then steered away. I could not blame them. I must have looked pretty pathetic, bent forward under the weight of my backpack like a turtle, holding on to my chest with both hands while coughing out phlegm into some of the Turkish paper napkins, I still had. Patrick and I had bought them from a street vendor while in Istanbul, when we both came down with what seemed to be the flu. But except for dealing with the chest pain I was not worried; the x-rays taken at the hospital in Salzburg had been negative for tuberculosis. After what I had gone through in the last three months married to Patrick, coughing and looking sickly was the least of my worries. *This is not the time for me to dwell in the past,* I reminded myself. *I'm home now, so get with it.*

I knew I was back in the United States because that was my destination, but an alien awareness had taken over my senses. There was no one waiting for me. No Welcome Wagon, nothing to endorse my mere existence except for the throbbing pain throughout my body, providing me with an odd but explainable amount of pleasure. *I am alive, I am alive!* I repeated it in my mind over and over again until it dissipated when I pushed away all preceding recollections by going blank. Holding on to my belongings like a hoarder, I walked through the revolving door and stood on the outside pavement staring at the sky's doomlike shadows. I took in a deep breath. It wasn't cold for a winter's night. There wasn't even a breeze, only the movement of the cars driving by. Some stopped to let out passengers followed by long goodbyes. Others picked up passengers which only involved short hellos followed by a quick departure. Thick raindrops began to fall on the pavement hammering down like a child's two fingers on a keyboard for the first lesson. Then the sounds of the teacher took over demonstrating to her pupil the steady beat of each note growing in a crescendo speed as the skies opened for the grand finale. A sudden gush of wind ran though me. I retreated back into the airport building to hide in its warm womb and stood still against a wall. Patrick was no longer there to guide me. After following him through Europe like a puppet on a string, I felt his absence. *Oh my God, I can't think. I'm so tired! Where do I go from here? How do I get home?* I expected an answer. I tailed after some passengers who seemed to know where they were going, but once around the corner they all went in different directions. After asking a few people how to get to Hayward, I gave up. My hearing was still non-functional. I sat on the floor pinching my nose and pushing hard to unclog my ears. A chubby security cop approached and I could tell by his gestures he wanted to know if I needed help. "Sorry, but I'm deaf," I said. He stared at me so I pointed at my ears and shouted, "I'm deaf. Can you talk loud and tell me where I can take the BART?"

I must have looked like a sorry sight because he extended his hand to help me stand and said something while pointing to an escalator.

"Yes, of course, thank you officer," I yelled. I slipped my backpack over both shoulders, the Turkish broom under my left arm, and pulling the luggage and the rolling cart, I made it down the escalator.

Get some change, said the voice in my head.
I did.
Get into the train.
I did.
Can't you see that you're in the wrong train?
"I'm sorry!"
Get out at the next stop.
"Okay I'll do that."
Wait! Don't forget your darn Turkish broom.
"I would die! I would simply die if I lost my broom." I turned around and thanked an old man that handed me the broom I had left on the seat. I wanted to cry but nothing floated out of my tear ducts.

Veronica, you're almost home.
"Really?" I mumbled. I stepped into the next train.
What's the matter with you?
"I don't know. I don't know what's wrong with me," I said aloud, and was surprised to hear my voice. Two young men seated across from me stared. "Can you tell me when we arrive at Hayward?" I asked them.

It was eleven thirty at night when I found myself at the Hayward BART Station. Even though Nancy, my sister-in-law, had instructed me to call her as soon as I arrived, I didn't have the heart to call her to come all the way from Sacramento to pick me up in the middle of the night. From my backpack, I took out my mini list of phone numbers. Below Nancy's number were Diane and Dexter, my schoolmates, who lived in Hayward. Since Dexter was my ex-boyfriend I decided to call Diane instead. I was about to hang-up when I heard her sleepy voice. I did what everyone does when they wake someone and are too embarrassed to admit they should have known better.

"Hi Diane. I hope I didn't wake you."

"Who is this?"

"It's me, Veronica, from school. Remember?"

"Oh, my God! Veronica?"

"Yes, it's me."

"I don't understand, it sounds like you, but… we were told at school you had died with Patrick."

"No, I'm alive, only Patrick died."

"Oh, my God. I can't believe it. I'm so happy to hear your voice. Where are you?" I heard her crying.

"I'm here in Hayward at the BART station and I have no place to go. I need your help. Can I stay with you until the morning when my sister–in-law will come to pick me up?"

"I'll be right over."

I used the time to call Nancy to let her know I had a place to stay for the night. In less than ten minutes Diane arrived in her car. She was in her pajamas and robe. Everyone at Life West Chiropractic College had been told I had died with Patrick while honeymooning in Europe. She had prayed along with the other students in my class, and they had even observed a minute of silence for us.

Diane made a bed for me in her living room couch. I had so much to tell her; I couldn't shut up. It was three thirty in the morning when I lost my voice. I could detect a sign of relief on Diane's face as she went into her bedroom to sleep. I lay down on her couch and stared at the ceiling. I was wide-awake listening to the ongoing tune in my head playing non-stop since I had arrived in Amsterdam the preceding week. "I'm never going to dance again, lalalalalalalala I should have known better than lalalalala I'm never gonna dance again the way I danced with you lalala."

I woke up to the smell of freshly brewed coffee and Diane moving around in the kitchen.

Three hours later I was on my way to Sacramento, with Nancy and her husband Sean. Less than a month prior, Nancy's brother Patrick had been hospitalized in Salzburg, Austria, when his esophagus suddenly ruptured during dinner at a fancy restaurant. Nancy had flown from California to see her brother for the last time and to give me moral support after losing my husband. Our mutual tragedy bound us like sisters.

Nancy's parents, Bonnie and Roger, were waiting at the doorway of their mobile home. They were the first to hug me, followed by Patrick's first wife, Christina, and her children, Lauren and Paul. Patrick's brother Josh and his fiancée, Susie, cried as much as the children. They all had one thing in common—they were happy to see me and they were concerned about my health. I never felt so loved in my entire life and cried along with them.

Bonnie had lunch ready and we ate in silence except for the occasional, Would you pass the mashed potatoes? Perhaps a little more gravy? This is delicious! Another slice of roast beef, anyone? Your apple pie is the best! Afterwards, we all gathered in her living room. No one asked me any questions about what happened; they only asked if there was anything they could do. I shared with Josh and Susie my desire to know the words to the song in my head. I hummed it and Susie had heard the tune before, but was not familiar with the title or the words. She agreed with me; Patrick was trying to send me a message from beyond. She cried.

Bonnie asked me to sit next to her armchair and then leaned towards me and said in a soft tone that I interpreted as not being for anyone else to hear. "I must know, did my son change in any way for the better? Did he find peace before dying?"

"Yes, he changed for the better, with each day that went by." Out of love and respect for her I added, "He grew more and more serene and I believe he died peacefully." She kissed me on both cheeks and her tears wet my face when she held me in her arms.

At the end of the day I went home with Nancy and Sean. She sat in the back seat with me and told me funny stories about Patrick, when he was a kid. She was a good storyteller and had me laughing with her. "I only have one regret," she said. "I should not have let you go to Portugal by yourself after Patrick died. Staying in Germany by myself, while waiting to take the plane back home, were the loneliest days of my life." We hugged, crying.

When we got home, she asked if I would like to have my own privacy and sleep in the room above the garage or if I would rather she made a bed for me in her living room couch. She was my security blanket and if I could have it my way, I would keep her in my pocket and once in a while I would take her out and give her a hug. I chose the couch.

"Tomorrow we'll have lunch with Mom. She has something for you."

The next day, before we had lunch, Bonnie said, "I closed Patrick's bank account the day after you called and told me he was in the hospital and might die." She took an envelope from her apron's front pocket and held it in her hand as she spoke. "I was worried the bank would put a freeze on the money to pay for his charge cards and bills. You were only married a couple of months and I did not feel you were responsible for paying the bills he incurred before you got married. This money was your money." She handed me the envelope. "It's only right you get it back."

"That's right," said Nancy. "You put that money some-where safe. Meanwhile, don't you worry about anything, Sean and I will take care of you for as long as you need us."

My son Steve lived in New Jersey with his wife, Diane, and their two children, Jacob and Shayna, and Ralph, my eldest, was in Oregon attending Western States Chiropractic College. But I did not feel alone. Patrick had given me a very precious gift—his family.

How odd that while we were dating, Patrick told me to write down his family address and directions because I would need them someday. Even though we got married, it was as if he had a premonition about our future going in separate directions.

Patrick's body arrived from Austria that same week. His folks were busy making arrangements to have him cremated and they were organizing a memorial service for March 16, at 2 pm at the Christian Church he used to attend with Christina and their children. My son Steve could not make it because he did not have anyone to cover him at his music store, but Ralph made arrangements to get away from school for two days and was flying in.

My nights were spent mostly trying to make sense of what had happened in the last three months. To make it even worse, I had forgotten most of the words to the song playing in my head like a broken record except for the phrase, "I'll never dance again..." which kept repeating over and over and over.

I did my best to act normal in front of my family by cry-ing at the appropriate time when the occasion arose but what I really wanted to do was scream as loudly as I could and pour out of my system the emotional abuse I had endured while married to Patrick. I had to keep reminding myself, *Family and friends tend to cope well with someone crying over the loss of their loved one, but if that person turns into a screaming maniac they will not be so understanding.* The only thing holding me back from losing my mind was the thought of scaring *my* family away. I had to remain strong for them and also for my own sanity.

I could tell Bonnie was aware of her son's mental issues, but I did not feel I had the right to tell her the truth. The truth was better off buried in the darkness of my memories.

On Saturday, Nancy and Sean invited the family to their favorite Mexican restaurant. After ordering a chile relleno—stuffed green peppers with cheese—I excused myself to go to the bathroom. Seated on the toilet, I began taking account of my surroundings. The bathroom was mine, all mine! Across from me stood a small, clean, white sink and a dainty pump soap bottle. The small window to my right had the shade pulled down and was dressed with a white, handmade cotton curtain with yellow and green stripes. On my left within reaching distance was a wooden rack with magazines. I picked up one of the magazines and flipped through one of them admiring the latest styles for women. I remained seated on the toilet appreciating the clean floors and the soft colors of pink and green walls. Putting the magazine back I reached for the toilet paper, not a little square piece of toilet paper, like in some of the countries I had traveled in the last few months, but a complete roll of supple, downy paper, which I could use as much as I needed. Before wiping myself, I squeezed the toilet paper between my fingers, and brushed it on my cheek, enjoying its super soft texture. Pressing down the toilet handle, I watched the cascade flow of water. I flushed the toilet one more time, just to admire its wonderful technology. I turned the sink faucet handle to the left just enough to get the right warmth water temperature and used the perfumed soap to lather my hands. I took in a deep whiff. I became inebriated by its smell of vanilla.

I dried my hands with a paper towel from the automatic towel dispenser and stood back upon getting a flashback of the toilets with a hole in the ground in some of the countries of Europe and in the Middle East I had used while traveling with Patrick. Someone was knocking.

I opened the door to find Nancy with a line of impatient women waiting.

"Are you alright?" she asked. "I came to check on you. We were getting worried."

"My, you sure took your time in there," said the woman in the front of the line.

I blocked the door as I said passionately, "Has anybody looked inside this bathroom? I mean, taken a real good look? It's luxurious! It's the most beautiful bathroom I have ever seen! It's amazing, completely amazing!"

"Are you kidding? It's just a washroom in a Mexican restaurant!" said another woman in line.

"Yeah, what's the big deal? Where are you from, some foreign country?" said the woman in the front of the line.

Nancy came to my rescue. "She has an accent but she's an American. We just got back from a long trip overseas and some of the bathrooms there were deplorable, to say the least."

"Oh, I have been to Europe!" said another woman. "I know just what you mean. Some parts of Spain I visited, the bathrooms didn't even have toilet paper."

"I'm so glad you understand." I made room for the woman in the front of the line to go in and then announced to the others, "There's even heat in this bathroom!"

Nancy grabbed my arm and we walked to our table, where my family was patiently waiting.

That afternoon, Nancy, Bonnie, and I went to a florist to buy flowers for Patrick's memorial service. When the florist asked me how much I wanted to spend I said boldly, "What are your cheapest flowers?" Ironically, the cheapest were daisies, Patrick's favorite. I chose a small, heart-shaped wreath.

Michelle, Nancy's sister, flew in from Arizona to attend the services for her brother. When we hugged, I could not let go of her and cried shamelessly. She looked like Patrick. She was beautiful.

The church was filled with family members and friends as well as some of the congregation members. I sat in the first row with Ralph on my right side and Nancy on my left. They both held my hands. Patrick's picture stood on a long table in front of us, surrounded by several flower arrangements and wreaths. My heart-shaped daisy wreath stood to the side, on a wooden easel. I had the following written on its yellow ribbon, *"As long as you hold my hand I'm not afraid of climbing."*

It was my way of saying thank you to Patrick for saving my life. While climbing on the east side of Pamukkale Mountain in Turkey, he had reached for my hand and pulled me up just as I had lost my footing on the ice along the ridge.

I sat quietly staring at the flower arrangements wondering what happened after death. Patrick was forty-two years old, ten years younger than me. If it was true we had a soul, where did his go? Where was he? Was he still stuck in Austria, across the world where he had died? If he had a soul, was he aware of how many lives he had messed up?

"Mom, look!" Ralph pointed to my daisy wreath. I squeezed Nancy's hand and brought her attention to the daisies. An invisible force was moving the wreath back and forth as if pulling on it. One of the daisies was pulled out and then fell gently on the floor. The wreath stopped moving.

"Nancy, oh, my God, Patrick is here. He just tried giving me a daisy like he used to." Then I whispered to Ralph, "He's asking me to forgive him."

Of all the people in the church, we were the only ones that witnessed his visit.

After the service I stood, picked up the daisy and pinned it on my jacket's lapel. Patrick always gave me a little love note and a flower, usually a daisy, when he apologized for making me cry. I had no doubt in my mind he had been present at the service. He had pulled the flower from the wreath. There was life after death, after all. Maybe not life as we knew it, but definitely something kept the spirit going.

Before leaving for Oregon, Ralph promised to fly back during one of his school breaks and then we would drive back up to Oregon to spend a week together. "Mom, you'll love Oregon. It's a beautiful state." He did not have to convince me; I needed to get away and connect with nature. Ralph was not only my son, he was my best friend, and I was in dire need of a friend.

Sean was the owner of a very successful landscaping business and a craftsman of Native American flutes. What had started as a hobby had bloomed into exquisite professional instruments sold privately and at Native American specialty stores. Sleeping in their living room gave me the chance of hearing Sean play as I closed my eyes and felt surrounded by the magic of music. He stood about two or three feet away from me, playing soft melodic native tunes every night. I got a feeling he did it on purpose, to bring me peacefulness. Like the children's tale of *The Pied Piper* who played his magic pipe Sean's tunes also had a hypnotic effect as they easily transported me into a calm dream-like state.

I was being fed and nurtured by my newfound family, and with each day I felt like I was getting stronger. My lungs were healing. I no longer coughed.

Nancy and I were having lunch with Bonnie and Roger and when Roger went outside to smoke, Bonnie said, "You probably don't know this, but Patrick had a personal bank account and I feel you should go there and at least try to get the money out even though your name isn't on it."

Nancy offered to drive me to the outside teller machine. First I used the code numbers Patrick had given me for the storage place in Hayward, where we stored all our furnishings before we left on our honeymoon. When it didn't work I entered every number combination I could think of including his Social Security, his birthdate, and even the usual 1234. I took a chance and went to talk to the bank-teller.

"Excuse me, but my pin number isn't working. Can you help me?"

"No problem, honey, just enter your bank account number and then a new five-digit number here." She pointed to the small counter machine.

I could not believe she did not even ask for my identification.

I took a chance and dared the impossible. "Any chance you can tell me my balance? My husband and I just got back from vacation." I smiled.

"Let's see here." She viewed the account on her computer. "It looks like you have a total of $1,850." She smiled back.

I took all the money out except for five dollars so I wouldn't create any suspicion.

Nancy was waiting in her car and when I told her what happened she laughed. "We better get the heck out of here, before we get caught." She put the pedal to the metal, as they would say in New Jersey.

I got a phone call from my school friend Leila, in Georgia. No warning or checking ahead to make sure I was in town. She had bought a plane ticket and was arriving the next day. "I want to make sure with my own eyes that you're okay," she said.

They say if a person has one real good friend through life, they should consider themselves lucky. I was extremely lucky. Either that or I had done something awesome in my previous life and was getting payback.

Once I told Nancy about Leila coming over, she went to air out the apartment in the barn for us to share. The "barn," as she called the large building, got its name from having a barn-shaped structure but it was far from being a real barn. The bottom was used as a garage for Sean's landscaping trucks and tools and the second floor had two spacious apartments with two separate entrances. One apartment was his flute workshop; the other was a large studio bedroom with a kitchenette and a bathroom. Nancy's daughter, Susan, liked to stay there when she was home from college. The apartment was furnished with two beds and many dainty antiques including some very beautiful old quilts from Nancy's prized collection.

Leila and I had been friends since first quarter at the chiropractic college in Georgia. After my scholarship in Georgia ran out at the end of a year I moved to California to attend Life West Chiropractic University.

She had gained a little weight but otherwise she had not changed. It was good to see Leila again. She was just as wild and full of life as ever.

How I had unloaded onto Diane on the first night I arrived in the US was nothing compared to what I did to Leila. Every night I would pull my cork as if I were a champagne bottle and I exploded, crying out all my feelings of resentment and anguish to a very nurturing and almost saint-like friend. She listened and listened and not once did she tell me to shut up. By the third night, I realized that even though Leila had been a professional psychotherapist before becoming a chiropractic student, I owed her at least one night of jokes and positive thoughts. She left believing she had helped me emotionally but I was still far from being my normal self.

Leila who also used to be a food caterer before being a psychotherapist, insisted on shopping for food daily and cooking it for us. Every night there were pots and pans all over the kitchen with veggies flying everywhere, and sauces splattering in all directions. Leila made enough food to feed an army—from hors d'oeuvres to dessert. The cleaning afterwards was beyond what words could describe, but Nancy remained composed and even laughed at times over Leila's humorous and joyful attitude. But I could tell Nancy was not enjoying the shindig wholeheartedly when her usually spotless kitchen became more like a campground. I believe that when Leila left for Georgia, Nancy was quite pleased.

One morning after Nancy and I finished cleaning her inground pool to be ready for the summer ahead, we sat in the reclining chairs enjoying the sunshine. "Veronica, you don't have to go back to school," said Nancy. "Sean and I will be very happy if you stay living with us."

"I feel very fortunate to have you in my life and I thank you from all my heart for making me feel so loved, but I can't live without a purpose. I need to move forward, finish college, and get my degree in chiropractic. That was my dream before I met Patrick and once again it's starting to call me. I need to finish what I started."

She was very understanding. I knew she was not a saint, but an earth angel, definitely.

The following Monday I left Sacramento and drove to Hayward in the white Nissan 300ZX that I had inherited from Patrick. Gosh how I missed my red automatic Saturn, which had been sold to pay for the honeymoon trip to Europe. I could not handle the stick shift in the Nissan. Having to constantly change gears was not my forté; it was also a real pain in the neck to park on a downward incline. Not that it was much different on an upward incline, as I found out soon enough. Either way I was guaranteed to slide into the next parked vehicle.

I went to my old bank in Hayward and deposited the twelve thousand dollars that Bonnie had given me, all in five hundred dollar denominations. That money was for one purpose only—to start my practice—and as such, it was untouchable, even sacred, until I graduated. Then, just to make sure it was still there, I checked my safe deposit box where I had stashed away the revolver I had brought with me when I moved from Georgia to California.

I had parked on an incline as there were no cars around, but when I came out of the bank, I was now sandwiched between two cars and had to ask a passerby if he could move my car out. Then I went to visit Mrs. Krum, the maintenance lady, at the apartment complex in Castro Valley where Patrick and I had lived before getting married. The rent had gone up. I would have to find another place to live. I told her she could keep the bird feeders Patrick had asked her to take care of while we were away.

Before leaving for Nancy's I took a walk through Life Chiropractic College and tried to do my best not to get emotional. I could feel the vacuum of Patrick's absence. The school no longer enveloped its arms around me. The hallways were cold and unsympathetic to my crying.

I was not ready to start classes but I signed up for the summer quarter anyway. So I would cry for a while. Like Mama used to say, *Put your right foot forward and start walking* or like Aunt Heydee would say, *Get over it!*

Donna and Cody, my old schoolmates, were walking in the hallway at the college and when they saw me, they had the same response as Diane when she heard my voice on the telephone. They already knew from Diane that I was alive, but seeing me in person was still a shocker. I reciprocated their nurturing hugs. We exchanged phone numbers and since they lived together they gave me their address and said if I came back at the end of the spring quarter, they would help me find a room to rent. "Are you okay if we tell Dexter that we saw you, and give him your phone number? He'll probably want to call you. He still loves you, you know," said Donna. Dexter had been my boyfriend before I met Patrick. He was also a chiropractic student and we knew each other back when we attended the chiropractic college in Georgia.

When I got back to Sacramento, Nancy told me Dexter had called. I called him back and we talked for an hour. Before hanging up he said, "Veronica, remember you can count on me for anything." We would always be friends; I had no doubt.

I wrote to Patrick's friend in Holland whom we had visited during our travels. I also wrote to Dio and Lydia, the two Greek doctors at Santorini Island, who let us use their summer home at no charge for over a week. And I wrote to my family in London thanking them for their hospitality. I told them all that I was sorry, but I had to let them know that Patrick had died unexpectedly while we were in Austria.

The only ones who wrote back with their condolences were my family from England.

On Saturday, my family treated me to lunch at their favorite Chinese restaurant. They took great joy eating family style, where an array of main courses was served on a rotating tray, called a "Lazy Suzy" in New Jersey. I went to the bathroom and while peeing, I got a flashback of Patrick in the hospital in Salzburg being prepped for surgery as I watched them put a catheter into his urethra. The inner pain I felt in my bladder became so real I thought I was going to pass out. I bent forward, still seated on the toilet, crying out of control.

I stood at the sink to wash my face. *Pull yourself together,* I said harshly into the mirror. *You look pathetic. How dare you ruin your health crying over someone who doesn't deserve you losing a single tear for his miserable life. Now, get out there and be thankful you are alive and home!* I splashed copious amounts of cold water onto my red eyes and then went to join the family. I sat next to Bonnie hoping her motherly instinct could not read in my face how much I had witnessed her son suffer.

The weeks went by with family outings, playing table games in the evening, telling funny stories to each other, and during quiet hours, reviewing the schoolbooks and notes I had kept from my last quarter in chiropractic college. One morning I woke up and to my surprise, the tune that used to play in my head like a broken record had stopped. But I was far from being well. A word, a thought—no matter how small or insignificant—would trigger the painful flashbacks from the past.

I learned from Nancy that Patrick had tried to stop his family from seeing Christina after the divorce, but they refused to abandon the mother of his children. Nancy also told me why Christina was so deep into debt. "She was only seventeen when she married my brother; they were both very young. But he was very possessive and very frugal. During the fourteen years they were married, he had complete control of what she could spend. When they got a divorce, she found herself free to spend what she earned, and could not help going overboard. Now she's making up for all those years."

My heart went out to Christina every time I saw her. She was a sweet, loving, kind person. When I hugged her after returning from Europe I told her, "We have something in common. We loved the same man very dearly, didn't we?"

She cried with me.

"I understand how you feel," I continued. I didn't tell her what else was on my mind. I was sure that like me, she had suffered a lot being married to the man we both loved. But now he was gone and in her mind he was a wonderful husband and father. I knew better.

Every day I had to hammer into my brain, *I must put aside the past and go forward into the future.* That trend of thought helped but it did not take away the panic of going back to college alone and away from my family in Sacramento and that my old friends and classmates had moved on.

Monday morning I drove to Hayward to meet with Donna and Cody. They had called me about an ad in the local newspaper for a room to rent in a private home on the hills of Hayward, about a fifteen minute drive from school. They felt I was better off taking care of my lodgings now instead of waiting until the summer quarter started as then I would be overwhelmed by moving and starting school.

The homeowners were in their early fifties and they lived in the house where they rented the room. Mrs. Ahmed's first name was Susan and she was an American. She was a third grade school teacher. I liked the way she smiled; she radiated an unpretentious kindness. Mr. Ahmed was business-like, but very friendly, and I felt at ease talking to him. He had a Middle Eastern accent and I thought he might be Jewish because of his dark eyes, dark hair, and olive skin. The house was a large split-level and there were four bedrooms, with three that were being rented. My room was conveniently located on the ground floor next to the kitchen. To go in the room, I would have to go into the kitchen first. It was big enough for a single bed, a small desk, and the TV and stereo equipment that I had inherited from Patrick. A large window faced a California-type garden with a lemon tree, lots of cactus plants, flower pots, and a huge built-in swimming pool. The bathroom with a shower was to be shared, and it was located next to the playroom downstairs, which was off limits to everyone. That room was where the owners relaxed and watched television. Susan told me I could plant vegetables and herbs in the garden if I so desired. I gave them a check for $1500 to cover two months' rent and signed a contract. I had two weeks to move in.

I told Mr. Ahmed that I had a large storage unit filled to capacity with Patrick's possessions and needed to have a garage sale. He said I was welcome to store everything in his spacious, almost empty, double car garage until then.

I could not have found nicer people to rent from. I only needed one piece of furniture—a twin bed. Before leaving for Sacramento, I bought a bed and made arrangements to have it delivered to my new address.

Two weeks later, I said good-bye to my family. Before I drove away, Nancy gave me two twin-size soft blankets. I promised to visit during the holidays and whenever I could get away for a weekend.

I went directly to the storage unit in Castro Valley but my car could only hold two small boxes that were filled with kitchen utensils and clothes. I was going to need a moving truck.

Ralph flew in from Oregon; it was his spring break. The timing could not have been more perfect. I rented a huge truck and with his help, we stored everything in Mr. Ahmed's garage. Some items I threw out without even showing them to Ralph. I was too embarrassed to let him see some pictures Patrick had taken of women he knew and some personal papers he had written including a detailed account of his clandestine meetings with a woman he had a relationship with while he was married to Christina. With Ralph doing most of the work we threw away Patrick's antique double desk; a humongous, heavy monstrosity that would have taken up a major part of Mr. Ahmed's garage.

I did not have much of my own; most everything had belonged to Patrick. Ralph set up the entertainment center in my bedroom and connected the speakers, tape recorders, record player, and the television. Anything technical with electrical wires was beyond my scope of knowledge. "If you have to move again and I'm not available, you can connect everything by yourself," he said. "All you have to do is match the colored tags with the matching numbers that I put on the wires and in the back of the system."

Ralph and I accomplished the impossible in a day and a half. The garage was filled to the top and Ralph and I were ready to leave for Oregon the next day. We were exhausted. Ralph was ready to sleep in a sleeping bag on the floor in my room, but Mr. Ahmed was nice enough to let him use the comfortable sofa in the playroom downstairs.

My classes would be starting July 8th but I planned to be back in California by July 1st and spend the 4th of July with my family. Afterwards, I would leave for Hayward and have a garage sale before classes started. By then I would also know more about my government student loan, and how I would be paying for my living expenses until I graduated, hopefully at the end of next year, to be exact eighteen more months to go.

Before we left for Oregon, Ralph took a slow walk around my car. "Sweet!" he said enthusiastically. "Do you mind if I drive your 300ZX to Oregon?" He emphasized the Z and the X, and then as if he was providing me a service from the goodness of his heart he added, "You can just sit back and, enjoy the ride."

"It's all yours." I gave him the key. "Just get us there safely."

Being a passenger was conducive to talking. It didn't matter that I had already poured my heart out to Diane and Leila; I was still obsessed by what happened during the three months prior to getting married to Patrick and the following three months of marriage. I also needed a priest and I needed to confess. I needed Ralph sympathy. I needed to expose my anger, my grief, and the guilt tearing up my insides. The more I expressed my feelings to Ralph the more vivid the images became. I blamed Patrick for dying. I blamed him for allowing me to love him and for making me hate him.

"In Turkey it got so bad I asked God to kill either me or Patrick because I couldn't take it anymore." I clenched my hands and then twisted them like a blood-soaked rag. Should

I tell Ralph the truth? I stared at my hands and then held them tight between my knees. In one straight breath I let it all out, "Ralph, I killed Patrick."

I knew he was paying attention but his face showed no emotion.

"I killed Patrick!" I cried out, losing all restraint.

He gave me a slightly furtive look. "You did, huh?" He took a deep sigh and shook his head.

"I was desperate. Ralph, I prayed to my mother's spirit and promised her that I would buy the pink tombstone she had asked for before she died if she became my guardian angel and helped me to get rid of him. My wish came true, so I killed him."

"Mom, you can't be serious. I doubt your mom had anything to do with your wish. God is the one that saw your situation. It was God's decision, not yours. You can wish all you want but if God does not agree, it does not happen."

I hadn't thought of it that way. It made absolute sense and only Ralph with his natural engineer common sense could have grasped the truth. I promised never to blame myself for asking for God's help if in the future I need it again. But I also made an internal thank you to Mama just in case she had been my intermediary angel.

"When you become a father," I said, "you will make a good one, because you have a lot of patience mixed with a lot of common sense."

"Thanks, Mom. I know you want grandkids, but I'm not ready yet."

We were laughing but our laughter stopped abruptly when we saw dark smoke coming up from under the hood. Lucky for us, a police car appeared out of nowhere and he called a towing company. Our car was taken to a nearby gas station, but we were told the car needed to be towed a little farther to a Nissan dealership in Redding.

Good thing Ralph had brought his camping gear along as we now had the opportunity to use it. The dealership gave us a loaner car and we drove to a campsite nearby. I had never camped before. We picked up some fast food, beer, and firewood. We sat on wood logs by a small campfire and ate hamburgers and French fries and I even joined Ralph and drank half a beer. We stayed up talking about starting a chiropractic practice together even though Ralph would probably graduate before me since I had lost two quarters. "When I was stationed in Tucson, Arizona, I loved the weather and the scenery there and I was thinking we might like to practice in Tucson," he said. "I took a trip last summer to check it out."

"I remember you telling me about it. So how was it?" I took a gulp from my beer bottle at the same time as him, and couldn't miss the Universe smiling at us from above with its glittering diamonds and the ghostly hint of time standing still, just for us.

"Tucson didn't seem to have the same appeal anymore. Maybe we should check out La Jolla, in California. I heard it's gorgeous, like living in paradise."

"Sounds better to me than Oregon, where it rains all the time."

"It doesn't rain every day," he said defensively.

There were only two snags with camping—getting up during the night to go to the bathroom while wondering if there were any wild animals prowling around, and sleeping on the hard ground. Even though the sleeping bag had a tag guaranteeing high technology thickness, I could still feel the pebbles cutting into my back, and when I lay down sideways—my favorite sleeping position—my hips ached from the lack of softness that only a real mattress can offer. But I did not complain; physical discomfort was a slight price to pay for the happiness I felt being in Ralph's company.

The next day we were back on the road after I charged my Visa $2,500 for the engine repair.

Ralph's apartment was a typical two bedroom, no frills, student hangout. His bedroom had a bed and a desk; the other bedroom was occupied by his roommate, who paid for half the rent. The living room became my temporary bedroom as it had a futon that I slept on. We didn't spend much time at home. Ralph, being the perfect host, was bent on showing me all the wonders and magic of Oregon. He took me on daily trips to Mount Hood, the seashore, the Rose Garden, and the Oregon Zoo.

"Ralph, you're right. Oregon is a beautiful state—very green and the people are very friendly, but I really don't care for the rain."

"It's not rain, Mom. It's liquid sunshine."

He made me laugh and I could see his point of view, but I was partial to *"solid"* sunshine, as in California, and could do without the *liquid* part.

One evening I expressed to Ralph that I would like to learn more about our religion and someday, even learn to read Hebrew. So before I left Oregon, Ralph surprised me with the Torah written in English, and a beginner's book on how to read Hebrew. He went over each letter of the Hebrew alphabet and said, "It's not easy, Mom, so if you forget the pronunciation, just call me."

I drove back to California as fast as I could in the hope of not being stuck on a highway all by myself, hundreds of miles away from the nearest Nissan dealership. Two hours into driving, the engine began making burping sounds and was spitting smoke, but not as profusely as before. As I left the highway, there was a Nissan dealership at the corner—I couldn't believe my good luck! I was told there was a screw missing to hold whatever it was that needed to be held together. The other dealership obviously had forgotten to put it in. I was charged $850 for the screw.

When I got back to Hayward I tried to get the $850 back from the first dealership, since they had not done the job correctly. "The screw must have fallen off and we are not responsible for it since when you picked up the car it was running fine," was their answer.

The car breaking down on the way to Oregon and then on the way to California cost me a small fortune, but it didn't matter. It didn't matter how many times I got tripped along the way, I still had my legs to stand on.

~ *Chapter Two* ~

Back to School

Summer of 1996

Nancy had encouraged me to sell everything I had inherited from Patrick and keep the money to live on, but I couldn't do it. The same way Bonnie felt I was not responsible for Patrick's bills after being married for only three months, I felt I did not deserve to keep the things that might have more meaning to his family. When I got back to Hayward, I called Josh. Patrick had left his pickup with him for the sole purpose of getting the brakes fixed. I told Josh he could keep his brother's truck and the motorcycle that Patrick had left in storage. I gave Patrick's rifles to his father, knowing he could pass them on to his grandson Paul when he got older. There were three bicycles in storage. I gave Nancy Patrick's very precious possession—his practically brand new mountain bike. If anyone could appreciate it, Nancy would, as she loved mountain biking. The other two bikes were older and were of a lesser quality so I kept them to sell at the garage sale.

I removed all the quarters from inside a large glass bottle that Patrick had been filling for many years and took all the quarters to the bank. It amounted to $525.50—enough money to keep me stacked with groceries for a long time.

It wasn't easy going through Patrick's possessions and deciding what was going to be sold, what to keep, and what should be given back to his family. Mr. Ahmed offered to buy the refrigerator in exchange for one month's rent.

I put Patrick's two Kinkade posters under my bed with the intention of giving them to his daughter, Lauren, when she got married. I kept the collection of old glass bottles Patrick had found along the train track where he used to live. I also kept all the broken glass pieces he had collected from Pebble Beach in California. I loved glass, stones, and pottery items; those were things I would keep. They made me happy. The Indian beads he had taken from the Indian graves had to be returned to the earth, but until I found the proper place to do that, I put the small plastic container with the beads inside an old purse, in the bedroom closet, away from sight.

Instead of having the garage sale before the school year started as I had planned, I opted to be with my family in Sacramento that weekend. There was plenty of time to have the garage sale once I got settled in.

While visiting, Nancy asked me if I would mind going into the woods by her house and picking some wild flowers that we would take to her mom when we visited her that afternoon. There weren't too many flowers to be found, but there was lots of greenery.

I walked into Nancy's kitchen with what I thought was going to make two nice flower arrangements.

"Oh my goodness! Veronica, you picked poison oak! Whatever you do, don't put them down. Let me get you a garbage bag, no, better yet, please go back to the woods and get rid of them."

"They're so beautiful, though. Are you sure they're poison? I'm not itching!"

"Please get rid of them and then come back. I'll help you to get washed up outside, in the garden, and no matter what, please don't tell Mom. If she finds out, she won't allow you in her house. She's highly allergic to poison oak."

I had always wanted to have a sister or a daughter but I had something even better—I had Nancy. When I got back from the woods, I stood on her patio as she sprayed me lovingly with the water hose and I used soap to wash my hands, arms, and legs. I laughed along with her as I twirled around so she would get me from every angle and then I went inside to take a real shower.

Classes started and as I had expected, I was invisible among my new classmates. I knew I was to blame; I made no attempt to connect with anyone. I went through the motions of saying hello and talking over the usual trivialities that students have in common, but my heart was not in it.

When I went into the computer lab, I took a brief look at the desk where Patrick used to sit while waiting for students who needed his assistance. Somehow I expected him to be there. School had a different feel; I no longer felt protected by the security blanket of its walls, and I missed my old classmates.

Dexter was two quarters ahead of me and so were Donna, Cody, and Diane. They were the only connection I had with my past but we weren't in the same classes anymore and as such, we didn't see each other except for the occasional hallway encounter. We were all on a very demanding, full-time schedule with very little time to socialize.

Margie, a student one year older than me, had been married to a neurosurgeon for twenty-five years, got into a bitter divorce, and even though they didn't have any children, like Leila, Margie received a substantial alimony check every month from her ex-husband. It was enough to pay for her rent, tuition, and all her personal needs, but she was far from being Leila. Margie was used to having everything her way and was very bossy. She didn't ask if she could borrow my notes, she would say, "Give me your notes, I need to go over them." I stayed away from her as much as possible.

It was probably psychosomatic, but once I began reading the Torah and practicing the sound of each letter of the Hebrew alphabet out loud just before I went to sleep, I noticed the next day that my brainpower seemed to have increased and that I was more open to learning. Whenever I got stuck, I called Ralph. He was always glad to help no matter what time I called him. I was lonely and still sad and angry, but I was doing okay.

One afternoon, Al called from New Jersey.

"Ronnie, (he still called me by my nickname) I feel very hurt that you didn't write or call me to help you when your husband died."

"I'm sorry, but you and I have been divorced for a long time. It didn't even enter my mind."

"I'm going to send you fifty dollars a month, whether you like it or not. So don't say no. Ralph told me what happened. I'm sorry you went through some hard times, Ronnie. It will make me very happy to help you, so don't say no or I'll be very upset."

I thanked him from the bottom of my heart since the expenditure of fixing my car had thrown me for a loop and the cost of living in California was much higher than in Georgia. Fifty dollars a month was more than I could ever hope for and it would definitely keep me afloat without me having to touch my savings.

"Patrick was a lucky man to have you as his wife," Al said.

"I'm the lucky one to have you as my friend. Al, if you ever get sick or need help in any way you can count on me for as long as I'm alive."

He had never done me wrong for the thirty years we had been married, and he was the father of my two sons. The downfall of our marriage had been mostly my fault; I was still growing up when we got married and inquisitively wondering like a newborn about all the wonders life had to offer.

Susan, Mr. Ahmed's wife, and I became friends. When I got home from school she would be sitting at the kitchen table, and after greeting me joyfully, she would ask about my day. I began joining her on Saturday mornings for a brisk walk to the nearby park where she liked to take her old Schnauzer. "Old Bucky is old and almost blind," she would say in her spirited, almost childlike manner. "But his snout can still detect the opposite sex. If I don't hold him tight he'll take off on me."

I rarely saw the other roommates except for Rod, who lived in the room next to mine. He was of medium height and could be handsome if he wasn't carrying a few extra pounds. He was only thirty-five, but his natural afro hair displayed a few thin patches on the very top. He attributed it to some kind of scalp fungus. I liked him because he had an amazing sense of humor, was very spiritual, and had a positive attitude about life. We usually talked in the kitchen while making dinner. Seven years prior to moving in he had owned a cheesecake company and was a "very successful entrepreneur," as he liked to call himself. "I was doing so well that I bought a large sailing yacht where I held parties on a regular basis," he said. He showed me some pictures of the boat and the people on it and confessed to having a weakness for beautiful blonde women. I did not have the courage to ask him what went wrong, why he had lost everything. I felt that if he wanted me to know, he would have told me. Except for losing his blonde "Barbie dolls," as he called his ex-girlfriends, he appeared to have accepted, for the most part, his new way of living in a rented room and working as a dispatcher for a moving company.

Jack, the roommate upstairs, possessed a dried prune-like face and his thin frame seemed to lack any body fluid, as if he had lived all his life in the desert. He wore his greasy, thinning, straight blond hair parted in the middle. He was most likely in his late fifties, but I could be wrong, since when it came to guessing someone's age I was usually way off. We were always polite to each other when we met, yet I hardly knew anything about him. One Saturday morning he saw me in the kitchen and said, "I have a doctor's appointment at the VA hospital and my car won't start. Do you mind taking me to my appointment?" I sat with him in the waiting room at the hospital when suddenly he put his arm over my shoulders, and putting his mouth to my ear said in a tone that gave me the creeps, "It feels great to have a woman like you interested in me."

I yanked his arm away and stood. "I have no idea what you are talking about. You asked for a ride …"

"Don't deny your feelings. I like you a lot too."

"I'll wait for you outside, and I'll drive you home, but afterwards we have nothing more to talk about with each other." It had taken a lot out of me to speak my mind. Confrontation of any kind made me physically sick; I could feel my stomach twisting tight inwards and my hands shaking.

The drive home was an emotional ordeal for me; Jack wasn't taking no for an answer. As soon as Mr. Ahmed came home, I told him about Jack's behavior and he said he would take care of it.

The next few days when I left my bedroom or returned from school and had to walk through the kitchen, if Jack saw me, he would turn his back on me. It was an awkward roommate situation, but at least he left me alone. Then one morning I woke up exactly at five in the morning to guttural sounds by my bedroom window. I took a peek through my shades and saw Jack practicing some sort of martial arts. With a huge backyard in which to work out, he had chosen the space next to my bedroom window. I had no question in my mind he was doing it on purpose. But I didn't complain to Mr. Ahmed because I was afraid of what Jack might do next.

I was faced with a major issue when I went to have a tooth filled. Dr. Roth's breath was ghastly. I kept my mouth open while he was poking at my tooth, but all kinds of thoughts were going through my mind. For the sake of other patients like me, he needed to know. I had to say something. But if I did, he was going to get offended, and he did have a drill in his hand. I could take the smell of sweat, but when it came to a smelly fart or bad mouth odor, I could not differentiate—they both made my stomach turn and my stomach was turning. If I puked in his face without warning him, he would be really upset that I didn't allow him to get prepared. Maybe he was not aware of his breath and he would be thankful for my tactful way of saying he needed to brush his teeth. Maybe he would be so thankful for my honesty he would not even charge me for the visit. If I was in practice and one of my patients told me I had bad breath or a piece of spinach stuck between my front teeth I would be grateful for their honesty. I pushed on his chest gently to move him away from me.

"What seems to be the problem?" he asked.

"I'm sorry, but ..." Oh dear, I had to think of something quickly and yet had to be polite. "Um, would you mind wearing a mask, please?"

"A mask?" He frowned.

"You know, one of those things surgeons wear over their mouth so they don't breathe germs into their patients while doing surgery."

"I'm not a surgeon. I'm a dentist. I don't have to wear a surgical mask."

I pointed to my mouth with my index finger and said, "Your breath is far out!"

He backed away. "Are you telling me I have bad breath?"

"Yes. Sorry, but would you mind brushing your teeth?" I waited a beat and added with what I felt was a friendly, encouraging smile, "I'll wait." I crossed my arms over my chest, so he would get the message that I really wasn't in any hurry.

"I brush my teeth every morning before coming to my office. No one has ever complained about my breath."

"I believe you brush your teeth, but maybe there's something wrong with your stomach. I'm very sorry but I have an asthma problem. Maybe it's why I'm so sensitive?"

I hoped he would be more sympathetic if he believed I had a health ailment and not be too aggressive with the drill.

He was angry and obviously holding a grudge because he left the room after he finished doing the filling. He was also hardheaded because he didn't wear a mask during the procedure. I could tell he did not want to see me again.

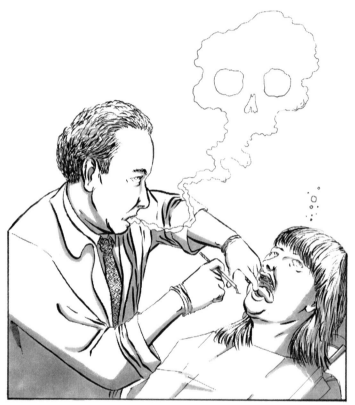

Help... I can't inhale!

When I got home from school on Monday, I had a message on my answering machine from the Jewish Community Center in Lisbon, Portugal. "Please call immediately; it's urgent." They must have called earlier in the day—an eight-hour difference meant it was too late for me to call their office. The phone rang at 3:45 in the morning. Papa had been hit by a car while crossing a street and was taken to the hospital, but he was dead upon arrival. The news of his death could not sink into my head.

I called Luisa, his caretaker in Portugal. "He was living with me," she said. "But we had an argument a few weeks ago and he moved out without telling me where he was going. I have not seen him since." She then added without emotion, "The authorities found him walking the streets and put him in a home for the elderly because he could not take care of himself. This is all I know."

I knew exactly what had happened. Crossing the street? My foot! No way! He committed suicide!

A long time ago, Papa had made his plans very clear to me. "The day someone puts me in an old folks' home, I will kill myself."

I wore my sunglasses to school. Margie saw me in the hallway and wanted to chat. I told her my father had died and that I would like to be left alone. She asked my father's age.

"Ninety-four."

"Oh, well he had a long life!"

I controlled myself from calling her an idiot and went outside to cry. So what that my father was ninety-four years old! There was no such thing as being the right age to die. How dare she say something so heartless!

Papa knew the last time we saw each other that we would never see each other again. When I came by his apartment in Lisbon to let him know I was going back to America after Patrick died, he held my face in his hands for what felt like a long time. His eyes had teared, and he looked at me the way one looks at someone for the last time. I felt it too, but I didn't share those feelings with him since there was nothing I could do to convince him to leave Portugal. It was easier to simply act like death would never come to either of us and one day I would return to Portugal to visit him once again.

I put an ad in the local newspaper and held a garage sale over the weekend. I did better than I expected. Patrick had collected a lot of fishing gear, yard and work tools, records, clothing, shoes, and books. I sold the two old bicycles for $350 each. The furniture sold quickly too, since he took good care of all his stuff. I made $3,500 even though my little jewelry box where I had my two wedding rings and a few gold trinkets disappeared. I paid what I owed on my charge card and put the rest into my checking account. I also called Al and told him to stop sending me money. The student loan paid for everything I needed and if I wasn't extravagant, I could even save some money.

Mr. Ahmed and his wife decided to have their own garage sale. According to him, all their possessions that had been in storage for twelve years had become damaged by mildew. With a garage sale they would be able to recoup some of their money before everything had to be thrown out.

Since we had become good friends, I told him about Jack's workout in front of my bedroom window at five in the morning. It paid off to complain; Jack was asked to leave at the end of the month.

The California coast reminded me of Portugal—blue skies, blue oceans, and majestic rocky cliffs with smooth, clean sandy beaches below. On weekends, if I had finished my studies by Saturday, I took Sundays off to drive to the shore. I always took a bag lunch and one of the blankets Nancy gave me. Even if it wasn't cold or windy, I liked wrapping myself in it. Meditating while staring at the ocean and breathing in the salty air was very comforting. I also spent a great deal of time thinking about life in general. I asked myself why I had always been in one bad relationship after another. What was I doing wrong? Then I recalled Ralph's words, "Mom, why do you always have to get emotionally involved? You need to learn to enjoy meeting someone without immediately getting into a serious relationship." He was right; I needed to distance myself from developing lovey-dovey feelings right away. I told myself that there is nothing wrong with being alone. Being alone is better than being with someone else and being miserable. I really like being alone; I feel very happy this way.

What a pleasant surprise to receive a check from the Internal Revenue Service! I could not understand why everyone was always griping about the IRS. I felt obliged to call and thank them for the $350 check. The woman I spoke to thanked me for thanking them and she told me they never had anyone calling to show appreciation for their thoughtfulness. Poor guys, they were only doing their job.

Jack moved out. But it seemed that if there wasn't one weirdo around, another one would take its place. Mr. Ahmed introduced me to our new tenant and roommate. I thought I was going to pass out. He looked like Patrick and his name? Patrick!

Late that evening I was in my bedroom when the front doorbell rang. I went to open the door when Patrick came running downstairs to get the pizza he had ordered. It was the wrong size. He went on a screaming fit which brought Mr. Ahmed out of his playroom downstairs where he was watching television with Susan. He got to Patrick in time to stop him from punching the pizza deliveryman. I went into my bedroom, locked the door, got into my bed, and covered myself with blankets. I did not get up during the night to go to the bathroom. I was scared to bump into Patrick in the hallway.

When I got back from school, Mr. Ahmed told me not to worry; Patrick had been asked to leave.

Good thing I had not changed my last name when I married Patrick. I was indebted to Roberta, my roommate in college. I was dating Patrick at the time and she had made me promise her that I would not change my last name when I married him or I would be sorry. She could see into the future.

The astronomic bill for Patrick's stay in the hospital in Salzburg, Austria, arrived at Nancy's address. Nancy advised me to stay cool and not do anything about it. "Maybe they'll give up if we don't answer," she said. "They don't have your name or address."

I didn't have much faith in that happening. They had found Nancy's address and sooner or later I knew they would find me.

I was proud of my technique of remaining focused in my studies when I got home. Before the quarter started I had covered my television screen with an old cactus poster. Two months had gone by and not once did I have the need to remove it. I could not wait to be done with chiropractic college. The sooner I graduated, the happier I would be. I was eating healthily, taking brisk walks in San Francisco and drives to the shore, and whenever possible, spending the weekends with my family in Sacramento.

Diane called. "I'm very concerned about you," she said. "You're physically and emotionally subluxated. You need to go see my chiropractor as soon as possible and get your spine adjusted."

I smiled about her diagnosis of my malady being a subluxation. We had learned at school that when the spine was not properly aligned and caused pressure on the nerves, it was called a subluxation. A subluxation could understandably cause several health issues but I knew better than that. What I was really suffering from was called Post-Traumatic Stress Disorder. After being married to Patrick and then being a witness to his death during our honeymoon, of course I experienced anxiety and flashbacks. Just to make her happy I made an appointment with Dr. Blaze for early the following

Saturday. The plan was to get home afterwards to study the rest of the day.

I guess I was a bit too anxious and arrived at Dr. Blaze's house a half hour earlier. I parked in her driveway and waited a few minutes before I decided to see if she was home. Perhaps she could treat me sooner. I knocked on the front door but nobody answered. The living room window by her front door had no curtain. I took a peek. The inside reminded me of my old friend Nanette's house, in New Jersey. There were newspapers, books, laundry, boxes, and fast food bags all over the place. The way her house looked on the inside took away my confidence in her healing skills. She was a hoarder. I began walking back to my car when I heard a raspy voice, "Who are you? Are you soliciting?" A woman wearing a wrinkled cotton dress with a mound of hair in dire need of brushing stood by the gate in the fence.

"I'm here to see Dr. Blaze. I'm Veronica, her eleven o'clock patient."

"Oh, I guess I can see you now," she said, waving at me to follow her into the backyard and then into the back room, which had an adjusting table and a curtain in the background, evidently covering the "dirty" side of her living room. She sat by a small desk and before asking me any questions about my health or why I was there, she wanted me to pay her a flat rate of one month of chiropractic adjustments before she would treat me. Since I had lost my confidence in her attributes but hated confrontation, I told her I had to leave immediately for another appointment across town. She charged me $45 for not canceling the appointment the day before. I felt embarrassed and gave her a check.

When I got home I called Diane and told her Dr. Blaze had been a great disappointment. She made me promise her I would keep looking for professional help.

I made an appointment with Dr. Markham, the school psychologist. Maybe if I talked with a professional shrink I could learn to let go of my grief and stop driving everyone insane listening to my stories about Patrick. I needed to forgive him so I could be at peace.

When Dr. Markham shook my hand like a wet noodle, I automatically assumed he was not qualified to help me either. Patrick always told me a man's handshake was a sign of his own security. Dr. Markham asked me to sit down and closed the door. I decided to be cooperative and gave Dr. Markham a condensed version of what went on during my honeymoon and then asked, "Can you help me to get rid of my anger?"

He got up from behind his desk and stood in front of it, about four feet from where I sat, and stared at me while leaning forward towards me as if I were a specimen under a microscope. "Are you having suicidal thoughts?" he asked.

"Quite the contrary," I said smiling. "I want to live. That's why I'm here."

"When was the last time you wished to die?" He sat at his desk and clasped his hands together under his chin as if he were contemplating making a thoughtful chess move that required his undivided attention.

"Like I said before, when I was in Turkey. But that's because I was at the end of my rope. I don't feel that way anymore."

"Are you repressing thoughts of suicide?"

"No, I don't have such thoughts. As I said, I just want to go back to having a normal life. Can you help me?"

"I can only help you if you tell me the truth. Are you contemplating killing yourself?"

He made me uncomfortable. I also wondered if he had a hearing problem. "No, I have no such contemplations. Besides I'm too chicken to take a chance and hurt myself." I gave a little grin, trying to get him to relax enough so he could give me some professional advice.

"After listening to you, I can't even begin to imagine how you made it through. You're suffering from post-traumatic syndrome and you need to start accepting your feelings of anger and understand that being depressed is perfectly normal."

I began crying. He was right. I should be depressed after my ordeal and wanting to kill myself would be more of a normal reaction. Obviously something was wrong with me. I should be suffering a lot more. I cried harder.

"I'll see you again this Friday," he said, walking to open the door for me. "How about four o'clock; is that good?"

"Yes," I cried uncontrollably. "I'll be back this Friday at four. Thank you for your help, doctor." I moved closer to give him a hug.

He backed away into the wall as if I were a vampire.

"Sorry." He put both his hands up in a defense movement. "I'm your doctor. I'm not allowed to hug patients."

Dr. Markham reminded me of Dexter, my ex-boyfriend who had serious behavioral issues with physical contact. I left crying without any control over my mixed emotions. Before I even left the building, I thought about what had just happened. I had gone into Dr. Markham's office looking forward to a spiritual recovery and instead I had come out crying my eyes out and feeling guilty for wanting to get on with life. As soon as I got home, I called his office and left a message on his answering machine canceling my next appointment.

I got a phone call a few hours later from Dr. Markham. He wanted to know why I had canceled my Friday appointment. If I were a doctor I would want to know the reason my patient was canceling. So, I told him.

"I'm sorry if I made you feel worse than when you came in," he said. "I'm just beginning my practice and I guess I have a lot to learn. I do appreciate your honesty. Will you still give me the opportunity to try helping you?"

"Dr. Markham, you did help me a lot. So much so that I no longer need any more psychology. You made me realize my happiness and future are in my own hands. So, thank you."

My schoolmate Margie was complaining about some skin tags on her neck and I offered to remove them. "Will it leave any scars?" she asked.

"Not with my method," I said confidently.

The next day I brought some thin brown sewing thread to school and we sat on the grass outside under the shade of a tree. I tied each thread around the base of each stalk to cut off its blood supply. I instructed her not to wash her neck or pull on the strings. After a week went by, she was getting impatient with the way she looked. She did look kind of bizarre with five skin tags tied with brown thread on her snow-white skin.

A week later she stopped me in the hallway and said angrily, "How long is it going to take for these ugly things to fall out?" She pointed to the skin tags that by now had turned black.

"Wow! They are definitely dying." I was proud of my work. And then I said, "Your skin tags were huge so it's going to take a little longer than usual." Seeing her frustration I added, "Use a turtleneck sweater—it will cover the tags and threads from sight and speed up the dehydrating process."

Three days later I saw her in the hallway at school and tried my best to avoid her but she called out, "Veronica, I woke up this morning and when I went to look in the mirror they were all gone! Thanks so much, and like you said, no scars!"

Tying skin tags with thin sewing thread was a primitive approach, and if anything, it didn't look too appealing while the tags dried up, but the method worked great. I used to do that to Al when we were married. He always had a few around his eyelids. I learned the technique from watching Aunt Heydee and Mama who knew many old fashioned medical procedures from their brother, a medical doctor. And what they didn't learn from him, they improvised.

Twice a week I treated myself to lunch at the school cafeteria. They made excellent veggie burgers and stir-fried concoctions of brown rice and greens, and the prices were affordable for students. The other days I brought my own lunch. I stored my frozen veggies in the student refrigerator at the cafeteria and at lunchtime, I put them in a bowl and topped it off with ramen noodles, water, and about half the included sauce pouch. Sometimes I would add fresh spinach, broccoli, or whatever I found on sale at the farmer's market. In class I always had a small plastic container with fresh fruit and nuts for snacks. When I got home I made a fresh green salad for dinner. I never fried or baked. It was either raw or steamed for maximum nutrients and I always drank the water from steaming or boiling vegetables. I made a lot of soup, too.

I joined a gym close to where I lived. I went for an hour, twice a week, including Saturday afternoons. I owed Patrick for teaching me the value of working out and how to properly use the machines.

I was going full steam with my classes, and I even added extra courses to catch up with the two quarters I had lost while married. I was focused on taking the extra classes so I could start my clinic training by September and hopefully graduate December of 1997.

The all-day classes and long hours of studying drove me into looking for a room at school where once a day, preferably during my lunch break, I could put my world on standby for a few delightful minutes of blissful sleep. A sign above a door situated at the end of the hallway just before exiting the east building read, *The Silence Room*. Until then I had always left school using the west side exit, facing the parking lot. I opened the door to *The Silence Room* slowly and allowed just my head to go forward, like a probe exploring a body cavity. The first thing to catch my eye was a male student sleeping on a long, overstuffed, brown leather couch. The room had no window and its neglected ambience was prevalent in the discolored tan walls and two ceiling lights barely lighting six small cubicles with particleboard desks and metal folding chairs. They say God helps those who help themselves and I was absolutely delighted with my finding.

The next day, as soon as I was done having lunch, I rushed to my little piece of heaven but found "my" couch already taken. I sat at one of the cubicles and waited in vain. There always seemed to be someone sleeping on the couch, but I learned that if I got to *The Silence Room* by 12:05, which was when everybody was having lunch, the couch was guaranteed to be free. Within minutes after I lay down I was fast asleep and amazingly enough I woke up refreshed within 30 minutes. Those little naps gave me the power to withstand so much brainwork. Patrick always took a nap in the front seat of his pickup after lunch. He called them power naps. I never thought I could enjoy a siesta in the middle of the day, but I had learned to appreciate its full value.

One Saturday morning while driving on Highway 80 to Sacramento, the driver of a red car began honking his horn while making angry obscene gestures at me.

Since I could not stop to ask what was wrong, I slowed down from 85 to 65 miles per hour and pushed my automatic window down.

"Your hazard lights are on!" he yelled. "Turn them off, you idiot!"

Hell if I knew which button to press. The car console on the Nissan looked more like the inside of a jet plane. Some buttons did not work, and others I saw no reason to even try. Gosh I sure missed my old automatic red Saturn. Just to get the wacko driver off my tail, I began pushing and pulling buttons hoping one of them was not the one that disconnected the moon roof. That was all I needed, for it to go flying off and cause a deadly highway accident. A few minutes later, but what felt like an eternity, the madman was still yelling and honking and then he did the inexplicable—he tried to push me off the road!

I quickly took the next exit and drove into the closest gas station. I was out of breath when I told the gas attendant about the crazy driver. "You very lucky you not get shot."

"Are you Spanish? *Habla espanol?*" I wanted to practice my Spanish at every opportunity I could get. With Portuguese being my first language, Spanish came easily to me but only practice could make it better.

"I'm from Mexico. Soy de Mexico." And he went on in Spanish, "Some of those people with road rage carry guns in their cars, to shoot drivers like you." He showed me the hazard light button and at my request, he helped me remove the moon roof.

I rode away with the top off happily singing my own made-up song as loudly as I could. I couldn't wait to see Nancy, Sean, and Bonnie and spend the day with them.

Being surrounded by my holistic chiropractic studies and listening on a daily basis to the benefits of a heathy diet in conjunction with the proper vitamins, I was inspired to do some research after hours at the school library. I wanted to learn more about the impact of vitamins in hopes they could help with my memory, slow down the aging process, improve my vision and hearing, and make my hair shiny like it used to be before I began coloring it black. I was astonished to find there were vitamins for just about anything. I made a list in order of importance: Coenzyme Q10 for reversing the aging process in the cellular level and to help with memory, Vitamin A for the eyes, Vitamin D and zinc for the hair and hearing, and Vitamin C to support the immune system.

Saturday morning I went to the local health store. I had never been to one before but expected to find a world of answers. An older couple was busy arguing behind the counter. Neither one acknowledged me when I walked in. I assumed they were husband and wife. I was disappointed they were both out of shape and wore glasses. Didn't they take vitamins? I took my time walking around the aisles when a young girl about 25 mumbled something so low I had to repeat several times, "What? What did you say?" She was asking if I needed assistance.

I bought the smallest bottle of Coenzyme Q10, to use only while studying for tests and not on an ongoing basis, because it was very costly. I also bought a bottle of vitamin A. All vitamins were expensive but I felt if I could pump up my brain and improve my eyesight, it was worth it.

I had three good friends in school, Tom from Japan who was in his mid-thirties, and Dan and Jan from Vietnam in their mid-twenties. Their names were a shortened American version of their actual names. We sat together in classes, shared notes, and soon began studying together at my house. It was a little crowded in my room but we managed. Like me, they didn't have much in common with the other students and maybe it was just our perception, but there seemed to be an invisible wall between the American students and the four of us. We talked about it once but none of us brought it up again.

To my surprise, Vitamin A made my bones ache, much like after eating chocolate. I didn't know what they had in common, but the result was the same, within two days of taking Vitamin A, I was crying from sharp debilitating pain and could hardly walk. Of course I stopped the Vitamin A intake but not chocolate, even if I suffered afterwards. I loved chocolate. Just the thought of chocolate melting in my mouth made me leave the house to go shopping for a chocolate bar. What a nasty addiction! I sympathized with drug addicts. There was no difference between them and me.

A hefty check came in the mail through the travel insurance that Patrick and I had purchased before going on our trip abroad. It took me by surprise that the insurance company sent me so much money when they had already paid for Patrick's transportation and funeral expenses.

Without a second thought, I sent the check directly to the hospital in Austria and added a letter stating, "This is all the Insurance Company is willing to pay for Patrick's bill and I'm sorry if this is all I can give you but I'm going to school on a government loan, so my finances are very basic, and I'm not able to send you any more money."

I kept my fingers crossed that they would understand my situation and leave me alone.

Autumn of 1996

Bonnie called. "Veronica, I'm making arrangements to have Patrick's ashes placed at a very nice cemetery close to our home. After checking several cemeteries, I found one that is very modern with a beautiful spacious avenue in its center and it's very well kept with trees and flowers all around the central avenue. It's a little expensive but I want the best for my son."

"That's not good, Bonnie," I was horrified. "I'm sorry but Patrick will be very upset if you put him anywhere else but in the cemetery where his grandfather is buried."

"How do you know that? Are you sure?"

"Every time we went to visit you and the family, he always took me to his favorite cemetery. He would walk around as if it were sacred ground and he stood by his grandfather's grave and would say something like, "I can't even imagine any other place better than to be buried here." Before we left for our honeymoon in Europe, he took me there once again and said, "When I die, this is the only place I will be happy, high up on the hill, surrounded by trees, and next to my grandfather."

"Oh my goodness, Veronica. I'm so happy you've told me this. I want him to be where he belongs. I'll look into it and call you back. Thank you so much for sharing his wishes with me."

Bonnie had bad news. The cemetery where Patrick would like to be buried had been classified as a historical site and they would not allow any more burials, not even ashes. She was going to hold a family meeting as to what to do next and call me back.

Patrick's burial wish came true. It was decided that we would dig a spot next to his grandfather's old tomb and then deposit Patrick's remains next to his grandfather. Nobody had to know about it, except us.

On Saturday morning, I put the little container with the Native American Indian beads in my backpack and drove to Sacramento. We all carpooled in two cars to the cemetery and some of the family members stood watching to make sure no one else was approaching. Nancy handed me the box with Patrick's ashes to empty into the hole in the ground, next to their grandfather's old tombstone and then I released the beads among his ashes and stepped away to allow the men to cover the hole. I blocked all negative thoughts and feelings and allowed Patrick to enjoy the moment by being in the cemetery of his choice. Like my father told me after he learned about Patrick's death, "Veronica, stop crying. You have no reason to cry. Your mission was to carry him until the end. It was because of you that he was able to travel to all the places he wanted to see before dying. God chose you to be the facilitator of his last wishes. You were his angel of mercy." When my father told me that, I didn't understand the meaning; I was confused. But when I dropped Patrick's ashes in the ground, I understood what Papa meant. I was still helping Patrick.

When I got home Sunday night I had a message from Dexter on my answering machine. "Call me as soon as you get in. You need to come to my apartment because I have a surprise for you worth the trip." His voice was so elated I could not say no even though it was almost midnight. When I got to his apartment he handed me a copy of a test supposedly to be given to my class the next morning. I told him no way it was going to happen at our college, but he said, "At least read it." I did and then went home. What a waste of an hour going to his place! I would have been better off staying home and studying.

The next day we had the test. It was the same test I had read the day before.

A week later, Dr. Samson, our teacher, walked abruptly into our class, slammed the door behind him, and threw a stack of papers on top of his desk. "Someone got into the office safe and made copies of last week's test." His sarcastic tone increased as his eyes looked at us like piercing arrows. "Yes, you all did supremely well in your scores, but they are worth zero!" He brought his index finger and thumb together to make a zero in the air. "Nada! That's what you get. I want you to know that anyone who answered more than eighty percent of the answers correctly gets zero credit for it. I will not put up with cheating in my class and I promise you that the next test will be a lot more difficult than this one! There will be no cheating in my class! Do you hear?"

Oh, the joy of seeing an honest-to-goodness professor! I had the urge to clap but I knew better. Instead, I looked up to him with admiration for speaking up. That was the reason I loved that school. The teachers were honorable and they cared—they were the best! I felt emotional about it and swore I was in love with Dr. Samson. But not everyone shared my feelings. About half the students got up mumbling some obscenities and started walking towards the door while one of them spoke out for the group. "How dare you accuse us of cheating? How dare you punish us for what some people in this class may have done? You have no proof of who saw the copies. We're marching out of here and we're bringing this up to the president of the college. We want justice!"

I remained seated with the rest of the class as the teacher followed the students out of the room. It was deadly quiet until twenty minutes later, when the teacher returned with the complaining group wearing a victorious look on their faces.

"I apologize if I made it sound like the whole class cheated." Dr. Samson's announced to the class. "I must be doing a great job teaching because 95% of you answered the test 100% correctly." He took a deep breath before he went on to say, "Let's go on with today's lecture and get ready for the next test at the end of this month, which by the way, you have nothing to fear—it will be only about what you have been taught in class." I loved the way he smiled.

When I got a copy of my test back, I belonged to the 5% who had missed a lot of the answers. When it came to memorizing something, it only worked for me if I understood the subject. Dr. Samson was a great lecturer but the subject was still a challenge, even after I had read the test with the answers the night before.

I got a letter from the hospital in Austria thanking me for the check I sent them. I didn't owe them any additional money for the hospital bill, and they had written off the balance. I was now debt free; thank you, God!

I had just finished doing my pecs workout at the gym by squeezing the machine handles across my chest when both forearms went prickly fiery red. The feeling went from itching to painful. I showed the rash to the gym manager who immediately said, "Our machines get cleaned all the time, and you have obviously caught it from someplace else, not here." What a bunch of sissies! Right away they thought they were going to get sued and failed to accept the responsibility that I had caught contact dermatitis in their gym.

I went to the bathroom and lathered my arms with soap and water several times. By the time I got home, the rash was gone. I began carrying a small towel to the gym and made sure I cleaned anything I had to touch. Live and learn.

Every once in a while Mr. Ahmed and his wife Susan invited me to sit with them at their kitchen table and have lunch. I felt like the three of us had developed a strong relationship.

One morning, Mr. Ahmed asked me to follow him to the backyard and said, "Because you're studying to be a doctor, I need to talk to you and see what you think. I'm very concerned about Susan. I took her to see our family doctor and he believes she's showing signs of Alzheimer's. I don't know what to do."

"She's a little forgetful, but aren't we all?"

"It's more than forgetful," he said. "Two years ago she left a pot on the stove and went shopping. As a result of the extensive fire damage, the kitchen and the bedroom you're in had to be completely rebuilt. We almost lost the house."

"I've left things on the stove; everybody does it sometime or another. My goodness, Susan is only fifty-four years old! She's younger than me. You should get a second opinion. That's my advice."

"I was called to her school where she teaches fifth graders and they told me that she's no longer able to do her job. Her mental capability is deteriorating rapidly. They were the first ones that noticed the changes and alerted me that something was wrong."

"Has she had any significant health issues in the past?" I asked.

"Meningitis, ten years ago. She almost died in the hospital; the doctors were surprised she survived."

A painful chill ran down my spine but I had to ask, "Prior to her illness, did she have any birds?"

"She did. I mean, we had a few but they died about a month or so before Susan got sick. She loved those birds."

I shared with him my own experience when Ralph, my older son, had developed meningitis as a baby after our two lovebirds died. His doctor had mentioned he might have caught spinal meningitis from the birds who might have been carriers of the dreadful disease. He had also been concerned that if Ralph survived, he might develop brain damage. Maybe that's what was happening to Susan, but they diagnosed it as Alzheimer's since she was an adult. I also mentioned some researchers who believed that cooking with aluminum pans could cause Alzheimer's, but once again, nothing was certain. I promised to talk to one of the doctors at the college even though I knew for a fact there wasn't any treatment available. Susan was in the prime of her life; I felt horrible for her. It was nothing but a slow death sentence. How could it be happening to someone so kind, so full of life? My feelings towards her were those of a sister, and I could not help crying.

Now I understood why Susan would tell me the same stories over and over again. One time she invited me to go to church with her but while she was driving, she would take both hands off the steering wheel while talking and I had to remind her to use at least one hand. After that trip, I no longer would get in the car with her. But in all fairness, she did not get lost going or coming back.

Mr. Ahmed went on, "Susan is about to lose her job as a schoolteacher. If her condition is not properly diagnosed, she'll lose financial compensation and health insurance. I have to work tomorrow. Would you be able to take her to the medical appointment? You just have to make sure the doctor, who is an independent medical examiner, states in a letter that Susan no longer can teach due to her loss of mental aptitude. Only then will she be entitled to get benefits."

The next day, I rushed home from school during my lunch hour to take Susan for her appointment. She was seated at the kitchen table with several large photo albums on the table and was holding one of them open on her lap. "We don't have to be there for another hour," she said. "Let me show you some pictures of when I was younger." I sat next to her. She put the photo album on the table between both of us and pointed to each picture and newspaper clipping covering her career as a teacher for the last twenty years. The photo albums covered her life achievements as a teacher, a frequent speaker, and an educational ambassador traveling across the US and to Japan. She was very proud of having won best teacher of the year for five consecutive years. Except for being a little dippy (and who isn't?) I found her to be an intelligent, witty person. How could her brain be dying? It was one of those devastating nightmares so many people wish they could be spared when they got older. But in her case she was still young. Maybe it was also happening to me. My goodness, I remember forgetting to turn the stove off several times years and years ago, and also driving to go somewhere and after a few blocks I had no idea where I was going. My brain was obviously still working or I would not be able to attend college, but I could not help wondering if that's how it all started. One year after another, slowly dripping like honey on a cold day, and then everything just freezes.

The trip to the doctor's office with Susan made me realize how much I hated medical doctors. The doctor asked me to come into his office where he stood as if in a hurry to get me out of there. "There's nothing physically wrong with Susan to stop her from going to work. I'm not able to give you the letter her husband wants."

"I know she can walk. She has no issues with her legs. The problem is her memory. She can't teach. Even the school staff brought it up to her husband. She goes to class but instead of teaching she plays with the fifth graders. We just need a note from you stating she cannot work in this condition so she can get some form of financial aid."

"As long as she can walk, talk, and drive, she can go to work."

I had enough with his insolence. "Isn't her brain inside her skull which is attached to her neck and the rest of her body?"

"What are you talking about?"

"You know very well what I'm talking about; her legs are moving, but her brain is not, get it?"

"Don't be a wise ass with me, or I'll have you thrown out of my office. You'd better leave."

I lowered my voice. "Sorry, I apologize. Look, she worked for twenty years as a devoted teacher and now she is unable to teach because of Alzheimer's. Your letter stating that is very important so she can have the proper health coverage. Can you please do that for her?"

"What part of no don't you understand?" He opened the door and I left but I was not leaving without making sure the five people in the waiting room heard me. "He is a pathetic, lousy insurance doctor! Independent medical examiner, yeah, right! Guess who pays him? He works for the insurance company! That's who pays for his 'independent' opinion." Susan held my hand as we walked out of the waiting room and said, "You're my friend. Thank you."

I had never seen Mr. Ahmed get so angry, "I don't understand why you could not get a letter from the doctor. Did you forget to ask? What was the problem?"

"I did ask, but he is an IME. He could care less about Susan; he works for the insurance company. That's what an IME does; they get paid to decline claims."

"I'll get a lawyer, I swear. I'll sue the hell out of the insurance company, just wait and see."

That week he threw away all their cooking pots and bought new ones.

It was late in the evening when I drove home on Sunday from Sacramento and stopped at a gas station in Hayward to get some gas. An old beat-up pickup truck was parked next to the other gas pump. I went to pay for the gas, and when I was walking back to my car, I saw two young Latino men walking around my car.

"How much you want for car?" said the oldest.

"It's not for sale. This is the only car I have."

"Give us your address and we come by and pay cash for it."

They had to think I was an idiot. There was no way I was going to give them my address. Putting aside my natural instinct which told me not to talk to them I thought, what if they are really interested and want to buy the car. I could use the money to buy myself a "real" car.

"Why don't you make an offer now?" I said.

"We follow you home and we talk about it, there."

"Here is my school phone number. Call their office if you're serious, and then we can talk."

As soon as I gave them the number I could see they were not happy. They were speaking Spanish but spoke too fast and among themselves for me to hear what they were saying.

I got into my car and made a right hand turn out of the gas station. They got into their pickup and made a right turn after me.

My very next thought to myself was, *Remain calm. Your imagination is taking over again. Make a left hand turn at the next corner and then a left again and see what happens.*

They followed me with each turn I made.

I saw the red traffic light ahead. I had heard how car thieves wait for their victims to stop at a red light to rob and kill them. *Test them! Don't stop at the red light. Go through it.*

They followed me through the red light. That was good enough for me. My heart was beating so fast I could hardly breathe. That late at night there was no traffic. I was at their mercy. *Let's see how fast this thing can go.* My foot went down, as down as it could and moving the clutch into the next gear I drove like a mad car racer. I was out of their sight within seconds. There was no way their old pickup was going to keep up with me. I made a few turns here and there just to make sure I had lost them. When I stopped in front of my house, I raced in, bumping into Rod who was coming up the stairs.

"Wow, girl, what's up? What happened?"

I was shaking all over, including my legs. "I… I believe I just escaped from being hijacked or… killed or both…" I was out of breath. I followed him to the kitchen.

"Sit down." He pointed to the kitchen chair. "I'll make you some chamomile tea. What happened?" He put some water in the kettle and turned the gas on.

I told him.

"Good thing your car was faster than theirs. They were definitely out to get you."

"I gave them my school number," I said panicking. "They know where I go to school."

He handed me his Snoopy mug with hot tea. "Here, drink this." He laughed. "You have nothing to worry about. Most likely they think you called the police by now and since you saw their faces they could not be that stupid to go looking for your car on campus." He laughed again. Rod was able to eject an exuberant yet comforting tone to his voice every time he laughed, and he did laugh about most anything. But it was never a senseless laughter. He knew how to tone it, and like a musical instrument, he used it according to the incident at hand.

I calmed down.

Marlene, a student I met at the school cafeteria, seemed to have the same interests as me. She went dancing every Friday night and wanted to know if I would like to go with her. She gave me her address and I was to pick her up at eight on Friday night.

I got dressed appropriately for an evening of fun and dancing and arrived at Marlene's place promptly at eight. Her house had no lights on. I knocked at her front door and heard her voice from inside, "The door is open Veronica, just come in."

I walked down the dark blue hallway towards a dim light coming from a room. I started to think, *This is weird, really weird. What the heck am I doing here? What if she's a wacko or even worse, a vampire?* When my mind got going, it was very fertile.

She was lying under a bunch of blankets and was propped up by pillows.

"What's wrong?" I asked. I was only being polite.

"I think I've come down with something, but I'm not sure." Her voice was a faint whisper and the sweet feeble look reminded me of a young Hollywood movie star on her deathbed, suffering from tuberculosis. She murmured, "Are you disappointed, that we can't go out tonight?"

"Oh no, I understand," I lied. "If you're not feeling well, you should stay home. I have to study anyway. Do you need anything before I leave?"

"You're leaving already? Can't you stay a little longer? We could talk."

"No, I have to go. Maybe we can go dancing another time, okay?" I left.

She must have been sicker than I realized since she didn't have the strength to get up and call to let me know she couldn't make it.

"My" couch in The Silence Room had become a pirate's treasure. Not only was it more comfortable than my bed, but I was fully energized after my nap on it, *and* it even paid me back for sleeping on it! The first time I was about to get up, I found a quarter playing peek-a-boo from the back of the middle cushion. I lifted the cushion and to my delight, I found three and a half dollars in small change. I looked around to see if there were witnesses to my crime, but it was lunch time and no one was in sight. On another day, I made a real killing. While lying on the couch for my usual nap, I slipped my hand behind the back cushion and not only found three quarters, but also a rolled-up five dollar bill. The money had to be falling off the students' pockets when they used "my" couch. Never in my whole life had I ever found money. As a kid I used to feel a certain jealousy towards my brother Max-Leão who always found at least one or two coins next to the benches in the parks we frequented. I was making up for lost time.

At midterm, Ben, a fellow student, suddenly developed an interest in harassing me. Because he was in most of my classes, I tried to ignore him by looking away, and when he sat next to me, I moved to a different seat. He was probably in his mid-forties and looked Italian with olive skin, thick dark hair, and dark eyes. I could tell he worked out, but his behavior made him ugly enough for me to hate the sight of him. When I told him to go away and leave me alone, he took my response as an invitation instead. One morning he came over to where I sat in class and bending over, whispered in my ear, "You have such beautiful breasts. Were you a topless dancer before you decided to be a chiropractic student?"

My first impulse was to quickly look at my chest, and when I did, I realized that I was just wearing an unflattering, loose T-shirt. I picked up my pencil and pointed it at him. "If you don't go away, I'll stab you with this."

"When I look at you, I can't help but get an erection!"

"You have a serious problem and I hope you die from it."

"Babe, I can satisfy you."

I put my notes and books in my backpack and walked out of the classroom to wait for the teacher to come in before I returned to my chair.

When I got home, I called my friend Diane and told her what I was going through. "I'm going to turn him in at school for sexual harassment," I told her.

"Veronica, good luck with that. It will be your word against his. You'll be wasting your time and energy."

The next day I was seated in class when Ben came over and stood next to me. "Do you know what you need?" he asked with one of his smiles that turned my stomach. I looked up, wondering what next. He winked at me. "Think about it. You know."

I needed to stop the bastard.

Shooting him would stop my career as a chiropractor. I lay in my bed that night meditating. I woke up in the morning with the solution and shared it with Diane during lunch at the cafeteria.

"You've got to be out of your mind! What if he jumps on top of you?" she said.

"I hate him so much that I believe if he did that I would cut his balls off."

I promised to keep her posted.

My plan to get rid of Ben went into effect the next day. I sat next to him for our first morning class in Neurology. "Sweet," he said stretching out the word and looking me up and down as if I was a piece of steak. "You must need it badly," he said. "But don't worry, I'll be gentle."

"Oh, no, I like it rough. The rougher the better, don't you?"

It was easy to flirt with him; all I had to do was play off his words and smile at him playfully. After the class was over he was convinced I found him irresistible. He asked me to spend the night with him. I whispered back in his ear, "How about Friday night, a cozy, romantic dinner at a fine restaurant, just the two of us, alone. And then see what happens? I bet you can come up with something, hmm?" I smiled with pure hate in my heart which of course he took as being just the opposite feeling.

Friday night I put on my tightest, sexiest dress that showed lots of cleavage. It was a very short white lacy dress that I had bought years prior but never had the chance to wear. When I came out of my bedroom, Susan and her husband were sitting in the kitchen finishing dinner.

"You must be going out on a date." Susan winked and smiled. "You look very nice."

"Thanks, Susan."

"Can I give you some advice?" she asked.

"Of course you can," I said. I loved Susan. "Your advice is always welcome."

Her husband left the kitchen and went downstairs. I guess he could tell what she was going to tell me was for women only. She wore a mischievous look in her eyes when she gave me a piece of paper and a pen. "Here, make the letter T on this paper, like this, big. On the top, here to the side write "Good," on the other side of the T write, "No Good." When you come back from your date tonight, write everything you liked about him on the Good side and on the other side, what you did not like. That will give you a good idea if you want to go out with him again."

I thanked her but I didn't tell her the purpose of the date was to get rid of him. I also wondered if perhaps she had been misdiagnosed, as what she showed me made a lot of sense.

I heard the honking of a car horn. It was Ben. As I got into his car he immediately put his hand on my thigh. I picked up his hand and put it on the steering wheel. "I'll feel a lot better if you keep both hands on the wheel so we don't have an accident. I want to enjoy our first night together with all our parts working, get it?" He smiled back at me and I went on. "I have so much to give you, Ben. This is going to be a memorable experience for both of us. Tell me more about yourself."

I had heard that if a rapist kidnaps a woman, the best thing she could do to keep herself from harm is to keep the criminal busy talking. This was my chance to try and see if the speculation was correct. It did keep me busy listening and his rude attitude helped to reinforce my opinion—he was nothing but a conceited jerk.

He yelled like a crazy nut at the other drivers, and by the time we got to the Italian restaurant, he already had told me his ex-wife was nothing but a mad bitch, and women only belonged in two places, the bedroom and the kitchen.

Living in California like so many movie stars did gave me the empowerment of being an actress, and with such a thought in mind, I maintained my "toothpaste ad smile" as we sat across from each other at the small cozy table in the Italian restaurant of his choice. While he was busy complaining to the waiter about the loud chatter from the customers at the other tables, I took the opportunity to make my already low cleavage more prominent. Aware of his weakness for breasts, I brought my chest forward and over the table. His eyes were on me, and I knew I had his complete attention. Until our meal came, I just nodded to show my complete understanding of his life story as a bodyguard and an electrician before deciding to become a chiropractor. I was waiting for the right moment to strike him down to his knees.

I took my time slurping each noodle and licking my lips afterwards. I knew I was addressing his senses when he put his fork down and after picking up my hand, he started rubbing my left index finger. "Everything about you stimulates me physically," he said.

Improvising had always been my strongest asset when taking acting classes many years prior, but when it came to remembering lines, I was a complete loser. I went on with what felt most natural. In the end I only had one goal—to scare him away badly enough that he would never approach me again. Maintaining what I felt was a sultry look I said, "I've never been with a man your age."

"How old do you think I am?"

"59?" I wanted him to feel old and decrepitated,

"I'm 54..."

"Oh, that's good. You're only two years older than me!" I gave a slightly dramatic sigh of relief and then went on. "My second husband was ten years younger and he died during our honeymoon."

"Are you pulling my leg?" He laughed loudly but did put his fork down. Ha! Finally my plan was starting to have an effect.

"No, I'm not. To be exact, he lasted exactly three months. But maybe I shouldn't tell you." I kept rolling my fork around the noodles on my plate. Come little stinkbug or maybe he liked to be called bedbug, which was probably more appropriate. Either one worked as my spider web did not discriminate against evil insects like him.

"What happened?" He was all ears. "What did he die from?"

"The honeymoon. You know, sex! Everybody in school knows what happened! Didn't you hear about it?" I was taking a huge chance that my lying was going to kick me in the face but I was willing to gamble.

"No. What happened?"

"He had a weak heart. Believe me, it was a complete surprise when he died that awful, awful night. We only had done it five times, and when I got on top of him everything was going fine until he suddenly stopped breathing." I took a deep sigh. "He just wanted to make me happy, that's all." I paused for a moment, and then went on. "I must be honest with you, Ben. I need someone that can go on *all night long*." I stretched out the words "all night long." "Do you know what I mean?" I made sure to slurp one more linguini noodle.

"You said that was your second marriage, so what happened to the first one? Did he also die?" He forced out a chuckle.

"Oh no, he's still living, in New Jersey, but I'm afraid he's not doing well. He used to be a very healthy individual when we first got married. But he's twelve years older than me and once his penis couldn't hold up, I had to ask for a divorce. I mean, what else could I do?" I looked at him as if waiting for a response and added, "In many ways you remind me of him since you also smoke." I smiled as innocently as I could, but I could see that his face was deadly serious and he was listening to me intently. Then I said, "Well, you know what happens to the extremities when you're a smoker for many, many years. By the way, I mean, you don't have to tell me, but are you starting to have some problems, too?" I didn't give him time to answer. "We settled our differences with a divorce. He's looking forward for me to get married again so he can stop paying me a sizable alimony every month."

"How much money does he send you every month?" He seemed genuinely interested.

"Let's see." I shrugged my shoulders and kept them up as if my head needed support to think the question through. "I don't really keep track, you know." I let my shoulders down quickly and giggled long enough to show him how airheaded I was about money. "He pays for my school tuition and all my living expenses, and..." I raised my shoulders again and added earnestly, "anything I want, I simply charge it. He takes care of the extras that way. This will go on until I get married again, hopefully very soon." I pouted my lips with a fake little smile and blinked my eyelids at him several times, as if saying, how would you like to be my man?

He had stopped looking at my breasts. When we left the restaurant he drove me directly home saying he was a bit tired after a long week of tests in school. He wasn't the least interested in a hug when I said, "Good night, Ben. I had a great time." He remained seated; I closed the car door and ran into the house. Ha, I had gotten rid of him for good!

When I got in, I grabbed the piece of paper Susan had left on the kitchen table and just for the fun of it, I wrote on the good side of the T, *Ben paid for dinner,* and then I called Diane. She was still awake waiting for me to tell her everything.

Harassment payback

Leila called me one evening with some very good news about a very bad instructor we had. Our old teacher at the college in Georgia, Dr. Frickenson, was going to jail for lying about his credentials. The cops came into his classroom and handcuffed him right in front of the whole class. I bet the students were exhilarated. He was neither a medical doctor nor a lawyer. He was a crooked man with a vicious attitude and I was very happy to hear they got him. There was justice after all.

Ben had not approached me since our date. He sat in the back of the room whenever we had the same class. Diane and I talked about him and what had started as a nuisance became a fun, private joke between her and me.

Marlene waved when she entered the school cafeteria and then pulled up a chair next to mine. "I'm so sorry about the other day. How about you and me go dancing this Friday night?"

"Are you sure you're up for that? Are you okay now?" I asked.

"Oh yes, I feel wonderful and can't wait to see you."

"What's the name of the dancing club we're going to? I can meet you there."

"You know, I've been there so many times, but I just can't remember the name. You know where I live; just meet me at my place at eight this Friday, okay?"

Like an idiot, I said yes. And once again I learned the true meaning of déjà vu when I got to her house. I knocked, she said, "C'mon in, the door's open," and when I reached the bedroom doorway, there she was in bed. I stood in the bedroom doorway. "You're sick, again?" I asked, controlling myself from adding a curse word or two.

"I just don't feel good enough to go out tonight," she said, putting aside a magazine she had been reading.

"So, why didn't you call?" I remained stiffly in the doorway.

"I wanted to see you." She pulled herself up on one elbow. "I just love your positive outlook on life and I thought we could spend some time together, just talking."

"Talking? Are you out of your mind? Marlene, I can't afford to catch whatever it is you keep getting. I'm sorry, but I have to go." I left frustrated and wondering if her selfish attitude had to do with being from California, even though Nancy and her family were just the opposite.

Marlene and I were just school acquaintances; we weren't even in the same classes. The next time she asked me to go out with her the answer was going to be, sorry, but I gave up on dancing.

Radiology class started promptly at seven thirty in the morning. The teacher pulled the shades down on the only window in the classroom and then turned off the lights. The idea was to make the room as dark as possible so we could get a more detailed picture of the X-ray views being flashed on the screen. Dr. Stewart's voice was mellow, soft, seductive, and within a half hour of sitting at our desks staring at the dark "mysterious" slides, most of us succumbed to a state of natural rest. An hour later the two gray metal doors opened to let in the blinding sunlight, like a lighthouse beacon shining into our dungeon.

Feeling guilty but refreshed, I followed the path to the next class across campus. Then one morning a miracle happened. One might even call it a revelation! A sleep expert came to one of our classes. After introducing himself as the Sleep Doctor, he asked, "How many of you are having a problem staying awake during classes?"

No one raised their hand. "Don't feel guilty!" The Sleep Doctor's boisterous voice matched his triumphant look of, *I know you all do.* "If you'd slept enough hours the night before, you would not be dozing off during the day. You're having problems staying awake during the day because you have sleep deprivation!"

What a reality check! The idea that our grogginess and inability to concentrate could be wiped out simply by going to sleep an hour or two earlier made perfect sense. I started going to bed at ten o'clock.

Over the weekend I bought an Andes music tape. I was in Spain with Patrick the first time I heard a street band from Peru playing Andean music. I remember how each musical note had joyfully entered my being at a time I wished to be dead, and I saw the rain as a blessing as it washed my tears away. On that rainy day, I promised myself that if I returned to the US some day and went back to my normal life, I would dance to that tune to celebrate the meaning of being alive.

As I jumped up and down in my bedroom to the music, I thanked God for everything, and was also thankful that no one lived under my room!

I got a lot more done when studying on my own, except for studying for orthopedic and neurological tests, where hands-on was a must. What started as a very promising study group in my bedroom on Saturday mornings with my colleagues, Jan and Dan from Vietnam, and Tom from Japan, soon fizzled out to just Tom and me. At first he and I were very disappointed but after studying together twice we realized we got a lot more accomplished with just the two of us. With a large group there was too much socializing. Tom was just as concerned as me when it came to passing the clinic entrance exams. Neither one of us could afford to fail. "After studying so hard all these years and investing so much financially," he said, "I would lose face with my family if I failed."

I stretched out my hand to him. "Let's shake on it. You and I are going to kick butt when we take our entrance exams."

"Kick butt?"

"Yes, that's a short descriptive American term for, when we take our entrance exams we're going to pass them with flying colors and we'll be the best doctors the world has ever seen."

He was a very quiet person but his eyes lit up and I knew he felt the same excitement I did.

On the way home from school, I stopped at a garage advertising a special on oil changes. "How can I help you?" asked the man behind the glass counter while putting out his cigarette and looking a lot like my old-time idol, James Dean. The masculine tone of his voice and the way his freshly shaved face gave out a slight hint of cucumber made my heart go into tachycardia, or in less medical terms, really turned me on. It took me by surprise since at that point in my life I thought I was done with romance. I kept my face down, trying to conceal my blushing. "I need an oil change, I mean...my car needs an oil change." I chuckled a bit awkwardly.

He chuckled back and said, "Don't worry, I know what you mean."

I wondered what it would be like to kiss him on the lips and was glad he couldn't read my mind. He looked at my key chain lying on the counter, picked it up, and said, "Interesting, why a spine?"

"I'm a chiropractic student." Then I added quickly. "Next month I'll be in a clinic working on patients. I have to treat 350 patients before I can graduate." I knew I was bragging but I felt the need to impress him.

"I could use an adjustment," he said massaging his neck with his right hand and giving me an encouraging smile.

I did not even blink. "It can be arranged." My goodness, I would be able to touch him! Then more nonchalantly I added, "By the way, I love your pen." It was only right that I should give him some kind of compliment concerning his exquisite taste.

"It's a gunmetal and walnut bolt action bullet pen," he said.

"Wow!" I was somewhat speechless with such a description.

"Very special," he said. He looked at me as if he wanted to say something more. Was he calling me special? He put the pen in his front shirt pocket where he carried a pack of cigarettes. A tag above it read, *Derrick,* manager. "If you fix my back, the pen is yours." Derrick's dark blue eyes made me melt. It was pure physical attraction and while I sat waiting to have the car serviced, I rummaged through some magazines while looking up at every opportunity to look at him attending to other customers. Once in a while we caught each other looking and smiled. It was flirting in the first degree. The idea that Derrick smoked didn't bother me, if anything it made him even sexier in a wild non-conforming James Dean way. After paying him for the oil change he said, "I'll walk you to your car." I wondered if he walked all his customers to their car. It was parked right at the entrance and there wasn't much of a walk. It crossed my mind that perhaps he felt the same way as I did. He opened the car door for me and said, "If you need anything, anything at all, I'm here every day, just call me." He remained standing in the parking lot looking in my direction as I took off.

The next morning on the way to school I drove straight to his garage. I walked into the tire showroom and before he could say anything I handed him a piece of paper and said, "I'm on my way to school." I kept my voice and demeanor as if I was rushing for time. "This is my phone number, if you call me tonight, I would love to talk to you. I believe I have something important to share with you." I ran out like a schoolgirl, waved back, and said, "Bye!"

I waited until midnight. I was going to be a zombie in the morning. I had obviously let my imagination take the best of me. He probably had spent the night laughing with his beer buddies and telling them about the crazy woman customer coming on so strong to him.

The next morning on the way to school I was going by Derrick's garage and without a single ounce of self-pride I turned into his parking lot. He must have seen me because he came out to greet me. "I'm so glad you stopped by. I couldn't call you last night. You said you had something to tell me?"

"Yes. I heard chiropractic adjustments have been proven to help people stop smoking. Some chiropractors in Florida swear by it and I would like to try it on you, that is, if you want me to; if you want to be my patient. I won't charge you anything because I'm not working at the clinic yet. I'll be doing this as a personal research project."

"If you can make me stop smoking I'd be very thankful. I've tried it several times. It's not easy to stop. I sure could use some help."

It was confirmed that I would call him at work later in the evening after I spoke with Susan or Mr. Ahmed to make sure I could use the playroom downstairs to see him. When I got home I asked Susan, and she said I could use the room as long as it didn't take more than an hour.

I called Derrick and we made a date to meet at my place at ten, Saturday morning.

Friday went like slow motion as I eagerly waited for Saturday. When Derrick knocked at our front door I was more than ready. I had all the needed paperwork on a clipboard to write down his history and the physical exam findings. Most of all I couldn't wait to be close to him. He followed me to the playroom and I pointed to the couch for him to sit down. I sat next to him. Being aware of our proximity and my heart beating loudly enough to be heard, I moved slightly away from him while holding my clipboard as a protective shield against my chest.

I cleared my throat and said, "I will need to take some information, okay? Hmm...your full name?" I wrote his name on the very top of the paper. Then, I asked his age.

"I'm thirty-eight."

Okay, so he was a lot younger than me; I wasn't going to hold that against him.

"Are you married?" Of course he was not. I only asked the question because it was part of the intake.

"Yes, I am," he answered.

Even though it felt like a bucket of ice water had just been thrown over my head, I didn't even blink. Everything I had felt towards him up to that very moment shut down, much like turning off the switch on a circuit breaker. I immediately switched gears to focus on him as a patient, since it would have been pathetic to say, "Well, since you're married, I can't help you. Good-bye and good riddance." I had stepped into a mud hole and it was up to me to get out of it gracefully. I had read his intentions wrongly, I rationalized. He was not interested in me, he liked me as a customer, and he liked me even more after he found out I might be able to help him quit smoking. It was nothing more and nothing less.

I was still far from being finished doing the orthopedic and neurological examination when Susan came into the room and gave me the signal the hour was over. Derrick said he was more than happy to return the following Saturday. I was thankful to Susan for standing next to me as Derrick gave me a hug before leaving, which I reciprocated while maintaining my dignity. Okay so he didn't wear a wedding band, but the reason was quite evident even to a fool like me; he worked with grease and couldn't take a chance of the ring sliding off his finger.

Later in the evening when Rod and I met in the kitchen, he asked me how it went with my first patient. By then I was used to confiding in Rod on just about anything, except telling him about my personal blunder. I stuck only with the facts. "Learning from books and in lab classes with other students is totally different from being with a 'real live' patient." I sighed. "I didn't even take his blood pressure; I didn't feel secure enough," I confessed.

"Girl, there's only one way to learn—practice, practice. Every day starting right now I'm at your disposal for an hour." This time he laughed in a nurturing manner. He definitely had a different laugh for every occasion. It was truly quite amazing. "Go ahead, take my blood pressure," he said pulling his sleeve up. I fumbled with the cuff and the stethoscope and had to re-take his blood pressure several times.

"This is so frustrating," I muttered. "Thanks for letting me practice on you."

"You bet, girl." His throaty merriment possessed a reassuring sound quality much like when a friend gives you a slight nudge on the arm and says, *C'mon, you can do it.* He said, "What's the secret of success in anything we do?" He brought his index finger up and down, like a teacher reprimanding a classroom. "Practice," he said. "Go ahead and say it with me." We said it in unison—practice, practice, practice.

Rod was not only my roommate, he was my best friend.

The next morning Mr. Ahmed knocked hard on my bedroom door. He scared me, with the way the arteries on his neck were popping out as his voice rose to an unrecognizably high decibel. "My wife told me about you using the room downstairs to see someone." He didn't give me a chance to tell him that I had asked Susan, since he was out of town for the weekend. "How dare you," he raged. "This is my house and you must abide by my rules. You're not permitted to bring strangers into my living quarters. If you want to have guests, they will have to visit you in your bedroom. Do you hear me?"

That meant Derrick could not return.

I stopped by Derrick's garage and told him I no longer could see him but I would look for an experienced clinician to treat him until I was licensed to treat him at the clinic. "I will not go to anyone else," he said. "Will you consider coming to my house, meeting my family, and continuing with the exam?" Gosh, I had really misunderstood his intentions. I told him I was looking forward to meeting his wife and his eight-year-old daughter.

Derrick's wife was leaving the house when I arrived. She looked like a model, young, tall, blonde, and very beautiful but far from friendly. She hardly looked at me when I said hello, and simply got in her car and drove away. Their daughter, Molly, looked a lot like Derrick with her brown hair and blue eyes. She asked me if she could carry my doctor's bag inside the house. She sat next to her dad, watching what I was doing. I was a little upset at his wife for leaving, but having his daughter there made me comfortable enough to go on with the exam. His blood pressure was way above normal but it crossed my mind that perhaps he was a little nervous causing that to happen. I checked his upper and lower reflexes with a rubber mallet and they responded well but when I used a pin to test symmetrical feeling in the arms and hands he had decreased sensory at C5 and C7 on the right side. The decreased feeling on the right side in comparison with the left side was definitely an indication of pinched nerves in the neck at the C5 and C7 levels. Because of that and the results of some of the tests I had just performed, I told him it was very important he went to the chiropractic clinic to have neck X-rays done before I began adjusting him. I would have someone from the clinic call him the next day for an appointment. When I finished putting the stethoscope into my bag, Derrick offered to give me a tour of the house. Molly followed us. He was obviously proud of his home even though when he showed me all the rooms in the house I wondered if his wife would have been that open to showing me "their" bedroom. I felt like I was invading her personal space and couldn't wait to leave. When we returned to the kitchen, Molly left. I reached for my bag from the kitchen table and Derrick grabbed me by the hand and then bringing me closer to him, he put his arms around my waist and pulled me into a long embrace. *At first I thought, Okay, this is his house and he is hugging me completely aware that his wife or his daughter can walk in on us at any time. So this means it's just a very close and warm embrace, an innocent act between two people.* Yes, it was a long thought but so was the hug which turned into his lips being too close to mine. I wiggled out of the embrace and said irrationally, "I'm very lucky to have you as a friend. You're a good person."

"I'm the one that's lucky. You're the sweetest woman I have ever met. Veronica, you make me feel alive."

"Thank you, Derrick, but I have to go." Sweet Molly came in at the perfect time, and she hugged me before I left. Molly and Derrick stood by the driveway waving good-bye.

I didn't make arrangements for someone at the clinic to call Derrick for X-rays. I didn't call him either. I knew it was over between us, but it was not official unless I never saw him again.

Derrick called Tuesday night. "Veronica, I miss you so much. I think about you every day," he said. My brain waves were traveling in different directions. I didn't know what to say. "I need to see you," he said. "Don't you feel the same way?"

I was horrified by the mere thought of a relationship with a married man. The security of being on the phone versus a face-to-face confrontation strengthened my position, and the words just came flowing out. "Derrick, I have also been thinking about you and your family. You have a beautiful wife and an awesome little girl. My happiness is to know that you and your family are happy. I can't see you anymore."

"Please don't say that. I don't want to lose you. You mean a lot to me."

"Derrick, do you love your family?"

"Yes."

"Then you must think about them, not us. I thought I could help you but I can't and I'm sorry if I gave you more hope than help."

"I have very strong feelings towards you and I can't imagine losing you."

"Derrick, I don't feel the same way. Please don't call me anymore." I hung up.

I thanked God for giving me the strength to speak up, even though I couldn't help shaking. Being assertive took a lot out of me but it had brought me back to the reality that all men were created equal. Dexter, Patrick, Derrick, Michael— their names didn't matter, they were all a bunch of losers.

My next oil change would have to be at another garage even if I had to pay full price.

The clinic entrance exams went beyond what I expected. I felt well-versed enough to work in an emergency room when it came to my diagnostic skills but there was a lot of emotional anxiety while waiting silently in the hallway facing each small examining room where we were being tested. When I saw Tom standing in front of one of the examining rooms with a serious look on his face I smiled and gave him a thumbs up. I found that when I encouraged someone else to be fearless, I was also pumping up myself. Inside the rooms, a professor and a volunteer acting like a patient awaited each student. We only had so much time to answer the questions and act upon it. When the next student came out, it was my turn to enter. In one room I was to adjust a pregnant woman, and in another, I was to diagnose the condition of someone who had been in a car collision. In another room there was a "patient" lying prone. The examiner pointed to the region of the patient's kidneys and asked me what were the names of the two small organs and what did they do? I said in Portuguese, *rins.* And then I went blank.

"What did you say?"

"Rins." I began panicking since I could not think in English.

"I'll give you one more minute to give me the correct answer." Dr. Russell had a serious look on his face.

"I'm sorry. But I'm thinking in Portuguese and all that comes to my mind is *rins.*" I wanted to cry.

"So you are Portuguese?" He cocked his head slightly to the side with a deep expression of interest. "So, what does *rins* mean in Portuguese?"

"Kidneys..."

"Got you!" he said with a big smile. "Now tell me what do the *rins* do?"

"They balance our internal environment by making hormones which help regulate blood pressure, they make red blood cells and help make bones strong, and they are also amazing filters. They filter the blood to produce urine, which is composed of wastes and extra fluid."

Gosh, how I loved the teachers at this school! They were absolutely amazing.

Except for the *rins* incident I thought I had done well. Now it was a question of waiting for the results.

"Hi, Veronica." It was Donna on the phone. "Cody and I and some other students are planning to go to Delicias, Mexico, during our winter school break and work there as volunteers at their hospital. We want to invite you to come with us."

"No. Not Delicias. Donna, I can't go." There was no way in heaven I would go to the same town and work in the same hospital that Patrick and I had been to before getting married. Just the thought of it made my chest close down so hard that breathing became difficult.

"It will do you good to face your fears and..." She took a slight pause. "We need you to help us with translation."

"I'm sorry," I said, terrified. "I just can't do it. You're asking too much from me." Nothing would make me return to Delicias ever again.

What an incredible Saturday morning. The cafeteria was covered with balloons, flowers, and lots of bright decorations. The music was upbeat. There was happiness, excitement, and lots of energy from the room that was filled to capacity with students, teachers and staff, family and friends. Ten graduates were leaving the clinic to enter the outside world as chiropractors, and nine new clinicians like me were entering the clinic for one more year before graduating. Appropriately dressed and wearing a white doctors' jacket, I stood along the back wall with some of my colleagues, waiting to have my name called. A student from a lower quarter stood next to me and hugged me. It was Mustafa.

"Is your husband here with you?" he asked.

"I'm not married."

"That's too bad. A woman like you should be married."

"Thank you." My name had just been called.

I began walking down the aisle, the bride without the groom. I needed my parents. I wanted my parents to see me and be proud of me. Why couldn't they have lived longer? Everybody was clapping as they did for everyone else. The clapping had rhythm like music. I felt alive again and did a few skipping steps along with the beat. I was sure Patrick was watching from the other world somewhere above us. He had already shown me that nothing was impossible when it came to returning from beyond. I had no doubt in my mind my parents were there, too.

I accepted my clinic ID badge with a smile. I had worked very hard for it and it felt like a medal of honor when the clinic director pinned it on my lapel. I thought about Patrick. He had lost a very precious moment of our lives. I was overwhelmed by anger and sadness.

After the ceremony, Mustafa found his way to me. "Congratulations," he said. We hugged again. The first time I met Mustafa had been a year prior when he was in first quarter. He was helping some students sell used books in the school parking lot. I remembered him because Patrick had asked me why I was talking to Mustafa when I was looking at the used books. Since Patrick and I had just started dating, I thought Patrick loved me so much that he was jealous of any man I spoke to.

In the last few months since I returned back to college, I probably had seen Mustafa three times as we hurriedly crossed paths between classes. Except for the one day when he saw me in the hallway and asked if I was okay. I told him I felt like I was coming down with a cold. He took me by the hand to the cafeteria and bought me a cup of lemon tea and added some honey to it. I had to be honest—I liked his olive skin complexion, his dark eyes and dark hair, and I especially enjoyed the way he looked at me, as if he were completely taken by my charms. He treated me with respect but in a very sexy way. I found him exquisitely attractive. He was from Morocco.

"My mother is visiting from Morocco," he said. "And she's staying with me for four months. Will you treat her, now that you're a doctor? You're the only one I trust to treat my mother."

I was moved by his confidence since we hardly saw each other except for the casual encounter in the hallway between classes. He knew nothing about me. I told him I would be honored to treat his mom. His mom would be my number one patient. Only 349 more patients to be eligible to graduate!

When I got home, I got a phone call from Leila. She had signed up with the chiropractic group going to Mexico and insisted I join her there. I gave her every excuse I could think of but she had her mind made up. "Veronica, how can you say you don't want to go? I miss you. I'll buy your airplane ticket if you can't afford it. You have to go. Just imagine, we'll be working together as chiropractors helping many people that otherwise would be without health care." She just went on and on and I did not have the heart to put a damper on her enthusiasm. Even Howard, the hugger from the college in Georgia, was joining her on this mission. I called Donna and told her of my change of plans. We were leaving for Mexico on December 15th.

I was seated at the library when Mustafa sat next to me. We did not hug. We smiled at each other. It felt natural that way, but even at my age I could feel myself blushing, probably from the sinful thoughts rapidly crossing my mind.

"Do you still want me to treat your mom?" I was hoping he had not forgotten his request.

"Yes. Her back and neck cause her a lot of pain. She could use your chiropractic skills."

"I'm leaving for Mexico at the end of this week. But when I get back I'll call you to make an appointment for her to see me at the chiropractic clinic, okay?" And I was thinking, *My goodness his eyes are so dark and mysterious. He is so sexy.*

"Are you going with your boyfriend to Mexico?" he asked.

"I don't have a boyfriend. I'm going with a group of student friends from this college."

"Maybe next time I can go with you?"

"That would be really nice." I felt my face turn red again.

There was a moment of silence.

"I would like you to meet my mother before you leave for Mexico," he said. "Can you make it tomorrow?" He gave me the directions.

Mustafa's mom only spoke Arabic. She insisted on serving the food and would not allow me to help her. I felt like the Queen of Sheba as Mustafa kept offering me small pastry delicacies filled with ground lamb meat. His mom was taller than me, looked underweight, and her complexion was pale and marked by her age of seventy-four years. "I should help her set up the table." I tried to get up from the large floor pillow, but Mustafa put his hand on my shoulder. "My mother would be very upset. Even though she suffers from constant back pain, she is used to it. When you get back from Mexico, I hope you can help her."

I promised him I would do my best. She spoke and he translated. "My mother says she admires your long dark hair, so shiny and beautiful."

"Please tell her that her hair is also very beautiful."

"My mother says your skin is flawless like that of a baby."

"Please tell her I say thank you and her skin is also very nice." I had the hardest time receiving compliments.

"My mother says you're very smart, going through school and becoming a doctor. She admires you."

I got a feeling that all those compliments were not exactly what his mother was saying and it was his excuse to say nice things to me. When he told me he was thirty-five years old I said to myself, *shit!* He is seventeen years younger than me. It's a curse, I swear! Everybody says I don't look older than thirty-five. Will I ever get old? I was not complaining. I just prayed to God that when I finally started aging I didn't suddenly wake up one morning all wrinkled.

I didn't share my age with Mustafa. It didn't feel appropriate to do that in the middle of having dinner or when he kissed my hand, or "translated" something nice to me. I would tell him how old I was when I returned from Mexico. As much as I was attracted to him, I had no intention of getting in a serious relationship with him or anyone else. I had good friends at school and that was enough for me. My freedom was very satisfying and too valuable to lose.

~ Chapter Three ~

An Affair to Forget

December 15, 1996

Donna and Cody and I flew from San Francisco to Phoenix and then to El Paso, Texas. Flying in small airplanes always affected me more than in the super large ones where supposedly the air pressure was better controlled. I yawned, blew my nose, swallowed my saliva, both sipped and gulped large amounts of water, chewed on carrots, crackers, and numerous pieces of chewing gum. I also took two Benadryl capsules before each takeoff to help with drying my sinuses. It made me sleepy for about fifteen minutes and then nausea took over. Each time the plane landed I cried from the needle sharp pain in both my ears and the agonizing deep pain of my brain swelling while trying to escape from inside my constricting skull. When we landed the second time, Donna and Cody took me under their wing and used their hands to signal me to follow them to a taxi that we shared to take us to the border and into Juarez. We all carried our own portable chiropractic adjusting tables and I was glad I had kept Patrick's table which was a lot lighter than my old one. Thank God by the time we went through customs and the border—which took over an hour—most of my hearing had returned. They asked me how much the adjusting table was worth. I had learned a lot from my last trip to Mexico and told them in my most convincing Spanish lingo, "Oh this beat-up junky old table that cost me five bucks at a garage sale? I can only hope it doesn't break down when I use it to treat at no cost, some poor patients at the hospital in Delicias."

Even though I advised Leila to do the same, later I found out she decided to be honest and told them four hundred dollars so they made her pay seventy-five dollars for "border" taxes.

I was fine until I sat in the bus to Delicias. The idea of going back to the same town where I had been with Patrick had me petrified. My friend Sara in Georgia had told me I was psychologically messed up in the head because I was addicted to making people happy. Yes, I liked being surrounded by happiness. But if I liked happiness so much, why was I in the bus to Delicias? Because Leila wanted me to go and I wanted to make *her* happy!

Donna sat next to me and asked what had really happened to Patrick. I wasn't sure I could tell her everything during the seven-hour bus drive, but I did. Well, it almost took seven hours; sometimes I stopped to cry.

It was ten at night when we arrived at Delicias. There were three taxis available to take the other eighteen chiropractic students and the three of us, plus twenty-one portable adjusting tables and the usual bit of luggage. I sat in the back on Cody's lap and managed to stick my upper torso and head between the two seats up front. In Mexico it didn't matter how many passengers chose to ride in a taxi so with three rows of passenger seats, it was basic math: if you divide twenty-one by three taxis, it equals seven passengers per taxi plus the driver. Donna gave me the name and phone number of the hotel where she and Cody were staying and I was dropped off at the hotel where Leila and Howard had made reservations.

The last time I had been in Delicias, Patrick and I had stayed at a no frills motel and I had taken for granted that it was the best they had to offer in such a small town. I was wrong. My present hotel lobby boasted the splendor of dark wood wall panels going up a large stairway lit by a huge glass chandelier giving the round lobby the look of a grand hotel in New York City. But no one at the front desk was aware of any Leila staying there. I gave the lady at the front desk the phone number Donna had given me and she was nice enough to call the other hotel. Donna came to the phone and encouraged me to leave my adjusting table at the front desk, take a taxi, and join them for dinner. There had been a serious miscommunication between her and Leila and it just happened that Leila and Howard had been at the other hotel waiting for all of us to show up for dinner.

According to the directions at the front desk, the other hotel was only three blocks from where I was. I decided to walk even though it was snowing. I didn't know it snowed in Mexico, much less in Delicias, where I had come close to having a heat stroke about a year prior. Except for the crunching of the fresh snow under my shoes, it was a quiet, silent night. There were no cars and no people and the few stores along the way were safely enclosed with steel burglar-proof doors. It was snowing but it wasn't cold. I could have walked without my coat but the guilt of being alive and the anxiety of being in a place where once I had loved some-one who turned out to be my worst nightmare took over my whole body making me shake so hard my teeth began chat-tering. I was freezing from the inside out. Being in Delicias was the worst place I could be. I started to cry. I had no tis-sues with me, not even my usual used ones for emergencies like the one I was in. Between the tears and the wind depos-iting moist, sticky snowflakes on my eyeglasses, my vision became seriously obstructed. I stopped against a building, took my glasses off, and slipped them into my coat pocket. I bent my head forward to allow my nose to drip on the ground along with my tears.

A young woman dressed in what seemed to be an over-sized fur coat must have been trailing behind me. I became aware of her when she went by and after giving me a quick stare she muttered, "Jesus Christ!" She didn't even look back. I stopped crying. "Jesus Christ, you are right!" I said out loud and with plenty of conviction. I took my gloves off and put them in my coat pocket. I stretched my arms out and turned my palms up to collect enough snow to wash my face, and then I used my gloves to wipe the snow off. I put my glasses back on and started walking at a fast pace.

At the end of the street I saw the hotel at the corner. Donna, Cody, Leila, and Howard were seated in the patio-like lobby eating and talking. Leila saw me and came running towards me and we hugged and jumped up and down and then holding hands like children, we danced briefly in the style of "Ring Around the Rosie." I loved Leila; her child-like manner was no different from mine and was one of the reasons we always got along like sisters. Howard the hugger, as he had been labeled at the college in Georgia, stood waiting patiently to greet me in his usual way. In anticipation of his precious hug I put my hand out. "Wait," I said beaming with happiness. I took off my backpack and then my coat as fast as I could and put my arms around his neck waiting for the much-needed hug. This was a different hug from what I remembered him doing in Georgia. First he hugged me in his warm, comforting way and then without letting go, he gently but firmly moved every bone on my back with some very distinct "pops." He had integrated the science of chiropractic into his hugging technique. I was impressed.

He sat next to me during dinner and kept giving me compliments about how nice I looked and how glad he was to see me again. The last time we had seen each other had been in Georgia, when he came to my apartment under the pretense of wanting to give me a massage, which was really weird since we were only school acquaintances. At the time I was glad to get him out of my apartment. Now in Delicias, years later, my feelings had not changed, I enjoyed his hug but that was as far as it went. His continuous polite praise throughout dinner and the way he stared at me like a weasel annoyed me.

When Leila and I went to the bathroom I asked, "What's with Howard? Didn't you tell me he has a girlfriend?"

"Yes, he does. He's engaged to be married and madly in love with her. All he does is talk about her all day long!"

That put me more at ease. He was being nice because we had something in common; we had been students at Life University in Georgia. But it was a small table and it was hard for me to look at him with a straight face. His extra thick eyeglasses did a serious shrinking effect on his eyes reminding me of fish eyeballs inside a pair of binoculars. It was two in the morning when we finished eating and socializing. Then I found out the reason "my" hotel did not know anyone by the name of Leila as Howard had put the reservations under his name when they arrived the night before. The bad news was that Leila and Howard had gotten the last room available and the hotel where Donna and Cody were staying was also sold out. But according to Leila their king size bed was big enough to fit six people comfortably and I was welcome to join them until something else became available. Unless I joined Leila and Howard, I had no place to sleep.

"If it's that big I have no problems sleeping with the two of you. I'm exhausted." I was not looking forward to sleeping in the lobby's chair and then in the morning having to carry my adjusting table to the hospital and work all day.

A smirk and then loud laughter came along with Cody's remark, "Hey Howard, you lucky dog, that's every man's fantasy to sleep with two women!"

His remark did not bother me. Leila was my best friend and Howard, for whom I had no physical attraction whatsoever, was engaged and in love with his fiancée.

The room was eighteen dollars a night, which meant six dollars each. It was decorated Texas style and the bed was indeed humongous. Our private bathroom was luxurious beyond words, with ceramic Roman tiles, a tub, and a large stone shower with plenty of hot water.

Leila went to take a shower. I took my pink silk pajamas out of my backpack and sat next to Howard at the foot of the bed, waiting for my turn to go next.

"Veronica, I'm so sorry about your husband dying. Will you accept my condolences?" He put his arms around me and gave me a strong, long hug. When he would not let go I figured he really was feeling sorry for me being a widow. I pulled away from him and went to stand by the bathroom door. "Thank you for the condolences, Howard," I said with a complete lack of actual thankfulness.

Leila came out wearing flowery colorful flannel pajamas and got into bed. I went in to take a well-deserved hot shower and brush my teeth. When Howard went into the bathroom, I lay in bed next to Leila. She was busy reading the Bible.

"Do you mind if I read to you aloud while Howard showers and then we all go to sleep?" she asked.

"Of course, go ahead. I'd like that."

Her monotone voice, not to mention what she was reading, made it hard for me to keep my eyes open. I would have fallen asleep if it weren't for the sound of the cold breeze coming through the cracks around the closed windowsill on my right. There was no heat in the room. I had brought the wrong pajamas with me.

Howard came out of the bathroom wearing flannel pajamas with a Scottish plaid pattern with a matching robe. Without glasses he looked like a slim Jack Lemmon. He sat on the bed, put on a pair of socks, took off his robe, and got into bed. I commented how smart he was to wear socks because my feet were freezing. "I can warm up your feet with my hands," he said. I had a premonition and said, "No, that's okay, I'll be warm soon." Leila turned out the light on her side table and said good night as I said good night and so did Howard.

Suddenly I felt one of his hands gently caressing the top of my head. It was the way a mother comforts her child to sleep and I could not resist his touch. I should have said something but part of me longed for that tenderness. I kept my eyes closed even though it was dark enough that I could not see anything anyway. *What do I do? What do I do? Leila is way off on the other side of the bed but she's in the same bed! What do I do? Is this a dream or a nightmare? I should stop him. No, I don't want him to stop.*

He took his time touching my head, face, and brushing his fingers through my hair. I did not wait too long to respond. I cuddled closer to him. I needed to be held more than ever in my life. And he was willing to do just that. Aunt Heydee, who was my mentor while I was growing up and was definitely a very wise woman had been right when she told me many, many years ago, "In the darkness of the bedroom you don't have to see your lover's face as long as he provides you with what you need." I finally understood what she meant, because Howard was definitely not my type and even though he was becoming my lover, I did not love him. He kissed my neck as if savoring a rare fruit, slowly moving his lips to the next spot not even an inch away. I had never experienced lovemaking in such way. I did my very best to reciprocate back, taking my time kissing him the same way. In the back of my mind I was hoping Leila had fallen into a deep sleep-like a coma, since there was no sound or movement coming from her side of the bed. I got closer to him. I stopped when I could not be any closer, unless I got under his skin. Our lips met.

"Sorry guys," Leila said as she got out of bed. "I believe I'm suffering from insomnia. I'm going down to the lobby if you two don't mind." She put her robe on and left the room.

We did not stop to apologize. The night was not long enough for us to get any sleep and when the alarm went off at seven we quickly got dressed to go to the hospital.

When we met with Leila at the hospital ward where we would be working, she informed us that Howard and I could have the room all to ourselves. She had made arrangements to stay in another room with another student.

Except for Leila and me, no one else spoke Spanish. Leila was from Argentina and her Spanish was impeccable. On the other hand, I at least got away with making myself understood because even though I spoke Spanish like a Portuguese and not a Spaniard or a Mexican, it was good enough to establish a dialogue. The hospital lobby was packed with patients waiting to see us that morning. According to the nurse in charge, there were 125 people with numbered tickets. We were given the hospital's large auditorium to treat patients. It was about the size of an American gym at a high school and had a raised stage with powerful ceiling lights, which some of the chiropractic students were using to read the X-ray films that a few patients had brought with them. I got busy doing physical exams, adjusting spines, and translating when needed. I was surprised the lack of sleep did not affect my judgment; if anything, I felt energized.

Howard and I had lunch at the hospital's cafeteria. We sat across from each other eating and talking about everything except the night we had spent together. Seeing him in the daylight took away any romantic ideas or feelings towards him. We were bed partners—nothing less and nothing more. Half an hour later we were back to treating patients at opposite sides of the room.

"I feel so much better in my lower back. Thank you, doctor," said Mrs. Carrera, a well-dressed woman who didn't seem to be like the typical patients we were treating for free. Mike, another colleague, came over and asked if he could borrow my Activator Instrument. His patient was too acute to be adjusted manually which was the preferred method being used by him and all the other students. The small handheld spring-loaded instrument I had brought with me was ideal to deliver just enough impulse to the vertebrae and remove pressure from the nerve causing pain, without thrusting hard into the painful joint. Mrs. Carrera went on talking, "Will you be here tomorrow? I would like you to treat my husband, too. He's been suffering from neck and right shoulder pain for ten years. Can you help him?"

"I can try," I said. There were no appointments being set up as people simply came, sat, and waited patiently for their ticket number to be called.

Mike returned in less than five minutes and handed me the Activator Instrument. "I can't help the woman. I can't even use the Activator on her; it's very frustrating. She starts to cry as soon as I touch her. Do you think you can see her since you speak Spanish?"

"Oh, that's my sister Madalena," said Mrs. Carrera, pointing. "Don't pay any attention. She's always complaining about her back."

I walked over to Madalena who was lying face down on the adjusting table. Her upper body was twisted to the right and her lower back was bent to the left with her left knee bent. She was sobbing into a large white handkerchief that she held in both hands. Unlike her sister, Madalena wore a simple cotton dress and was not wearing shoes. I bent forward and said in Spanish, "Madalena, my name is Veronica and I'm a doctor of chiropractic. I would like to help you. May I touch you?"

She looked up briefly with pleading eyes and a slight forced smile touched the corner of her lips. She was a lot younger than her sister. She nodded her head in agreement and then went back to crying. I said, "Just breathe deep in and out when I touch you, okay?"

I put my hand over the back of her head and caressed her just like Howard had done to me the night before, kindly. I said what felt natural to say or at least what I would want to hear if I were in her place. "Madalena, you are loved. Don't cry anymore. Let go of the pain." I ran my hand gently down her spine looking for subluxations so I could proceed with an adjustment. She stopped crying. Her body began to relax and she was no longer stiff and guarded as her body straightened out. I took a step back and looked up at everybody. Even her sister was quiet. I was afraid to do anything else and decided to skip the Activator adjustment.

"Madalena, if you feel better, you can get up," I said.

She stood and put both hands to her face looking at me in disbelief. Then as if embarrassed she murmured, "You fixed my back." Her eyes opened wide in wonder and she smiled. "Thank you, doctor, for taking my pain away," she said. I stretched my arms to her to hug her. She looked a bit surprised but then she hugged me back. "May God bless you," she whispered to me.

She left with her sister. I began sobbing uncontrollably. "I did not adjust her spine! I barely touched her!" I said.

Good thing Leila led me outside the auditorium. Crying in front of patients was not the coolest thing to do.

"She was starving for affection!" I cried. "That's what cured her, the human touch." And I cried and cried. "I swear that from now on, I will come to Delicias every year. If I can help someone like Madalena again, I can say that becoming a chiropractor was well worth it."

I tried to pay close attention to the variety of adjusting techniques used by other students. That afternoon I learned from Dr. Stewart—a chiropractic student who was an expert on extremity adjusting techniques—how to treat temporo-mandibular disorders. At five o'clock we all walked out of the hospital and headed for dinner at a local restaurant. There was a lot to talk about regarding what went on that day.

Except for looking furtively at each other, not once did Howard and I hold hands or show any affection towards each other. No one dared to ask us what had happened the night before; most likely Leila had already shared the news with everyone. It was a little after midnight when Howard whispered in my ear, "Let's go?" We left feeling unashamed and while walking to the hotel, we made up for not display-ing affection to each other earlier in the day by kissing every few steps and laughing hastily at everything we said. The snow was still falling and everything was white; it felt like Christmas. Our room was freezing cold and we rapidly found ourselves taking a hot shower. It was the first time we saw each other naked. Howard was in very good physical shape and when I complimented him on his assets as a lover he said "I take a lot of pleasure from satisfying a woman."

I didn't pay attention to how long we showered but we stopped once we ran out of soap. When we opened the bathroom door there was enough steam coming from the running water to heat the bedroom. "What do you say we keep the bedroom warm by leaving the shower running?" I said playfully. Soon the bedroom was comfortable enough to pull the covers off. I had fantasized a few times in my life about making love with the one I loved while traveling across the Universe. Such a fantasy was probably induced from having watched the movie *Barbarella,* many years ago. Being surrounded by fluffy clouds of steam was most likely the closest I was ever going to be to touching the sky.

Across the Universe

Like everybody else, Howard also wanted to know what happened to Patrick and me, so I told him. He confided he had also been in several bad relationships. He had been married twice and the second one was worse than the first. But at present he was engaged to someone he really loved. I thought, "So much for undying love." I just listened. When he found out I had been in Turkey with Patrick he got all excited because when he was in his early twenties he had been a member of the Whirling Dervishes. "When I was in Turkey I wanted to go see them so desperately," I said. "But Patrick considered them devil worshipers just like the Pope.

"Your husband was a very confused man," he said. "I'm really sorry about what you went through." He rocked me back and forth slowly in his arms, and then as if stricken by a whimsical idea he said joyfully, "I know the words and music by heart. Would you like to hear some Sufi chanting?"

"Oh, my God! Yes. Please," I responded excitedly. I moved slightly away from him and bent my right arm up to support my head with my right hand. I had no idea what to expect, but I was ready to see and hear something amazing.

"I'll start with some Rumi poetry," he said while also bending his left arm to support his head. Then with his free hand as if it was a feather floating in the air he softly landed it over my left breast caressing it. He lowered his voice and spoke each word slowly and only for me to hear, "Since in order to speak, one must listen, learn to speak by listening. If your thought is a rose. You are a rose garden, if it's a thorn, you are fuel for the bath stone." And then he began singing what sounded more like a chant. His voice was deep, mellow, and sensual. I felt a heated sensation spreading throughout my body and it was not a hot flash. I guess he sang in Turkish because I did not understand the words, but the sound and rhythm of his voice drove me into seventh heaven and I would do anything to make him chant all night.

We fell asleep an hour before our alarm went off. We had just finished getting dressed when we heard repeated loud knocks at our door. It was Leila and the gang. She wanted to show the bed to our friends. It sounded like a reasonable request. "The only way to measure it," she said, "is to have everybody lie down on it." That meant all six of them plus Howard and me. Someone got up and snapped a picture of all of us on the bed. From there we stayed on the same floor and followed Mark, another chiropractic student, who wanted to show us his room. A huge old-fashioned metal bathtub stood in the middle of his room. It had been painted with colorful blonde mermaids on a bright green background. We all got into the tub, and once again someone took our picture. Our hotel décor was unique and everybody had just become aware of each room being outrageously different. We all agreed to meet at the end of the day at the hotel's basement for a game of pool among their bigger than life-size wine barrels and then gorge ourselves on their seafood buffet dinner.

Once again, the day at the hospital was busy treating the local community. At noon we received a call from a hospital in another town asking if some of us could go over to treat their patients. They were willing to pick up the volunteers and bring them back. Leila offered to go with six other chiropractors. That meant fewer of us to take care of the many people where we were, but we managed. Howard and I did not have lunch and did not leave the hospital until 5:30.

While walking back to the hotel, Howard and I got caught in a blizzard. It was hard for me to believe I was in Mexico; it was more like winter in New Jersey. Howard asked me if he bought a bottle of tequila would I drink some with him, and of course I said yes. When we got to our hotel, Leila and the gang were already there waiting for us to play pool and have dinner. We all posed for group pictures in the hotel cellar. The decorative motif was gothic but in a Mexican Western kind of way.

It was one in the morning when Howard and I headed back to our room. We kept the shower going to heat up our bedroom but we used the bathtub to soak in. While curled up in his arms he said, "Have you seen the movie *The Bridges of Madison County?*

"No. What about it?"

"It's a love story. Very similar to what has happened to us."

I did not respond. We barely knew each other. Having sex intertwined with talking was still a physical thing and it had nothing to do with love. He was in love with someone else, and I was done with love forever. Probably the reason I was so relaxed about our situation.

He lay in bed on his back with a couple of pillows behind his head and after asking me to sit on top of him, he removed the bottle of tequila from under his pillow. He took a gulp and then passed it to me.

I could not keep myself from reading the label. It was a habit I had developed while in chiropractic college. It read, "Hornitos" and at the bottom of the label, "100% de Agave." I did not know much about alcohol and had no idea what Agave meant, all I saw was that it was 100 percent. I had no intention of drinking and then getting sick from it. I took a taste, just enough to wet my lips and wondered what I could do to refrain from drinking another sip.

We kissed.

"I love the taste of your lips," he said, closing his eyes.

Howard obviously liked tequila and that opened the doors to my salvation. I took a small swig from the bottle but did not swallow it. I very carefully delivered a drop at a time into his mouth. He was ecstatic and so was I. He drank the whole bottle, drop by drop, in between kisses. I felt like a professional sex connoisseur, for lack of a better word.

He became talkative about his personal life. "Once I found out how much women liked hugs it was my ticket at school to get them into my arms and closer to my body. I would walk the hallways just to feel a woman without getting into trouble. They welcomed my hugs. Did you ever meet Susie Smith? She was in fifth quarter. I loved going over to her apartment and spending the night with her. She always opened her door wearing shorts and a lacy bra. She had the cutest butt I've ever seen. She committed suicide last year. What a waste!"

I did not know how to respond except to listen.

"I hated my second wife. She would not give me a divorce so I bought rat poison and began adding it to her food every day but I was afraid I'd get caught. I wanted her to die so badly! Lucky for her, she gave me the divorce. I have a patient now in clinic and I can tell she likes me a lot. She's a young black woman and when I look at her I know it's just a question of a few more visits before we have sex."

I was glad when he passed out. I moved to the other side of the bed as far away from him as I could and cried over Susie's death. I never met her, but I thought it was very sad that she was remembered for having a cute bottom and no other assets. Next to me lay a lover I no longer wanted anything to do with. Only a criminal would use rat poison to kill another being. I was still awake when the alarm went off.

I doubted Howard could remember what he had told me the night before. It reminded me of a book I had read as a child, where the protagonist, in order to learn the truth from an older woman, got her so drunk that she spilled the beans. "Do you remember falling asleep last night?" I asked him.

"I only remember your sweet kisses putting me into oblivion," he said smiling while putting on his pants.

I had no reason to tell him what he had shared with me during "oblivion," as he called it. I now lacked any further warm feelings towards him but I was thankful for his presence in Delicias. He had helped me more than he could ever imagine. He had showed me the healing power of the human touch, whether treating someone like Madalena or myself. He had reinforced my lack of faith in men but had also taken away my guilt of returning to Delicias alive and without Patrick.

The day went smoothly at the hospital until a mother brought in her one-year-old baby. She held him in her arms as the baby had problems holding his back and head up. I panicked because I had never adjusted a child, much less a baby. Excusing myself, I told her I would be right back and ran to Gary, another chiropractor who had a lot more experience than me. I told him about the floppy baby.

"What do I do?" I said. "I've never adjusted a baby."

"Does the baby have a spine?"

"Yes, of course. But can you adjust him and I'll watch?"

He came over, took a look at the baby and said, "Your patient needs manual adjustment of the neck and back." I backed away a few steps with a panicked look on my face. He continued, "Do what you have learned in school. This baby needs you."

That's all he had to say. I palpated the child's spine and instead of using the Activator Instrument, I manually adjusted his mid and upper back. Then I put him face up and I adjusted his neck. To the mother's amazement, the baby sat up. I was also dumfounded. The mother started crying, "My son, my son! You fixed my son!" She was hugging him. I was thinking, "My goodness! My goodness! Chiropractic really works! How many times do I have to witness the healing power of chiropractic before I feel it in my own heart?" I answered the question myself with what made the most sense, *It's going to take time.*

I encouraged the mother to bring her baby the next day for another adjustment. I would be leaving early the next morning back to the US but some of the other chiropractic students would be staying for another week.

At the end of the day, Howard and I joined Leila, Donna, and Cody once again for dinner at our hotel. The food was very good and half the price of all the other places. It was one in the morning when we said good night to all our friends. Donna and Cody reminded me that I needed to be at the bus station at four-thirty and they would be coming by to pick me up in a taxi. Howard said he needed a cup of coffee and we sat at a small corner table.

"Veronica, these days have been the happiest days and nights of my life," he said with a serious look on his face. "I don't want it to end."

"I know what you mean, but we have our own destinies to follow." Being emotionally detached helped me to be creative in the drama department. It was a perfect scene from Casablanca.

"Do you know the song, "Torn Between Two Lovers"? He sang a few notes and then said, "That's how I feel at this moment. I'm torn between you and my fiancée at home. I've been thinking about this all day. I'm willing to move to California to be with you and we could attend school together."

I didn't like Howard's suggestion. He had killer tendencies and was a cheater. I didn't hate him, but I didn't like him either. I owed him for bringing me back to life in the last few days, but it didn't mean I was obliged to him for the rest of my life.

"Howard, I really want to thank you for being my friend through this moment in life when I really needed someone just like you." I was being honest about that and then I made up the rest as I went along, "Howard, I don't love you like you and your girlfriend love each other." *What a joke.* "You have something very special there and I will not break the special bond you both have." *If he believed that one, he would believe anything.* "Can't we keep what we have, the way it is? We can write, and we have each other's telephone number." *The farther apart the better.*

"You're the most amazing woman I have ever met."

I looked apprehensively at my wristwatch and said, "Wow, it's almost two in the morning; I have to be up and ready to leave in less than two hours. I really need to get at least an hour of sleep. Do you mind?"

"I'm very tired too."

We took turns at brushing our teeth and then lay in bed under the covers without taking our clothes off. I fell asleep instantly. Thank God Leila came knocking at our door to wake me up. It was four o'clock and my alarm had not gone off. I was ready in a split second, and after giving brief hugs to Howard and to Leila, I joined Donna and Cody in the taxi that was waiting outside. We made it to the bus station by four-thirty but when the bus finally arrived, it was two hours late.

It was always good to get away but it was even better coming home. I was ready to celebrate the end of the year and the start of 1997!

I intended to use the weeks left before classes started to study for the National Boards. I wasn't taking them until the end of the next quarter, but when it came to being prepared, I was like a Girl Scout.

I called Ralph and gave him an abbreviated version of what went on in Mexico. I finished by saying, "It was a lot of fun and now we are just friends."

"I'm proud of you Mom for having a good head on your shoulders. It's about time you learned to enjoy going out with someone without getting into a serious relationship or worse, getting married."

I received a package from Howard with three cassette tapes of Sufi music and a few pages of written poems in English. Along with it came a card and a letter. The card said, *Dear Veronica, my arms long to hold you and my lips hunger for the sweet taste of your tequila kisses. I miss you so very much, but at the same time I feel blessed for the precious hours we shared which will always unite us in spirit even if we don't know where our mortal souls go. With love, Howard.*

Wow, how romantic he could be, even from far away. Then I read his one-page letter, about his trip back to Georgia. He ended it with, "...I'm writing to you just a few steps away from my fiancée who is in the other room, absorbed in writing Christmas cards to friends and relatives. I can still smell your perfume, feel the softness of your skin, taste your lips, and remember the sexy way you always held me in your arms. I desperately need you but my desire for you clouds my common sense. I want one hundred kisses of tequila and nightly hot sudsy showers while we hold onto each other tight. I'm scared that we'll never again have what we experienced in those nights together so forgive me if I can't help dreaming about them..."

That was not love, not for me and not for his fiancée as he called her. I wished I could have the opportunity to hit him across his face with a rock; my fists could never do justice to what he deserved.

I crunched the letter into a ball and threw it into the wastebasket. He was despicable. That explained why sometimes men were referred to as dogs, but in all fairness, some women were also bitches.

The next morning I rented *The Bridges of Madison County*. I didn't cry at the end of the movie like Howard had warned me I might. I didn't see anything that even resembled a beautiful love story to compare it to what we had experienced in Mexico. He must have been referring only to the bathtub scene. It was raining and I felt it appropriate to listen to Howard's Sufi recordings. While listening to the languid music, I began writing to him. I titled it *Yesterday,* because I was influenced by the hypnotic sound of Sufi, and as such, it provided me the vivid flashbacks of our encounter in Mexico. I wrote one page about our erotic encounter. When I was done, I had to take a deep breath because I knew he would be touched by the memories still lingering. I was not sorry about the experience. If anything, I knew it would live forever in the back of my mind as my return from the dead, or more explicitly, it was an awakening. I turned off the Sufi music and in complete silence I wrote a one-page letter and named it *Today.* It started with trivial stuff, like what I had for breakfast, and then studying for the Boards, having lunch, talking on the phone to some friends from school, having dinner, studying some more, and then getting ready to go to sleep. Then I wrote another page and named it *Future,* and told him how I felt about him and his letter, and that this would be the last time I would write back. I wrote nicely but straightforward about our relationship and if he wrote again, I said I would not have time to answer. I was getting ready for my *future* and had no time to indulge in the past. I thanked him for the music and the poetry, and I wished him luck.

~ Chapter Four ~

Dr. Esagui

Winter of 1997

I decided to take Ralph's advice and sign up for a correspondence course to earn a BS degree. It helped that I already had accumulated a lot of the credits and according to their curriculum, if I stayed focused I could complete the program before the end of the year, maybe before I graduated from chiropractic college.

Besides the clinic and getting ready for National Boards III, I saw my school curriculum of GI/GU Diagnosis, Radiology, Extremity Adjusting, Managing Spinal Disorders, Extremity Management, and Chiropractic Philosophy and Principles as an easy quarter compared to the previous ones. I didn't consider listening to a guest speaker once a week at the Chiropractic Seminar as a subject.

Rod sat on one of the kitchen chairs patiently waiting for me to show him my new dress. I came out of my bedroom wearing a long, black cotton dress that had a little white flower pattern on it, and I also had a long-sleeved black sweater with a trim around the neck of white flowers that matched the pattern on the dress.

"You told me you bought a gorgeous dress but it's just a plain dress," said Rod.

"It's my first professional dress. So to me, it's a very smart dress, in a professional way."

"But you're all covered up. That's far from sexy." He laughed heartily as he always did.

"We're not supposed to be sexy while treating sick people," I said. "The female clinicians' dress code is that the neckline has to be above the collarbone, the skirt length below the knees or longer, and sleeves are never short. Shoes are to be flat, with closed toes. We can wear pants if we like, but they must be dress pants. And I have to wear a white jacket over my clothing which is actually very good as I get to save on buying new clothes, so while in the clinic I only need two outfits."

Rod reminded me of Al who would not have approved of the dress either. Men were all the same, even nice ones like Al and Rod.

Prior to working in the clinic, my wardrobe to school had been a pair of shorts and a cotton shirt. Many a time I had been told I looked like Ellie May from the Hillbillies and everyone admired me for not freezing in the winter. I never told anyone I suffered from hot flashes.

The first time someone called me "Dr. Veronica" at the clinic, it didn't quite register, even when they said it again. I finally looked back and asked with my eyes, *Are you talking to me?*

I loved working at the college's chiropractic clinic. The idea that I was treating patients under the guidance of a supervising doctor who was ready to discuss the case with me and go over every small detail to ensure the proper care of each patient was to me, the most valuable gift anyone could give me. It was probably the way horses felt after running on a track and then being given a carrot. Treating Mustafa's mom was exhilarating. According to him, she was doing much better and had a lot more energy. I had been attracted to him since the first time we met but juggling my regular curriculum, studying for the boards, and working at the clinic made it impossible for us to get together. He offered to pick me up the following Friday evening and take me to his favorite coffee shop in Berkley where the atmosphere was very conducive to studying. I was impressed with the way he drove. On the way to Berkley, he told me he was having trouble learning the several adjusting techniques the college offered. He was in his third quarter and was concerned about finishing school. I gave him some hints on how to tackle the more demanding classes and I swore vehemently that if he remained focused on his studies he was going to be fine. "Am I not proof enough that it can be done?" I asked.

"Yes, the reason I admire you so much. You are a woman but very smart."

Did he mean I was a rare female specimen? "I'm just average," I said defensively. "There are women in our school who are geniuses, compared to me and all the other students." I added a certain emphasis to *all the other students,* as I was implying both sexes. "Some of the women are on the Dean's list and graduating Magna Cum Laude and Summa Cum Laude."

He didn't respond. Come to think of it, whenever we talked, we never exchanged opinions; he never asked me any questions. Instead he said, "In Morocco, coffee is served two ways: black, or what Americans call a small espresso, or nous nous, coffee with milk. I like nous nous."

Okay, great, I just learned something important about him; he likes coffee with milk. He picked a quiet spot at the coffee shop and ordered a café au lait. I had a cup of hot water with a twisted slice of lemon; coffee would have kept me up all night besides giving me the jitters.

He got busy studying and I appreciated that he didn't make conversation while I was reading. About an hour later he closed his note pad and piled his books to his right side. I did the same and then looked at him wondering what was it about him that I was so attracted to when we really had nothing in common besides attending the same college. He put his elbows on the table and crossed his hands under his chin. "When I graduate I'm going back to Morocco to practice," he said in a calm, composed tone; there was even a hint of a smile across his full lips. But in the second sentence his words struck me like nails on a chalk board. "As my wife you will have to wear a hijab as that is the law in my country." He reached for my hand. I instinctively moved my hand and put it flat against my chest. Marry him? Was he out of his mind? Going out for a cup of coffee and we were engaged to be married? I would never get married again and much less to be dominated again in another relationship. He was crazy. That's it, I thought, I liked him because he is crazy, and I am attracted to crazy men. Okay, I must remain calm. I have classes early in the morning. I need him to drive me home.

"Mustafa, you are a wonderful man and I appreciate your offer but I'm here with you because you invited me to study together. We are just friends, school friends."

"That's good, I understand," he said pensively. Then he whispered, "Can I share something with you?" I nodded my head. He looked around as if he wanted to make sure no one else was listening. He leaned towards me and said, "I have other friends, they talk to me, I hear them," he pointed to his skull. "Here, inside my head they talk to me, they guide me on what to do on a daily basis."

After what I had gone through with Patrick, that kind of talk was freaking me out. I began putting my books in my backpack but he was oblivious to my reaction.

"I'm jealous of the Jews," he said, remaining seated. I put on a deadpan face to cover my Jewish face. He went on, "I can't tell this to anyone, I can only share it with you because I trust you." He took a quick look around as if checking the room for possible intruders or spies, pulled his chair closer to mine, and bringing his upper body forward he whispered, "I know you are going to be surprised but I wish I had been born a Jew instead of a Moslem. Jews have a more direct connection with the mystical powers of the Universe, that's why they have survived for as long as they have. Most antique cultures have vanished, but not theirs. You're not to tell this to anyone. Swear it."

"I swear. My lips are sealed." I put my thumb and fore-finger together and moved them as if zipping my mouth shut.

Driving home, he was back to being Mustafa again. He liked the blouse I was wearing, and he had enjoyed our evening together. Before leaving his car, I wanted to make sure he knew where I stood. "I will not be studying with you anymore," I said. "I'm very busy getting ready for the National Boards and need to concentrate by studying on my own." And then I repeated the whole thing again before saying, "Thanks for driving me to the coffee shop."

"Dr. Ichaca, please come to the front desk," I heard over the clinic speaker. A few minutes later I heard it again, "Dr. Ichaca, please come to the front desk, you have a patient waiting."

I did not know they were calling me until Liz, the front desk person, came to get me in the hallway. "Doctor Ichaca why didn't you come to the front desk when I called your name?"

"I didn't hear you calling me." I was wondering about my partial deafness.

"Dr. Ichaca, I personally called you over the intercom twice!"

"Oh, I see. You're saying my name wrong. My name is Esagui, not Ichaca."

"Yes, that's what I have been saying Ichaca."

"No, not Ichaca, it's Esagui."

"Oh, okay, Dr. Ichaca."

"Look, from now on call me Dr. Veronica, okay?"

"Okay, Dr. Veronica." She smiled and added, "That does sound a lot better."

We were both happy.

My second patient at the clinic (after Mustafa's mother) was Mrs. Palmer, a woman with neck pain radiating down her

right arm and into her thumb. After I did a physical and followed all the necessary tests appropriate for her first visit
including X-rays of her neck, I made an appointment to
see her two days later. I needed those two days to put the
puzzle together—her history, the exam, the X-ray findings,
the evaluation of each exam I had performed, and have it
all organized with a diagnosis for Dr. Thompson, my supervising doctor. He drilled me with questions like what I had
found, what I was going to do, how I was going to adjust my
patient, the treatment plan, the report of my findings, and
so on. After forty-five minutes of discussion, Dr. Thompson
agreed with my clinical findings and told me I was ready to
treat Mrs. Palmer. The next day, Dr. Thompson came into
the treatment room to supervise Mrs. Palmer's adjustment.
As clinicians we could only adjust patients under a doctor's
supervision. Before Mrs. Palmer left, I gave her my home
phone number in case she needed me for anything that might
come up before the next appointment.

The following morning I got a phone call from Mr.
Palmer.

"I don't know what you did to my wife, but she can't get
out of bed now. Her lower back is killing her."

"I'm glad you called me," I said panicking. "She needs
to come to the clinic immediately. Can you bring her in right
now?"

As soon as I got to the clinic, I ran to my supervisor's
office.

"Dr. Thompson, remember Mrs. Palmer, the patient
with a bad neck? Her husband called this morning to tell me
I hurt his wife's lower back and she's coming in this morning
in a lot of pain."

"That's complete nonsense. I was there when you adjusted her neck. How is her neck?"

"Her neck doesn't hurt anymore. But her lower back
hurts a lot."

"Dr. Esagui," he said shaking my hand. "Congratulations on fixing your patient's neck. Apparently she also has a problem with her back and it needs to be addressed. Don't forget to take X-rays of her lower back before treating her."

My time was divided between classes, studying for my BS and the National Boards, and working at the campus clinic, but I spent a lot more time at the clinic. When there was a walk-in patient, the girls at the front desk always knew where to find me, studying in the doctors' lounge. There was a television in the patients' waiting room and *Toy Story* was always on, to keep the children entertained. Every time I briefly saw it when I went by, I thought it looked like one of those movies for all ages. Once I graduated, that would be the first movie I was going to rent. At home, my television screen remained covered with the cactus poster. I had three goals in mind, pass the National Boards, get my BS degree, and graduate from chiropractic college.

One morning as I turned to flush the toilet at the clinic, I noticed the toilet water covered with blood—bright red blood. Since I had a partial hysterectomy many years ago, I knew better than to think I was menstruating. We all know we are going to die sooner or later but when we are facing our own mortality it's difficult to accept the obvious. Overwhelmed with intense fear, a fear I had never experienced before in my life, my heart stopped beating and moved up into my throat. My legs shook so badly I had to hold onto the wall inside the stall. Then pulling my pants up, I ran out into the deserted hallway looking for the first doctor I could find. *Blood! Cancer! This is it. I'm a goner! Oh my God, I survived being married to Patrick and have worked so hard to be a chiropractor, and now I'm going to die just as I'm almost done with school. This is not fair. No! I refuse to accept it.* I saw Dr. Grossman and ran towards her.

"Excuse me, Dr. Grossman," I said, trying to catch my breath. "I need to ask your opinion. I just went to the bathroom and I'm bleeding profusely from the rectum and the urinary track, all at the same time. What do you think is wrong with me?" I did not want to hear the answer, I knew the answer, but I had to ask, maybe just maybe she would say, "Oh, that's nothing, my dear."

"I hate to say this but cancer is a good possibility," she said without any sign of compassion. "But it can also be from something you ate. For example, beets can give a pretty good scare the next day."

Beets? Beets! That's why she was a doctor and I was just a clinician learning the ropes. Beets! That's what I had for dinner. A large bowl of beet salad!

I went back to the bathroom to pee and enjoy its harmless red color and then I thanked God for sparing my life.

Studying for a BS was going according to plan. Once a month my college received my tests from the University of New York, and I was taken to a private room where a staff person handed me a sealed envelope. The staff member stood standing in the room watching while I took the tests. When I finished, I put the tests in an envelope, sealed it, and handed it to the supervisor in charge of mailing it. My school offered this service at no cost. I believe the reason I was able to handle the extra curriculum for my BS was because I had the best teachers I could possibly wish for when it came to my regular curriculum. They were inspiring and incredibly helpful. But also, the time I had spent previously at Life University in Georgia having to study on my own, and not being able to rely on most of the teachers there, had actually made me quite a self-sufficient and independent student.

I was studying at the library with other students a lot younger than me when one of them said, "Every time I ask you something, you know the answer. You have such a good memory. What's your secret?" Instead of saying, I don't waste my time partying like you do, I said, "I take Coenzyme Q10, a supplement that guarantees to reverse the aging process at a cellular level and increases brain power."

That's how I got the nickname Ms. Coenzyme Q10.

One morning I found my car, along with all the cars parked on the same side of our street, vandalized. Except for my windshield, all my windows had been smashed in. I took the car to the Nissan dealership and it cost me a pretty penny for new windows, not to mention that I had to rent a car, I missed my first two classes, and I was late for the third. Still, I was thankful to God for everything, and that included my health and working at the clinic treating patients. If all went well I would reach my 350 number of patients goal before the end of the year. Still, once I hit the 350 mark to graduate I had no intention of leaving my patients until I had the *canudo* under my arm. *Canudo* was the Portuguese slang word for a tube since a diploma usually comes rolled up like a tube and tied with a string.

Over the weekend, four chiropractic clinicians and I shared a small table at the local Farmers Market in Hayward. The clinic supplied us with a small tent and encouraged us to "go out there," and "offer your services." Speaking on a one-to-one basis to complete strangers about the benefits of chiropractic services and encouraging them to sign up on the spot for care was not easy for me. Stuart, the other chiropractor next to me said, "This isn't easy for me either; I feel like a car salesman."

Funny how someone can say what you're thinking but the intonation and the perception of their words can reverse your personal thoughts. I responded, "We are far from selling cars and just in case someone tells us they don't believe in chiropractic or do believe in chiropractic, it's not a religion and it's not magic. We are simply providing a natural and safe way to heal." With that in mind, my perception on how to speak to someone changed right then and there. Two people signed up with me for Monday. One was a young girl who had been suffering from daily headaches all her life and the other was a seventy-eight-year-old male who was experiencing moderate mid back pain since he lifted a heavy bag of cement a week prior.

Before leaving the market, I had a chance to try a persimmon and thought it the most delicious fruit I had ever tasted! The name "persimmon" made me think of Persia and all the imaginative stories I used to read as a child. I bought half a dozen.

Leslie, the girl with the headaches, responded well to chiropractic and her chronic headaches were gone after the second neck adjustment. I put her on a once a month maintenance treatment plan. Mr. Lawson was not so lucky. The X-rays I took of his mid back showed a compression fracture at T8. I called him to remind him of his next appointment but he said, "I can't come to see you anymore. I told my medical doctor about the results of the X-ray and he advised me against seeing a chiropractor."

"Why would he say such thing?"

"He said you would do me more harm than good."

I wanted to say he was most likely going to be treated by the good doctor with the usual three meds they gave everyone, but he beat me to it. "He prescribed me some medicine," he said. "A pain killer, an anti-inflammatory, and a muscle relaxant."

Jo, a chiropractic student from Thailand, had borrowed my class notes once and we became friends. He had a wife and two children in Chiang Mai where he had been practicing as a podiatrist for ten years. Many medical doctors from other countries came to the US with the purpose of returning to their homeland as chiropractors. Amelie from France and Diya from India were both medical doctors in their countries. Amelie had told me a degree from the US would give her a lot more recognition and a better chance of being a successful doctor when she went back.

I was at the library when Jo stopped to talk. Since he was a podiatrist I told him about the painful callus in my right foot, right between my third and fourth toes.

"Those are painful," he said. "How did you get that?"

"Walking for three months in the same hiking shoes, while in Europe. What do you recommend I do?"

"I can remove it for you right now," he said excitedly. "It will take me just a few minutes."

"Well, I would love that, but we're in the library." I pointed to the students.

"So what?" He got on his knees. "Let me take a look at it." He took my sneaker off and examined my foot. He removed a small file from his pocket and announced with a confident "podiatrist look" on his face, "This is easy. Once I file it off it won't bother you again." He went right on filing as some students went by and snickered, others smiled, and two of them stood watching.

I had no problem developing X-rays on my own but I always requested my X-ray supervisor to inspect the way I positioned my patient and until he gave me the okay to go ahead, I did not push any buttons on the X-ray machine. I loved radiology and the thought crossed my mind that after I was done with chiropractic college, I might pursue a few more years to become a radiologist. To me X-rays were like a much-needed map while traveling in a foreign country.

Before taking a chest X-ray on a new male patient, I asked if he had any metal or pins in his body.

"Do pierced nipples count?" he asked.

"You mean… actual pins?"

"I can show you." He took off his shirt.

I stared at him, particularly at his nipples, and blurted out what I was thinking, "My goodness, what if it gets caught on something?" I did not give him a chance to answer. I said, "Just… stay right there and I'll be right back." I ran to Dr. Banjoul's office to ask him what I should do.

"You can't be that naive. You mean to tell me that you've never seen or heard about nipple piercing?"

"No, I've never heard or seen anything like that in my whole life. Why would a man put metal loops into his nipples? Don't you think that's really strange?"

"Dr. Esagui, we're across from San Francisco. There's nothing strange about anything you see here. You just go ahead and take the chest X-ray and make a note on the X-ray logging about the piercing. And please, do me a favor; don't stare at the poor guy."

I could not ask for a better roommate than Rod. I could talk to him about anything. It was like having a brother. When I got home, Rod always asked me if I had any fun patients that day. Of course without saying names I would confide in him, as he was always eager to listen. I told him I had a new patient, a young woman suffering from lower back pain. "And she is also complaining of bladder infections. She keeps getting them one after another since she got married three months ago." I sighed. "At her next visit I'll have to provide her with information concerning the honeymoon curse, and I don't know yet how I'm going to tell her."

"What's the honeymoon curse?" he asked laughing, as if it were the funniest thing he had ever heard.

"You don't know?" I had just opened Pandora's box and I knew he wasn't going to stop there.

"Well, no I don't know but it doesn't sound too good. So what is it?"

"I can't tell you. I'm too embarrassed to give you the details." I went to the refrigerator and began taking out some spinach, radishes, and a cold boiled egg. Boiled eggs were great to add to salads, or use to make an egg salad sandwich inside pita bread.

"You're a doctor and you can't talk about a health issue that will help your patient?" He was genuinely curious but I wasn't going to go any further.

"It has to do with sex, okay?" I began slicing the radishes into a small bowl.

"Ah, I see." His mind was actively searching for a way to get me talking. "So what? You know that I'm your friend, so talk to me. Make believe I'm your patient."

"I don't know if I can do that; you're a guy..." I began smashing the egg with a fork.

"Does it help if I put my hand on my waist and act girly?" he asked with a high-pitched voice and acting the part.

"That's a lot better," I said delighted with the opportunity to playact how I should address the subject with my patient. "Okay, *Mrs.* Rod, it's like this. You have just gotten married, so you're having a lot of sex with your husband, right?"

"Uh huh," Rod nodded his head in agreement, still with his hand on his waist but paying attention.

"In the excitement of being a newlywed, sometimes the hands go from the anus to the vagina or by having intercourse in various positions, the penis can contaminate the urethra which is connected to the bladder. The result is a bladder infection. You should go from the front to the back, never from the back to the front. That's why little girls who are just learning to wipe themselves, if they wipe from the back to the front, they are more prone to developing a bladder infection."

"Wow! I never knew that." Rod dropped his act and stood nodding his head up and down. "Thanks for sharing it with me; it makes a lot of sense actually." He repeated, "Wow, I never knew that."

"Most people don't. I didn't, until I went to school."

Because of Rod, I was very comfortable the next day when I talked to Susie. Her response was, "Is it okay if I bring my husband with me to my next appointment? I'm too embarrassed to tell him what you told me."

Spring of 1997

I passed all my classes and was looking forward to starting my next quarter soon. During the spring break, I spent my days studying mercilessly for my BS. In the evenings I attended a seminar for National Boards III, which had been highly recommended by students who passed the boards and who swore the high price tag had been well worth it.

In my quest to find a different place to study and still enjoy the outdoors, I went to the Japanese Gardens not far from where we lived. I took my books with me and sat under a wooden gazebo overlooking a pond filled with colorful koi fish. It was peaceful but I couldn't study, as sitting more than ten minutes on wood without some kind of cushion was hard on my buttocks. There were also mosquitos welcoming my presence and a bee kept buzzing around my head.

Studying was best done in my bedroom, as at the school library there was always someone stopping to say hello and who then remained chatting. I would begin studying in my room for one hour, then I'd get up and do Thai Chi for five minutes. Another hour later, I'd dance to the sound of Sufi. After another hour, I'd jump up and down to the sound of Andes music. Keeping my blood circulating at the end of each hour revitalized my brain, helping me focus.

One Saturday Rod and I went to the movies. He loved *Star Wars*. I felt if I had seen one I had seen them all, but I went anyway. He was fun to talk to and like me, he had no problem going to the bathroom at the end of one show and then sneaking back into a different featured movie without buying another ticket. That afternoon we saw *Star Wars, The Empire Strikes Back*, and *Return of the Jedi.* We got home late.

Paul, my stepson, and Mark, his friend, drove from Sacramento to spend the weekend with me. They set up their sleeping bags on my bedroom floor and Friday night we had a pajama party, ate junk food, and talked most of the night. In the morning I did a physical exam on both of them, just because I liked practicing on as many people as I could. I wanted to be more efficient and being a visual/hands-on person, that was the only way I improved on what I already knew. Paul was shocked to find out he had a hearing deficit on the right side. He wanted to join the Navy and I felt bad having to tell him my findings. "I could be wrong," I said. "But I doubt they will take you in, as a soldier in battle who can't hear is a dead soldier."

"I'm still going to try and see if they'll accept me," he said. "If they don't take me, I may look into becoming a chiropractor. I've been thinking about doing that for my father."

"For your father? How about what you want?"

"My father is living inside of me since he died. He's always with me."

Poor kid. He was sixteen years old and he was still traumatized by his father's death. I wasn't sure if he was ever going to recover from the loss. He was the product of an abusive relationship but it *was* his father, and just like any other child, he longed for his father's presence and to be accepted by the man he most likely had hated, but now revered.

"I understand how you feel. But trust me when I say he does not live inside you. You are the only one living inside you."

"When I went to Disney with the family last month I saw a man that looked just like Dad," he said. His lips moved up at the corners as he tried to smile, but his eyes were tearful. "I followed him all day, that's all I did, hoping he would look at me and talk to me." He broke down crying.

He had missed being loved as a child. I understood the hurt he felt, and now covering his frustration with an imaginary father was all he could do. I handed him some tissues and said with the most convincing expression, "You probably don't know this but your father was very proud of you. I have been meaning to write to you about it, but I feel this is better said in person. While we traveled in Europe he always bragged about you, how smart you were, and how much he admired you."

"He said that? He said that about me?"

"Yes, he believed in you wholeheartedly. I remember him saying one day, 'I know that sometimes I lose my patience with Paul and may have said some very hurtful things but I was only trying to make him tough. It was my way of telling him how much I loved him even if I chose the wrong words. That kid is so smart; whatever he decides to do with his life, he'll achieve it on his own. He doesn't need me to tell him what to do.'"

"He really said that to you?"

"Yes, and a lot more. He could talk about you for hours. Sorry if I don't remember everything he said, but it was all good stuff."

We hugged each other, his tears were gone, and a sunny smile lit up his whole being.

Yes, I had lied, but I was proud of it. White lies were born specifically to change one's perception of the truth and thus boost one's miserable life into a happier one. I knew God would forgive me, and if not, I was sure Patrick would interfere on my behalf, for his son.

On Sunday morning before Paul and Mark left for Sacramento, we went for a hike in the woods close by where I lived. On the other side of a deep narrow gorge, we noticed what looked like the skeleton of a large animal. "Maybe it's the skeleton of Big Foot," said Mark. I couldn't stop them. They took off running down the cliff yelling, "Yippee!" and "Heehaw!" like the rambunctious teenagers they were and didn't stop until they reached the bones. They carried their treasure back and when we got home, I kept the deer's skull and the lower spine. They took everything else. There was just so much one could do with a whole deer skeleton. It was a fun weekend overall, and it reminded me of the days when my two sons and I played together.

I put the dirty stained bones in a bucket of water with some Clorox and left it all in the backyard. On Tuesday morning, the bones were bleached clean and white. I wrapped them carefully with paper towels and put them in a shoebox.

Someday I would display them in my office to show patients what the bones of the spine looked like with dehydrated, worn-out discs in between the vertebrae.

Everything was going along smoothly. Three more quarters to go and I would be done with chiropractic college. Yahoo!

My new curriculum was: Obstetrics/Gynecology, Geriatrics, Psychiatry, Neuromuscular Disease, Cardio/Pulmonary Diagnosis, and the usual Chiropractic Seminar once a week. From the six Technique Electives, I chose to master Activator, Sacral Occiput Technique (SOT), and Motion Palpation Extremities until December when I expected to graduate.

Rod invited me to run with him in the San Francisco Bay Breakers event on May 18. Except for running with Patrick a few times because he insisted I had to do it, I had never done anything so ambitious.

I was very excited about participating in such an event. "I have always wondered what it would be like being surrounded by physically fit racing pros," I said

Rod laughed. "There will definitely be professional runners, but the majority of the people participating are like you and me, just regular folks having a fun time."

Still, we took it to heart and early in the evening when he got home, we began training by running together for about an hour, twice a week. Once I began huffing and puffing I took a few seconds to catch my breath while he kept going, looking back at least once with a smile of triumph. Of course he beat me—he was twenty years younger than me. The second week I was a lot more energized but he still kicked my butt.

Kim was a chiropractic student who had been born in the US and was five years younger than me. Her Japanese parents had been confined to a camp in the US during World War II. It was now 1997 and her parents were still alive. I assumed they were very young when they were prisoners. I could get Kim to smile once in a while but it was a lot of work; she would rather do battle. The more passionate she got the more she stuttered, but it did not slow her down. Quite the contrary, once she got going, it was like watching a train without brakes on an incline, her speech impediment got in the way and in the effort of moving her tongue to deal with some longer syllables, I was guaranteed to receive a spray of saliva across my face. Once I recognized her contradictory nature, I kept all opinions to myself and we got along great. A few students called me a saint for putting up with her. I didn't have to put up with her, we didn't talk about politics, religion, or sex; we studied for exams. When it came to doing an orthopedic test, there was nothing to argue about; we just followed the instructions in our books.

I was surprised when she invited me for sushi to celebrate my birthday on May 7th since she was far from being a spendthrift. I had just started mixing the soy sauce with a little wasabi when she said as if in premeditated slow motion, "I want to work with you when I graduate." I could see the sushi rolling around inside her mouth as she kept talking. "I propose you start the practice and when I graduate I'll join you." My jaw dropped and I lost the grip on my chopsticks; the California Roll remained soaking in the little saucer. I stared at her, speechless. "Don't worry," she said as she swallowed the contents in her mouth and pulled a dry smile to the corner of her thin lips. "I have the money. I have all the money we need to open the office right here in Hayward. We will be equal partners." Her lips remained in the same position and I was sure she was trying to project a confident grin.

"Thank you so much for your offer," I said. "It is very nice of you but my son Ralph and I already made plans to practice together."

She shrugged her shoulders, shoved another piece of sushi in her mouth, and stuttered, "Somehow I expected you would say that."

I could have asked her what did she mean by that, but I knew if I did she would start an argument so instead I said, "So, we are still friends?"

"Sure," she lied through her teeth.

I bought myself two pink frilly chemises. I paid fifty dollars for both and they were my belated birthday presents. One had transparent embroidery in the front and closed with two mini rose buttons. The other had little white pearls sewn all around the chest and the material reminded me of butterfly wings, delicate and slightly transparent. The first one I wore was the one with the rose buttons. Inside its softness, I dreamed about love and when I woke up in the morning, I felt complete from within. *I don't need a man to be happy. I have finally grown up*, I told myself. *When I wake up next to someone I will ask myself, do I want to wake up next to this jerk every single morning of my life? The answer will always be the same—NO!*

I finished the San Francisco Examiner Bay to Breakers race as number 27,863 out of a total of 75,000 participants. Rod advised me not to overdo it because the enjoyment came from just being a part of it more than anything else. I didn't intend to run the whole time anyway; it was very hot and I knew better than to get overheated. In less than a minute, Rod and I got swallowed by the running crowd and we lost sight of each other. I appreciated when some of the cheering crowd standing along the roads handed us water bottles and others got a little more creative as they sprayed us with their garden hoses. I cheated a bit, as I ran at the start of the race and at the end, and in between, I speed-walked along the side of buildings where there was shade. Everybody else ran in the center of the street under the scalding sun. Along the way, I had the courage to pull my camera out of my belt pouch and took a few candid shots of some men wearing nothing but sneakers and others dressed as women. The whole event was nothing but a festive street party; probably the same way it felt being part of the Carnival in Rio de Janeiro, Brazil—just fun, fun, fun! But there were of course, real racers running all seven miles, and tragically, one must have died because a body was covered with a white sheet on the side of the road, next to an ambulance.

In the end, I got a well-deserved T-shirt for doing my best and a copy of my picture as I crossed the finish line with my arms up in the air proudly displaying my racing number tagged on the front of my shirt. My first race had been accomplished, except that I couldn't find Rod and I didn't have any money to take a bus home. I sat on the ground by the finishing line and waited. Two hours later I heard Rod's recognizable laughter as he made his way to where I was seated. He had taken his time walking, mingling with people, and having a great time.

One Sunday Mr. Ahmed knocked on my bedroom door. "I made extra food for lunch. Would you like to join Susan and me?" He prided himself on making the best barbecued chicken. Susan had made mashed potatoes and she liked to add sour cream to it. "Everything is delicious," I said.

"You should try some yogurt on the chicken and mashed potatoes," he encouraged, and passed me the plain yogurt container. I put a spoonful on the side of the dish. He said, "In my country we use yogurt with just about everything."

Susan said, "He likes yogurt a lot because he is a Moslem. I like sour cream because I'm Protestant and you, what's your religion?"

I pondered a little about the connection of dairy product consumption and religion but seeing Susan's childlike smile, I felt comfortable sharing with them that I enjoyed yogurt and I was Jewish.

"You don't look Jewish," Mr. Ahmed said. "I'm very surprised." He put his fork down as if he had just lost his appetite.

"Well, you don't look Moslem either." I smiled. He did not.

If anything, a clear look of shock had taken over his features as he stared at me and said "You and I are cousins. The Moslem religion came from the Jewish religion. Brothers against brothers it has been since then. But Allah is the only one!"

I made believe that I didn't hear his last remark and instead I decided to play on the idea that we were related. "I'm not surprised to know we may be cousins. They say if each of us was to go way back in time, we are all family."

He did not answer and left the table abruptly.

I helped Susan to clean the table and put the dishes in the dishwasher then I went back to my room but couldn't study. I felt I had made a mistake letting him know about my religious background. The next evening I was just sharing with Susan that I had found a small market where they sold freshly baked pita bread for only fifty cents and I enjoyed stuffing it with fresh veggies for my lunch. Mr. Ahmed was cleaning the kitchen counter and said with a snicker look on his face, "Perhaps you're richer than you think. Maybe some of your family that died in the concentration camps stashed away their money in a Swiss bank." His tone of voice tinted with disdain creeped me out. I stared at him. He went on, "Think of all the money you could put in your pocket. You should check it out! Then you don't have to worry about buying cheap bread."

Anything having to do with the words "concentration camp" reminded me of my two cousins, Ellen, age thirteen, and Marion, age sixteen, who along with their schoolmates had been murdered when the Nazis took all the children from their school in Holland and into a concentration camp to be gassed. Even though I did not follow the Jewish religion, I felt like he was kicking me in the guts by mentioning money in my pockets in association with the concentration camps. I said good night and went into my room.

Maryanne, one of my patients, kept inviting me to a special seminar where people with personal problems could learn to deal with them.

"The first seminar I attended," she said, "I voiced how devastated I was after my boyfriend left me for another woman, even though I had given him one hundred percent towards the relationship. And the speaker asked, 'If you really, really loved your boyfriend and did not want him to leave, why did you not give him two hundred percent?' His comment made me realize what a fool I had been and I was able to recover emotionally and return to my normal life."

I wanted to say, if it helped you return to a normal life, why are you still attending the seminars. Instead I said, "Maryanne, I've never been so happy in my life. I'm doing well in school and at the clinic, and I have good friends. I'm very content. I have no reason to go."

"You're a doctor, you owe it to your patients to be able to steer them in the right direction when they need help like I did. Come once, just once with me." It made some sense and I agreed to go. As she was leaving she turned around and said, "Oh, before I forget, I'm bringing a friend of mine I would like you to meet. He used to be a district attorney in LA. You'll like him."

"Great," I thought, "now I'll have to put up with some loser who can't get a girlfriend on his own."

I stared at the opened newspaper Mr. Ahmed had left on the kitchen table after he and Susan had lunch. I doubt Susan had done it. It was his message, his way of dealing with someone who once had been family and now he hated. The full-page article with a picture to boot was about the containers that were found with the heads of Jewish prisoners from Nazi concentration camps. The shameful feeling I had sensed so often throughout my life for being part of the human race came when it was at its worst came washing over me like ice through my veins and I thought I was going to vomit. I went back into my bedroom and could not stop crying. Why did God allow so much cruelty to exist? I needed an answer or I would go mad with the despair I felt. I looked in the Yellow Pages for a Jewish temple. Maybe a rabbi, since he was educated in the Jewish law, could provide me an answer I could live with.

The synagogue was in Hayward. At the end of the service on Friday night, the rabbi, a man in his mid-forties with an amazing operatic voice, invited the small congregation of fifteen people to his house for dinner. It was an old home with small rooms and one bathroom but somehow the dining room was long enough to fit the table and chairs for everyone to sit with plenty of elbow room. I did what I could to help his wife, two teen daughters, and a few other women who had brought serving dishes and pans with already-cooked food. The environment in the kitchen was festive, like a potluck party. We took our seats and after a few prayers of thanks we sipped the ceremonial Kiddush wine and sang two hymns. Then we all went back to the kitchen and took turns at the sink for the ritual hand-washing. Luckily one of the women helped me recite the prayer before returning to the table in silence. When everyone was seated, the rabbi recited the blessing over the challah bread and distributed the pieces dipped in a little salt. It had been a long, long time since I had been to a Friday night Shabbat dinner. The last one had been when I was attending college in Georgia and Leila invite me over to her house. I had forgotten the whole ceremony. The meal consisted of chicken soup with matzah balls, pieces of gefilte fish, greens beans, fresh greens and cabbage salad, baked salmon with pineapple-grapefruit salsa, apricot chicken, sweet brown rice, and for dessert, apple crumble and double chocolate fudge brownies. No one rushed through the meal; we exchanged stories, laughed, and sang songs. Being surrounded by such loving people was a divine warm feeling confirming that some human beings were simple and good down to the core. Outside it was dark and raining; I was not in any rush to go home.

I waited until most everyone was gone before approaching the rabbi. I told him how heartbroken I felt after reading in the newspaper the despicable things some humans did to each other. "How could the Germans commit such atrocities and still live with a clear conscience? How come God allows these kinds of atrocities to happen?" I asked.

"God gave us the brain and heart to make our own choices. God does not want people to be like sheep just saying yes to everything he says just because we are afraid of Him. It's up to us to make the right decision, and that is what makes us noteworthy of Him. Some people choose evil and others do not. It is a personal choice, not a race choice."

I accepted what he said because he knew more about God than me, but if I were God, I would personally kill anyone that was a menace to humanity.

On Saturday night the phone rang. It was Maryanne letting me know she was on her way with her friend Allan and should be arriving in twenty minutes. I stood by the front door waiting for them. She introduced me to Allan and after we shook hands, we began to talk as if we had known each other all our lives. She cut us off, "We're running late. If you don't mind Dr. Veronica, go ahead and sit with Allan in the back seat. You guys can talk all you want there."

I found him charismatic and I could tell he liked me too, but our attraction for each other felt more like a spiritual connection. He was my age, but didn't fit in the category of a fifty-three-year-old man; he was attractive in a youthful way. He liked to travel and like me, he had been to thirty-two countries. We had a lot to talk about.

The hotel ballroom where the seminar was being held was filled to capacity with hundreds of people neatly seated in rows. It was still early and Maryanne asked Allan to save the two seats on each side of him. "Allan," she said, "we girls need to use the powder room. We'll be right back. C'mon, Dr. Veronica." I followed her to the bathroom; she wanted to talk "girl talk." She had a mischievous twinkle in her eye and asked, "What do you think? Isn't he handsome?"

"Yes, he is." I had no reason to lie.

"I've known Allan for many, many years and once I met you, I knew you were both made for each other."

Then she told me there was a twelve hundred dollar fee per year to become a member of the group to be able to continue to attend the seminars, and with each meeting, you were required to bring at least one or two guests. The more guests you brought in, the more points you were awarded and the better chance you had to climb the ladder of success in the organization.

"There's going to be one motivational speaker tonight and the main subject is 'Life is what you make of it,'" she said.

No kidding! I thought to myself. *Who doesn't know that!*

The speaker was a man in his mid-thirties dressed in a dark blue silk suit and enough diamond studded gold rings to make any woman jealous. He asked each person seated to take their turn standing and then state what was in their life that they needed to have resolved. He then gave his recommendation. This went on with each row, and everybody basically was griping about something or another. When it got to Maryanne she stood and said, "I'm looking for a good paying job, but I don't seem to be able to find it."

"If you were really looking for work you would have found it by now. Next." The speaker's tone was half authoritative and half sarcastic, mostly sarcastic. I didn't care for his pedantic attitude.

It was Allan's turn. "I'm trying to decide if I should quit my job and change careers," he said.

"What is your present profession?"

"I'm a lawyer."

"Are you making a good living from it?"

"Yes, I am."

"And what would you like to do instead?"

"I know it sounds strange but I would like to get a small food cart and sell hotdogs or something like that."

The speaker waved at him as if he were an idiot "That's not a career. Stick with what you have now." He shook his head and taking a deep breath, he pointed at me. "Next."

I stood. "Sorry, but I don't have any problems. I'm very happy with my life." The silence that followed told me I had better come up with something. I recalled Mr. Ahmed's change of heart towards me. I said, "I do have one wish."

"And what is it?"

"I would like for people to stop hating each other in the name of religion, color, or personal choices, you know, prejudice."

"Don't you have a personal aspiration for yourself?"

"I already have everything I need. But Peace on Earth would make me very happy."

"Keep dreaming. Next," he said.

I could hear some people laughing and others looked at me as if I were nuts. I felt out of place until Allan said, "I like what you said. Will you go to the movies with me next Saturday night?" He had no malice. I said yes. When I got home, Mr. Ahmed was in the kitchen drinking tea. I had a feeling he had been waiting for me. He said, "I want to inform you that from now on I expect you to clean the inside of the kitchen oven once every other week."

"I don't use the oven."

"It doesn't matter if you use it or not. You live here, you clean the oven."

"Mr. Ahmed, I always clean the top of the stove and the sink after using it. And once a week I wash the kitchen floor, as you know, without you even asking me to do it. I have never used the oven since I moved here so why should I clean something that I don't use?"

"These are the rules of the house. I have been too lenient with you. And by the way, I'm thinking about suing you for divulging my wife's condition to other chiropractors."

I did not answer, he was back at punching me with whatever his narrow, ignorant mind dictated him to do. What he was saying made no sense since when Susan was first diagnosed with Alzheimer's, he asked for my opinion and had encouraged me to get as much information as I could on the subject. I told him I was going to ask for advice from one of my teachers at the clinic and he was all for it. He knew very well I would not do anything to hurt Susan. I even took time off from my studies to take Susan back and forth to medical appointments.

It didn't stop there. The next day he said flat out that I had stolen two potted plants from his backyard since they were nowhere to be found. I never went into his backyard and if I had taken his plants where would I put them, under my bed? From the day he found out about my religion he had turned into a poisonous, religious snake. I felt sad and very confused about my situation. I had no intention of cleaning his oven; it was a matter of principle, even if it meant I would have to move out.

Allan picked me up the following Saturday night and after going to the movies he took me home, but we stayed in his car talking. I thought I was better off listening; men liked women who listened. He had been married twice and for the last seven years he had abstained from alcohol and drugs. He was very proud of his new lease on life and no matter where he traveled, he always made arrangements to connect with someone from AA as soon as he arrived at his new destination. When he was into drinking, he had been with a lot of women. I told him I would like for us to remain friends as I enjoyed his company. We exchanged phone numbers. It was two in the morning when we said good night.

Bonnie and I talked on the phone once a week. She was the closest I had to having a mother. Even though Mama had proven after she died that she did love me when she saved my life, as my intermediary angel, I could not help feeling cheated growing up not having the same warm relationship that I had with Bonnie. I remembered Mama had once put her hand on my head to check out my fever when I was a child. I recall the occasion because she left her hand on my head for perhaps a minute and it felt like the touch of an angel. We rarely had a conversation of any kind. She was the mother, the queen, and I was a mere subject. She was preparing me for the future, I learned later on. She wanted me to be independent of her so that I would be able to survive on my own. She sent me away to America, to the other side of the world, but as long as I found happiness she was willing to make the ultimate sacrifice that only a mother could. She was willing to never see me again. But I would gladly give up everything I had to have her in my life. Bonnie called to see how I was doing and then brought up the same subject she had been complaining about for months. "I would love to taste food again. My sense of taste has stopped working; I get no pleasure from eating. I was told to see an Ear, Nose, and Throat specialist and hopefully something can be done. What do you think?"

"Why don't you try and stop using your inhaler so often? That is what is killing your taste buds."

She called four days later. "The doctor said I have a deviated septum and if I have it fixed my palate may return to normal again."

"That's the biggest lie I've ever heard. And what does he mean by 'it may return,' what kind of guarantee is that? Please don't do the surgery."

"Oh, he told me it's a simple procedure and I'll be out of the hospital the same day. Don't worry honey, I'm in good hands; he's a very good doctor."

"Bonnie, please don't do it. I don't trust doctors, principally this one; he is lying to you." I started crying, hoping it would affect her decision. "Please Bonnie, I have a bad feeling about this. Don't do it."

Nancy called a few days later. "Mom is home. The surgery went well. She is resting now, just wanted to let you know about it since I know you were dead against it."

That evening Nancy called back. It was hard to understand her because she was crying. Finally I understood her saying, "Mom died...she died...we found her dead, lying on the floor."

I closed my eyes and sat on my bed, and then I joined Nancy crying on the phone.

I woke up early in the morning hearing several taps on my bedroom wall coming from Rod's bedroom. He could not get out of bed due to acute low back pain. He asked me to call his chiropractor. Within half an hour, Dr. Hammond was at our place. After he adjusted Rod's back, he asked if I would adjust his, since I was a chiropractic clinician. I took Dr. Hammond to my bedroom where I had an adjusting table and adjusted him with my Activator Instrument. He was so happy with the technique and how he felt afterwards that he made an appointment for Monday to come to the clinic and officially be my patient.

When Dr. Hammond came to the clinic, I took his history and then left the room after asking him to undress and get into a patient gown so I could perform a physical exam. When I got back to the room, I was very good at controlling my reaction when he showed me his underwear. "Dr. Veronica I need to show you these bloodstains. I'm very concerned. What's your opinion?"

"How long have you been bleeding?" I was thinking about beets.

"For about six weeks."

"Hemorrhoids can do that. I'll be right back."

I ran to Dr. Thompson's office, my clinic supervisor. I was advised to go on with the physical, and then send my patient to get a blood test.

Dr. Thompson called me to his office. Dr. Hammond's blood test had come back positive for the HIV virus.

"My God, that's terrible; that's a death sentence," I said. "He's my friend. I can't give him the bad news. Can you do that for me?"

"No, Dr. Esagui. You're his doctor and as such you have to face that responsibility."

When I got home, Rod said, "Any interesting patients today?"

"No, nothing new really, just my usual patients. How was your day at work?" I knew better than to share Dr. Hammond's situation with Rod. It was a private issue.

I was a nervous wreck when I sat next to Dr. Hammond the next morning.

"This is your blood lab result." I handed him the report.

He stared at it and then stared at me. His eyes teared.

"Dr. Hammond, I'm sorry."

"This is not possible. How can it be?" He held his head in his hands, weeping.

"I'm supposed to tell you that if you have been with other men or are presently in a relationship, you must let your partner and the others know about your condition." I said exactly as I had been instructed by Dr. Thompson.

"I have only been with a man once and it was many years ago."

I was thinking, it only takes once and it all depends on the luck of the draw, very much like gambling. Sometimes we win and other times we lose.

"Will you still be my chiropractor?" He wiped the tears with the back of his hands.

"Yes, absolutely, but I was informed that you need to come in as the last patient of the day."

Dr. Hammond chose his own treatment plan, three times a week, until I graduated in December.

Rod became my patient. He had been rear-ended by a semi-truck five years previously. He was lucky he survived and even more lucky when he made a real sweet deal with his insurance company. Instead of accepting a large settlement, he asked to have chiropractic coverage for the rest of his life. But I treated him at home at no charge. Whenever his back was hurting, I adjusted him on my adjusting table in my room. Since his chiropractor was now my patient, Rod trusted me completely.

I was leaving for school Monday morning when Mr. Ahmed stopped me in the hallway. I said good morning but in the back of my mind I knew he was ready to do battle. He went straight into it. "I noticed that Sunday afternoon you brought a date into your bedroom."

"I'm not dating," I said. I shook my head in disbelief.

"You were both seated next to each other on your bed." He emphasized the last three words.

"Yes and you saw us because I left the door open. I have nothing to hide; Allan is my friend."

"Isn't that sweet," he sneered.

"We were sitting on my bed because there's no place else to sit. I was showing him some of my family albums. Like I said, we're only friends."

"You are a..." he stopped as if looking for the proper word to insult me and then said, "I have been too easygoing. You shouldn't be bringing students into your room either. From now on you're no longer allowed to bring anyone into your room."

"Mr. Ahmed, Allan is not a student, he's my friend and if that bothers you, I won't bring him in anymore. But please, I need to study with a partner when it comes to hands-on studies for the clinic and when practicing adjusting techniques. You've met Jan; she's an adult and a very responsible person. Do you want me to close the door? Are we making too much noise?"

"It does not matter if the door is open or closed. You want to study with someone, you go study at school. I don't want strangers in my house."

"This is not fair. You have met Jan and Tom. They are the only ones I bring over to study with. You know they're all nice people. Why are you doing this to me now?"

"I'm the owner of this house and if you don't like it, it's too bad."

"Very well then," I said without a second thought. "I'll be out of here as of the end of this month." I was late to school and drove a bit hazardously. Mr. Ahmed must have found another renter to pay him more than me, was my first thought. But if that were true, why didn't he just raise my rent? No, it had nothing to do with money, my guests, or cleaning the oven, which I refused to do. It all had to do with prejudice, racial prejudice of the worst kind. The idea of moving again had me stressed out, but during my lunch, I began looking in the newspaper.

I thought I had found a nice apartment until I took Rod to see it. He advised me against it unless I carried a loaded gun in my pocket.

Jan recommended I take a look at the college's bulletin board.

During my lunch break I found an interesting ad with a colored picture of a white Siamese cat sitting on a green pillow. Underneath the photo it read CAT CONDO written with a thick red magic marker and decorated with tiny sparkle paws. The ad read: "Condo fully furnished and ready to move in. Only $450 per month! For details call…"

I pulled the ad off the wall and ran to the next phone. The owners were Lisa and Bryan, who just happened to be chiropractic patients at the clinic.

At the end of the day I went to see their apartment. I had never met them at the clinic as patients. I was very impressed with the private garage under the building complex and the metal gate that opened and closed when I used the code numbers. Once Snooky, Lisa's cat, rubbed himself against my legs, they said it was all they needed to see that I was the right roommate for him.

~ *Chapter Five* ~

The Cat Condo

Lisa and Bryan had been together for six months since they had met at the chiropractic clinic while waiting to be treated by their clinicians. It was love at first sight and soon afterwards, Lisa moved out of her condo to go live with Bryan. But Bryan's apartment complex did not allow pets and Lisa could not bear the idea of leaving Snooky all alone in her condo, for which she still carried a mortgage. The whole apartment had become Snooky's kingdom; he even had his own room with not one, but two litter boxes at his disposal. Snooky sat on Lisa's lap purring while she lovingly stroked his long white hair. "Don't ever feed him anything but cat food," Bryan said and Lisa added, "My Snooky will expect to sleep with you at night. He loves to snuggle up on those chilly nights."

"Really? How cute of him." I could feel Snooky's cold piercing eyes staring in my direction. I told them I would be delighted to feed their Snooky and clean his litter boxes, but I did not tell them that at night, Snooky would be sleeping in his own room. I did not sleep with creatures with dander and who spit hairballs; I had no intention of waking up with itchy eyes or clogged sinuses. There was a good reason why a pregnant woman should not handle a cat or clean its litter box. Their feces could transmit Toxoplasma gondii, a microscopic parasite, and there were also tapeworms, round worms, and hookworms to be aware of. So even though I was not pregnant, what's good for the goose is good for the gander. I would clean his litter boxes, pet him, brush his fur, and feed him his cat food, but I was not going to take any chances with him carrying in his paws and then into my bed, the feces which could very well harbor bacteria such as salmonella, giardia, and intestinal worms.

Mr. Ahmed chose not to be home when I left. Susan thanked me for the twin size bed I left behind since my condo came with a queen size bed. "We can use it for the next renter," she said. We hugged and a twinge of remorse hit me as I knew it was the last time we would see each other again.

Nancy and Sean came from Sacramento to help me move to my new apartment. Rod offered too but I was afraid his back would give out. I was also concerned that once we were no longer roommates we would get busy and drift apart. I promised to have him over as often as I could or at least once a month to have a home cooked meal.

Thank God Ralph had taped all the wires to my stereo entertainment center with matching numbers and color codes. I was very proud of my technical abilities when I connected everything and it worked. The apartment had security alarms all over the place. It was like living in some top-security prison, except I could leave anytime I wanted.

Snooky's bedroom was far from being decorated for a human. It was a badly thrown together storage room—a labyrinth of boxes and furniture—a perfect playroom for a cat. The living room and dining room were overcrowded with furniture and knickknacks. I needed to be able to walk through the apartment without hitting my knees on some tight corner. Except for a round oak dining table and four chairs, a blue velvet loveseat, and a small coffee table, I moved all the rest of the furniture, knickknacks, and boxes of my personal stuff that I couldn't come up with a good reason to open yet, into Snooky's room. I bought a seven-foot collapsible table to be used as my desk, and carried it all by myself into the apartment. I put it in the living room with all my books and papers and aligned it neatly against the wall. Snooky seemed to be as excited as I was; he followed me closely and I had to be careful not to trip over him. The sliding glass door in the living room opened to a very small veranda facing the street, but it was still big enough to fit two small chairs. My wall-to-wall bedroom closet was filled to the brim with Lisa's "skinny" clothes, apparently obtained before she gained an extraordinary amount of weight. Both Lisa and Bryan were obese, but next to Bryan, Lisa looked trim because she was half his weight and height. I didn't have much of a wardrobe but I needed space for about six hangers so I bought two tiered hangers each designed to hold multiple pants, shirts, and blouses. It was very organized and took up a minimum amount of space.

Coming home was like entering my own private palace. Snooky had become an interesting roommate. He greeted me with a meow, which I took as, "I missed you, where have you been?" He followed this by rubbing his face and then his body along my legs. It was definitely a cat hug and I returned the loving gesture by putting him on his back and scratching his belly. I gave him his food, changed his litter boxes, took a shower, and then made my dinner before sitting down to study at my new super big desk.

Sandy, one of the staff members in the radiology department at the clinic, was horrified when I told her my new address. "Oh, my, my! You sure have moved to the worst part of town. When it comes to crime, it can't get any worse. You have to get the heck out of there as soon as you can!"

She had to be confused about the area where I lived. I had been there five days so far and had not seen or heard anything bad. Besides, there was probably more security in the building I lived in than at Fort Knox.

However, on Friday night I found out why Sandy had labeled my neighborhood the worst part of town. In my opinion it should have been called, "The gang's all here." Around the corner from my new residence was a bar, and on weekends, that's when things got heated, with drunks fighting and people shooting guns. No cops showed up. If I were a cop, I wouldn't show up either. On Saturday night, I saw two cars parked under my window with couples having sex.

Even though my bedroom faced the street where the night shootings were happening, I wasn't worried. At night I kept the light in my bedroom off and I walked bent over, until I got into bed. Even if a bullet came through the window, my bed was at a lower level. As long as I was cautious, I felt perfectly safe where I lived.

A week had passed when Lisa and Bryan came by to see how I was doing and to visit Snooky, whom Lisa missed desperately. Bryan told me he used to be a CIA agent and that one day he was flying a helicopter still in the experimental stage, when it suddenly collapsed to the ground, killing his co-pilot. Bryan awoke in the hospital, in critical condition, with pieces of scrap metal lodged in his spine. The government had refuted the story and diagnosed him with a mental disorder.

"I look fine to the naked eye because no one can see the constant pain I have to live with for the rest of my life," he said. "The morphine I take every day no longer helps. I'm permanently disabled. The government owes me, they owe me plenty. Sooner or later they are going to pay. I'm doing all the legal paperwork myself and I'm going after those bastards." Lisa's story was just as dramatic. "Joel, my stepfather, used to rape me and then beat me. I was very young." She lowered her eyes; tears fell. "C'mon, give me one of your smiles, you," Bryan said, throwing his long arms around her like a life preserver. "You know I love you and will never let anyone hurt you again." Then he made a little joke and started to tickle her until she began to laugh. They were such a sweet couple; they were perfect for each other.

I was aware of Lisa's past. When I first cleared out the

living room and was putting the furnishings into Snooky's room, a few handwritten pages addressed to her stepfather fell from inside an old *Life* magazine.

Ralph and I made plans to drive to La Jolla during our next school break. He had heard La Jolla was one of the most beautiful places in California to live and work. It was a long trip for him since he would be driving from Oregon to meet with me in Hayward but he felt it was worth the drive to see if we liked it enough to open our practice there. I couldn't wait to see him.

I didn't know what to make of Lisa and Bryan's "drop in" attitude when they showed up unexpectedly two days later. They didn't even knock; they used their key and walked right in. I was cleaning the kitchen after dinner and was startled to see them standing in the hallway like two apparitions. "Don't worry, it's just us," Bryan said. "We came to see our Snooky. Lisa was feeling a little depressed today and I thought it would be good for her." They sat on the living room couch with Snooky purring on Lisa's lap. It was nine in the evening when I gave them a subtle hint, "Well, it was fun having you over but I have to get ready for bed. As you know, classes start at seven-thirty in the morning." They didn't leave until eleven but it was my fault because I kept politely answering their questions and listening to their patter of life experiences.

Her name was Martha. She was only fifty-five years old. Multiple sclerosis had put her in a wheelchair. Not able to walk or even stand up on her own, she was at the mercy of her husband Jorge who wheeled her into the clinic like a piece of meat to be pounded until tender. Jorge was a re-tired medical doctor who insisted on bringing Martha in two times a week to be adjusted "hard."

He lifted her from her wheelchair without the slightest tenderness, and would throw her on the adjusting table face down as if he hated her. Then he stood over me, overseeing what I did and saying things like, "When you adjust her spine, go hard at it. Do it hard, damn it!"

Martha was skin and bones and osteoporotic. She did not speak except for when I asked her how she was doing, and then she would slur out, "Fi...ne. I feel fi...ne."

About fifteen years ago, Martha was crossing a street when a car hit her and threw her into a building. She never recovered from the trauma and a year later she developed MS.

Having finished my quarter and feeling like all my exams had gone well, I was excited to take on an adventure with Ralph. We took our time driving through the southern towns of California and found a motel to spend the night in La Jolla. The next morning we drove around the town and stopped at La Jolla Cove. Its familiarity, even though I had never been there, filled me with an eerie feeling. "Ralph," I said, feeling like an elephant's foot was pressing on my chest cutting off my breathing, "this is going to sound really odd to you, but I have a déjà vu feeling about this beach. I can't explain it, but it's not a pleasant feeling. I have to get out of here." Ralph didn't laugh or make fun of me; he took my arm and escorted me to the car. But what really changed our minds about practicing in La Jolla was seeing what kind of people lived there when we became witnesses to a car accident.

We were stopped behind a line of cars, waiting for the light to turn green, when suddenly a car literally came flying over the cliff and dove like a flying saucer into a huge bush on our right. As quickly as it dove into the bush, it came out the other side like a rocket. It kept on going until it finally stopped when it flipped over on the sidewalk, about five cars down from where we were. Yet no one got out of their cars to inquire if the driver and the passenger were alive! Ralph and I ran to see if they needed any help. The drivers waiting for the light to change just looked the other way. We were shocked. The two women were not complaining of any injuries and one of them used her cell phone to call for help. The idea that nobody showed any sign of concern was a warning; we did not belong there. We would not be happy living in a town where people were selfish and too busy to care.

We were only gone for three days, but Snooky had a few surprises waiting for me when I got back. He had decided if he was going to be abandoned and left alone at home, he was going to poop and pee wherever he felt like it and he purposely picked the entry hallway. I barely missed stepping on it when I opened the door to the apartment. He knew he had been bad, because when I walked in, he took off and hid in his room under a dresser.

After visiting La Jolla, Ralph was convinced Oregon was the only place we should practice. He was graduating in September. Because of the time I had lost from school while being married to Patrick, I would not be graduating until December.

I still had a week left before returning to school and Lisa and Bryan made me an offer I could not resist—$100 a day to work for them while on my school break. My job was to make them lunch and clean their apartment and drive them to wherever they wanted to go. I told them I would be available as long as I was home by seven to study for my BS degree, which I was working hard to finish before the end of the year.

While they lay in bed watching television, I did mounds and mounds of dirty laundry. I also colored their hair. They liked the same color, platinum blond. One morning after cleaning the bathroom and kitchen, I took out the trash and began moving some boxes that were in the middle of their living room against the walls, to make some space to walk

Room Service

from the front door to their bedroom without tripping. They lived like packrats. Bryan called out from their bedroom, "What are you doing? Don't move anything around. We like it the way everything is."

I was grossed out when Bryan requested that I use one of the five-pound bags of ground meat they had in the freezer to make four huge bloody burgers. He wanted them fried in deep oil followed by frying up a huge amount of French fries.

"Why so much oil?" I could not help being curious.

"We have to have a lot of grease in our food so it will coat our stomachs," said Bryan. "The drugs we take can make holes in our stomachs if we don't coat it with grease. We don't have a choice in the matter."

It did not make me feel any less guilty that I was helping them clog their arteries.

They spent the days in bed watching television, and I served their meals on trays. Once in a while they would ask me to take a break, sit on their bed, and listen to their stories. They needed a friend to talk to.

"As you can see, we have a very packed apartment and don't have any space available to sit," said Lisa. "That's why we live in our bedroom." They both giggled.

"I'm trying to get a morphine implant to help me with dealing with the back pain," said Bryan. "But it's not easy to convince my doctor. If it wasn't for chiropractic care providing us some relief, Lisa and I would most likely commit suicide."

The last two days were a lot more pleasant as I drove them to the shore and we watched some people paragliding. Bryan and Lisa paid for my lunch. I had fun taking their pictures at a sunflower farm where the plants were even taller than Bryan. We did get along pretty well when just having a good time, and I did not have to get up early the next morning for school. For seven days of being their housemaid and chauffeur they paid me $700 in cash.

Summer 1997

The summer break came and went as I kept busy studying for the boards and my BS degree, and enjoyed late movies with Allan and sometimes dinner out. Rod was working two jobs and barely had any free time but I got him to come over once for dinner and just to make him happy, I went with him to a business meeting which turned out to be a pyramid business scam. But it was fun and as always, I enjoyed his company. My next quarter curriculum consisted of Ethics,

Clinic, Pediatrics, Differential Diagnosis, Toxicology, and the usual once a week mandatory seminar. It was going to be a breeze.

I was seated at my desk at home when I heard the phone. "Hi Ronnie, it's Al." He never waited for a response. "I received a notice to pick up a registered letter addressed to you from the post office. It had no return address and I thought it was kind of suspicious and maybe it was from the hospital in Austria trying to collect money from you, so I wrote on the envelope, 'Moved, unknown forwarding address.' I thought you should know. Are you doing okay?"

"Yes, and you?"

"Good. Take care."

I was used to his abrupt one-way conversations, but his sister Ruth who still lived in Long Island, couldn't get used to his manners even after a lifetime of phone calls. "I swear he drives me crazy," she would say when we spoke on the phone. "He calls me at least once a month which is very nice of him, but all he does is talk about himself and never, ever waits to hear what I have to say. It's like he could care less."

It wasn't that he didn't care. He had a hard time hearing and the way he handled the situation was to put no effort into listening. He called and if we answered the phone, it meant we were still alive and that was all that mattered to him." I understood his frustration. I had been lucky to have at least one good ear.

I wondered who could have sent me a registered letter with no return address. It was from someone who apparently wanted to contact me but wanted to remain anonymous. There was only one person in the world I could think of—Michael. The love we had felt for each other and what had become a secret affair five years ago, had taken a dive into a black hole when I left for school and he moved to South Carolina with his family. If indeed he was looking for me,

I wanted to know. I called Tracy, my old friend and theatre partner in New Jersey. She was my only hope.

We chatted about the good old times and all the people we had worked with for almost ten years and then I said casually, "And what about Michael? Remember him? I wonder what happened to him." I waited for a response while holding my breath. "Oh yeah," she said. "Funny you should ask. He called me about two weeks ago from South Carolina where he lives with his mother. He asked me for your address. I gave him Al's address since I didn't have yours in California."

Oh my goodness, it was him, after all! I needed to find the last letter he had sent me as his address was on it. Five years ago I had slipped it in one of my photo albums. I had seven photo albums if I were to count the three with just my baby pictures. I once mentioned to Mama my intention to throw two albums away and she was panic-stricken. "No, you can't throw them away, those pictures are alive! Promise me you won't throw them away. You'll have bad luck from then on—it would be the same as committing suicide."

I apologized to Snooky for disturbing his territory and began digging into one box after another; the photo albums were in one of them. I lacked organizational skills when it came to writing the contents on each box. The only way to find the album with the letter was to go at it, box by box. Which one, which one had his letter? A painful thought crossed my mind—perhaps during one of my moves or while in storage, the letter had fallen from its hidden pages. He was going to be lost forever; I would never see him again. I prayed, *Please God, I just want to find out if he's okay.* Maybe something happened to his mom. Maybe he's in trouble and needs my help. Maybe he still loves me. Maybe we still have a future together after all. There it was! An envelope was peeking out from behind the photo of a much younger me proudly holding a shoe box. It contained the miniature set I had built in full detail for the production of *Ten Little Indians*, a play I had produced at the Kobe Japanese restaurant, many years ago.

I held the envelope with both hands against my chest for a few minutes before I read his letter inside. Then I wrote: *Dear Michael, I believe you sent me a letter to my old address in New Jersey. I live in California now. Tracy told me you called and asked for me. If you are looking for me, here I am. It's been a long time since we saw each other. What have you been doing all these years? How is your mom and family? I will be graduating from chiropractic college, hopefully by the end of this year. I'm doing well and I hope you are too. You can write to me if you like; I would love to hear from you. Ronnie PS. I no longer go by that name of Ronnie like I used to in New Jersey. Now that I'm a student I have to sign all my papers with Veronica, my legal name."*

Lisa and Bryan's visits began to increase and it got to a point where I never knew if when I got home, they would already be there, seated in "my" living room waiting for me. They were very nice people but it was as if they had adopted me. I knew it was Lisa's apartment, and the cat belonged to her, but as a renter, I felt I was entitled to some kind of privacy. One Sunday morning I practiced over and over in front of the bathroom mirror how I was going to talk to them about my lessee rights. "It's like this," I would tell them as I stood erect while maintaining an air of dignity mixed with some compassion in my tone of voice. "As a renter, you must give me a day's notice." No, that would mean they would be at my apartment every day. I started again. "As a renter, you must stick to once-a-week visits with Snooky and they have to be on Saturdays when I don't have classes the next day, and not in the morning because I would like to sleep late on Saturday, and on Sunday, too. Oh yeah, and you must call me before coming and never stay more than two hours." I rehearsed it over and over again but after a while it lost its spontaneity. I was better off speaking from the heart.

Sunday afternoon I got home after going shopping for groceries and they got up from the couch to hug me with words such as, "So nice to see you," "We've missed you," and "Lisa can't wait to show you how to cut Snooky's nails." Then Lisa added, "Oh yeah, and we bought a new brush for his fur. It's always good to have two in case you misplace one."

Bryan handed me a small bag of catnip. "Snooky loves it." He laughed mischievously. "And for you my dear, we brought you a box of chocolates." I did not have the courage to say anything concerning their uninvited visits. He opened the box and laid it on the coffee table. I was thankful they ate them all before leaving three hours later.

Monday evening I came home from school and found them comfortably seated on the couch eating a bag of potato chips, taking turns dipping into a dish of guacamole. I sat on a chair across from them and after saying no thanks to the chips I spoke without putting a second thought to my words, which had always been the best way to express myself. "I would like to request some privacy. When I come home from school I'm too tired to play hostess and I have to make dinner and study. I can't have you here every day visiting Snooky. Also, you probably don't know this but I'm basically deaf and when you walk in without any notice you scare the heck out of me."

"You're in luck, sweetie," Bryan said. "I'm an electronic engineer and an inventor. Why do you think I worked for the CIA?" He winked at me and laughed joyfully along with Lisa. "I'll make you not only a hearing aid, but also a special attachment for the telephone in the living room that will alert you visually as well as with sound when it rings. Let's go home, honey," he said to Lisa. Then he said to me, "I'll have them both for you the next time we come over." They hugged me enthusiastically and left.

While working at the clinic I became aware that the adjusting techniques I had been taught were becoming a natural unconscious action, like a musician playing an instrument by ear versus reading the music. I understood that quite well because when I used to play the guitar or the banjo, in the beginning I had to look where I put my fingers, but after a while, my fingers just knew where to go. Prior to adjusting a person's neck or back, I started performing spinal distraction to relieve the pressure on the nerves and to get the patient to relax, and then I adjusted the spine accordingly. My patients loved the procedure. One lady even brought in a silk scarf so I could use it to perform the cervical distraction; she liked it better than the cloth towel I used as a leveler. I was very careful when I worked on her not to mess up her wig. She suffered from alopecia.

Between working at the clinic, studying for my BS, and doing my regular schoolwork, the days were going by fast. Plus, a week had gone by without Lisa and Bryan coming by; I could not be happier.

When Allan called Saturday morning to ask if I could come over to his apartment across town, he sounded terrible and I knew something was up.

He had just been diagnosed with Diabetes II. My poor friend, life had been far from kind to him. At eleven years old, he had caught hepatitis C after having a blood transfusion in the hospital for an appendectomy, and now this extra hepatitis C finding was not easy for him to handle. I didn't leave his place until he was feeling more positive about life. When I got home, I found Lisa and Bryan seated on the sofa drinking from two oversized soda cups. They had just finished eating several fast food burgers and containers of fries and the vestiges of shredded lettuce and ketchup, mustard, salt and pepper packets, including the bags and wrapping paper, littered the small coffee table and the carpet. The overwhelming smell of fried food permeated the room reminding me how much I hated that fast food odor. Like children, when they saw me they got up and just about jumped on me taking turns at rocking me back and forth in a hug lasting longer than a minute each. I did not know how long they had been waiting for me in the steaming apartment, since there was no air conditioning, but their faces glowed with sweat and excitement. "We were worried about you," said Bryan. "You're usually home on Saturdays. We have something wonderful to show you."

"Yeah, wait till you see what my Bryan made for you," Lisa said enthusiastically. And he added in the same exuberant manner, "Wait until you see your new toys!" Lisa handed him a shoe box from which he took out a thin metal wire with what looked like a large bullet hanging from it. "Just stand still, so I can hang this around your neck." He held the "necklace" with both hands as if he was about to slip a purple medal of honor over my head. "This is your brand new hearing aid!" he said, slipping the long metal wire around my neck. It was long enough to reach to about the middle of my sternum and then he tugged on the "bullet" and hastily slipped it into my left ear. "The sound can be easily controlled," he said, "by twisting to the right the protruding end like a wheel. Like this," and he turned it.

"Ouch!" I shrieked, pulling away from him and pulling the bullet out of my ear. The feedback had been so piercing I feared I had blown whatever hearing I had.

"No problem, little missy," said Bryan. "I'll take it home and tweak it a little more." Then he proceeded to work on the phone using a screwdriver to attach a wooden box and a round lantern to it. I had to give him a hand; he did not give up easily. He sent Lisa to call me from the phone in the lobby. The phone rang with the earsplitting sound of an ambulance siren, while the lantern, like those from old police cars, began to spin from the top of the wooden box, which was attached to the back of the phone. The lights that projected over the living room walls and ceiling created a psychedelic imagery of bright red and glowing whitish yellow. Snooky took off yowling into his room and if he had hands I was sure he would have closed the door behind him.

"Isn't this wonderful?" Bryan asked. "From now on you will never miss a call! He winked at me and then with a beaming smile said, "Isn't this the most amazing thing you've ever seen? And I created it just for you, our buddy and friend. If by any chance you can't hear the siren, you'll definitely see the lights!" He lifted me up in the air as if I were a baby and after they took turns hugging me over and over again, they left.

It was a living nightmare, but I lacked the courage to burst their bubble after he had worked so hard to create such monstrous creations.

On Saturday mornings, Allan drove over and we began taking hikes at the nearby park and sometimes we speed-walked a few laps around the local high school track. I was impressed with his stamina when he climbed the grandstand two steps at a time without stopping to take a breather. One morning I shared with him a bunch of funny jokes about lawyers. He didn't find them funny so I switched to chiropractic jokes.

"How many chiropractors do you need to change a light bulb?" I asked.

"How many?" he rolled his eyes a little but did smile.

"Only one, but he'll need to come in three times a week to make sure the bulb is working."

He laughed.

Over the years I had gotten a lot more assertive than I used to be but I was still unable to express my feelings in situations where I had to face confrontation. I needed something to happen to give me permission to fight for my rights. Thursday night was the clincher.

I got home after making a stop at the food market, and there were Lisa and Bryan seated on "my" couch eating their fast food dinner. It was like being on *The Twilight Zone.* They were far from finished and remained seated munching away. Lisa stretched her arm towards me to hand me a hamburger, still wrapped. "Here you go sweetie, you must be hungry after a long day at school."

"I don't eat meat, thank you," I couldn't help lying. I went into the kitchen and started putting away my groceries. My brain was on overdrive looking for what to say or do next but I couldn't think of a thing.

Bryan followed Lisa to the kitchen and they both stood there watching me wipe the counter, which wasn't even dirty, I just didn't know what to do. "How was your day at the clinic?" Lisa asked.

"I'm still working on your hearing aid," Bryan said. "You saw a few patients today, hmm?"

I really did not want to have small talk. All I wanted was to be alone. I said, "I had a good day and I did see some patients and it's late. It's 8:30 and I need to unwind and get ready for bed." I walked past them and said politely, "Excuse me folks, but as *you know*," I emphasized the words you know, "I have to get up early. I'm going to take a shower and get to bed, so good night and let yourselves out."

I went into my bedroom and took my time to get my pajamas, although when I came out, they were *still* seated on the couch. I went into the bathroom and purposely took a long shower but when I came out, they were still seated on the couch petting Snooky who sat between them. They had no intention of leaving. I began turning the lights off and then I opened the front door and yelled, "Get out of here, now! You're impossible! Don't you get my message? I'm in pajamas for goodness sake what more do you want me to do? I've told you I have to go to bed. Leave! NOW! Or I'll start screaming even louder!" I was screaming pretty loudly already and even if I wanted to yell higher, that was as loud as my voice could go.

"My, my, you're really stressed out. You don't have to yell at us. But don't worry, we're not upset about it, we're your friends. We understand, you're tired," said Bryan helping Lisa to get her coat on.

"Yes," Lisa said as she hugged me. "We're here for you, and we love you. Tomorrow I'm coming to the clinic because I would like you to be my doctor. Bryan will stay with the doctor he has now. But I want you to treat me from now on, okay? Love you." She planted a kiss on each of my cheeks.

They left and I cried out of despair. I could not believe I had lost my self-control with such sweet, loving people.

Mr. Cornell saw me two times a week for the treatment of back pain. When he came in the first time, he bluntly informed me, "I'm a schizophrenic and bipolar. Sometimes I lose it completely and I can become dangerous to others." I was taken by his honesty but I was also taken by what to do. I chose to remain silent and see what else he had to say or do since he was seated by the only door out of the treatment room and I was seated on the other side of the room. He was also three times my size, and I became very aware that if I showed any fear, like trying to run out, all he had to do was extend his arm and squeeze my neck with his long fingers. He said, "You will be smart to leave the treatment door open, because I'm not to be trusted." I looked straight at him and said, "I'm your doctor, and if you hurt me, no other doctor will even come close to you. You'll have to suffer for the rest of your life with back pain. So the question is, do you want me to treat you?"

"You're a very courageous woman."

"No I'm not courageous, quite the contrary. I'm a doctor and I want to do everything I can to help you to get better." I stood, walked slowly towards the door and stood facing him.

"So, do you still want me to do the exam and treat you?"

I found out later from Dr. Thompson that Mr. Cornell was telling the truth. I was advised to keep the door open and whoever was in charge that day was to be nearby in case I called out for help.

I began leaving the door halfway open and sat next to the doorway while having Mr. Cornell seated on the other side of the room while taking his intake prior to adjusting his spine. He always handed me a chocolate bar after getting adjusted. I was a chocoholic and I never threw away chocolate, but after he left, it went into the trash can at the end of the hallway.

When I got home Monday afternoon, I opened the door slowly expecting to see Lisa and Bryan, but they were nowhere in sight. I had some leftover soup and a fresh salad for dinner, and then sat at my desk to study. Snooky joined me as he always did, on "his" chair next to me. After an hour of studying I felt it was appropriate to celebrate my privacy by having some strawberry ice cream. I studied another hour, scratched Snooky for about ten minutes and with plans to go to sleep earlier I went to my bedroom to get my pajamas.

I had to look twice at my bed, however. Someone had been sleeping in my bed and I knew it was not Goldilocks. The top bed sheet was tucked neatly under the blanket— something I would never do. They either took a nap or, had sex in "my" bed. Maybe both! I was horrified by the mere thought. They had violated my bedsheets and my pillow, and they had robbed me of my privacy, my very personal privacy. I would have to call Allan for advice. There had to be a law against this type of intrusion, but first things first. I knew it was getting late so I took all the bedding to the laundry room in the basement to be washed in hot water, and rushed out to get my car and drive to a hardware store, not far from where I lived. I bought a lock for my bedroom door. I was the least mechanically inclined person in the world and had no concept of how to change a lock. But I was determined to figure out how to remove that door lock so I could put a new one in. I did it! Ha, ha, ha! Now I was the only one with a key to my bedroom! *Oh happy days are here again,* I sang. That night I fell asleep with a smile of accomplishment on my face. In the morning I woke up with a solution of how to get back at my intruding landlords. Ralph would most likely advise me to call Allan and get his lawful expertise on how to handle the case, instead of being so passive-aggressive as he would describe my way of handling impossible tasks. But I couldn't help myself—I truly enjoyed coming up with solutions that were a lot more creative than laws.

As soon as I got to the clinic I took Diane, my school buddy and friend, into the bathroom and told her about Lisa and Bryan using my bed. Although she knew about their constant "visits" she said, "You have got to stop them. This one takes the cake." She was as horrified as I was. I told her I was ready to teach them a lesson, but I needed her help. They were coming in that afternoon for their chiropractic adjustments and since she was Bryan's doctor, all she had to do was play along.

When I saw them seated in the waiting room, I went to get Diane and we both entered the waiting room. I said loudly enough for the three other patients who were seated to hear, "Diane, please do me a favor. Before you adjust Bryan, you need to inspect his whole body. He and Lisa, his fiancée, might have contracted some porous dermatitis from sleeping in my bed last night."

Everybody in the waiting room was paying close attention. I wanted to shame Lisa and Bryan even if it meant I was the carrier of some horrible skin disease.

"Why on earth would you sleep in Dr. Veronica's bed?" Diane said to Bryan.

"Lisa and I were tired and decided to take a nap while we visited our kitty." He wore a sheepish grin.

"We didn't know about your skin condition," Lisa said to me. "You never told us about it. Is it contagious?"

"Of course it is. It is highly contagious," I said vehemently. "If you lay on my bed sheets and sweat, it goes right through your skin like... osmosis." I was proud of my cockamamie story. The patients seated in the waiting room exchanged looks with each other.

"Oh my goodness," Lisa pulled her sleeves up and started looking at her arms.

"Bryan, you better come with me right away," said Diane. "I'll have to take a careful look at your skin. Have you been scratching at all this morning?" Diane winked at me as she followed him to the treatment room.

Lisa sat on the adjusting table and said, "We got tired of waiting for you and decided to take a little nap with Snooky."

"Snooky was also in my bed? When I get home I better check under his fur for purple crusty spots."

"Oh, my poor Snooky!" Her eyes filled with tears. "Will you take him to the veterinarian if he does? Please?" Snooky was not allowed in my bedroom much less in my bed, but since Lisa was so distraught in general about his skin disease, I felt lucky that she didn't pick up on this.

"Of course I will," I said quickly changing her focus away from Snooky. "But now let's check your skin and make sure the fungus has not already started attacking your internal organs."

"What kind of skin disease do you have? Your skin doesn't show any spots."

"Lisa, sorry about this but if you caught what I think you have, I will need to send you to a medical doctor so that you can get half a dozen shots of penicillin. I have to have shots twice a year to control the fungus."

"Oh no, I'm allergic to penicillin! Come to think of it, my arms and legs feel itchy." She began scratching her forearms and then the back of her head.

"If by tonight you notice a loss of vision or your tongue turns black," I said, lacking any remorse, "more serious measures will have to be taken."

"No, please don't tell me that, what can I do? What can Bryan and I do?"

"Hmm, good question," I rubbed my chin between my thumb and index finger as if pondering. Then I said, "You and Bryan need to stay home and drink a lot of water for at least a week. Oh, and…no sunlight during the one week of incubation period."

Afterwards, Diane and I met in the bathroom and we were laughing our heads off. We could have gotten into a lot of trouble for what we did but it felt good to be bad.

While bending over a patient to palpate her thoracic region, my darn nose started bleeding profusely. I said hurriedly, "Excuse me, I'll be right back." Trying my best to stop the blood avalanche from staining my white jacket or the hallway cream colored carpet. I used my hands as cups and ran to the bathroom. I believed my nose bled from being smacked across the face by my father when I was a child. Trying to repair the damage, my mother used to take me to a doctor to have my nasal lining cauterized, which I believe caused more harm than good.

I had become an expert at rapidly stopping a nosebleed. Once in the bathroom, I blew hard a few times and then firmly held the base of my nose for a few seconds. Then I blew again to get rid of any clots that once they got hard, if even barely touched, they would start the bleeding again. I took my white jacket off and washed the blood with cold water.

I was terribly embarrassed when I got back to the treatment room and found three bloodstains on the back of the patient's light blue shirt. I prayed that when she put her shirt in the laundry basket, she wouldn't notice them.

After one peaceful week of no unexpected "guests" in my apartment, I made the mistake of lifting the phone when the siren rang and the flashing lights went off. It was *them.* At least they called, I reasoned with myself.

"Hi, Veronica," said Bryan. "We're downstairs. Can you buzz the door open?"

Lisa's voice joined in bright and cheery, "Yes, honey, we're here to see you and Snooky, but we don't want to just 'pop in' unexpectedly." She giggled along with Bryan.

Wow! I had made an impression on them after all. So I thought. After they sat on the couch Bryan said, "We noticed you put a lock on your bedroom door. That was a very good idea, because this neighborhood is known for some criminal activities and at least you'll know they can't get into your bedroom." He laughed with what seemed to me a mocking tone.

So, they had been back to my place during the week and had tried to go in my room! Ha, ha, ha, I could just imagine their faces when they found the door locked. The only criminal minds around were *them.*

I got a letter from Michael. After two months of waiting for his response, I had given up on him. If he had a good excuse such as he almost died in a car accident or had been detained in the hospital in a coma, then perhaps I would understand the delay. He didn't answer my questions and finished the short letter with, "I'm writing to you because I love you and I don't want to lose you again." How could he be in love with me after so many years of complete silence? He woke up one morning and saw the light of love? No way! He used to say we were an odd couple because he was twenty years younger than me. He was right. And now five years later we probably had even less in common. I took a good analytical look at my past. In those days, I wanted to find undying love so desperately I had convinced myself that Michael was my

Prince Charming, right out of one of my romance books that I used to be addicted to as a young girl. I told myself, *Michael is a ghost from the past and I must leave him buried. Some day I will find my true soulmate.* I crunched his one-page letter into a ball and threw it into the wastebasket.

Diane called. She was going to pick me up in ten minutes to go for a hike. Whenever she suggested a walk in the park, I knew she wanted to talk. She was sure her husband was cheating on her and even though she felt miserable about it, she loved him so much that she was willing to forgive him. I sat outside on the curb waiting when a pickup truck went by with two Latino men in it. They blew the horn and whistled at me. My first reaction was, Wow! I've still got what it takes to make men whistle. Then I took a closer look at myself. There was nothing to whistle about. I was over half a century old, 53 years old to be exact, and I was wearing an old, stained, oversized T-shirt and baggy sweatpants. There was nothing exciting or seductive about my looks. I was just a woman and that was all that mattered to them. When another car went by and the driver yelled out, "Hey babe, you wanna go for a ride?" I gave him the middle finger. Bunch of freaks!

My last quarter at school had become a drag except for Public Health, X-Ray Pathology, and Office Procedures I felt like I had learned everything I needed to know in a classroom environment and the bureaucracy of keeping us occupied until we graduated was a waste of energy and time. I preferred to spend my days at the clinic treating patients. That's where I really belonged.

I spent most of my free time at the doctors' lounge entering patients' files, studying for my class assignments, or socializing with other clinicians. It was a simple room with comfortable chairs where we sat waiting to be called by the front desk person when our regular patient arrived, or we lucked out with a walk-in patient. Seth, who was one quarter behind me, had been sitting next to me for the last two weeks while waiting to see his patients. His slightly receding silver white hair was held back neatly in a small ponytail, matching his well-kept small beard and mustache. He was 49 years old. He rarely smiled and I felt that was the reason he looked older. His dignified looks and superior intellectual attitude came across on our short conversations as intimidating. But I was attracted by the idea that I could flirt yet remain detached. He invited me to dinner on the following Friday night.

He drove a black car. "Nice car," I said as he opened the door for me. I knew men liked that kind of compliment.

He walked around the back of the car and when he got into his seat he said, "It's a brand new Mercedes. They're very comfortable to drive." I went on to tell him I used to have a friend in New Jersey and that was the only brand she bought. To which he said, "Smart woman." I was out to impress him with my Mercedes connections and told him my oldest son Ralph had a friend in New Jersey who worked at a Mercedes dealership and he could only say good things about it. To which he responded, "I also have a Porsche, but it's last year's model."

"Oh, wow!" I said. "That's impressive for a student. Are you a millionaire?"

"I don't consider myself rich. There are a lot of people with more money than me."

Yeah, I thought, *like the king of Spain.*

He found a parking spot in front of a Greek restaurant and asked for a table by the window so he could keep an eye on his "wheels." I was hoping dinner would not be gyros as I had overdosed on them during my trip to Greece with Patrick. "I have been here several times, and I know what's really good," he said. "If you don't have any dietary restrictions, do you mind if I order the food for both of us?"

"As long as it's not gyros I'm open to try anything," I said delighted with the idea of getting pampered and not having to put any effort into what to order. The vegetable soup reminded me of Portuguese cuisine and the lamb dish was just as delicious. Sitting across from each other eating and talking, I succeeded in making him smile. He became more human, as if the conservative shell he had worn all those days we sat next to each other had finally cracked open. Out of habit, I offered to pay for my meal but he said, "I invited you and I can afford to pay for dinner." On the way back to my apartment, he asked if on the following weekend, I would like to go to Calistoga, the land of wine, and to a hot springs spa that he frequented every time he was in the region.

"I would love to. I've never been to a spa, but I must warn you, I don't drink," I said.

"Good, I'll drink and you can be my assigned driver. I'll bring the Porsche."

Early Saturday morning Seth picked me up in his black, open-top Porsche. I felt special being on a date with a man who appreciated my company and trusted me to drive his car if he drank too much. Gosh, it was good to feel like a woman, a modern, desirable woman. I let my long hair fly to the open country breeze, and like a movie star, I wore oversized, prescription sunglasses which allowed me to appreciate the famous manicured vineyards of Napa Valley on the way to Calistoga. Napa Valley put to shame the French countryside that I had so admired when I had driven through it with Patrick while on our fateful honeymoon.

I didn't have time to buy a bathing suit for the occasion but on the other hand, I couldn't recall the last time I went swimming so saw no reason to buy one. I tried on my old sleeveless black bodysuit, I had been using for working out and I opted to use it since it made me look appealing in a sexy way. It was over ten years old and considerably worn out; but I checked the seams to make sure they would hold me in when I went into the hot springs pool, which Seth had described as being very hot. I wore my jean shorts, and Patrick's Hard Rock Cafe black T-shirt from Puerto Vallarta, over the bodysuit.

I knew I had made the right choice when at the spa's dressing room, a woman said, "Wow, you're not wearing a bra under that bathing suit. You're in very good shape."

Wrapped in the spa's large white towel, I emerged from the dressing room and blinked in the bright sunshine. I waited until Seth, who was sitting on the side of the pool, looked in my direction. I threw him a kiss and removed the towel. The woman in the dressing room had given me the confidence to feel secure in my nakedness. Carrying the towel nonchalant over one shoulder, I walked up to him and put the towel next to him. Then I walked down the steps into the pool. It was as deep as my waist. I had to hunch down to get my neck wet. He joined me and we waddled in the water, laughing. After twenty minutes or so I sat on the side of the pool, with my feet dangling as he stood in the pool looking up at me. I knew the bodysuit material had thinned out enough through the years to be almost transparent when wet.

Seth had come prepared with tanning lotion. He rubbed the cream lotion firmly over my back, arms, and legs. When he handed me the tube saying I should apply it to my chest and face for protection, I smiled and said, "Can you do it for me? I may miss some spots." I was being bad but I needed to know if he was able to provide a more loving touch. He did. I returned the favor by taking my time to massage the lotion just as lovingly to his forehead and face while paying close attention not to let the lotion get on his beard.

We spent close to two hours going in and out of the water. It was as hot in the water as it was out of it. Sitting by the pool, Seth ordered red wine and I asked for a large glass of ice cubes to crunch on. He told me about his younger days when as a hippie he had lived on a farm commune. "Those were the good old days. I've been playing with the idea of starting something like that again, once I get my chiropractic license."

"You want to practice on a farm?"

"I wouldn't be practicing. I'd be running the commune."

"So why bother to go to college to be a chiropractor?"

"I have to prove myself to my parents."

My goodness, he was a child in a grown man's body! We stopped in downtown Calistoga, a typical old western town that looked like something out of a cowboy movie except for the boutiques selling expensive trinkets. Seth wanted to check out a certain boutique where he always stopped to buy body soap. He bought a white robe and several soaps. "Aren't you buying anything?" he asked.

"I already have a robe and lots of soap." I didn't have the courage to tell someone so rich that I lived on a student budget and that my priority was to save enough money to someday open a practice with my son. On the way home, we stopped at a vineyard, where we had a late lunch. Seth ordered a bottle of red wine with his meal and I had club soda with a twist of lemon.

I couldn't wait to drive his car.

"I gave my wife everything she wanted but she never had enough," he said, after a few glasses of wine. "After the divorce, she found a sugar daddy. She's spending his money like there's no tomorrow. She's doing well." He took a sip from his glass of wine and said, "He already bought her a house in Malibu."

"Wow!" I took in a mouthful of a delicious mushroom that was stuffed with crab meat. "If I wanted, I could buy a house, too," he said pensively. "I just don't feel like I need one right now." He shrugged his shoulders. "My parents have set me up with quite a lump of money in a trust fund for when I graduate. Meanwhile, anything I want, my mother takes care of. That includes my living expenses and tuition."

"Wow!" I repeated. There was something about bragging about being born with a silver spoon in his mouth that bothered me. It wasn't that I preferred to be with a pauper, it was the attitude of not once mentioning he worked for what he had coming to him.

Of course I also didn't care for the stick shift on his Porsche, but he didn't seem to mind every time I put it in the wrong gear.

While checking my emails at the computer at the school lab, I was shocked to find an email from Michael. I answered, "Yes, you have the correct email. It's me, Ronnie."

He responded, "I can't believe I found you! Ronnie, I'm so happy to hear back from you. If you give me your phone number, I'll call you. I have so much to tell you."

I kept my message to one chilled line, "This is my number:.. You can call me tonight between seven thirty and nine Eastern time."

At the magic hour of seven thirty, I sat on the sofa brushing Snooky's beautiful white coat, waiting for Michael's call. The screeching phone's siren and the blinding show across the living room and kitchen hit me hard at eight o'clock sharp. Snooky looked at me for a split second and then sprinted out of my lap like a speeding bullet into his labyrinthine quarters.

After our initial exclamations back and forth of "Wow, that's you," "I can't believe it," "So good to hear your voice," and "How have you been?" he said, "How would you feel if I were to come to California at the end of September?"

"That's just one month from now," I said, taken quite by surprise. I chuckled nervously. *Should I be happy?* I asked myself. Then my thoughts out loud, "I don't know. It's been years and at present I'm dating someone."

Except for his breathing, silence crawled from the phone receiver. I waited until he spoke again. "I love you and I still want to see you." He sounded adamant. Didn't he hear me say I was dating someone?

"It's been a long time." I counted on my fingers to be sure, and said, "It's been five years since we last saw each other."

"I know you'll never forgive me. I saw the look on your face when I told you it was more important that you follow your career than waste your time with me. I just wanted what was best for you." He sounded like my mother. I remained silent. He said, "I saw you crying when you drove away that day. You thought I was breaking up with you forever and didn't love you. You were wrong."

"You did break up with me. When you tell someone to go away even if it's for their own benefit as you say, it means breaking up." It was my turn to pause and then I added, "I have no plans for the future."

"I don't either," he said. "I only know I must see you."

"I'm dating someone," I repeated, just in case he had missed that part of our conversation.

"I understand you're dating someone. I understand how you feel after all these years of silence. Ronnie, how about if we don't make any promises until September and see how it goes when we meet?"

"Okay, let's wait until September and see what happens."

"I love you, Ronnie."

"Me too." I meant I loved myself.

Snooky and I had become study buddies. He liked to sit on the chair next to me. He liked making believe he was sleeping but he kept a close watch through his slanted, semi-closed blue eyes. When he decided I had studied enough, he would put on a theatrical stretch, walk over my lap, hop on the table, and sprawl belly-up all over my papers and books. He expected me to scratch his belly and head. The problem was that he was very demanding when it came to getting scratched. A five-minute scratch was no longer acceptable. Snooky may not have been able to hold a conversation, but his body language and actions clearly showed what was on his mind, "Scratch me or I'll remain sprawled all over your paperwork meowing until I drive you nuts."

One day I was making a tuna sandwich for lunch and he stood in the kitchen doorway yowling. I knew exactly what he wanted; that's how close we had become. But against my better judgment and specific orders not to do it, I gave in. The next time he heard me opening a tuna can he came running to the kitchen entrance waiting for his share. If the owners found out, I could lose the apartment. So I told him, "Look man, I was kind enough to give you some of my tuna once, but that does not mean I'm going to do that every time I make a sandwich. You have your own cat food." So, what did he do? He looked at me for a few seconds, his silent stare speaking loud and clear, "How dare you talk to me like that?" Then he backed away to the center of the living room and squeezing himself as hard as he could, he pooped on the carpet. I swear he was smiling, with a nasty, triumphant, feline look on his face.

The next time I was opening a can of tuna, I wrapped a towel around the can so he wouldn't hear the sound of the can opener. But he heard it! When I looked at him, there he was, straining himself again in the middle of the living room. I caught him just in time to throw him into one of his cat litter boxes.

I stopped eating tuna sandwiches at home after that.

It was eight in the evening and I had just finished studying for a test when the phone went off in all its grandeur. Bryan and Lisa were calling me from downstairs and asked if I could buzz the front door open. I let them in. They wanted me to drive them to Fry's Electronics.

"Bryan, you drove here, so why don't you just go to Fry's? You know it's close to my bedtime."

"We'd feel better if you'd drive. Our medications affect our sight at night."

"Yeah," said Lisa, "we'd feel a lot safer if you'd drive."

"They'll be closed by the time we get there."

"Oh no, they're open until nine and I promise that you'll be home at the latest by nine-thirty and in time to get your beauty sleep," said Bryan lovingly, squeezing one of my cheeks.

"Nine-thirty I'll be home?" I knew I was being taken by their charming smiles.

Their heads were bobbing up and down. "Yep, we promise to have you back here by nine-thirty. Here are the keys to our car."

They sat in the back seat as they always did when I drove them around. I turned the key and said, "Bryan, have you noticed that your gas meter shows your gas tank is empty?"

"Oh, don't you go paying attention to that, little lady." He laughed loudly and cheerily along with Lisa. "We have plenty of gas. It's only a twenty minute drive, anyway."

It was 8:45 when we got to the store and before I could blink an eye, they disappeared like phantoms, into one of the aisles. After checking out some cameras, I began searching for them. They were tall, especially Bryan, they were large, and they were very blond, but they were nowhere to be found. Someone was announcing over the speaker that the store would be closing in five minutes when I caught them speaking to one of the employees at the end of aisle three. "There you are," I said, relieved. "Let's go. They're closing."

"This young man is helping us and we'll soon be on our way," said Bryan. By the time we left, it was nine-twenty. I gave up on the idea I would be in bed by nine-thirty.

Not even ten minutes of driving went by when suddenly the car coughed a few snorting sounds and stopped dead, right in the middle of the highway. I turned the wheel to my right, hoping as if by some magic force that the car would know I wanted to be out of the swiftly approaching traffic behind us. Horns were blowing and brakes were screeching as the cars swerved around us and before I could say or do anything, Bryan opened the car door and jumped out screaming, "Just stay at the wheel and turn when I tell you. Lisa, c'mon honey, help me push the car off the highway."

I rolled my window down and shouted, "There's no shoulder to pull onto."

"So what, we'll push the car until we find a space. Don't you worry, Veronica, you just stay at the wheel!"

Great! I had a double human bumper! As if their bodies were going to help me when we got rear-ended by a semi-truck. I could just imagine reading the headlines the next morning, *"Invalid couple living on morphine, give up their lives pushing their car off the road while the driver, a chiropractor, did nothing but pray while seated comfortably at the wheel."*

Lisa and Bryan

Feeling like a turtle in the middle of a racetrack, I had no difficulty visualizing our bodies dismantled by the impact of the cars speeding by us at more than 75 mph. If we were lucky, our lives would cease right upon collision, however there was always the possibility we would wind up in a pile still alive but with body pieces missing. It felt like forever before they were able to push the car close to the highway's side railing where the narrow shoulder lane lead up to a ramp and an exit.

Bryan helped breathless Lisa to the back seat and he sat next to me in the front. I looked at him, and then her, and then feeling like a fool I said, "Now what?"

"Now we must remain calm and wait for road help," said Bryan.

"You mean cops?" I said.

"They're called highway patrolmen," he said.

Thirty minutes went by. Bryan got out of the car, opened the trunk, and handed Lisa a small orange plastic gas container. "We can't stay here the whole night," he said. "I'm going to remain with the car. You two go see what's up there by the exit. Hopefully you'll find a gas station. This container will give us enough gas to get home."

When Lisa and I got to the top of the hill, it was pitch black. We took a chance and crossed the long bridge over the highway but there was nothing on the other side except a dark, narrow country road. We crossed the bridge back and kept walking towards a distant dim light. I was no longer checking my wristwatch. It was a cool pleasant night, perfect for a long walk. The light came from a small gas station! Lisa had the gas container filled and insisted on carrying it back. As we approached the corner to walk down the exit ramp leading to where we had parked, we saw a police car with the lights flashing and two policemen with flashlights looking into the car. Lisa dropped the gas container on the ground and began running towards them screaming hysterically, "Bryan! Bryan! Where's Bryan? Bryan! Bryan!"

One of the highway patrolmen yelled to us, "Get off the road and walk behind the metal railing!"

I did as he said, but not Lisa. Suspecting Bryan had been taken away since he was nowhere in sight, she kept running towards the cops with her purse and fists flying in the air. "Where's my Bryan? You pigs! What did you do with my Bryan?" I feared they were going to shoot her when they grabbed her by the neck forcefully and made her get on her knees trying to stop her from hitting them.

Just then a brown car stopped and let Bryan out. "Hi fellas," he said in his usual joyful mood. "I'm the car owner. I was concerned about my wife and friend and went looking for them. I even borrowed a large can of gas from the gas station up there." He pointed to the opposite road where Lisa and I had walked from.

It was two o'clock in the morning when I finally got into bed, but I was so stressed out that I couldn't sleep.

On Friday, Seth invited me to his apartment for the first time. It was exquisitely decorated with modern furniture, equally wonderful metal art works, oil paintings, and ceramics. It was a blend of antique and modern pieces but my favorite was the couch. I liked the way its plump, soft cushions bent slightly in the middle and brought us closer. His lips were so close, it only felt natural for me to kiss him. I was finally in the arms of a man closer to my age. He kissed me and then wrapped his arms around me, bringing my body closer to his. The phone rang and he went to answer. I thought that was rude. Why would anyone pick up the phone when kissing the girl of his dreams for the first time?

"A sales call," he said. "I'm hungry. How about if I take you out to dinner and we see a movie afterwards?"

"That sounds like a great idea." I didn't have the courage to say I would rather remain kissing. There were several explanations for his behavior, I thought. Either food was more important to him than lovemaking, or he knew he had me and there was no need to rush the inevitable, or kissing was going to be as far as we would ever go because he was an older man and all he needed was a friend.

He sat across from me at the restaurant. "I would like to recommend the filet mignon & lobster tail combo, he said.

"They are both my favorites." I said happily.

"You are not at all like other women I've dated. They always order a boring salad. It's so much more fun to share dinner with someone that enjoys the same food I do." He drank red wine and I had my usual, club soda with a twist of lemon. While munching on the crispy asparagus, I slipped my right shoe off and touched his leg with my foot. I had seen that done in a James Bond movie and was dying to try it. He said, "I like your sexy, groovy attitude."

"Groovy?" I asked, and laughed. "Sorry for laughing but isn't that from the 60s hippie generation?"

"Well, I was a hippie. I even attended Woodstock. Didn't you?"

"I wish I had, but in those days I was a full-time mom."

He let me pick the movie. I selected *Logan's Run.*

"You surprise me," he said. "Women usually pick romantic stories."

"I'm okay with romance, but I love adventure and fantasy movies dealing with the future."

"Why is that?"

"The future is a fantasy; it doesn't exist until we reach it. No one can predict or rebuke what has not yet happened. So I keep my mind open to all possibilities. If I'm lucky, I'll be able to experience in the future what we now watch but for now I'll consider it a fantasy." He stared at me. I added, "There are lots of options on the way to the future." *Had I said too much?* I asked myself.

"You are a bit odd," he said, "but I like you anyway."

Oh my, he sounded so much like Al. Me and my big mouth. When was I to learn not to go into any philosophical conversations unless I was talking to someone like Allan or Rod who were on the same mental level as me?

In the theatre, Seth put his arm around my shoulders and I put my head on his shoulder. I loved feeling loved.

When we got back to his apartment, he adjusted my back and neck on his adjusting table and then I did the same to him. "Let me show you how I adjust my own back when I can't make it to the clinic," he said. I laid on the white plush carpet next to him and watched him use a small rubber ball to press his back into it. I was far from impressed. It was nothing but a massage to the paraspinal muscles; it had nothing to do with adjusting a specific joint. We talked some more while lying next to each other, his arm being used as a pillow for my head. The room was softly lit by a tall metal lamp in the shape of candelabra. The time was right to bring our lips together once again. That awesome feeling of "the first time" passion of the moment folded over us in a sweet emotion of pleasure. It was my humble opinion that nothing could compare to the first time two lovers had sex. But right in the middle of what I considered a steamy moment, he stopped, and getting up from the floor said, "I'm not like other men."

Great! Here it goes again, another weirdo in my life. I hope he's not into pain or some freaky stuff. I waited with apprehension.

"I don't like to finish quickly. I like to stop, go do something and then come back for more. This way I can be hard for hours. Would you like some vanilla ice cream with fresh strawberries?"

I smiled with relief, even though my favorite ice cream flavor was not vanilla, but I did love strawberries. "Is there anything else I should know about you?" I asked courageously.

"Oh yes, just one more thing. I like to wear certain clothing items that make sex more exciting."

"If that brings you more pleasure, I'm all for it." But I thought that seeing a middle-aged man with white hair and white beard parading in front of me in a bra and panties was going to be too much of a freaky experience. If that's what he meant, I wasn't looking forward to it. Wasn't anybody normal anymore?

After the ice cream treat, he put on some Frank Sinatra music, which was as exhilarating as elevator music. But I guess that helped him get back into the mood because we had sex on the floor and he didn't stop for a break. Afterwards we sat on the couch as he was eager to watch the news. I couldn't wait to go home. I guess he also had enough excitement for the day because when I looked at him, he had dozed off. I got up carefully and wrote on a napkin, "Had a great time. If you want to get together again, call me." I put the note on the coffee table next to the couch and left.

Once in a blue moon Rod and I spoke on the phone but we were going in different directions with our lives. Allan and I maintained our friendship by still going hiking once or twice a month and having dinner at his apartment. I found him physically and intellectually attractive but the idea of possibly catching hepatitis from intimacy kept me on guard. I never invited him to my apartment.

After we hiked one Saturday morning, he drove me home and we remained seated in his car talking as we always did. "I'm so depressed lately," he said. He pushed his seat back and closed his eyes. "It's very hard for me to accept that I can never father a child because of my hepatitis."

"I understand how you feel. It must be awful," I said, reaching in my head for all possible philosophical answers. Thank God he was far from having the same dismissive attitude of Seth; Allan and I could talk philosophy for hours and still maintain respect for each other's opinion. "But as cruel as it may sound," I ventured into the positive side of negativity and said, "don't you agree there's a reason for everything in life?"

"You know I do."

"Then why do you feel so sad?"

"Not being a father makes me a loser. I would give anything to have a child of my own."

"That's very greedy and selfish of you since you know that you can't have it. You would be messing with the Universe. Beware of wishes!"

"Still, it depresses me not being able to leave a legacy. Once I die there's no one to continue my family line. I feel like I've failed as a member of the human race."

"You might have seriously failed if you did have a child and it turned out to be the worst experience of your life, like so many parents have, and there's nothing they can do about it." I watched him bring the back of his seat forward and as he sat up he turned his body towards me, listening. "You told me several times that you're a great believer in *The Twilight Zone,* like me, right? So, what would you say if I told you that maybe, just maybe, your child would have been born with three heads, or even worse, another Hitler. But just like in *The Twilight Zone,* you have been given a gift by someone who loves you very, very dearly and made sure you got hepatitis to protect you from becoming the father of your worst nightmare. You should be thankful that you're saving the world from who knows what."

"You're right. You make sense in a rather unusual way, but I can't question it. I guess I really shouldn't be complaining." He smiled contentedly and gave me a hug.

In the past, Allan had been the one to lift up my spirits when I was down in the dumps. I was glad to return the favor. We were good for each other.

Friday night, Seth and I got together for our second rendezvous at his apartment. He opened the door wearing men's lacy black underwear.

Somehow I was a bit disillusioned as I expected something totally outlandish. That evening I got to see two more pieces of his most intimate underwear, a silky yellow thong and a dark blue thong with red dots. He was trim and in excellent shape but his long white hair and white beard just seemed to throw things out of context. I asked him if I should get a few sexy undies for myself but he said he'd rather see me naked.

It was always dinner at a nice restaurant, a movie, sex, and the news on television. Seth's love for watching the news and then falling asleep or talking about the news made me depressed. It reminded me too much of Al. According to Seth, one day out of the blue, his ex-wife asked for a divorce because she was bored. I understood her completely.

"Have you read *Men Are from Mars and Women Are from Venus?*" he asked me during a TV commercial break.

"I heard about it, but I never read it."

"Well, you should. It will teach you to be more like a woman. You're more like a man."

"How is that?" I was not sure if I should be offended.

"Well, one thing you do which is not at all like a female is after we have sex, you don't cuddle up to me telling me sob stories and asking me if I love you. The women I've been with have always done that, so in that case, it's refreshing that you're different. But it really annoys me that after I open the car door for you to be seated, and I come around to put my key in my car door, you reach over and open it. That spoils what I have just accomplished as a man. You're far from being a woman from Venus!" He handed me the book from his coffee table. "Here, take it with you. You need to read this book and make some changes."

I was good, I was very good. I acted like Snooky and did not say what was on my mind, *I'm proud to be an Earth woman. But you must be from Pluto or Uranus. Let's see how you feel the next time it's pouring rain and I let you stand outside the car fumbling for your keys. See how it feels to be out with a selfish Venus woman!*

I "forgot" to take the book home with me when I left.

The next Friday evening I came to the realization that I had conquered Seth's heart, or at least his confidence, because he took me on a tour of the rest of his apartment, including his bedroom and office. He showed me where he kept his most precious possessions—the antique mini clocks, oil paintings, and other artifacts that he had collected since his wife had left him seven years ago. But the trust and sense of confidence he showed towards me did not take away the overall gloom I felt every time I left his apartment. Although we shared the same career, we didn't seem to have that much else in common although the sex was pleasant and I enjoyed the free dinners and movies.

Rod's former chiropractor and my current patient, Dr. Hammond, who was diagnosed with HIV, spoiled me with gifts. He brought me flowers, gift certificates to restaurants and supermarkets, and once, a potted tomato plant. He even gave me a brand new front door mat with the words *Welcome to Chiropractic*. "This mat is for your office when you start your practice; I want you to always remember me and remember how much you helped me."

One day he brought me an ultrasound machine. I got the feeling he was giving me his equipment because he was quitting his practice. He needed to get back to facing life versus contemplating death.

"No more presents, please," I said. "As your doctor, I believe what you need is a voyage to somewhere special. Is there a country you would like to visit?"

"I would love to visit Denmark. Maybe even move there. But I don't know. My life is at the end."

"Not necessarily. I'm your doctor and I'm the one that says if you are at the end or not. You need to make plans to go to Denmark. If you want to live, you will live. Unless you already gave up and have decided to get buried."

"No, I want to live."

"Well then, give yourself two months of eating right, lose some weight, start a workout plan at the gym, get pumped up about your existence, and get a plane ticket to Denmark at the end of the two months. What do you say?"

"I really love your idea. I have to think about it and maybe I'll take your advice." We hugged.

The advice I gave him was something I would give myself if I were in his shoes. Most people know what they have to do but they just need a little push.

I passed the National Boards part III; I could finally take a deep breath and relax until November when I would start preparing for the National Boards part IV. I was still waiting to hear about my BS degree from New York University. After that, I was free to fly away like a bird in the sky with no direction but up, up, up.

While visiting the family in Sacramento, Nancy took me to visit a chiropractor looking for an associate. I could tell Nancy was hoping I would settle in Sacramento and practice close to the family. I was willing to see what the chiropractor had to offer, what his office looked like, and basically get the feeling for what to expect when I graduated in December.

Dr. Marcus was a nice person and so was his practice, but I still wished to work with Ralph.

I was done allowing anyone to adjust my spine. All my ligaments were lax from all those years of so-called adjustments by students practicing on me with no idea of what they were doing.

When I turned in bed at night, my neck cracked like a firecracker and it hurt as it got stuck. Also, when I drove and had to turn my head sideways, my neck popped and then it locked up in a most painful manner. I should have listened to a student friend who upon graduating from Life University, advised me to be wise and not allow students to practice on my spine. By the time she graduated, she was a mess. But it was tough saying no to anyone when they also allowed me to practice on them. My clinician prescribed me Ligaplex pills to help strengthen my ligaments.

I brought my dilemma to my adjusting teachers. I had enough experience to confidently manipulate the spine and had so proved it by working at the clinic as a clinician. They agreed and I became officially exempt from having hands-on by other students.

Leila called one night. Poor thing, she had to be the most sensitive person I had ever known. "Veronica, I can't handle dissection class. I can't stand the thought that these cadavers are being cut without a second thought. They were once people just like us. They had a mother and a father; they were once alive." She cried.

"Those people offered their bodies to science so that you and I can better understand the human body. You should feel honored to be dissecting them. By getting upset about it, you're taking away the respect they deserve and that's not nice."

She calmed down and I changed the topic to funny events. I prided myself in still being able to make her laugh. Some day she would become an awesome chiropractor!

Every day I learned something new at the clinic. I should never tell a runner that they were not to run anymore just because their knees were trashed. I should never tell a patient with degeneration of the spine not to ride their horse. Most got upset when they learned the truth. Would I stop telling them what to do? Of course not. Doctor meant teacher, and teaching was my profession. Win some, lose some. When would I learn the lessons of everyday life? Like everyone else, probably never. They say to err is human, the reason history keeps repeating itself. When Tara, a young chiropractic student, came over to my apartment to study for a test, I could tell she had been crying. Her eyes were bloodshot and she did not smile.

"What's wrong?" I asked.

"My boyfriend left me last week," she said between short little sobs. "Two years. Two years we were together. We were starting to talk about getting married. He left me for another girl."

Boy, she was in luck! If I could just make her see men the way I did, I could save her from any further grief.

"He'll get what he deserves, don't you worry," I said with authority.

"Richard was always wonderful to me; it was that girl who turned his head."

"Yeah, his head all right. Trust me when I say he is not worth a single one of our tears. Love them and when you're not happy, leave them. That's my motto. And I don't mean love them as with love, I mean use them and throw them away for good when you're done with them."

"I don't know if I can do that," she sobbed.

"Look, I'm older than you and I have experienced many, many relationships. I have even been married twice and I'm telling you, they are all jerks. If you keep your heart closed you will never get hurt again." I got up to get some tissues from the bathroom. "Here." I handed her the tissue box and sat next to her again. "Just have fun, and don't get seriously involved with anyone. Promise me that from now on, you'll only love yourself. Promise me that."

"Okay, I promise," she said, wiping her tears. "He was such a disappointment, the bastard!" She blew her nose and then cleared her throat. "Since he left, I haven't been doing well in school, and I haven't been able to concentrate on my studies; I'm a wreck. I'm sorry, but I have to go; I can't study."

"That's fine, you need time to recover, and I hope you take my advice."

We hugged, and before leaving she said, "Thanks for listening. From now on I'm going to be like you, cold as ice."

I was proud of myself for having helped her. She was never going to suffer again over some egotistic, selfish, good-for-nothing jerk. My goal in life would be to save every woman I met who had been used by her man.

I woke up during the night crying. What had I done to Tara? What kind of monster without feelings had I made of myself when I was the one that messed up by making the wrong choices? I had contaminated Tara with my polluted negative thoughts. I had not been happy since I started going out with Seth. I was the one who had lost my values. Sex with him satisfied my body but not my soul. In Mexico, I thought it worked out well, three days of honeymoon and then I was free. But now I realized "so long and farewell" only worked for those who had already lost their soul, their heart. Was I heartless? I was, because I felt empty and very unhappy.

When I got to the clinic, I went looking for Tara. I took her to one side and said, "Tara, I want to apologize for my stupid behavior yesterday telling you to use men and not to love anyone. Listen to me. Better to love and cry like you did last night than not to know what love is. Please do love someone again and if you get hurt, oh well, that's life."

"What you said yesterday showed me you were also crying but from inside here." She pointed to her heart.

"You're so young and so wise."

"I'm not that young; I'm thirty-two years old and have been dating since I was sixteen. I don't look it but I do have a lot of experience," she said, grinning playfully, "like you."

"The man I love is coming in September."

"I'm glad. So you're opening your heart to love again?"

"I'm actually looking forward to it. And you opened my *eyes,* thank you." I hummed, "Whatever will be, will be."

We gave each other an exuberant high five and went our way.

I called Seth at the end of the day and asked him to meet me at a coffee shop that night.

"I owe you an apology," I said as soon as he sat across from me. "I have been using you for sex. I'm breaking up with you. You deserve someone better than me."

He stared at me as if I had just sworn, then he said, "What's the matter? I thought we had a good relationship. I'm shocked."

"Trust me, our relationship is not based on truth. I love someone else or at least I believe I do. His name is Michael and I haven't seen him for years but I used to love him. Either way, he's coming in September. Only a month from now and we're going to try and see if we can make it work."

"When September comes and you get tired of what's his name, you'll come back to me," he said. It was hard to see if he spoke out of anger or jealousy. The beard covered most of his features and his upper body remained erect.

"I'm sorry if I hurt your feelings but I'm being honest with you," I said.

"I was starting to have strong feelings for you. I intended to ask you to be my fiancée and now you do this to me."

"I'm sorry…"

"Never mind." He took a deep breath in and blew it out noisily. "This is payback, I know. Some people call it karma. I did the same to a woman I met at a grocery store about two years ago. I just wanted her for the night. We got together twice and then I left her because twice with her had been more than enough. Did you have more than enough with me?" he asked with an ironic tone, pushing his chair back to leave.

"You have been very nice to me, but I don't love you."
I looked down at my hands on my lap and remained seated.
When I looked up, he was gone.

When Seth saw me at the clinic the next day, he said
hello but kept walking. We never saw each other again.

~ *Chapter Six* ~

My Prince Charming

I sent an email to Michael with the news about my breakup with Seth. He responded, "I'm so happy to know you're no longer seeing someone; I would really like to make our relationship work." The email had started on a positive note, but as I kept reading, a dark cloud loomed over my common sense as if lightning were about to strike. I tried not to read between his lines and to remain optimistic even though after so many years he was still no further in life than when we had last seen each other. He was still living in a trailer with his mother in the forsaken woods of South Carolina. "I was doing well, until I lost my job a year ago," he wrote. "It's hard to make a living without a job but I have been plenty busy taking care of my mother and paying her bills." Did he mean he was helping his mother by driving her to the next town, since they lived out in the middle of nowhere? Was he buying her groceries there and then mailing her bills at the local post office? He's gone one whole year without work? Where did he get the finances to pay for her bills? What did he do all day, go hunting? "If it's okay," he wrote, "I'll move in with you and then apply for a computer job in Silicon Valley where the world's largest high-tech corporations are located. With all the experience I have from my last job, it will be easy to get hired. There are lots of computer companies around where you live." It sounded like he had done some inquiries about Silicon Valley. He sounded very secure in his qualifications; I was glad about that. "I never told my mother or family about our previous relationship," he wrote. "But I intend to tell them how much you mean to me when we visit them later, perhaps next summer if you're up to it." I read and re-read his email while fighting mixed feelings over every word he had written as I repeated over and over again that I was being oversensitive and should be focusing on the positive, because love would take care of everything.

That night I prayed, "Dear God, please make it a reality for Michael and me to always be happy and in love, no matter how many hardships come our way. Being forever happy is all I ask for, even though he is twenty years younger than me and doesn't seem to have his life together. Thank you, dear God!" But I couldn't fall asleep. My instincts told me I was dreaming.

Mario, my Mexican patient at the clinic, caught me by surprise when he handed me a large crystal pendant on a silver necklace. "It will always bring you good luck," he said.

"It's very beautiful. Thank you, but you shouldn't have."

"You deserve it. If it weren't for you fixing my back, I would have lost my job. Please don't get offended, but I'm in love with you."

"It's not love Mario, you're suffering from the Florence Nightingale effect. I helped you get better and as a result, you have feelings for me."

"No, no, I know how I feel about you, it's called love, not Florence."

"Thank you then but I already have a boyfriend."

"American men not as good as Mexican men. We're devoted to our family. I will always love and respect you."

I accepted the crystal because he insisted and I did not want to offend him. Besides, the crystal would always remind me of Mario.

On August 29th I flew to Oregon from San Francisco with my/Patrick's family to attend Ralph's graduation from Western States Chiropractic College. My other family members from New York, and Washington were there too—even Steven, Ralph's childhood friend, who also came in from New Jersey. Al sat next to me during the ceremony and we watched with pride as Ralph walked across the stage wearing his black graduation cap and gown to receive his Doctor of Chiropractic degree. At the end of the next quarter—in December if everything went well—I would also be accepting the same honorable degree. After the excitement of the graduation ceremony at the Convention Center in Portland, we all went to a fancy restaurant where Roger my father-in-law, asked the waiter loudly enough for everyone to hear, "Is my dinner gonna cost me an arm and a leg?" The waiter snapped, "More like both your arms and legs." Each person ordered their own main course and was responsible for their own bill, but we shared the appetizers. Everything was delicious but as expensive as we had been warned about. Nancy was concerned about her father acting like a joker during dinner and embarrassing her since he had this thing about going to the bathroom and walking out wearing the toilet seat paper around his neck, but he was fine. However, it was some of the other adults that in the excitement of the occasion seemed to be in their third age, throwing spitballs at each other. Before heading south the next morning with my California family, we joined all those who still remained at Ralph's girlfriend's apartment for some socializing and hors d'oeuvres. Steven and I reminisced about the old days in New Jersey and he said, "I'll always remember you as the coolest mom I've ever known. You were completely involved in the lives your sons as well as in the lives of the other neighborhood kids like me. We all looked up to you." I was touched.

Ralph and I also had a chance to talk a little. He didn't have the finances to open a chiropractic office but he was excited about practicing in Portland, Oregon as a mobile chiropractor. His brain was still working like an engineer and he had researched all venues regarding how to make mobile chiropractic work effortless. He was going to buy a Toyota RAV 4 because he could easily slide in his adjusting table and therapy equipment in the back of it.

He asked me to work with him once I graduated in December. I wasn't attracted by the prospect of carrying an adjusting table, with my bad back, to people's homes and offices. That was not what I had in mind when we had talked about practicing together. Even though he had all angles covered on how to do it, it sounded like too much physical work for me. I told him I had to think about it.

Autumn 1997

The weekend after I returned from Oregon, Allan and I went to the beach and spent four hours lying on the sand, talking. I wore a hat and a jacket but as always, I was wearing shorts. It wasn't that hot as it was already September but I guess I didn't give enough credit to the sun's rays. My legs got so severely burned that I couldn't even cover myself that night with a bedsheet, plus in the morning, I woke up with a sore throat and runny nose. My head felt double its size. I knew I was running a fever. And every time I sneezed, I had a bloody nose to boot. I called Nancy. She said, "You probably caught the cold from being on the plane from Oregon and breathing all those people's germs." If she was right why didn't she and everybody else catch it?

Michael called. He would be leaving South Carolina on September 21st and arriving on the 26th. I needed to recover quickly. Soon I would be hugging the man I loved! That night I prayed again, "Dear God, please protect Michael when he crosses the US in his old beat-up red pickup truck and please help me get rid of the flu."

The fever was gone by the end of the day but the cold lasted three long days.

Bryan and Lisa invited me to dinner at the Olive Garden. I was wondering what they were up to when they said they wanted to make me an offer they knew I would not be able to resist. Bryan spoke for both of them. They were going to buy a large motor home and travel all over the US and wanted to hire me as their full-time private chiropractor/driver/cook. I was to name the price because whatever I wanted they could afford it. The idea of treating and being the nursemaid to two patients for the rest of my life was unbearable. Let's see, was it worth a billion dollars every six months? No, not even two billion a day. I said thank you very much, but I had already promised my son Ralph that once I got my chiropractic license we would be working together in Oregon. They were sad but understood and that's how I got out of that one without hurting their feelings.

Sunday, September 21

Michael called from St. Louis saying he expected to arrive in about three days. Soon I would be in his arms. I spent the day cleaning the apartment including Snooky's room. I wanted "our" nest to be perfect. I brushed Snooky's fur once in the morning and again in the afternoon and because I wanted to share my happiness with him, I gave him a whole can of tuna, not just the juice. My goodness, I had asked God so many times for true love and happiness and it was finally happening! I was getting a career and looking forward to each day with Michael. My life finally had a purpose.

I called Nancy and told her about Michael and just like a sister, she was very happy for me. "You'll have to bring him over so we can meet him. If you love him, we will too."

Wednesday, September 24

I didn't sleep much; Michael was arriving sometime in the afternoon. In the morning, I ran to Kinko's to make copies of the notes I had been studying and then came home and started to cook. One could never go wrong with Italian food. I used fresh ground meat to make small dainty meatballs and then added them to my homemade marinara sauce with tomatoes, garlic, fresh oregano, salt and pepper, onions, capers, olives, and a dash of wine, to be served over spaghetti. Even though I could not drink without getting sick, I splurged on a bottle of red wine. I was willing to have a glass with him that night. It was a dinner celebration; a celebration of love. "If someone is willing to wait long enough for their soulmate, it will happen sooner or later," I told myself as I set the table and put the wine bottle in the center next to the small bouquet of fresh flowers I had bought at the market. I called Lisa and Bryan and told them about Michael and before I could ask, Bryan said they understood I would need some privacy for a few days. "That's right," I said, amazed at his perception and added, "thanks."

"Don't mention it. We understand completely." I was shocked as he sniggered in a sexually perverted tone and said, "You better take it easy to start with since you haven't had sex with anyone for a long time." I could hear Lisa's giggles in the background. He had me on speakerphone! I played along, "Oh, okay you two, I'll be a good girl."

"Yeah, that's what we're afraid of." Oh, what funny people they were.

"Thanks for caring." I hung up.

I lay on the couch feeling like I had drunk a gallon of coffee and tried to breathe deeply in and out, slowly in and out, in and out. It didn't work; Snooky was lying on my chest. I sat crossed legged on the living room floor and Snooky took it as an open invitation to sprawl on my left bent knee. Once it started to cramp I got up to watch television. Click, click, click, nothing good on. I called Diane and then Donna but all I did was talk about Michael. They were not interested, and were just being polite. Those hours of waiting felt like forever. I wondered if he had changed much; I knew I did. I was older and my innocence was gone. I was a mature woman. It was four in the afternoon. I knew he would be exhausted after driving across the United States without stopping.

I finally could not contain myself and called his mother. I needed a friendly ear.

Her raspy smoker's voice was unmistakably recognizable. But it was a voice from the past that still projected the same warmth and kindness. "Ronnie, it's so good to hear from you!"

"How are you? I miss you." I meant it.

"I'm fine, honey. Yes, I miss you too. It's been a long time."

"I know. I called also to let you know Michael is still on the road but should be arriving later today."

"Ronnie, I don't know how to thank you for not giving up on him. He really needs you."

"Madeleine, you know that Michael and I are in love, right?"

"Ronnie, I always knew that you loved each other. Neither of you were very good at hiding your feelings."

"And how do you feel about our age difference and all?"

"Honey, age means nothing. I'd rather see my son happy with you than miserable with someone his own age." I had her blessing and she insisted I call her once a week to let her know how I was doing. I loved that woman!

Monday, October 20

Hard to believe a month had gone by since Michael moved in. It felt more like a lifetime. I was still in love with him but I was not happy. My prince charming needed help. He was a chain smoker, a serious alcoholic, jobless, and addicted to the internet. I could see the reason he had brought along a computer. He needed something to do besides watching television. The first week he talked about getting settled before looking for work. I agreed. The second week he told me he had inquired over the internet and there were no computer jobs in the Bay area. I was surprised. The third week I said, "Any job that helps to pay for food and expenses is a very good job." He hit his closed fist on the desk table—the one I used to study on, but since I no longer studied at home, it was now his computer table. "Getting a job below my qualifications is not acceptable. I won't do it!" He lashed back at me as if I had said something offensive. Something else was missing in our relationship—intimacy. It didn't matter if I prepared a romantic candlelight dinner and wore a sexy negligée, he was always tired. Snooky and I were stuck with the worst kind of roommate. He lacked good hygiene, and the body odor mixed with tobacco and alcohol bothered Bryan and Lisa enough to keep them away from visiting us. Every night Michael stayed at his computer playing games until three or four in the morning. When I left in the morning for school, he was sleeping.

I did not look forward to going home. Besides my regular set of courses, I was spending more time studying at the library and was putting in extra hours at the clinic. Any reason to stay away from home was my salvation for not having to deal with my personal life. After I was done with my school assignments at the library, I read medical and chiropractic journals, trying to find something on the side effects of chocolate. All they said was that it could cause a headache; otherwise it was actually good for you. Humbug! Then why did I get bone pain from eating chocolate? Something was being hidden from the general public. The research became a daily mission and I stayed at the library until they closed.

One of the treatment rooms at the clinic went under quarantine. They put a sign on the door, *Contaminated room! Do not enter!* It was a bit melodramatic. They could have just locked the door. It all started when I took a history on Mr.

Martinez, a new patient, and he said, "I probably should tell you this, I have tuberculosis."

"Really? You have TB?" I immediately stepped away from him as he nodded his head. "Okay, just stay seated and I'll be right back." I closed the door behind me and ran to the office of Dr. Howard, my new consulting advisor. He freaked out and started asking me questions like, Did you touch him? How close did you get to him? How long where you in the room with him? And then I was asked not to return to the clinic or classes until Mr. Martinez was seen by a pulmonary physician.

The tuberculosis case turned out to be a false alarm. Mr. Martinez's X-rays showed an old scar, just like the one I have from having TB as a child. I was back working at the clinic, but I had already reached my 350 quota of patients' visits needed to graduate. I could not take any new patients but I was allowed to continue treating my regular patients until I received my chiropractic degree in December.

When I came home, Michael's breath wreaked of alcohol. He didn't kiss me. He hugged me—a very strong hug as if he were trying to stop me from inhaling. I didn't like it. If I forgot to inflate my lungs with air, I couldn't catch my breath, so I held my breath in until he let go of me. I felt vulnerable; he could easily hurt me. Also, when he drank, it seemed to affect his common sense and for some unexplainable reason he would go into a fit over tofu, arguing it was nothing but a rich man's food. We could be having broiled chicken and rice pilaf when out of nowhere he would start preaching about tofu. When he did that, I just ate my food quietly hoping it wouldn't escalate into an angry fit, but it always did. Drinking did not make him a pleasant companion. I didn't understand him; I didn't know what he wanted. No matter how late I got home, I always made dinner and lit table candles to see if he would mellow out, but nothing helped. Michael was now a stranger; a shadow of the man he used to be.

Dr. Hammond had been busy making some positive changes regarding his health. He became a vegetarian and joined a gym. One evening, since he was the last patient of the day, we had a chance to talk a bit. He said, "I bought myself a round trip ticket to Denmark. I'll be gone for one month. When I come back, I'm going to start practicing again."

"That's awesome, I'm so happy for you!"

"Like you said, life is what you make of it."

He made my day.

It was Sunday and Michael had been on the internet all morning. "Let's do something special today," I said. I had interrupted his viewing of *South Park*, an adult animation show he watched religiously. "How about going to San Francisco, what do you say? We can take the BART."

We went by train because driving with him meant he was going to smoke in the car. Reasoning with him again that it wasn't fair to subject me to secondhand smoke was a waste of time. His answer was always that I never complained when we lived in New Jersey. Of course I didn't. We were not living together or seeing each other every day.

We walked through Chinatown and snacked on egg rolls, then took the bus to Castro Street, where I had been with Dexter and Patrick, and had enjoyed the eclectic mixture of people, shops, and restaurants. However, this time we didn't make it far from the bus stop. He went bananas when he saw the cultural diversity. He was homophobic! Drinking as much as he did, which was every day, seemed to have taken away his gusto for life, his sense of humor, and his loving heart. His mind was drowned deep in liquor and he could no longer appreciate the rich colors and diversity of life

One evening, under the pretext that I could use the hands-on practice, I listened to Michael's lungs with my stethoscope and did the usual fremitus palpation as he repeated "ninety-nine" every time I touched his back. There wasn't much resonance of the left upper lobe. He could not talk without clearing his throat and coughing. I was not a pulmonologist but I suspected he was developing emphysema. Being a chiropractor and having adopted a holistic view associated with my profession, it was very difficult for me to see the man I loved smoking to death. "The only way I could stop smoking is if you tied me to a chair in a deserted island," he said.

Over the weekend, I took Michael to meet the family in Sacramento. He was absolutely charming and as I expected, everybody liked him. He spent a lot of time smoking with Nancy's father outside the house. When it came to drinking, he didn't have a drop. No one in the family drank.

Michael was supposed to go for a job interview the next Monday. I was confident once he got a job he would have more self-esteem and would be back to the way he used to be, the Michael I loved.

I came home earlier from the clinic; I couldn't wait to hear the good news. He was sleeping in front of the television. He had drunk himself into a stupor and never made it out of the house for the interview.

I mentioned getting a temporary job at Burger King or McDonald's but once again he got insulted.

One day he gave me one hundred dollars. I found out his mother sent him money every few weeks. "Here," he said, "this should help with the bills." I made it a big deal that he was giving me so much money, and that it was going to help a lot!

The next day he used his charge card to buy a new computer at Fry's and then had the audacity to ask for my help with the monthly payments. When I said, "Sorry, but no dice," he said, "It's only until I have a job, then I'll pay you back." I grabbed the hundred-dollar bill still tucked in my purse and handed it to him, saying, "Here's your money back. Now I don't owe you anything."

Ralph flew in from Portland where he was teaching Anatomy and Dissection at Western States College as an adjunct teacher. We spent a week heavily engrossed with studying for the National Boards Part IV. He was very proud of me for having finished my BS and he was convinced I would be graduating with flying colors from Chiropractic College the following month, December 7th.

Ralph and Michael got along great. Ralph took me aside and said, "Mom, Michael really loves you."

If Michael loved me, *really* loved me, he would stop drinking and smoking and would get a job.

After we took the National Boards, Ralph went back to Oregon. We would know the results in January. I thought I did pretty well but when it came to taking tests it was never a sure thing with me. Now with Ralph I had no worries; he was a wiz at taking tests.

Sara, my friend from Georgia, sent me a letter. She had lost financial aid and had been selling her blood, her job did not pay enough to cover tuition and food, and she was thinking about dropping out of college. A day before, Michael had asked me for eighty dollars to help him pay for his storage in South Carolina where he kept his stuff. "Sorry, but no dice," had been my response once again to his "borrowing." It was a polite way of saying definitely not, instead of a flat out, "No." Over dinner I told Michael about Sara's situation. "I'm going to send her two hundred dollars to help her out. It breaks my heart to know she's selling her blood."

He had a fit. "She sounds like a loser!" he screamed. "I'm in a bad financial situation and you're going to help her but not me?"

I screamed back, "How dare you call her a loser and say your situation is worse than hers! You have a roof over your head, and food on the table, and I love you enough to put up with your costly addictions. She doesn't have anyone to turn to." I got up and went to my bedroom. He followed me and said he was sorry and we made up. But I did not lend him any money.

For my graduation dinner celebration I wore a short red silk dress. The same one I had worn when I had visited Mama many years ago. Knowing how much she liked me wearing that dress and believing that her spirit was present on such a happy occasion, I wanted to please her. I wanted her to smile from heaven above and be proud of me. But it was December, so I stopped at Goodwill and was lucky to find a long black wool coat with a red silk lining for five bucks. It was a perfect match.

Ralph's and Patrick's whole families flew in to attend the graduating ceremony. As we were all waiting to walk into the auditorium, I met Gloria, Patrick's second wife, for the first time. I didn't know that she worked part-time in the admission's office. She introduced herself and wished me luck in the future. We hugged each other. I knew that like me, she had been a victim of the man we both had once loved. As I walked into the auditorium to receive my degree, I looked back and saw her standing motionless, her petite frame melting like a shadow against the wall behind her. I felt sad for her. No one in the family had acknowledged her.

Ralph stayed for the weekend. His gift for my graduation was to be a surprise and I was asked to go out and not come home until six in the evening. I went to the mall, met with Rod for lunch, and then went to the movies with Allan.

Before I even entered the apartment, the delicious smell of fresh herbs and homemade food permeated the hallway outside. Ralph had gone with Michael to the food store early in the morning and bought all the ingredients to prepare a very arduous, gourmet, four-course meal. He had followed the recipes from his favorite cookbook—mushrooms stuffed with lobster, butternut squash bisque with French bread, and Linguini Alfredo with crab and shrimp. (He knew I loved seafood.) It was a feast fit for a king, or in my case, a queen. His thoughtful present moved me to tears and that night before I went to sleep, I thanked God for my son Ralph and even Michael's mere existence in my life.

Being done with school was an exhilarating experience of freedom. I had served my time, and even though I enjoyed it fully and would do it again if needed, I felt that leaving the Bay area and going on a trip to somewhere special would be a treat, a confirmation of my freedom, the start of a new life. I shared those feelings with Michael who agreed it was a good idea. "How about going south," I suggested. "Mexico isn't too far. We could go just for a few days and on the way back we can visit the famous San Diego Zoo and Disneyland."

"I'm all for it. We both deserve a break."

On our first night in a Los Angeles motel I made a futile attempt at being amorous. I kissed him on the lips but there was no response except for, "I'm due for a cigarette." He went outside to smoke. For dinner he ate barely anything but he drank enough to pass out on the bed when we got back to the room.

The next day I drove through customs and into Tijuana, Mexico. He went berserk yelling, "Keep the windows up! Lock the doors! Let's get out of here! Drive faster and don't stop the car for anything! Let's get out of here! We're going to be mugged or killed if they grab us!" I tried to calm him down and convince him we weren't in any danger, but his face had gone pale and he showed such a look of terror with his body all tensed up against the seat as if trying to crawl down it, and his hands were moving as if trying to push away invisible monsters. He was so emotionally disturbed over the Mexican surroundings that I had no other choice but to take the next U-turn back to the US border.

What had happened to Michael, the man I had fallen in love with in New Jersey? What had I seen in him? How could love be so blind? But then I reasoned, "He lived most of his life in the rural countryside of New Jersey, then he moved into the woods of South Carolina for the last five years, so what else can I expect? He's a country boy! He's a gringo suffering from culture shock.

Our next stop was the San Diego Zoo; I believe he enjoyed it as much as I did, particularly when we stood by the underground glass window watching the hippopotamuses swimming underwater as graciously as ballerinas. I was mesmerized and could have stood there all day. Disney was our next stop and it was wonderful to see Michael enjoying himself, smiling, and willing to stay until they did the fireworks display, which was worth the wait. The idea was to drive back to Hayward that same night. I should have known better. It had been a long day, with lots of driving and walking. I was more tired than I thought because within an hour of driving I was falling asleep at the wheel. I put the radio on full blast but it didn't help. I asked Michael to tell me stories, but nothing could keep my eyes open. We were lost on some long, winding, country road and the surrounding darkness was very conducive to sleep. I told him, "The first motel we see, we need to stop. I'm not going to make it; I'm too tired."

The hotel was $150 for the night. I bargained a little and the manager agreed to let us have the room for $125. When we got into the room, Michael said, "This is a really nice room, well worth $150," and then he added sarcastically, "but you had to Jew her down to $125, hmm?"

I did not answer. In the three months he had lived with me, his non-Jewish contribution to our relationship had been nothing but sadness and disappointment in my life. I took a shower and did not come out until my tears had dried. I got into bed and told myself, *It's now officially over between the two of us. I need to leave him but I have to figure out how, without hurting his feelings. Thank you dear God for giving me the opportunity to see for myself the end of an imaginary love that never existed except in my mind. The truth is, since he arrived, I've been separating myself from him, a very wise decision.* I was proud of myself. *By pulling myself away from him I have saved myself from suffering a sudden jolt of misery. It's no different from taking little tiny bits of poison every day, until you build a resistance to it versus taking the full dosage straight up and dying.*

Two days before New Year's, Ralph and his girlfriend came by our apartment and spent the night with us and then they drove south to spend New Year's night in Tijuana, Mexico. I did not share my fears or concerns about Michael with Ralph then. I probably should have.

Winter of 1998

Life is like a circus. Much like their performers, some of us get shot from a cannon hoping we don't land on our heads, while others of us laugh like clowns and act like silly ballerinas pirouetting unsuccessfully. The crowd cheers on enthusiastically and then goes home without a second thought for the sculptured bodies who are earning their living by holding onto a horizontal bar hanging from just two ropes and who have a complete disregard for the lack of a net. If we fell (but we won't because we're professionals) there would be a massive, echoing "Ohhhh nooo!" and except for the children who would look away, or perhaps peek between their fingers, some adults would leave wondering who was going to pick up the pieces afterwards.

I knew how to recognize the signs of depression; I always idealized some philosophical idea, a deterrent to keep my brain occupied from addressing reality. I needed someone to talk to. I went into my bedroom and began dialing my friend Leila. But Michael came in and lay down next to me reading a book. I canceled the call.

It was January 13th and I was still waiting to hear if I had passed the National Boards. I needed a job soon. I sent out applications to chiropractic offices advertising for chiropractic assistants.

One evening, we were having dinner and I shared with Michael my plans to start taking aquatic aerobics. "I need to do something to maintain my figure." I smiled.

"Don't you think it's ironic that you're paying someone for that?"

"Of course I have to pay for the use of the pool. What are you talking about?"

"Why don't you just work the field? It's a better workout than waddling in the water."

"The field? You mean like picking potatoes or string beans? What do mean by the field?" I was too stupid to realize he made no sense because he was drunk, so I went on, "Working in the field is not the same as exercising specific parts of the body."

"Oh, yeah?" he said with the look of someone who had just been told he was an idiot. "You go shovel coal and you'll learn what I mean in a hurry." I stared at him. He kept on going, "You're telling me that the men out there shoveling coal need to exercise? Isn't that enough work?" His drunken laughter was demonic. He took a bite of the broiled chicken and kept talking with his mouth full, "Tofu is tasteless!"

"I know you don't like it," I said. "That's why I made chicken." I reinforced it, "You are eating chicken."

"Tofu was originally created to feed the starving poor and now that some rich guy made it fashionable, we eat it."

"You're so right about that," I said, trying to remain composed while he kept raving on. I was glad when he finally ran out of steam and went to sleep on the couch. I cleaned the table, did the dishes, and talked to Snooky who sat on top of my feet while I stood by the kitchen sink. "The place smells," I whispered to him. He looked up and meowed faintly.

The next morning I attempted to convince Michael to attend an AA meeting. The organization was very close to where we lived. "You're the one with the problem, not me." He went back to his computer game.

That evening I attended the AA meeting but left after half an hour. Michael was the one who needed to attend those meetings, not me.

I called Ralph with the bad news I received in the mail. "I don't understand how you could have failed," he said. "We studied together and you knew the material as well as me."

"I do know the material, but I have dyslexia."

"No you don't. The problem you have is that English is not your first language. Mom, you need to give yourself some credit; you are doing better than a lot of people that were born in the US. You graduated from chiropractic college, and you have your diploma. Look how far you have gone. I'm very proud of you."

Ralph always knew how to make me feel better about myself.

I would have to re-take the National Boards in May. I would do better the next time. I just had to work harder.

I applied for a job that I saw advertised in the newspaper. Something about selling time-shares. Anything to get me out of the house and provide me with some cash was worth trying. I had spent $450 on the trip to Mexico and the bills kept coming mercilessly.

I was hired to work Saturday evenings and Sunday morning. When I got home from the interview, foolish me,

I thought Michael would be delighted I had found work. "Great, you spent a fortune to become a doctor and now you're going to work selling time-shares?" He yelled in the familiar high nasal tone that by then had become as annoying as the phone siren. "Don't you have any pride?" He walked away and sat at his computer.

"I can't do anything with my degree until I pass the National Boards IV. I have a job and that's all that matters to me." Maybe he believed that sitting around the house all day long, playing games on the computer, watching television and drinking, sooner or later someone was going to knock at the front door and offer him a CEO position in a major computer company.

I went into my bedroom, closed the door, and got busy reading the information my boss gave me about Maui, Hawaii.

My first day on the job, I sold two time-shares. I just talked about the beauty of the island and asked the two couples, "What more can anyone want than a vacation in paradise?"

The boss called me to his office at the end of the day to tell me that they were very impressed with my skills. My paycheck in two weeks would be showing the hefty commissions I had made with each sale.

Bryan and Lisa were keeping their distance. I called them to see how they were doing. Bryan said, "We want you to know that we still love you, but Lisa and I can't stand the smell of cigarettes. Our lungs can't take it. Please don't take this the wrong way, but we don't think that Michael is good for you. Every time we come to visit Snooky, your boyfriend is in a deep drunken stupor."

Michael was in the room. I said, "Thank you for calling. You're right. I'll talk to you tomorrow, okay?"

Michael left to buy some groceries and I took the occasion to call his mother. Her response was more than I expected. "I have feared this call for a long time," she said. "If anything, we're all very concerned with your safety. Has he tried to hurt you?"

"He does act a bit strange when he drinks but he's never hurt me. Should I be worried? What are you trying to tell me?"

She didn't answer; her son-in-law came on the phone. "I hate to tell you this, but Michael is dangerous when he drinks too much. We've witnessed him going into the kitchen and throwing knives in fits of anger. You need to keep sharp objects out of his way and get out of the house when he acts crazy."

Except for squeezing the breath out of me when he hugged me, or going off on tantrums over tofu when he got sloshed, I found him harmless. I couldn't conceive of the idea that he could hurt me. But it did bother me that a few days prior to the phone conversation, I came home and found my revolver lying next to his computer. My first impulse was one of anger. I felt he had no right to take it from where I had it hidden and then carelessly leave it loaded and out in the open. I knew he lost his common sense when he drank; was he contemplating suicide? Was he planning to shoot me? His family's fears about my safety were a warning I could not ignore. I quickly hid my gun under one of Snooky's litter boxes and except for the butter knives, I stored the sharper, pointed kitchen knives under the other litter box. There was no way in heaven Michael would look under them. Then I called Allan.

We met for lunch the next day. He heard me patiently. "You need to leave him as soon as possible," he said. "Michael doesn't sound emotionally stable." I promised Allan that I would be leaving Michael once I figured out how I would do it. Gosh, the idea of looking for another place to live was like a nightmare for me. I had no place else to go, but he did—back in South Carolina.

That night I couldn't sleep. I left early in the morning for the school library and sat at one of the desks going over how to best approach Michael. I could walk into the apartment and say, "Here's enough money to pay for gas. I want you to leave." But I could just hear him say, "You don't love me anymore? Are you trying to get rid of me?" Even if that was the truth that was just the kind of confrontation I wanted to avoid if at all possible. So okay, I could say, "I'm going to visit my family in Sacramento and won't be back for two months. You take care of the rent and the bills and oh yeah, don't forget to take care of Snooky." But what if his mother sent him enough money for two months and he found the kitchen knives and the gun? I knew, I *knew* exactly what would make him leave. "Michael, I'm very sorry but I've fallen in love with someone else; you have to leave." Bad idea, because under the pretext of being happy for me and wanting to hug me, he could squeeze me to death!

I went to Pizza Hut for lunch and then to a multi-theatre complex where after seeing *Liar Liar* with Jim Carrey, I sneaked into a variety of other movies. Finally I called Ralph. I told him everything that was going on and asked for his verbal wisdom as to what to say to Michael. "Mom, it's very simple. When you get home, just tell him the truth, that things are not working out between you two and that you're giving him a month to get out."

I took a deep breath and opened the front door to my apartment ready to speak up. It was six o'clock in the evening. The dining room table was set and he was in the kitchen tossing a salad. He smiled when he saw me. "Happy Valentine's Day, sweetheart," he said. Then he said, "I'm making dinner, I hope you like hamburgers with cheese. I even bought hamburger rolls and pickles." He had shaved and his hair was clean, not greasy; he had showered. For the first time since he had moved in, Michael had gone grocery shopping and prepared dinner. I was caught off guard and touched by his earnest gesture. Next to my dinner plate there was a Hershey chocolate bar and a small bag of M&M's and a Valentine's card he made on his computer. I had forgotten it was Valentine's Day.

Two days later, I came home earlier than he expected. As I opened the front door, I saw him rushing to hide two bottles of liquor behind the sofa. I had never seen his alcohol booty. He drank when I wasn't around, except for an occasional beer or a glass of wine with a meal. He was a professional at hiding his liquor. Seeing him hide the booze, while all along he acted as if I were the one with a problem, hit me like a hot poker into my guts. I banged the door closed, dropped my backpack on the floor, and experiencing a joyous rage, strode towards him right up to his face. "GET OUT!" came out of my throat like a roaring lioness. He could have easily pushed me away with one hand, but instead he backed into the side of the couch and looked at me with a blank look of astonishment—he had just been caught red-handed. I repeated, "GET OUT!! GET OUT OF HERE!" I did not realize I had so much bottled up inside; my words came out like rain water falling from a broken gutter. "It's been almost five months with no job, just sleeping all day, drinking, smoking, you don't clean up the place or yourself. It's over, get out now!"

"I'm sorry, Ronnie."

"I don't give a shit. Did you hear me? I want you out of my apartment right now." I closed my fists as if I were going to strike him. He moved his hands in front of his face and mumbled, "I said I'm sorry, didn't I?"

"I don't care how sorry you are, you miserable, drunken bastard!" I yelled from the top of my lungs. "I hate you, I hate your guts! I hate everything about you!" I wiggled one finger aggressively at him. "I want you out of my life right now." I poked him in the chest and pressed it in a few times as I demanded furiously, "Leave right now! This very minute, it's over! Do you hear what I'm saying? Get out of my house right now or I'll scream until the neighbors call the cops."

"Okay, okay, I'll leave. But I need to call my mother and get some money to get back home."

"Call your mother, call whoever you want. You're out of here today. Start packing now! The gravy train is over." I went into my bedroom, banged the door closed, and locked it. My heart was beating so hard I felt lightheaded, as if I were going to faint. I called Ralph, and once I heard his comforting voice, I calmed down.

It was six in the morning when I heard a knock on the bedroom door. "Ronnie, I just want to say good-bye. My pickup is packed with all my belongings and I'm leaving now." I put on my coat, and walked him to the garage under our building.

"I left my laptop on top of your desk. I want you to have it," he said. "I'm sorry things did not work out between us. You know I love you, don't you?" He kissed my forehead before getting into his truck.

He waved as he drove off, his old pickup spitting a cloud of dark, menacing fumes.

I ran upstairs to my apartment and locked the door behind me. Jumping up and down while clapping to the rhythm of my voice I sang, "I'm free, I'm free, I'm finally free!" Snooky stared at me from his bedroom entrance and then joined in the chorus meowing along as I cried out, "We are both free, we are both free!" I picked him up and twirled with him across the living room, like a ballet dancer that had just lost her marbles. He must have gotten dizzy because he extricated himself out of my arms and ran between my feet on his way back to his room. I couldn't stop singing, "Thank you God, thank you. Oh, what a beautiful feeling, oh, what a beautiful day! La di da da da la la!" I opened all the windows. "Let the sun shine, let the sunshine in, the sun shine in la di la di da." And then I went on a cleaning frenzy. It was my own Passover, the worst had passed.

Odd how the date coincided with the day my mother had passed away. I had a feeling, and it was just a feeling, but a strong, sweet feeling that my mother was still keeping an eye out for me. In the afternoon I got a call from one of the chiropractic offices where I had applied for a job. "The reason for the delay in calling," said the female voice with a Hispanic accent, "is because we just found your application behind our fax machine. It must have fallen there a month ago according to the date when you sent it to us. We're hoping you're still available."

"I am, I am," I said, controlling my voice from sounding too anxious.

"Good. Our associate chiropractor quit unexpectedly last week, and the doctor would like to meet you as soon as possible. Can you make it here by 7:30 tomorrow morning?"

The chiropractic office was in San Jose and it took me just over an hour to get there due to all the traffic." I was surprised to find Dr. Sharkey, my future employer, far from a model of health. He wore a shabby, discolored white shirt and brown corduroy pants, and he reeked of sweat, but that didn't seem to affect his successful practice. He hugged me exuberantly. "You can't imagine how glad I am to have you working with me," he said. "I treat about one hundred patients a day and I really need an assistant. Can you start tomorrow morning?" It was the opportunity of a lifetime. I would be working in the outside world and would accumulate lots of valuable experience in a real chiropractic office. I also planned on starting to study full force once again for the National Boards IV. With that previous burden of a malfunctioning relationship on my shoulders, I considered it a minor miracle that I had managed to finish my BS and graduate from chiropractic college.

My hours at the chiropractic office were from seven to seven, Monday through Friday, and on weekends, I sold time-shares in Castro Valley. I studied for the boards in the evening until I was too tired to keep my eyes open. It wasn't easy working at such pace but I was determined not to give up.

Four days later I got a startling wake-up call at two thirty in the morning. The phone siren went off followed by the light show. It was Michael. "I didn't want you to worry about me. I'm home."

"Oh, good," I said, lacking the least concern. "Thanks for calling but I need to get back to sleep. Have a nice evening. Bye." I hung up and closed the bedroom door behind me, feeling like I had finally closed the door on that part of my life.

~ Chapter Seven ~

Out and About

Between working as a chiropractic assistant and selling time-shares, I was doing more than well financially. I made my first payment towards my student loan and began putting money away for a new car. The maintenance was high on the old jalopy and when it came to the stick shift, it was a miracle I had not worn the gears to the ground. I just had to find some free time to go shopping for a new Saturn since the one I used to have had never given me any problems. I also began thinking of getting myself a hearing aid. The last time I had worn one had been some twenty years ago. I was hoping with the new advances in technology that there was something out there that would work more efficiently so I could better hear my time-share customers from across the table. To compensate for my hearing inadequacy, I talked a lot, but I still had to answer some of the questions that were muffled by both the loud, upbeat, Hawaiian music playing in the background, as well as the hustle and bustle of people talking at the other tables. When I got home, I had a hoarse voice from speaking above my normal level.

The next time Lisa and Bryan came by to see Snooky, they went on and on about Michael. "We couldn't breathe in this apartment with all that smoke, and every time we came over he was outright rude to us," said Lisa. "Yeah," said Bryan, "the first time we met him I told Lisa that he's an alcoholic. My father was one. His beatings and disregard for my brothers and me, and of course my mother, well, till today it still affects me emotionally." He cried. Lisa cuddled up to him on the couch and they hugged each other. They were such a sweet couple.

They were back to their daily visiting but I didn't mind as I was gone all day and usually didn't get home until eight thirty or later depending on the traffic.

When the phone bill came, I took a stroll through the college campus holding the laptop Michael had left me. I went up to the first student I came across and said, "If you need a laptop, I'm selling this one for $85.72."

"That's really cheap. What's wrong with it?"

"Nothing is wrong with it; you can plug it in if you want."

He found a wall socket nearby. "You must be really pressed for money," he said. "I'll give you a hundred dollars for it."

"Nope, I just need eighty five dollars and seventy two cents, exactly."

It was a matter of principle. Michael was going to pay for his phone bill one way or another.

Besides the hefty commissions from selling time-shares, the company offered to send me to Maui for a week, all expenses paid, as a token of appreciation. I declined the offer. I had no desire to travel anymore. Besides, I couldn't stop working for a whole week at the chiropractic office. I needed to pay for my soon-to-be new car and my hearing aid. And I needed to accumulate as much money as I could to start my chiropractic practice when I passed the National Boards IV, preceded by the State Boards, depending on which state I moved to. Such a decision was still up in the air. I felt pulled from all directions—Ralph in Oregon, Nancy in California, and my son Steve, his wife Diane, and my grandchildren Jacob and Shayna in New Jersey. Then there was the possibility of working at a hospital in Cairo, Egypt. It had grabbed my attention the first time I heard about it from Leila. I had always wanted to go to Egypt. According to my Aunt Heydee's investigation into the Esagui family roots on my mother's side, our ancestors had come from Egypt as perfume and jewelry merchants, across north Africa, and finally into Portugal where they settled. I asked Leila to mail me the application form since she was so close to Life Chiropractic University. The college was working with the hospital in Cairo and except for the poor sanitary conditions, the students had nothing but good things to say about their experience there.

Michael called. I could tell he was drunk. I said with composure, "Sorry, but I can't talk right now, I have company. Bye!" I was confident that sooner or later he would stop calling. After what his family had told me, the only person I worried about was his mother who had no choice but to have him live with her. His sister and her husband were lucky; they lived somewhere else.

One morning on the way to work at the chiropractic office, I put on the radio as I always did and found myself immersed singing along with a blasting tune from the Rolling Stones. It was only the beginning of March, but the sun shone bright and the skies were a celestial blue without a single puffy cloud—it made the very air around me feel magical. I was high on life. I glanced to my right side and a young truck driver, probably in his early thirties, with straight, dark, shoulder-length hair flowing in the wind, smiled at me. He probably had been watching my "dancing" performance of facial expressions, hand gestures, and upper body movements, but I doubted he could hear me. Most likely he did hear my radio; it was loud enough for a deaf person. I smiled back and gave him a thumbs up. He responded by putting his hand out of his window and doing the same. He maintained his speed along my side and kept looking at me. It hit me as funny; I smiled back at him. When he slowed down, I did the same, when I sped up, he did too. We were in different vehicles, never to see each other again, so I felt safe flirting. He flashed his headlights and I got in front of him. He crossed to my left and began driving along the side of my car. We did this type of courtship back and forth but when he made the motion for me to follow him to the next exit, I panicked. Playtime was over. I nodded my head and smiled. He got in front of me. As he was getting off the highway at full speed, I waved at him and kept going. I was well aware that it was mean of me to play with someone else's emotions but I needed to feel wanted even if for a fleeting moment. Besides, I have to be honest about it, I had a thing for truck drivers, monkeys, and trucks. I liked *B.J. and the Bear,* where a trucker and his pet monkey traveled the highways of America having nothing but fun and exciting adventures. Then of course, there was a film that was still fresh in my memory and was my very favorite Clint Eastwood movie, *Every Which Way but Loose,* where Clint played a trucker traveling with his pet orangutan.

Someday I hoped to travel in a truck with a monkey or a friend, most likely a good friend, across the US. Although there was a huge amount of gas needed to run a truck, it had to be exhilarating to sit way up there and watch the beauty of the land all around for as far as the eye could see.

There was no question my wages were extremely high and the first month working at Dr. Sharkey's office made me feel like I had won the lottery. But like everything in life—even in paradise—there was always something to muddy the waters. I called Ralph and told him about it. Anything less than one hundred patients a day and Maria, the front desk person, had a fit. My job was very involved and I did everything except adjust the patients. I performed the physical exams, re-exams, X-ray readings and marking, and physical therapy. I made a report of my findings and entered all data into the patients' files. Dr. Sharkey took a brisk look at the patient's file outside the room and in less than two minutes, he was in and out of the room. There was no relationship between him and his patients. Everything moved to Maria's drumbeat. I had never been in the armed forces but Maria was a natural platoon sergeant. Maria was from Mexico and so was her angel-like beauty, her eighteen-year-old daughter, Juanita. Her job in the office besides filing and billing insurance companies was to accompany Dr. Sharkey to court, as his assistant. Maria was proud of the way she had made it out of Mexico. One day she grabbed Juanita's hand, who was only twelve years old at the time, and they entered the US. She didn't go into detail on how she had done it, except for saying, "We ran."

Maria had a boyfriend, Mario, who also worked in the office. He was from Mexico and only spoke Spanish. Besides keeping the rooms clean during the day and vacuuming the carpets at the end of the day he also helped me with setting patients on heat or ice. One day I was rushing from one room to another to do the physical exams and he said, "Don't work so hard, it's not worth it,"

"I have to be speedy, or Maria will chew my head off," I said.

"I know, she thinks we are her slaves. But you just tell me which patient needs therapy and I'll help you, okay? She's always ordering me around too but I ignore her. You do the same." She never told me how Mario had come to the US, but I figured the same way as she had done with Juanita. The road signs in San Jose depicting a family running across the highway, warning drivers to drive carefully in such areas, were valid after all. I was impressed; I worked with three of them. Another day Maria shared a little more with me. "We lived on the streets for a while. I was completely destitute until I met a Jehovah's Witness who helped me find a place to stay and gave us food. Are you a Jehovah Witness?"

"No, I'm Jewish."

She took a few small pamphlets from her desk drawer. "Here, you need to read this and then join us."

I could not figure out how someone like Maria had given birth to sweet, gentle Juanita. I had exactly ten minutes to do a complete physical on a patient no matter what was wrong with them. Physical therapy, like Interferential was to be no longer than five minutes but the charts showed the time to be fifteen minutes for billing. We had a one-hour lunch break from one to two. Maria and Mario, always left for lunch. Whenever possible, I ran to the juice bar down the street where I bought a veggie sandwich and one of their freshly squeezed fruit juices. Dr. Sharkey's meals were from Burger King and he shared them with Juanita in one of the back rooms or in his office.

Besides being a chiropractor, Dr. Sharkey also worked as an Independent Medical Examiner (IME) for insurance companies. There was nothing independent about what he did. His job as an IME was to turn down patients from having further care with other practitioners. Interestingly enough his regular clientele were mostly people who had been in motor vehicle accidents and they came religiously three times per week for three months. He reminded me of the crooked chiropractor I had worked for in New Jersey. Like him, Dr. Sharkey worked closely with two lawyers who sent their clients to be treated by him. Ninety-five percent of the patients were Hispanic. Maria had one goal in mind; the more patients, the more money she made in commission and the sooner she could buy a house. Everyone attending her Kingdom Hall of Jehovah's Witnesses were Dr. Sharkey's patients. Juanita worked at filing and billing insurance companies while Maria took phone messages and did the appointments. At the end of the day, I was physically and emotionally exhausted but the paycheck was so exceptional I kept saying to myself that I could handle the stress.

It was creepy when Dr. Sharkey's eight-months pregnant wife came in one day at the start of our lunch hour and asked me where her husband was. I pointed to the last adjusting room at the end of the hallway. She found Juanita lying down on an adjusting table and Dr. Sharkey lying on the table next to her. The room was dark but when she opened the door, she saw that they were holding hands. She walked down the hallway crying," Son of a b...., he's nothing but a son of a b..... I'm getting a divorce and he is never, ever going to see his children again!" Dr. Sharkey came out running after his wife saying, "But honey, Juanita and I were just talking."

"In the dark, lying down next to each other, holding hands? That's how you talk to an employee? Screw you! I'm getting a lawyer." She gave him the middle finger and banged the front door closed when she left. Dr. Sharkey went back to the room where Juanita was and closed the door behind him.

I felt Dr. Sharkey's wife's assumption was pretty close to the truth. I had seen Dr. Sharkey hold Juanita's face in his hands and look very lovingly at her while he held her against the wall in the hallway, with his obese body pressing against her small frame. The scenario was very sexual, but I did not believe Juanita had any feelings towards him. She was doing what her mother wanted. Maria was the type that if Dr. Sharkey were to leave his wife and kids and marry her daughter, she would give them both her blessings.

During lunch one day at the office, Juanita confided, "I don't know what to do, Dr. Veronica. I'm in love with a boy named Jesus. He's my age and he loves me too, but I can't tell my mother; she would be very upset."

Compared to Dr. Sharkey, Jesus had no chance of being accepted by Juanita's mother.

In the local newspaper, I found a hearing aid center in Hayward advertising the latest, most sophisticated hearing aids on the market for a whopping twenty-five percent off the original price. I made an appointment to see Mr. Vorshes, the hearing aid specialist, who said, "Technology has advanced tremendously in the last few years, beyond your imagination. No more clumsy hearing aids sticking out of your ears or behind your ear lobe. Now they have these miniature digital electronic devices that once inserted, they disappear from sight." He put a sample in my hand. It was made of see-through plastic and was tiny enough to stand on the tip of my index finger. I was amazed. He went on, "With a special syringe I will be inserting a soft silicone material into your ear canal to take an impression. After ten minutes or so when it's dry, I'll pull it out and use it as a template to make your hearing aid fit perfectly into your ear and no one will be the wiser. Isn't that great? What do you think?"

"Let's go for it!" I said enthusiastically.

Mr. Vorshes held the syringe into my left ear canal and squeezed in the soft blue dough. It kind of tickled, just a little, and it felt cool but not unpleasant. He did the same to my right side, since he had also told me I should wear a hearing aid in both ears. We waited the required time for it to dry. The problem was that once the molds dried up, he could not pull them out no matter how hard he yanked on them. I cried from the pain. I believe he was also holding his tears back because he kept saying, "I'm sorry. I'm so sorry. This has never happened to me before." The thought of living for the rest of my life with my ears clogged with plastic dough was unbearable. He called the main company in San Diego and was told the reason for the mishap was because I had deformed ear canals. They offered me a plane trip so they could remove the material and they would then try to fit me with their hearing aids. I would have to stay in San Diego for two days. I told Mr. Vorshes, "Flying is like torture for my ears and besides that I can't leave my job for one day, much less two days. And what are they going to do, surgery?" He shrugged his shoulders then shook his head and said meekly, "I don't know. I really don't know." He looked like he was ready to cry. I wondered how long he had been doing this kind of work.

"Look," I said, trying to project a confident tone of voice, "I'll bite the bullet until you take the molds out and don't worry about it if I cry." Then I pleaded, "Maybe you can pull it out piece by piece, instead of all in one chunk like you were trying to do before?"

Piece by piece, he finally pulled the last crumb of dough out of my right ear. The left one took a lot more effort and it felt like an eternity. He was sweating bullets himself while I cried really hard praying for the torture to be over. There was no charge for the visit. He was glad to see me leave and my feelings were mutual. I had been partially deaf all my life and for the most part, I had adapted to it. I would have to do the best I could with what God had given me; one ear was better than none.

When I got home, I used a Q-tip to clean some of the gook that was still left inside my ears; the tip came out stained with blood. No wonder it hurt so much! I could only hope I had not lost more of my hearing in my right ear.

Selling time-shares over the weekends did not give me enough time to recover from working at the chiropractic office. And since it was an emotional letdown every time I had to ask my prospective customers, "What?" or "What did you say?" I felt it was in my best interest to resign. My boss offered to raise my commission if I stayed. Money was important to me, but not as vital as having the weekends free to review and study for the Boards Part IV.

If I were rich, my dream car would look like a piece of junk on the outside but would be packed inside with all the gadgets of a luxurious car, like heated leather seats, a stereo CD panel, and of course, a powerful engine. I settled for a brand-new 1998 four-door, golden-tan Saturn. I purposely picked a family car model so I wouldn't have to worry about being hassled on the highway and there would be less of a chance of it getting stolen.

The only thing I did not like about the looks of my new car was the back that had a raised panel across it. They wanted to charge me five hundred dollars more saying that it made the car sleeker.

I patiently explained to the car salesman that if I wanted a sports car I would not be trading in my 300ZX.

"I want a normal looking car, without that thing stuck on the top of the trunk."

"We don't have one in the color you like without a spoiler."

"Spoiler, hmm? That's a good name for it." I laughed at my own joke. Then I said, "It's ugly. I'm going to another dealership where I can get one without it."

"We don't want to lose you as a customer and we really like your Nissan even though it's an old model. I'll tell you what," said the salesman, "how about you take the car with the spoiler and we take an extra $1200 off?"

For that price, I got the car and I figured I could learn to live with the spoiler.

Spring of 1998

Something tickled my right eyelid during the night. I remember trying to brush it off with my hand because it woke me up. I went back to sleep but when I woke up in the morning, the eyelid was about three times its size. I could barely open the eye as gummy mucus kept oozing out from the top of the eyelid. Even though I could barely see from the right eye, I got myself dressed and drove to work. Everybody agreed it looked pretty nasty. During my lunch hour, I was encouraged to go see the eye doctor in the same building where I worked.

Only a spider could have caused such extensive damage, I was told by the eye doctor. She prescribed an oral antibiotic and an antibiotic cream to be applied to the eyelid. I ruled out a poisonous tarantula as then I would most likely be dead. They fitted me with a black eye patch so I would not gross out the patients. I was assured I would not lose my sight.

According to Portuguese folklore, spiders were supposed to bring good luck and I had never bothered them until the fateful day one of them bit me and then I became their worst enemy. They had brought it against themselves. I bought a set of white bedsheets on the way home. When I got into the apartment, I did a thorough search in my bedroom and got rid of my flowery patterned bedsheets. White had just become my favorite sheet color as it was easier to inspect for the little buggers before I laid myself to sleep. I intended to kill every spider I came across.

Michael was still calling. He called when his mother wasn't home or was asleep, and his mother called when he wasn't around. When he called Saturday night at eleven, it meant two in the morning over there. I listened to him as after so many years that we had known each other, I thought I owed him that much. "There's this girl I like," he said, while coughing and sounding like he was gasping for breath between each word. "She's married and pregnant with her second child. Her son is nine years old and he likes me like a father. If my father died, then my mother could start collecting some money or better yet, if my mother died now, it would be even better for me. I wouldn't have to wait to get on my feet financially, but then what? Everybody is crazy, everybody is doing me wrong. I'm sorry I was a disappointment to you. I'm so sorry." I could hear him crying.

I no longer hated him, but listening to his crazy perception of what was important to him triggered the worst in me. "Get off your can, you selfish good-for-nothing!" May God forgive me but his drunken talk was beyond my endurance. "You really don't give a damn about anyone but your freakin' vices. You remind me of the beggar by the post office here in Hayward, a burnout begging for pennies to buy his booze." The words were coming out of my mouth like a machine gun, boom, boom, boom. I spoke as fast as I could. "That's what's going to become of you when your mother dies and her money stops coming in and by then your liver and your brain will be burned to a crisp. You'll be a miserable man full of hate and disease. That's all I have to say to you!" And I hung up.

A week later my eyelid edema had decreased by more than half, but a small pimple was sticking out from underneath the top eyelid, looking a lot like a sty except that it constantly oozed out a viscous substance. I believed the spider had left one of its fangs deep within and a chronic infection had developed.

I was impressed with Dr. Eyeram, the eye surgeon I found in the yellow pages. His waiting room displayed a large collection of newspaper interviews and before-and-after photos showing where he had removed metal pieces and other objects from soldiers' eyes. I figured a spider's bite was going to be a piece of cake for someone like him. I made an appointment for the next day and the best part of it was that once they found out I had no insurance and that I was paying cash, they charged me half of their usual fee.

Dr. Eyeram had to make a cut and pry out the spider's deposit. The epidural shot was the most painful part of the procedure, but afterwards I didn't feel a thing.

The eye patch would have to remain for a day. Ho, ho, matey, give me a parrot and a bottle of rum! No, after the "Michael experience," I would skip the rum joke, just the parrot would do!

Ralph and Steve were more than my sons. They were my best friends. I could call them any time of the day or night and they were always ready to listen. But because Ralph and I were following the same career and had been schoolmates, we had a lot more in common. He got the brunt of my calls complaining about my chiropractic job.

"It's not just a factory where I work, there's no heart, no feelings for any of the patients," I said. "It's all about money. Yesterday, a mother brought her seven-year-old son into the office. He had been hit by a car while crossing the street. I got cut off by Maria, the front desk person, from finishing the exam because I'm only allowed ten minutes per patient. The child could have had a concussion and they couldn't care less. I really want to quit but I'm making a lot of money working there."

"Well, if money is that important to you, it sounds to me like you've sold your soul to the devil."

The next morning, I got to the chiropractor's office a little earlier than usual. I told Maria, "I'm here to pick up my paycheck. I no longer work for Dr. Sharkey. I quit." She did not answer; she went in the back of the office to talk to him. I turned to her daughter and said, "Juanita, you don't belong here, either. Get out while you still can."

She hugged me and said, "Thank you, but you know that I can't go against my mother's wishes. I wish you my very best in your future." Maria returned and handed me the check silently.

Poor Juanita, her only salvation was to run away with Jesus.

It was the middle of April; I had about a month to get prepared once again for National Boards Part IV. I made plans to leave for New Jersey right after taking the Boards and visit Steve and Diane and my grandchildren, Jacob and Shayna. Maybe I would stay in New Jersey and practice there.

I shared my plans with Lisa and Bryan so they could start looking for another renter. They said they would like to keep the collapsible table that I used as a desk and they gave me fifty dollars for it. I only paid twenty but they said it would save them from going out and buying another. They intended to rent the apartment to another chiropractic student and they figured the table would be appreciated by the new boarder.

Michael called. As soon as I heard his voice I said, "I can't talk. I'm on my way out."

"No, no, wait," he said. "I just called to say that I'm going to get professional help. I'm calling my brother to help me out. You were right, I can't stay this way."

I guess the way I spoke to him the last time had been very harsh but he listened. What a relief! He was going to be fine after all.

I called Nancy to ask her if I could leave some of my belongings in her garage until I returned from my drive to New Jersey.

"When are you leaving?" she asked.

"May 18th, right after I'm done with the Boards."

"How long do you think it's going to take you to cross the US?"

"I'm driving straight through. So I would say, probably about five or six days."

"Would you like some company?"

"Are you serious? I would love it!"

"Do you really intend to drive across in five days? It would be nice if we could take our time and get a chance to see the countryside."

"I thought I was driving by myself, but if you're coming with me, it's another story—it will be whatever time it takes us to get there. I'm not in any hurry; I don't have a set date to be in New Jersey."

"You take care of the hotels for us to stay for five days as if you were going on your own, and I'll take care of our lodgings for as many nights as we need afterwards, and that's including the gas. Is that a deal?"

"You bet!" I was jumping up and down. "Yippee! Hooray!"

I put a "For Sale" sign in the laundry room in the basement of my apartment complex to sell some of my things. The neighbor upstairs bought my acoustic guitar and banjo. I had wondered what he looked like since I could always tell when he had a girl spending the night with him. He asked me if I could hear anything from downstairs. I lied.

I was not going to jinx the results by saying I did well with the National Board exams. I called Ralph and told him I had done my best. I was leaving for New Jersey with Nancy and had no idea where I would be in July so I asked the Board to mail the results to Ralph's address.

As much as I wanted to work with Ralph, being a mobile chiropractor like him was not something I relished. I also didn't know if I wanted to practice in a place like Oregon, where it rained all the time. I didn't know if I wanted to practice in California where there were so many earthquakes even though I had only experienced a slight tremor once, when Michael was living with me I couldn't put aside the knowledge that California was earthquake country. Maybe if I passed the New Jersey State Boards I would practice there instead. Steve and his family would be close by. I could be more involved in my grandchildren's lives. But there was also the hospital in Cairo, Egypt. I still had the application form to the hospital tucked away in a box with all my books and school notes. After being in the safe environment of school for so many years where I was told what to do and knew what to expect on a daily basis, being out in the real world was like being in limbo. I was now facing major personal decisions and their consequences. Do I stay or do I go? Where and when and how do I get started? I faced several doors—door number one, door number two, or door number three? There was also a door behind the curtain with no number. What if I opened the wrong door and all I got was a bucket of ice water on my head? I understood how a war veteran felt upon returning to society and having to adapt to a different form of existence. But with all the changes and choices that blinded me as if lost in a snowstorm in the middle of Siberia, I really only had one choice—going forward, one foot in front of the other, and taking it like a woman.

~ Chapter Eight ~

Nancy and Me

On the morning of my departure, I went to the kitchen to make sure I wasn't leaving anything behind. Snooky had been following me all morning like a shadow. He jumped on top of the kitchen counter and then to the top of the refrigerator, meowing. He had never done that before. He knew I was leaving and was asking me to stay. He would not come off the refrigerator and I felt obliged to explain, "I have to leave but there will be another roommate moving in soon and he or she will be taking care of you." He couldn't care less and meowed even louder. I said, "Look, I would love to take you with me to New Jersey, but it's going to be a long trip and you know very well that Lisa and Bryan would never agree to that." The latter was true. He remained curled up on top of the refrigerator until Lisa and Bryan came by to say goodbye and get the house keys. The phone rang. It couldn't have been more inappropriate; it was Michael. He had not gone for help as he had promised and I did not tell him I was leaving California. I just said I was busy and had to go and then I hung up. I sat holding onto my cramped stomach and feeling nauseous. Michael affected my health that way. I wanted to vomit. Lisa made tea for the three of us. I had too much stuff to fit it all into my car. We sat waiting for Nancy and we talked. I was going to miss them.

Nancy showed up at noon. We divided my belongings between her car and mine and I followed her to Sacramento where she lived. We would spend a few days with the family and then leave in my beautiful dependable new Saturn. Nancy had already mapped our itinerary across the US.

The day before we left Sacramento, the family gathered for dinner at Nancy's house, and afterwards we played card games. Patrick's first wife Christina, said, "Traveling with Nancy is a real treat. She'll always find the nicest motels and the cleanest bathrooms along the road and ice cream will become part of your daily diet. But you'll have to keep an eye on the gas gauge; she is known for running out of gas."

We all laughed and teased each other just a little. Gosh, what an incredible family I had! If I hadn't wanted to see my grandchildren and feel the need to find my own destiny, I would have stayed in Sacramento for the rest of my life.

Nancy and I each had a small bowl of our favorite cold cereal for breakfast. It was eight in the morning, we had packed everything we needed the night before, and we were ready for our big adventure across the country. The first thing I did when Nancy and I got into my car was to take off my wristwatch and put it in the glove compartment. It was June 2nd, a perfect Tuesday morning.

"I'm taking mine off, too," she said with a huge smile. "Who cares about time? When the sun starts to go down, we'll look for a motel for the night."

"Yeah," I said eagerly as I turned on the engine, "and let's not get up until our eyes open and we feel like having breakfast."

After a few hours of driving, Nancy's body language became apparent that she didn't trust me behind the wheel. She kept her right hand tightly grasped around the door handle, and her torso looked as if it were glued back into the seat by Super Glue. She moved the seat as far back as possible, and her long legs were kept stretched out as if bracing for a head-on collision. Her language also spoke a thousand words. "Veronica, maybe you shouldn't drive so fast; we're going to get a speeding ticket."

"I'm from New Jersey. I can't help driving fast. They didn't call me Roadrunner for nothing." I laughed heartily but she only put out a forced smile.

"Don't worry," I said, "if we get stopped, I have an identity badge from the days I used to be a reporter for a local newspaper in New Jersey and it looks just like a police badge. I keep it next to my driver's license and it has gotten me out of trouble several times." I tried reaching for my backpack in the back seat with my right hand.

"Veronica, you need to use both hands on the wheel. You can show me the badge later, when we stop."

"I never use both hands on the wheel and have never had an accident because of that."

"The way you swerve all over the road, it's very scary," she said softly, her voice slightly trembling.

"Oh, I didn't realize I did that. I'll be more careful, I promise."

The next morning when I got in the driver's seat, I noticed she had assumed the seating position of *I'm ready to die*. I waved the keys at her and said, "Would you like to drive today?"

The look of relief that swept over her face was precious. "I would love that. I enjoy driving." Then timidly she added, "I wouldn't mind driving the rest of the trip, if that's okay with you."

I handed her the keys. She beamed with joy.

I put my feet up on the dashboard, relaxed, and prepared myself to enjoy the view. She did love driving, and followed the law like an attentive highway patrolman, except she followed the speed limit.

What Nancy and I had experienced in Austria and in Germany had been the saddest days of our lives after her brother, Patrick, had died unexpectedly. Now we were being granted the happiest days of our lives as we frolicked through the countryside expecting nothing but a good time.

Nancy and her husband, Danny, were expert collectors of American antiques like children's books, American stoneware, kitchen gadgets, and much more. We stopped at every possible antique shop we saw along the road, and if we came across an ice cream parlor, we stopped there too. Any sign that said "ice cream" made Nancy drive off the beaten track until we found that sweet treat. If the ice cream was really good, we would go back to get an extra ice cream cone before going on to the next state. Not once did Nancy complain when I would ask her to stop if I saw something that caught my eye, like when I picked up some salt on the ground at the Great Salt Lake. We never ran out of conversation. I began drinking a lot more water, almost as much as Nancy did, because it forced me to get out of the car and stretch before following her to the bathroom.

The beauty of our nation was enjoyed wholeheartedly and sometimes it was like an echo inside the car as one of us would say, "Wow!" always followed by the other saying, "Wow!" We enjoyed looking at nature as well as other sights including some very handsome cowboys trotting on horses alongside a fence as we drove by a country road in Pennsylvania. We even got to see some abhorrent aspects of sexual animal behavior as we caught sight of a sheep mounting a cow. The rainbows we saw were always spectacular.

One afternoon when we stopped at an ice cream shop, I commented to the girl behind the counter, "We saw a bunch of houses a few miles away with no roofs. They looked like doll houses with the tops open. What happened?"

"We got hit by a tornado just a few days ago." She calmly went about serving us ice cream.

Every night I plugged in my one-gallon water purifier that I had bought many years ago at Sears. In the morning, we were always guaranteed to have fresh, clean water to fill our plastic bottles. (Some states were worse than others, and we got to see a lot of strange, thick residues left at the bottom of the container.) After plugging in the purifier, I washed my underwear and took a shower. Nancy looked forward to seeing *The Brady Bunch* on television. Except for the movie,

Raiders of the Lost Ark, which I had seen at least ten times, I didn't care to see old movies or shows. But the truth was that after seeing how much Nancy enjoyed watching the show, I began liking it too. It was similar to hearing a tune on the radio for the first time and thinking, "That's the crummiest song I've ever heard." But once they play it over and over again, you start humming the tune and even buying the tape.

Once in a while we would brag to the hotel desk manager regarding how long we had been on the road, the states we had crossed, and the sights we had seen, and they would ask, "And how long will you still be traveling?" We always had the same answer, "For as long as we like or get tired of it." Their response was always similar; they were jealous and wished they had the time to do the same.

We zigzagged through Wyoming, South Dakota, Minnesota, Iowa, Wisconsin, Indiana, and Ohio, and had a few adventures along the way. Once we got stuck in the outskirts of Chicago and two hours later we found ourselves in downtown Chicago and no matter how many turns we took, we couldn't get out of the city. It was nine o'clock at night when we stopped at a McDonald's. Some people eating there tried to help us by surrounding our table to look over the map Nancy had spread out on the table. But it was like showing a treasure map to a blind group. One of the employees said, "We're local people, we don't drive on the highway like you folks."

Even though it made more sense to find a hotel nearby and stay for the night, Nancy made it clear that she did not care for the idea of spending the night in such a big city. It didn't matter to me one way or another and we got back on the road. We drove straight, and when we saw a bridge in the far distance, we kept our fingers crossed that it would lead us away from the city. She didn't care in what direction we were going, as long as it was out. After the bridge came the longest, darkest road of our trip. Usually by nine we were comfortably settled in a hotel, but it was now midnight, and we could have acted as zombies on a *Twilight Zone* ride. We saw a sign for a motel and headed straight for their parking lot. It was the only night we didn't follow our nightly routine. We crashed hard into a deep, delicious sleep.

The next morning we found out we were in Michigan and decided to check out the Great Lakes. We were not impressed. Maybe we didn't give them a fair chance to enjoy their scenic views. But once we realized we were close to Canada, we drove into the country with the goal of visiting Niagara Falls. I had visited Niagara Falls several times when I used to live in New Jersey, and once again I asked myself why it was such a tourist attraction. A woman and her friend who were standing next to us cleared up the mystery when she said to the other in Spanish, "Nice, but doesn't compare to the waterfalls we have in Argentina. This is what I call tourist propaganda." Nancy loved the falls; she had never seen them before. But not all was lost for me as I saw a raccoon for the first time in my life, not even ten feet away from where we were standing by the falls. He or she was probably twelve inches tall. It seemed to be standing on its back paws just staring at me. Its hairy face reminded me of Zorro wearing a mask. I just wanted to pet it, but I knew better than that as a neighbor in New Jersey had her hand bitten by a raccoon when she opened a garbage dumpster lid. She developed a bone infection and almost lost her hand. Still, I put raccoons on my list of favorite, cute animals beside monkeys and bears.

I did not tell Nancy what the woman from Argentina had said, as it would have taken away the admiration she felt for the waterfall. Like her brother Patrick, Nancy loved nature and we stayed overnight just so we could explore the area the next day with a guided tour under the falls. I took a lot of pictures along the way but by then I had learned not to show them to Nancy. She felt less than photogenic and was throwing them away as fast as my Polaroid Instamatic camera was spitting them out. So I had to hide them from her, including the one where we looked like large yellow bugs because of the yellow plastic ponchos we were wearing in order to remain relatively dry when under the falls. Nancy had a chronic facial rash which came and went and I had a bunch of pimples like a greasy teenager. I thought I was over that curse once I became an adult but while living at the cat condo, the pimples had come crawling back out. I believed I was allergic to Snooky's dandruff and now that I was away from him, I was counting on my skin returning to normal after a few more weeks of fresh air.

Nancy had some issues with her neck and back and asked me if I could give her a diagnosis, so I started doing orthopedic and neurological tests on her when we retired in the evening. It kept me up on my skills and if I passed the National Boards, I thought that I might as well take the New Jersey State Boards, just in case I wanted to practice in New Jersey.

In Vermont, Nancy fell in love with Lake Champlain. Considering it was the first day of summer, it wasn't too hot; if anything, it was more like a warm spring day enticing us to stay and enjoy. We stayed an extra day and just sat on our bedroom veranda looking out over the lake, sunbathing on our lounge chairs, and talking.

While driving around Maine we saw a group of seniors getting into a cruise boat. Instinctively, and mostly because Nancy and I had a slightly dishonest nature when it came to doing something adventurous even at the cost of getting caught, we parked the car and followed them. What could be the worst that could happen? We would have to buy tickets? We were welcomed aboard and neither felt the need to volunteer any personal information. The senior group had to know we didn't belong with them but no one said anything aloud, although there were a few who pointed at us accusingly and whispered to each other. We were a little worried that the captain of the boat, a jolly middle-aged man, might just throw us overboard since the average age of the group was late seventies and up. He walked up to us, most likely amused by our gutsy intrusion and said, "Do you girls want me to take your picture?" I handed him my camera.

I showed the Polaroid picture to Nancy but kept it in my hand. Then I slipped it into my backpack. I knew if she kept it, she would throw it overboard.

Except for the conspicuous looks towards us by some of the seniors, we had gotten away scot-free with a very relaxing hour-long lake cruise. When we returned to the dock, the whole group was being led in a straight line like a bunch of sheep, into a bus. "Where are we going now?" Nancy asked one of the old ladies.

"Lunch is included with the cruise," she said. "You know, steak and lobster and a delicious fresh salad at the Hotel Croisson. Very good for the price, don't you agree?" she continued, looking at us suspiciously.

Nancy and I debated if we should get on the bus but after weighing the risk of getting caught, we decided not to push our luck.

At a hotel in New Hampshire, Nancy saw me putting two bath towels in my small carry-on just as we were about to leave.

"You're not stealing those towels, are you? My goodness Veronica, I never thought you could do something like that."

"Everybody does it. Jeanne, my sister in-law in Long Island, collects them from every hotel she stays at. She told me hotels expect the guests to take towels as souvenirs and they automatically add it to the cost of the room."

"That's terrible."

I put the towels back on the bathroom's wall rack feeling like a real criminal. When I got back to the bedroom,

Nancy was holding a pillow under her arm. "I'm going to take this pillow to the car and I'll be right back," she said nonchalantly.

"You're taking the hotel pillow?" It was my turn to be shocked.

"You told me last night that Steve and Diane may not have enough pillows for all of us and I can't sleep without a pillow."

"That takes a lot of guts," I said disapprovingly. Then I added playfully, "Well, be careful or I'll have to go visit you in jail."

"Don't worry," she said laughing. "I'm going through the back door of the hotel; they won't see me."

Wow! Compared to her I considered myself a petty burglar. She was a pirate.

We walked the famous Freedom Trail through Boston's historic neighborhoods and went by Paul Revere's house. We also visited the King's Chapel Burying Ground and the Old State House. As much as Nancy liked antiques, she was far from being a city girl so after spending one day in Boston, we drove south and to the very tip of Provincetown where we basked in its history. We stayed one day at Martha's Vineyard visiting their quaint shops and doing a bit of shopping, then headed west through Connecticut where it was a must to stop at Gillette Castle and we gorged ourselves on the view below. After traveling for four weeks cross-country, we were ready to head on to New Jersey.

I was so glad to see Jacob and Shayna once again; they were now four and three years old. "They are absolutely adorable," Nancy said and then she pointed to Shayna wearing a cute purple dress and sleeping on the couch while sucking on her thumb. "Look at her; she is the most beautiful baby girl I have ever seen." I agreed with her.

Nancy could only stay one week before flying back to California. But having lived in New Jersey for almost thirty years, I had a lot to show her in that one week before she left.

I began by taking her to see my old house in Freehold where I had lived for fifteen years with my then husband Al, Al's mother, and my two sons. Except for Mrs. Fisher, our neighbor around the corner, everyone else had moved. When I knocked at her door, a mature older woman opened the door wearing house slippers and a robe. I asked, "Is Mrs. Fisher still living here?"

"Ronnie?" She wore a surprised look and her round, chubby face narrowed as she asked, "What are you doing here?"

"You know me?" I refused to accept that the old lady standing in front of me who appeared to be wearing the same outfit of thirty-four years ago was the same young, skinny neighbor I used to know. We talked for a short while; she had two daughters living with her and several grandchildren that she took care of. Her husband had died unexpectedly from a heart attack; I gave her my condolences before leaving.

The next day we took the bus to New York City but just like in Boston, Nancy felt claustrophobic. "It's too crowded," she said. "Give me the mountains, lakes, the forests, fresh air," and she reminisced about Lake Tahoe, in California. I drove her into the New Jersey countryside, where she connected with Mother Nature. One evening I took her to see a play at the Kobe Japanese Restaurant where I had produced dinner theatre for almost ten years before I decided to go back to school to become a chiropractor. The play was a slapstick comedy, written by one of the producers, but the acting, as well as the play itself, was lacking in quality. I felt obliged to apologize to Nancy after I had bragged so much about "my" professional theatre. After the show, Mr. Ounuma and his wife confided that my regular theatre patrons had been dropping off like flies. They were concerned about how long he could keep the restaurant open if the theatre was no longer successful. Mrs. Ounuma's eyes were teary when she said, "We miss you very much," and she forced a smile. As it turned out, the next time I returned to New Jersey years later, the Kobe Japanese Restaurant had closed down.

I took Nancy and my grandchildren to Sandy Hook, my favorite spot at the shore. Seated on a blanket that was covering the warm sand and watching the soft waves kissing the shore, we drank from our water bottles and ate our tuna sandwiches and potato chips with gusto. The sea sprayed the air, jolting the fond memories of my two sons and me visiting this six-mile barrier spit many, many years ago. Sandy Hook was our enchanting secret getaway where pirates hid their treasures in the ruins of what seemed to be an abandoned fort. But since then, Sandy Hook had been christened with a new name of National Recreational Park. They had taken away the mystery of the unspoiled terrain, which was now perfectly manicured and displayed unfriendly signs around the old fort saying "Keep out."

The next day Nancy and I went to Asbury Park Beach. In the old days, it was New Jersey's best area for beach-combers and families looking for some cool relief from the scorching summer heat. Yet for some reason, little by little, the businesses along the boardwalk closed down and Asbury Park became a dilapidated town with not much to offer except for the Stone Pony, a local bar where Bruce Springsteen had played in his younger days. For me, Asbury Park was a nostalgic reminder of the hot summer days when I used to take my two children and my mother-in-law, Nelly, to spend a day by the seashore. We would walk the busy boardwalk breathing in the salty air that was mixed with the delicious smell of burgers and fries. We went in and out of souvenir shops and the kids had to choose which one ride they would go on, as the children's rides were very expensive. Nancy and I got out of the car to take a quick look at the shore-line and then headed to Atlantic City. But after being in Las Vegas, Atlantic City could not compare to the impressive glittering experience of the Las Vegas strip and its casinos.

It was like comparing Saint Peter's Cathedral in Italy to a small, plain church somewhere in Pennsylvania.

A trip to New Jersey had to include a visit to Ferry Street in Newark where we had lunch in a Portuguese restaurant, and I gorged myself with pastries at several Portuguese bakeries. I had completely forgotten that to drive on the Parkway in New Jersey, we had to pay tolls and the beaches were not free as they were on the West Coast. I appreciated the beauty of the New Jersey countryside and its shores, but I missed the openness the West Coast offered to their people, free of charge.

After Nancy returned to her family in California, I visited all my friends, including Dr. Peruzzi. He was the one who first adjusted my back and as such, had played a significant role in my life. It took me a while to find his new address since he no longer worked from his home. He had sold his practice and moved to a retirement community. Poor guy, for it appeared that all those years he had worked out and paid attention to eating healthily and had gotten his spine adjusted on a weekly basis had been a waste of time as he was now dying from lead poisoning. Allegedly the water pipes in his old house were the source of contamination. He had always been a pessimist and now he was a very angry old man. I saw him twice and each time it was a one-way conversation of how much he hated everybody.

Diane, my daughter-in-law, was still working at the old Fitkins Hospital in the blood lab. I admired her dedication as a mother and wife, working all odd hours of the night and day and still managing to take care of her family. I regarded her as a superwoman. I spent my free time playing with my grandchildren when they were not in daycare.

Having owned three music stores in the past made me eligible enough to help Steve at his music store and he appreciated having some time off. I had a gut feeling I had passed the National Boards IV and I started using my free time to study behind the counter for the New Jersey Chiropractic State Boards. I also took advantage of having at my disposal such a large selection of musical instruments. Except for band instruments, which I had no experience with, I played the pianos, the acoustic and electric guitars, and the banjos, and when someone came in to buy a guitar, I showed off a little. But playing a musical instrument was no longer my passion. The music on the radio was just fine with me.

One day I went looking for my old friend Rosanna, who had gone batty on me a few years ago when I didn't meet her in Florida during one of my school breaks while I attended Life University in Georgia. According to her next-door neighbor, Rosanna had move to Florida and left no forwarding address. I knew Rosanna well enough to know she had done it on purpose to hurt me, as she did that to anyone she felt had done her wrong. I wondered how she was doing; she was most likely alone and brewing in her hate for her family and for me. I remember she liked it that way. I hoped she had made peace with her daughter and her son, but in my heart I doubted it; she held onto grudges like a miser.

Ralph called from Oregon. "Mom, I have great news! You passed National Boards Part IV with flying colors!" I signed up immediately for a seminar in Newark that was specifically geared to help attendees prepare for the New Jersey State Boards the following month. According to some sources, at the first try it was close to impossible to pass the boards, and a legal battle was going on to fight discrimination against stopping new chiropractors from practicing in New Jersey. There were a lot more medical doctors than chiropractors, and even more lawyers than medical doctors, and I did not see them trying to prevent others from practicing. The whole thing was ridiculous, chiropractors against chiropractors?

I was working Wednesday afternoon at Steve's music center when I got a call from Mike, a teenager to whom I used to teach bass guitar many years ago and who had also performed in some of my early theatre productions. "Ronnie, I heard from Steve that you're back in New Jersey. It's been what, twenty years or more? I miss you. Let's get together; I would love to see you." I invited Steve to come along Friday night, since they were friends but at the last moment, Steve could not make it. I was looking forward to seeing "crazy little Mickey" as I fondly used to call him after a police car chased him for speeding and he thought he could get away by throwing glass beer bottles out of the window with the intention of blowing their tires. There were other wild stories about him but the one that really made the news was when his car went too fast around a corner, flipped over, and he broke his neck. The last time I had seen him he was wearing a halo brace attached to his head with pins placed into his skull.

The meeting place was at a western bar in Lakewood. Mickey was no longer a teenager. He was a handsome young man wearing a complete western outfit, with boots and dark matching hat and a shiny belt buckle big enough to send SOS signals miles and miles away. We sat at the bar reminiscing over the old days. He had to be drunk out of his mind because he leaned towards me and suggested, "Ronnie, let's go to the shore, lie down in the sand, and wait for the sunrise together."

"I'm leaving," I said, reaching in my purse to pay for my drink. He stopped me by wrapping his arms around my shoulders and said in the most candid tone, "Please don't leave. I've loved you since I was a kid."

The voice, the same intonation of seventeen years ago, came ringing out of his mouth. Oh my gosh, now a mystery had been solved! The one and only obscene phone call I had ever received in my whole life had been made by him. Well, what the caller said on the phone would most likely not be classified as obscene, even though he did announce, "This is an obscene phone call. I want to fool around with you." Instead of confronting him now, I decided to act like a mature adult; he needed to come to terms with his childish obsession. "Mike, I was your bass teacher, your friend. You're confusing me with the mother you never had." His mother had put him up for adoption when he was one month old.

"No, Ronnie, I never, ever saw you as my mother. I wanted you as my lover. I still dream about you."

"My gosh, Mike, that's horrible. How can you even say that?" Of course he could say it, he was drunk. Like a good psychologist, I changed the subject. "Steve told me you're married. Do you have any pictures of your family?"

"I've been married twice, but I'm divorced now." He pulled out his wallet to show me the pictures of his two exes and his three children. At least he cared enough for his family to carry their pictures, which I thought was very sweet. Life was not going well for him. He had lost his driver's license for drunk driving and in order to meet me at the bar he had taken a taxi. He was absolutely sloshed and I felt obliged to drive him home to Bricktown.

While driving, I preached about the evils of alcohol and how he should pay better attention to his health. I felt like a mother, working for the Salvation Army. When he reached over to hug me before leaving the car, I pushed him out with my feet. He held his door open and put his head in to announce, "Ronnie, I'll always love you."

Great, I thought to myself, another alcoholic in love with me.

When I went to Newark to take the New Jersey State Board, I was feeling great until I saw three other students who had also attended Life University in Georgia with me. It was the third time for Richard and the second time for Lucy and Rose. If it were true that the New Jersey Chiropractic State Board was making it impossible to get a license, it didn't matter how well I did. That helped me to relax during the exams.

The only test that stumped me was the X-rays. No age or sex on the view, the pelvis was missing, including the femoral heads, and the film quality had much to be desired. When we left the building Richard said, "Those damned X-rays! I guess we'll see each other again at the next State Board exam. I'm not giving up, are you?"

"I don't quit easily either. See ya."

Ralph called. "Mom, I just found out that Western States College is offering their once a year courses on Minor Surgery and Proctology and they're starting next week. If you're still serious about practicing together, you need to fly to Oregon as soon as possible. You'll also need to brush up on Obstetrics and Gynecology. All four subjects are needed to be licensed in Oregon."

"Gosh, I thought I was done with school," I said. "I already filled out the paperwork to go to Egypt even though I took the New Jersey State Boards last week. Gosh, I'm so confused. Ralph, I really don't know if I want to live in Oregon and be subjected to rain on a daily basis." I babbled on. "It's either New Jersey or Egypt. I'm not sure."

"Mom, you want to live in New Jersey? Are you joking? The pollution there is worse than the rain over here! And why are you talking about going to Egypt? You told me you're tired of traveling and besides that, why on earth do you want to go to Egypt and take a chance on getting stomach worms or some kind of Nile virus over there?" He took on a deep-sounding, serious voice, "Don't you think it's about time you settled down?"

Ralph should have been a lawyer. He always knew how to present a case.

Getting a round-trip plane ticket to Oregon on such short notice was cost prohibitive. I was told at the travel agency that I was better off buying a one-way airline ticket and then return to New Jersey by train.

I was in luck; in his living room, Ralph had a futon that opened into a bed. His apartment was in Troutdale, not too far from the college where I attended Proctology and Minor Surgery classes every morning. In the afternoon, Ralph was an adjunct professor at the college and I went home to study what I had learned in the morning. And with any spare minutes left in the day, I played for the first time in my life with the world of internet dating. Leonardo was Italian and lived in Eugene, Oregon. He was five years younger than me. I had no idea what he looked like, since he didn't have a photo with his online ad. I answered his ad because I was attracted by what he wrote: "Pictures are not important, I'd rather learn about someone from the inside out."

Leonardo liked to work out and had a black belt in karate. I assumed he was in good physical shape but did not want to brag about it. I began doing sit-ups and push-ups every day, so I could write to him that I also worked out. I wrote, "I'm done with my classes and am leaving Monday for New Jersey, but I would like to stay in touch and I'll keep you posted when I return to take the Oregon State Chiropractic Boards."

He responded, "When you get back, do let me know. I'll come and visit you."

I had never been on a cross-country train ride but I knew it would take a long time. I made sure the train to New Jersey had a private sleeping cabin. The train was equipped with a rail car with windows on all sides and overhead so during the day, I sat there as we crossed through Washington and Montana. I was taken aback by the splendor of the mountains and the panoramic scenic beauty, principally of the state of Montana. Someday I will return there, I promised myself. At night, back in the comfort of my sleeping quarters, I missed seeing North Dakota and part of Minnesota, but someone told me there was really nothing to see.

I did a lot of writing in my daily journal, studied the notes I had taken in classes, visited the restaurant car for my three daily meals, and slept soundly every night. I also finally decided that once I arrived in New Jersey, I was ready to leave, permanently. The idea of working with Ralph had become more comfortable in my mind. Having spent four weeks with him reminded me how much we had in common and besides that, my California family was relatively close, close enough for a drive or a quick one-hour flight. My plan was to drive from New Jersey to Georgia and surprise my friend Leila. I wasn't in any hurry. I could spend a few days with her, and then head to California and pick up my belongings at Nancy's house and even spend some time with the family before continuing on to Oregon.

I was sleeping when the conductor's voice announced that we were in West Virginia and were then heading north. I got my clothes on and went to inquire why the train had not crossed from Wisconsin through Pennsylvania and then directly to New Jersey, instead of going south and then north again. I was told that that was the way they always went. The long trip was accentuated by stopping at every station along the East Coast.

It wasn't easy to say good-bye to Diane, Steve, Jacob, and Shayna. In many ways, I had given them false hope that I would be staying. Diane and Steve had even discussed moving from their apartment to a house so I could have my own bedroom. But I couldn't do it. Living with someone made me dependent on them, and I needed to be on my own. My ex-husband Al and I met up, he had finally come to terms that we were divorced, and we parted as friends.

Leila received me with open arms and she gave me her comfortable living room couch. On one of our walks around her neighborhood, she told me about the "living" trees that had been murdered. "They will most likely be used in someone's fireplace." She cried.

I lacked the courage to tell her I considered myself pretty sensitive to my surroundings but not to such an extreme. I did not feel the pain or a soul connection to a tree being chopped down just like I didn't have a connection to the chickens or the cows being sacrificed to feed the consumers.

I called Nancy and told her about my travel plans to go back to California at the end of the week to pick up my stuff from her garage before heading north to Oregon. She asked me if I would like her company driving to California. Of course I said yes.

"Is there a way you can stay with Leila for two weeks? I'm bringing you a surprise that will knock your socks off but you'll have to stay there for it to happen."

"Okay, okay, what's the surprise?"

"If I told you it wouldn't be a surprise, would it?"

I loved surprises as surprises. Being told there was a surprise coming and then having to wait for it, when I already knew a surprise was on the way, automatically canceled the surprise effect and it became more of an annoying burden of wonder. What could it be? Probably something I didn't need.

Leila insisted on buying the food and cooking for both of us. I was using her electricity and water and was eating her food, but she wouldn't accept any money. So I made an appointment to see the president of the chiropractic college with the intention of selling a piece of artwork—a clay foot—that Leila had made before she started chiropractic college many years ago when she was thinking about being an artist instead. She had approached several art galleries but no one had shown any interest. She had only made one clay foot, but she could always make more if needed. She pointed to her right foot and said, laughing, "I still have the original mold."

In my opinion, the clay foot was a unique piece of art. It was very possible that the president of the college would like the foot as much as I did and would purchase it to display it at the school library. I was going to ask $1200 for it.

When his secretary told me he was a very busy man, I told her I only needed twenty minutes or less of his time. An appointment was made for Friday.

Steve called. "I have great news! Mom, we opened your mail and you passed the New Jersey Chiropractic Boards! You're now legally licensed to practice here. Mom, come back. We miss you."

"I miss everyone too, but Ralph and I are planning to practice together in Oregon. This is something we talked about even before going to school. Also, and I don't know how to explain this, but I love the West Coast and the way people think over there. Maybe someday you, Diane, and the kids will come visit and then you'll understand why I feel this way. Who knows, maybe you'll all decide to move to Oregon once you see how wonderful it is on that side of the world." I didn't think it was the right time for me to share with him that Leonardo's emails had also influenced my desire to return to Oregon.

Every morning I drove to the chiropractic college to use their internet. Leonardo was an aficionado of fly-fishing. "I'm making you a fly hook and putting your name on it," he wrote. I had no concept of what fly fishing was in comparison with regular fishing and a fishing fly hook did not seem to me like a romantic present but it was definitely very sweet. I couldn't wait to meet him. I visualized him as tall and toned since he did hundreds of push-ups daily and was into martial arts. And because he was Italian, he probably had dark hair and dark eyes and was a lot more sentimental in person than his emails led me to believe.

I sat in the president's waiting room and lying on my lap was Leila's clay foot, wrapped in bubble wrap. After waiting an hour, I followed his secretary to his office. "He'll be in soon." She closed the beautiful heavy mahogany door behind her. I looked very briefly at the walls covered with multiple awards and pictures of when the president was in his twenties and excelled in football. My main focus was soon directed at scanning the top of his large mahogany desk. According to the story going around campus when I attended that college, the statue above one of the buildings was none other than a naked, true-life replica of the school's president when he was a football star and still in top physical condition. One day, to the surprise of some students who happened to look up before entering the building, they noticed the statue was missing its most important anatomical part. A few weeks later, rumors started that they had found the perpetrator of the crime and "it" had been returned safely in one piece to our beloved president. Supposedly he used "it" as a paperweight on his desk. I didn't see "it," and assumed that if the story were true, he had taken "it" home.

The president walked into his office full of energy and almost crushed my hand when he shook it. He was as I remember him with slightly wavy, thick, white hair combed back, tall with excellent posture, and just a little older. Once he sat down, I stood eagerly and handed him the foot bound in bubble wrap. "Here," I said. "It's a sculpture made by one of your chiropractic students and I'm hoping, I mean *she* is hoping you will buy it and display it in the college's library."

He unwrapped it carefully and lifted it up to his eye level to look at it more attentively. "It's a real nice-looking foot but I can't use it in the library." He put it on his desk and brushed his fingers over the sculpture as if caressing it and added, "This is a chiropractic college not a podiatrist school."

"The student who made it attended this college and I was hoping you would buy it for twelve hundred dollars but I'm willing to take a hundred dollars. It would be a nice gesture on your part and she could use the money." Leila was going to kill me for selling it so cheap, but if I got him to buy it, it could be the beginning of her career as an artist.

"I don't buy anything. I never buy anything." He picked up the foot again and stared at it with what I thought to be some admiration. "You give me the foot and I'll use it on my desk as a paperweight." Oh my goodness, he did have a thing for displaying body parts on his desk, didn't he? Where the heck was his penis? I looked once more over his desk. He went on, "I don't buy, I only receive. Did you see the clock at the entrance of our campus? It was given to me by the artist. I don't buy anything, much less a foot." He was cheap. I took the foot from his hands and started wrapping it with the bubble wrap.

He showed me the ring he was wearing. "A present," he said, beaming a glorious smile. I acted as if I needed both hands to carry the foot and didn't shake his hand.

Leila was very disappointed. I promised her I'd visit a few podiatrists; maybe one of them would be interested. I know I would if I were a foot doctor.

Leila took me to a dinner party in Smyrna at the home of one of her friends. The house reminded me of a plantation mansion like the one used in *Gone with the Wind.* Except this one had glass chandeliers in every room and a center, white marble stairway that split on either side on the second floor as it ascended to the third floor. The dining room table regally accommodated all thirty guests. Before we took our seats, Leila told me, "Miriam, the hostess, is Jewish and her husband was a Moslem. He died in a car accident two years ago. Their son, David, was in the passenger seat but he didn't even get a scratch. If it weren't for David's support, Miriam would have died. Her husband and she were very close." Leila brought her index and middle finger together to emphasize the closeness.

David stood at the head of the table. He wore a long-sleeved white shirt and dark pants. His slim face with dark olive skin was complemented by his shoulder-length, dark curly hair. He recited a prayer in Hebrew and then in Arabic before proceeding to slice the bread loaves that were then passed around the table on two large silver platters. I said to Leila, "This is going to sound weird, but David seems to be too young to radiate such intense kindness. Do you notice that too or am I imagining things?"

She leaned toward me and whispered, "He's seventeen years old but since his father died, he seems to have acquired certain spiritual powers. A lot of people have started wondering if he's going to be the Messiah."

Why couldn't we just accept when someone was a good person? Why did they have to have anything to do with the Bible? Of course I didn't express my views to Leila and just ate my food. After dinner, Leila disappeared and everybody got busy talking to each other. I stood by the window looking at the garden. I really did not feel like making small talk with strangers. I was not aware of David until he stood next to me.

"Would you like to read a book?" he asked, his dark eyes radiating light.

"I do like books, but I don't see any here…"

"The book you need is in my bedroom." As odd as that statement may have sounded to anyone else, it made sense to me, so I followed him. The furnishings in his bedroom were simple—a twin bed, a large wooden desk, a chair, and books. Wall-to-wall books! It was a bedroom library!

"I can guide you to seek the answer. You seem to be caught between feelings of anger and yet trying to forget the past," he said, as if I were an open book myself.

"You can tell all that by looking at me?"

"Your aura tells me a lot."

"I have an aura?" I was curious. "Does it have a color?"

"It's white all around you and it glows like a crystal, except for some cloudy spots. As soon as I saw you, I could tell you're a healer, but you need to heal what makes you hurt inside first, before you can help others. Do you have a particular subject you want to know more about?"

"Death," I answered without hesitation. "I need to know about death and how I can forgive my late husband. At his memorial, he was there. I mean in spirit. He gave me a daisy. He always gave me a flower when he wanted me to forgive him... I wish I could forgive him now, but I don't know how."

He pulled a book from one of the bookcases and handed it to me. "Here is the book you need. Take your time. I'll close the door behind me so no one disturbs you. When I see you downstairs I'll know you have found what you were looking for."

I read and cried, and read more and cried again. When the tears stopped, I closed my eyes and prayed, *Patrick I didn't know you could hear me. I'm sorry, but now that I know that you can hear me, I'm sorry that by hating you all these years, I stopped you from leaving. I didn't know about that until I read David's book. I promise you that I'll also write to your daughter Lauren, since I know that she also hates you for the emotional abuse she experienced while growing up. I forgive you with all my heart and I'm sure that she will too. I no longer hold you responsible for what you did. You can ascend peacefully! Please go on, everything is fine now.*

Before leaving, I thanked David and when we hugged he said, "I see a bright future ahead of you."

Nancy's surprise was no laughing matter. As soon as she landed and we hugged she said with an animated smile, "Brunhilde, our *Austrian Angel,* is arriving from Austria to-morrow morning! That's the surprise! That's why it took me two weeks to come and get you. I was busy planning the trip with her. She'll be joining us on our drive to California!"

Leila knew of my experience in Austria. She was adamant, "Brunhilde is not welcome in my house, and I do not wish to meet her." I was disappointed but at the same time, I could understand how Leila felt. Some people could forgive and others could not and Brunhilde's involvement with the Nazis during World War II could be very difficult to accept for some. My father, who had lost so many members of his family in concentration camps, not only forgave Brunhilde, but wrote to thank her for taking care of me when I was destitute and alone in Salzburg, Austria. No matter what she had done in the past, I had to forgive her just like my father did. Brunhilde had begged me for forgiveness for what she had done during Hitler's time, but I also saw her as a victim of those times. She had been fourteen years old when her family joined the Nazi party and she could not go against her family's political choices. I forgave her because she had been there for me when I was down and out but I couldn't speak for those who had been murdered. She would have to meet them when she died and ask them for their understanding.

Nancy and I said good-bye to Leila that evening and stayed the night at a hotel close by the airport.

Brunhilde had not changed. She was still as funny and as full of vitality as ever and so we began our cross-country drive with Brunhilde sitting in the back seat since I was Nancy's navigator. We talked and laughed and even though Brunhilde's English was not the best, it was good enough for us to understand her and hopefully she understood us, too.

Every time we stopped, Brunhilde would get into one kind of situation or another, even though her left knee was hurting her. In Tennessee, she sat next to two old men on a bench while Nancy and I went into a grocery store to get ice cream and by the time we came out, she asked us if it was okay if she went with them because they were her new friends. They were retired American war veterans. Not much younger than them, she was vivaciously flirty and they were absolutely taken by her English small talk of, "I like you," and "You are handsome American men."

I took Nancy to one side. "Remember how in Austria Brunhilde kept going back and forth from the past to the present as if she had two personalities, the Nazi one and the kind Austrian woman one?"

"Yeah, I remember. I like her better when she's in the present like now." She paused briefly and then said," Do you think I made a mistake in inviting her over to travel with us?"

"I'm worried about her wanting to leave with the two old guys. She's ready to follow them. It reminds me of when I was an activity director at an old folks' home in New Jersey and if I didn't keep an eye on some of the residents when we went out, they'd disappear on me, or simply follow someone they liked. That's a sign of dementia and we need to keep an eye on Brunhilde. We're responsible for her."

We agreed never to leave her alone.

When we stopped at a restaurant in Kentucky for lunch, Brunhilde said she needed to go to the bathroom. Nancy and I sat in the small lobby waiting for Brunhilde to come out of the bathroom. We waited and waited and finally we started wondering what had happened when she came out holding herself on an older woman's arm. They were laughing and having a good time. Supposedly Brunhilde had been brushing her dentures in the bathroom and the other lady was doing the same. Brunhilde asked if she could go with her and we said, no, you're with us, remember?

Brunhilde's main goal in life was to make as many friends as she could along the way. But when her left knee started to hurt her so much that she couldn't walk without us supporting her by the arms or she would fall, she lost her sparkle. Sitting for hours in the car with her knees bent was not helping her to recover. Her knee took a turn for the worse. We couldn't leave her alone, even with a bad knee we were afraid she would take off on us. She needed a babysitter 24/7. We gave up on doing any kind of hiking—something we had been looking forward to while traveling. By the time we reached Missouri, she could not sit in the car without moaning. She told us she needed to go home, back to Austria, and have knee surgery as they had told her she needed before she had come on the trip with us. It was eight in the morning when we dropped her and her luggage at Springfield Airport. We couldn't find a place to park the car so we left her right at the curb by the airport entrance with an airport attendant. Within less than ten minutes on the highway, both of us looked at each other and agreed that leaving Brunhilde the way we did had not been very thoughtful. Most likely Brunhilde was at the airport crying all alone without a helping hand, because her two American friends didn't care enough to stay until she got on the plane. Guilt ridden, Nancy drove back to the airport and after parking by a sign that said, "No parking allowed," we went looking for Brunhilde. She was seated in a wheelchair and there were two flight attendants next to her. She wore a gleaming smile while talking to them and we could see she was getting lots of attention. She was being well taken care of so we left without her knowing we had returned to make sure that she was okay.

After hours of monotonous driving, "Are we still in Kansas?" became our private joke. Eventually we found ourselves high up in the mountains of Colorado, seated in the living room of John and Susie Manson, Nancy's old friends from California. They had sold everything they owned three years ago and moved to Colorado. Susie and John were convinced that sooner or later, most likely sooner, the whole of California would slide into the ocean after "the Big One" shook the West Coast into the Pacific Ocean.

We were invited to stay the night. There was a twin size bed and an air mattress. I had always wanted to try an air mattress; Nancy got the bed. I couldn't seem to fall asleep being so close to the floor but when I finally did, I experienced a hallucinatory nightmare where Nancy and I were panic-stricken and screaming as we pushed each other up a mountain so we would not be taken away by the waves below. "The West Coast is gone," I cried, "Oregon is gone, Ralph and Leonardo in Oregon are gone!" Nancy cried, "My whole family and my beautiful house are gone too!" We held each other crying, then she took on a look of complete delight. "Look Veronica, look at the beautiful beach! Have you ever seen anything more gorgeous?" John and Susie were wearing bathing suits. "C'mon you girls," they said, waving at us, "come and join us." I began walking towards them. The sand felt cold and wet and I was shivering, but Nancy was smiling and said, "I love nature, I could stay here forever." Then she fell into quicksand and disappeared. I screamed, "Help! Help!" I woke up crying, my air mattress had gone flat, and I was lying on the cold stone floor.

When they served us breakfast, I made the mistake of sharing my nightmare with them and that convinced them even more that they had made a wise move to leave California. I felt the reason that I had such a frightful nightmare about California and Oregon sliding into the sea was their fault, because that's all they talked about. I felt that they were very gullible because when the conversation came around to deer, I said there should be a lot of them roaming those hills, but we hadn't seen any and I wished I could see one up close. Then Susie responded emphatically, "Don't even say that! Your thoughts can make anything happen and you don't want to hit a deer on the way home."

As we drove down the torturous mountain road, Nancy and I did our best to keep our minds clear from encountering a deer running in front of us, but once we got to the main highway, we were stopped and unfairly charged by a crooked highway patrolman. He knew by my California plates that we were from out of state. Nancy was very upset and with good reason. At first she tried to remain calm but when he wouldn't budge saying that she was speeding, she yelled, "You're a liar! You're a freakin' liar!"

"Ma'am, do you want me to arrest you?" he said in a monotone voice.

"It's not fair, this is not fair."

"It looks like you'd rather get arrested than pay me $125 cash."

She handed him the money and I tapped her arm and said, "Please, don't say anything; it's not worth it."

He put the money in his pocket and said, "Now ma'am, you drive safely, you hear?" He walked away towards his car where his partner had been waiting in the passenger seat.

"Highway robber!" she yelled out from her window.

Five days later, we arrived in California after driving through eerie Death Valley.

I planned to leave for Oregon the next morning.

I didn't have much stuff in Nancy's garage. But no matter how many times I tried to re-arrange my belongings inside my car, there was no way I could squeeze in five more boxes that held my stereo, two large speakers, and my television. I had no choice but to rent a truck and tow the car behind it. At the truck rental, I was told I would need an eighteen-footer because it had to be big enough to pull my car.

There was only one glitch. They brought us the truck with a metal trailer ramp, but they were not going to drive the car onto it or even offer to attach the belts to make sure the car remained on the ramp. They handed us the belts, screws, and tools, and walked away. They were not even allowed to supervise our work. If my car got detached while driving, it was my problem, not theirs. Welcome to California, the land of suing.

Nancy and I stood staring at the pulley and the car. "It looks a lot like the kind of railing one drives over at the car wash," I said, trying to lose my fear and get myself motivated. "I'm going to try it slowly."

"I can do that for you," Nancy said hesitantly. And then added, "If you like."

"Like?" I asked, amazed at her more than kind offer. "I will be forever in your debt." Goodness gracious, I would not be surprised if she could do it with her eyes closed; she had driven twice across the US!

Mission accomplished, we began tying the straps around the tires and using the wrench to tighten any screws we felt important enough to hold the car from moving. What if we had missed the most important hook up, the one instrumental in keeping the car from sliding out as I took off? Nancy encouraged me to call Ralph to fly over and then drive the truck for me. He was not available. The guy at the truck rental came out wearing a mocking grin and said, "Are you girls done yet?"

He looked briefly at what we had done then shook his head and said to me, "Whatever you do, don't back out."

"What do mean, don't back out, what about when I have to park?"

"Look for places where you can drive in and then drive straight out." His voice had taken on a maternal tone. "Someone should go with her," he said to Nancy.

"I know, but she's doing it all by herself and it's a long trip to Oregon"

He interrupted her, "I really doubt she's going to make it to Oregon." What in the world was he referring to? I mean, talk about a complete lack of trust! Did I look that incompetent, and was it written all over my face? How dare he think of me in those terms when he had absolutely no idea of what I could and could not do?

"Can't you at least tell us if it looks okay?" Nancy implored. "I don't want her to die driving this thing."

He mumbled something under his breath and then checked the attachments and tightened a few screws.

I promised Nancy I would call her as soon as I got to Ralph's apartment. Waving back at Nancy, I drove off the lot feeling a little nervous but elated by the opportunity to drive a large truck, even if it was just for one day. My longtime wish had become a reality. The only thing I was missing was a monkey to keep me company. But I was better off without one; I needed to remain focused on the road.

I had not gone far when I made a wrong turn and saw the sign, "Dead End." I had no choice but to drive up someone's driveway and then back out. I got out of the truck and made sure the car was still attached. I had done well and felt empowered by my maneuver. I had just proved to myself that I could do anything I put my mind to. Once I got on the highway, I felt I had everything under control. All I had to do was go north until I reached Oregon.

I had forgotten to take drinking water but it worked out to my advantage. I only stopped three times along the way— twice to fill the gas tank and once at a truck driver's diner.

Whatever was in the hamburger that I ate there, the cook must have added cough expectorant. For over an hour, all I did was cough up phlegm.

Once I was in Oregon, I kept my eyes open for signs to Troutdale where Ralph lived, but all I could see were signs to Portland. I was not sure if I had gone too far and decided to get off the highway and ask for directions. "Welcome to West Linn" read the quaint road sign. Not far from the exit was a Texaco gas station with an interesting wall mural depicting a 60s country gas station. "This is Hwy 43," said the gas attendant. "You need to get back on 205 and then take 5 north. Just follow the signs." I used his phone to call Ralph, who told me the same thing.

It was late in the evening when I arrived at Ralph's apartment. When I got out of the truck, my hands, as well as my whole body, would not stop shaking from holding the vibrating steering wheel, which shook as much as the truck did. It had been twelve long hours of straight driving. My dream of some day getting in a truck with a monkey and driving across the US was now more like a nightmare to me. I was done with truck driving.

Leonardo agreed to wait for us to meet until I finished taking the Oregon State Chiropractic Boards at the end of the month. Luckily for me, Ralph's roommate had moved out a few weeks ago so I had my own private room, and Ralph was happy to have me as his roommate. My days were spent studying for minor surgery and proctology but I didn't bother studying for gynecology or obstetrics. I had already taken those classes while at Life Chiropractic College and I had given birth to two children. When it came to giving birth, I already knew everything. What could they possibly ask that I did not already know?

Ralph made the news on television as Portland's mobile chiropractor. He was quite busy treating patients at their homes and offices. I was far from feeling enthusiastic about the business, however. I knew when it came to lifting the portable adjusting table, my lower back was not going to stand for it. My best bet once I received my license, or I should say *our* best bet, since we wanted to work together, would be to open a regular office where the patients came to us.

~ Chapter Nine ~

The Fishing Hook

Leonardo lived in Eugene and rarely drove to Portland but the time had come for us to meet. He sent me an email, "I'll call you to let you know when I'm close." I was very happy when Ralph promised to stay home that afternoon. After so many months emailing each other, all I knew about Leonardo was that he worked out, used to be a bodyguard for some very influential people in Las Vegas, was retired, and his hobbies were fishing and collecting old bikes.

At five twenty he called. It was the first time I heard his voice. "Is this Veronica?"

"Yes."

"This is Leonardo. I should be arriving at your address in thirty minutes. See you soon." He hung up.

I complained to Ralph, about the brisk call. Ralph said, "Well, maybe he's in a hurry to meet you." I felt better; it made sense. I went into my room and changed my outfit once again. I went from a sexy short black dress to blue jeans and a country looking shirt. I wanted to look natural, like someone a guy would take along fishing. I combed my hair for the fifth time and checked out my lipstick. I sat next to the window looking out for his arrival. When I saw a man in his mid-fifties with the same stature of Robert Mitchum, the actor, carrying a gray metal box under one arm and looking at a piece of paper in the other hand, I knew it was him. I was sure my fishing hook with my name on it was inside the gray box. I never liked Robert Mitchum's looks, and even though some women would consider Leonardo handsome for that particular reason, the fact that he did not smile and only of-fered me a brief hug lacking any type of emotion made me a little apprehensive. Ralph was in the kitchen and I called him to meet Leonardo. From that point on, they stood in the middle of the living room as Leonardo went on and on about fly fishing without even once glancing at me. I felt left out of the conversation and remained standing, waiting for my turn to say something important since I didn't know anything about fishing. Finally I got my courage up to point to the metal gray container he held close to his torso and asked, "Is that a treasure box you're holding?"

"Oh yeah, my fishing tackle box." He opened the lid and handed me a fishing hook. "Here it is. I promised to make one for you, remember?"

I had seen fishing hooks before and I didn't see anything special about this one. I didn't see my name on it as he had promised and couldn't even imagine how anyone could put a name on such a tiny hook. "Thank you," I said. "It's very nice. Another one like this and I could have some very original earrings." I smiled, but he didn't.

He asked, "Would you like to have dinner with me?" Perhaps it was because he didn't look at me when he spoke, or because I felt ignored when he first came in, or his greeting hug lacked any type of warmth, but the man I had exchanged emails with for months now reminded me of a robot. Perhaps he was stressed out or nervous, perhaps both. I pushed aside my disappointment and said yes to dinner.

He opened the car door for me and I did not open his door from the inside. I had not forgotten about men being from Mars and women from Venus and decided to follow the rules. He drove to a Mexican food cart which in his opinion had "real" Mexican tacos. "I always come here for lunch or dinner when I come to Portland," he said. I couldn't help recalling my mother-in-law telling me that from her kitchen window she had witnessed a food vendor in the street below spit on an apple and then polish it against his dirty trousers before adding it to his basket of apples for sale. Since then, I have been leery of food stands, wondering about the vendors' personal hygiene habits.

He bought each of us two tacos, a tall Coke for him, and a cup of water with lemon for me. We ate inside his car. I gave him the other taco since I didn't care for Mexican food. He talked a lot about bicycles, another subject I knew nothing about, so I listened. When he finished eating he said, "As you know, I collect old bikes. Do you mind if we go to SE Hawthorne? They have lots of antique shops there." After traveling with Nancy across the US, I had learned to appreciate antiques, but once Leonardo entered a vintage store, he would disappear on me and I had to go looking for him. On the way home, we stopped at an ice cream parlor close to where I lived. His conversation was about himself, his two sons who didn't want anything to do with him, and how wealthy he used to be when he lived in La Jolla, before his ex-wife took him for everything he had. When he took me back upstairs to my apartment, he bowed before saying good night, turned, walked down the staircase, and drove off. I guess I had been a disappointment to him as much as he was to me.

I was very surprised when Leonardo called the next morning. "We need to talk," he said.

"Okay, go ahead."

"No, what I have to ask you has to be in person. I should be at your apartment by noon."

"Okay, see you then." Having met him, I was no longer concerned to be alone with him.

He walked in with a very serious face and offered the same "cool" hug as the day before. I sat on the couch and he sat on one of the dining room chairs across from me. He kept twisting his hands together and looking towards the sliding glass door to the small veranda where Ralph's barbecue grill stood. "How was your drive up here?" I asked.

"How do you feel about me?" was his answer while continuing to stare past me and through the glass door.

I wanted to say, are you talking to me? Instead I said, "What do you mean?"

"Well, we've been writing for months and we know everything about each other. I like Portland and I'm willing to move up here from Eugene." He looked straight at me, his eyes emotionless like a fish staring out of a fish tank. Then he said, "When do you want to get married?"

"Married?" I straightened my back up and put my hands between my knees, then quickly moved them up to cross my arms across my chest. "We barely know each other!" I wanted to laugh, but didn't want to appear rude. "We went out once, that's not even dating." Then I added daringly, "We haven't even kissed each other."

He got up and bending over, he kissed me lightly on the cheek, and in the same non-committing fashion, kissed me on the lips. He returned to his chair and said, "Okay, now we've kissed. How do you feel about me now?"

What the heck was the matter with him? No, no, it was more like what was the matter with me? I attracted losers; I wore a loser's magnet. All the men in my life had been losers, except Al, of course. He and I just weren't compatible, but I hadn't picked him so I couldn't get the credit for it, my mother and her sister deserved all the praise. I was alone with Leonardo and if he was out of his mind as I suspected, I needed to remain calm. I tried to be as cool as possible. "I can't rush into anything right now, for as I said, we barely know each other."

He stood and started pacing back and forth. "All that writing between us didn't mean anything to you?"

"Yes it did. It's called 'Getting to know you,' I sang, 'getting to know all about you.'" I smiled. He stared blankly at me. He either lacked any sense of humor or he was not familiar with the tune.

"I thought that's what we did when we wrote to each other almost every day." He sat with his head down between his hands, like a kid who had just been sent to his room.

"Writing to one another doesn't mean we're making a marriage commitment. I've been married twice and I have no intention of getting married again. So if you want to stop seeing me I understand completely." I stood and walked to the kitchen.

Ralph arrived just then and I breathed a deep sigh of relief. They started talking about fishing and then Leonardo said, "Veronica, I'm going to take you to a Mexican restaurant that in my opinion has the best tacos on the West Coast."

I almost said, "Even better than the ones we had yesterday?" Instead I said, "Ralph, you want to come with us?" I pleaded with my eyes.

"No Mom, you go ahead. Francis is coming over."

Before we went into the restaurant, Leonardo opened the trunk of his car and lifted a black blanket covering three similar large leather suitcases, the kind used many years ago before the smaller rolling kind came along for easier transport. He opened one suitcase and when he saw me staring at the neatly packed stacks of hundred dollar bills, he said, "I don't trust banks." I had seen enough movies on organized crime to recognize the "hidden dough." He carefully pulled one bill from a cluster tied with a rubber band. I was ready to ask where he got so much money when he beat me to it. "For many years I worked for a corporation that hired me specifically to make cash collections from different businesses in Las Vegas." That was the extent of his explanation but having lived in New Jersey for almost thirty years and having heard plenty about the Mafia in New Jersey, New York and Las Vegas I was better off not saying anything just like I had not expressed to him that I wasn't fond of Mexican food. I kept my thoughts to myself and went along with the flow, which when I look back at those days, I recognize my complete lack of common sense to even go out with a man like that.

The restaurant was a small shack but did have seats. I felt like a taco connoisseur, the ground meat seemed to be less greasy and the shredded lettuce was crispier. Or perhaps the tacos were no different from the ones the day before, but having skipped breakfast and lunch, I asked for a second one. Afterwards, he took me back to my apartment and gave me some pointers on working out with weights. Then he gave me a peck on the cheek and left. His personality fit the job he had in Las Vegas and I wondered how many people he had shot while remaining as detached as he was with me. I could not help myself from wondering what if he got rear-ended and the cops opened his trunk or even worse, if his car got stolen, all his "savings" would be gone in the blink of an eye. I also wondered how much money he had inside each suitcase and what the total could be…maybe a million dollars?

Autumn of 1998

I must have been out of my mind to assume I didn't need to study for gynecology and obstetrics. The vocabulary they used in the tests threw me for a loop. I had no idea what they were asking. What a jerk! When I left the State building, I knew I'd have to re-take the Oregon Boards, all because of my stubbornness.

Leonardo called. "I'd like us to get together. How about tomorrow?"

"I really can't, I'm sorry. But we can talk on the phone." I didn't feel the least bit of a romantic connection between us, but having a friend, even if he was a bit strange, gave me some emotional balance. Except for Ralph, I didn't know anyone in Oregon. But Ralph was kept busy with his mobile practice, his girlfriend, and teaching at the college.

Leonardo kept me entertained in a depressing way. He told me about one son who was in jail serving life, another who was into drugs, and he talked about his ex-wife whom I felt he still carried strong feelings for, otherwise why would he complain about her not talking to him? My life compared to his was very simple and boring as I spent my days just studying. Come to think about it, we did have something in common; we were both lonely.

Perhaps I had been too harsh on him. Maybe all the money in his trunk had nothing to do with his Vegas job and it was his life savings. It was his prerogative not to trust banks. It was agreed; we would meet Saturday in Salem, halfway between Eugene and Portland. He was going to teach me to fly-fish.

Walmart was going to be our meeting point. As always, I got there a little early, something to do with, what if I get a flat tire and then I would be embarrassingly late. That was the first time I saw some form of exuberance at seeing me and I responded by giving him a warm hug. I was also surprised when he reached for my hand while we walked down each aisle looking for a gift for a five-year-old boy and the boy's mother. He said, smiling, "Since I own a few shares of stock of Walmart it's a good idea to support my investment."

It was the first time I saw him smile. *Well, at least investing in stocks makes him happy,* I thought to myself.

He bought a little red fire truck and a silky white robe saying the reason for the gifts was that he was on his way to spend the night with John, his buddy, and the presents were for John's wife and their little boy. Oh yeah, what about John, his buddy? Wasn't he going to buy him something too? Most likely he was seeing someone else he met on the internet. I really didn't care. At that point in my life I was just spending a few hours with a friend and I needed some time off from studying.

As he promised, he had brought a fishing rod and took me behind the parking lot of Walmart so he could teach me the technique of casting a fly-fishing rod. I was glad I was going to be a chiropractor. I would make a pretty bad "fishing woman."

After I
threw
a few
tosses, he
gave up and asked if
I would like to have lunch
with him. He really had a
passion for Mexican food from
a food cart. We sat in his car eating
tacos and he told me that he also used
to be a very successful art dealer when
he lived in La Jolla. Kind of funny that
he was from the town where Ralph and
I felt only selfish people lived. Then he
said, "Do you think I look fat? Do I
look disgusting to you?" He wouldn't
allow me to answer the questions as he
went on, "My ex-wife used to say my looks disgusted her.
When we were married, she wouldn't allow me to touch
her. She used to say my body grossed her out."

"That's a nasty thing to say to anyone," I said. "In my
opinion, you're far from being fat and most women I'm sure
would agree you're very handsome."

"Not my ex-wife, she used to laugh at me. It got to a
point where I wouldn't undress in front of her."

"Well, Leonardo, you asked my opinion, but it seems
you've made up your mind that no matter what I say, you'd
rather believe your ex." I took a quick look at my wristwatch. "Oh no! How time flies! I better get going. By the
way, Leonardo, are you still married?" I asked as I got out
of his car.

"No, I'm not. I already told you that I'm divorced. Veronica, I'm very serious about our relationship."

Meeting at the Walmart parking lot so I could learn
to fish, eating tacos from a street vendor, and spending an

hour inside his car listening to him complain, was not my dream date. Still, I did ask him if he wanted to come over for Thanksgiving, but he said he couldn't because he already had promised his friend John and his family that he'd be with them.

On my way home, I couldn't help wondering, how gross did he look when naked? Was his wife being honest or cruel or both? And then I wondered what had happened to the walks on the beach he had wanted to do when we were writing to each other and the museums and art galleries we were going to see…

Leonardo's phone calls were not getting any better. "I'm at the end of my life," he said one evening. "Can I come over?"

"What do you mean by the end of your life?" I wondered if he was contemplating suicide.

"So much is happening, Veronica. I'm overwhelmed by what choices to make at this point in my life. I just need a friend to talk to. You always give me good advice."

"I only have three days left to get prepared for the Oregon boards. Can you wait until Saturday?

I took the boards on Friday, and Saturday morning I drove to Salem to meet with Leonardo.

He was waiting inside Walmart and he hugged me for the first time without letting go. "If you don't mind," he said, "let's go to Sherri's, get lunch, and talk."

No tacos. It sounded very serious.

He ordered a Mexican fiesta salad with broiled chicken and I ordered a veggie burger and fries.

"I like the sweater you're wearing," he said. "Nice black and white pattern. What kind of material is it?"

A compliment, his first compliment ever—wow! I said to him, "Thanks, it's just something I found at Goodwill for five bucks. I shop there for most of my clothes."

"You're the only one I trust as a friend." He sighed deeply and then began crying uncontrollably.

"What's wrong?" I gave him my paper napkin.

"I no longer have the desire to live." He wiped his tears on the napkin and blew his nose. The rain depressed him; people all around him depressed him, including his ex-wife who was still living in La Jolla, California.

I encouraged him to get professional help but suggested he first move to a state with a sunnier climate. He mentioned Las Vegas where he still had strong connections, and he agreed he needed to move out of Oregon.

"Will you wait for me until I get back?" he asked.

"Leonardo, I've been meaning to say this, but my ex-husband is back in town and he wants us to try and save our marriage. I must give my marriage a second chance." I couldn't believe how good of an actress I was. My script had come into my mind impromptu. "I know that you understand this after what you've been through with your ex-wife."

"I understand completely." His tears kept rolling down his cheeks. I was glad he cried. Crying was a good start to help with healing and in his case, at least from what I could deduce, he had been bottled up for too long. I passed him another napkin from under my glass of water.

I felt sorry for Leonardo but I was glad he was officially out of my life. The lie about my ex came in handy many times later in my life, when I found myself dating a dud.

The next day I went to the Washington Square Mall. The way I figured, if I applied for a job at all their stores, I would likely be hired by one of them.

One afternoon I was a witness to the miracle of chiropractic. It was a reminder of what I was missing in my life until I got my Oregon license. A massage therapist came to see Ralph at his apartment. She couldn't feel her feet and the acute lower back pain made it difficult to stand straight. She barely made it up the steps. I stood in the living room watching him adjust her lower back on his portable adjusting table. It worked better than I imagined. She stood from the adjusting table and upon realizing the pain was gone, she gave him a very emotional hug. That was exactly what happened to me, many years ago, when I couldn't walk because of a herniated disc. Being a chiropractor was the most fulfilling profession I could wish for and I couldn't wait to start practicing!

The manager at a health store in Washington Square called. I wasn't going to wait for other calls in the hopes of finding a better paying job. If anything, working in a health store was ideal for me considering good health was a vital part of my future profession.

My first day at work proved that being a health store employee was the best occupation I could ever have at that time. Herb, the manager who was in charge of my training, was studying to be a naturopath and he was planning on leaving once he received his license. He knew everything about herbs, tinctures, and vitamins. The best part of my learning was that as soon as I received my license, I would be able to pass my newfound knowledge to my own patients. I followed Herb eagerly around the aisles as he would point to different vitamins and what they did. That alone made the meager wages they paid me worth a million dollars a day.

Herb lived in Vancouver, Washington, and even though he had had most every bone in his body broken from falling off his motorcycle multiple times, that was still the only form of transportation he used. Considering we lived in the rainy Northwest and how badly motorcycles handled wet pavement, I diagnosed Herb as suicidal. I told him about a friend who lost the use of his right arm after a wipeout and about another who never recovered from a brain injury. Nothing worked. He was adamant about the joys of riding his Harley-Davidson.

The other co-worker was Mitch and he only had one thought in mind, scoring with me. He could not carry on a normal conversation without sexual innuendos. He was from Alaska and appeared to have had a long, rough life even though he couldn't have been more than twenty-five years old. He was about four and a half feet tall but that didn't make him feel less of a man. His handsome face on his little body made me think of him as a teenager suffering from puberty. Having dealt with Leonardo's depression for months, Mitch's happy-go-lucky attitude was like a breath of fresh air even if he had a dirty mouth. His tenacious belief that sooner or later I would give in to his charms and fall into his arms made me smile as I knew I could easily send him flying across the counter.

I sent a bottle of Saw Palmetto to a friend in New Jersey whose husband was diagnosed with an enlarged prostate. I also told her to add pumpkin seeds to his diet. Every day I learned something new. "A lot of people assume if medicinal plants are natural, they're harmless, but it's not true, and they should be used wisely," Herb said. "A good example is Echinacea, which we sell a lot of, as it helps boost the immune system. But if it's abused, it will stop doing the desired effect. Once someone has a cold, they should take Echinacea with Goldenseal, but it shouldn't be overused either or the body will lose its natural ability to keep the immune system functioning properly."

Garlic, which I loved and had always heard how good it was as a natural antibiotic, if used to excess, could increase the effects of blood thinners. Even Licorice Root, which had been proven to help with ulcers, if taken in large amounts, could raise the blood pressure to high levels. Those were just a few of the things I learned from Herb. I also learned a lot from customers as they told me what worked for them. One item was Flor-Essence tea. According to one of my customers, she had been given one month to live two years ago due to breast cancer and since she had been drinking the tea, the cancer had disappeared. Other customers told me similar stories about the tea. But it was a little hard for me to believe. If it were true, how come people were still dying from cancer?

I must have been doing a good job at explaining to my customers how certain supplements worked. An older couple came into the health store and besides buying the last five containers of Coenzyme Q10, they asked me to order a dozen more bottles. They were moving to Spain and would be there for four years. I had told them that Coenzyme Q10 was known for reversing the aging process at a cellular level. They checked it out on the internet as being true and wanted my opinion on what other supplements they should take with them to Spain.

After I got home from work, I had dinner, studied for the Boards, and then spent the rest of the evening on the internet looking for my soulmate.

I called Leila. "The world is so big," I told her. "There has to be at least one normal man somewhere."

"Have you not heard that men are like parking spots?" she asked.

"Yeah?" I waited for the punch line.

"All the good ones are taken." When she laughed, she sounded exactly like Muttley, my favorite cartoon dog.

"It's funny, I guess." I put out a forced giggle. She could tell.

"Honey, all the good ones are either married or dead." Her laughter was contagious but I wasn't laughing wholeheartedly.

It took about thirty minutes to get to work in the morning but when going home, it was more like fifty minutes because of the traffic. After a full day of standing while helping so many people looking for the miracle pill and teaching them how to improve their health, I needed the long drive to unwind. The first two times coming home I wound up in Washington state because I stayed to the left on Highway 5 instead of taking the right lane towards Troutdale.

I loved crossing the Marquam Bridge to the other side of the Willamette River. The night view of the city of Portland, while crossing the bridge, could only be described as euphoric. It was like a mini New York City covered with huge diamonds projecting sparks of life in all directions but mostly directed at me. Every night when I drove home, the sparks of life hit me through and through, giving me a feeling of vitality, an unexplainable sensuality, a breathing, living mechanism so intense that a full orchestra played in my head transmitting its sounds through my lungs and ringing through my vocal chords as if I were a radio. It was a miracle I didn't get into an accident every time I drove on that bridge because I had no control of the vibrations crossing throughout my whole body. The music was so clear that I was able to hum each musical instrument, note per note, exactly the way I heard it in my head. It was effervescent and glorious as my whole being became possessed by its mere existence. It was as if God had opened all my senses by putting the whole world in my hands through the visible sound of music. I never questioned it and didn't tell Ralph about it either. He would think I had gone out of my mind.

It wasn't easy looking for a relationship on the internet. After Leonardo, I wasn't so willing to settle for anyone; I had to be certain I even wanted to meet such a person.

Ralph came home one evening and said, "Mom, this has got to stop. You need to go out and meet people and make friends in person instead of spending your evenings like a zombie seated at my computer for hours. You need to get a life." Ralph didn't understand my predicament.

Number One: I didn't know where to go and socialize. Number Two: I didn't drink, and bars meant going even deafer amid their ridiculously loud music, where I would end up just nodding my head every time someone spoke to me, and usually it was a drunk. Number Three: I worked all day, even weekends, and once I got home I was done with driving around or going somewhere by myself.

Where I lived there was nothing except for McMenamins, a restaurant/pub type hotel down the street from us. And as for the weather, it was rain, rain, and more rain. Everything was gray where we lived. The apartment complexes were painted gray and so were the skies. I missed the California sunshine! Living in Troutdale was like being on the gray side of the moon. There were a few stores around like supermarkets, but then what? How much food could I buy? Even if I made the supermarket a place to walk around in as I strolled from one aisle to another, the refrigeration was enough to chill my warm enthusiasm on starting a conversation about frozen items or icy cold lettuce. Of course I could stick around the bakery section and ask about their warm bread and desserts, but there was only so much sugar I could consume.

At least on the internet I could browse through an array of possible suiters while comfortably seated in the warmth of a heated room. I looked for men about my age, and I read what they wrote to see if it matched my philosophy about life. I wrote to two or three of them but it never went further than their return email which was all about themselves and always seemed to lack a sense of humor. So then they got deleted. It was that simple.

I really enjoyed working at the health store but I met some very peculiar people, which in many ways made me aware of the diverse afflictions affecting the general public. I could only hope that my future patients at my chiropractic clinic would be average people looking to be adjusted versus those who were coming in asking for "miracle" supplements, like a diet pill to take at night before going to bed so they would lose weight while sleeping. Why didn't they just stop eating so much? I suggested they skip dinner.

One young man asked me if we had anything that could put him into a trance so he could go without food or water for a week or more. He didn't want to die, he just wanted to separate himself from this world so he could travel in spirit form for a while.

"No, we don't carry anything like what the Native American medicine men would use to put someone in a spell, if that's what you mean," I said. "But if you go see a psychiatrist, you'll probably be put on a drug that will knock you out and most likely transport you to the spirit world you want to be part of."

Then there was the creepy woman with two babies in a stroller. She said, "Do you have anything you can give me over the counter to keep my children sleeping during the day?"

I pointed to the two sleeping babies. "You mean something to make them sleep at night?"

"Oh, they're sleeping now but that's just temporary. They'll be up anytime now. I just can't take it anymore, if you know what I mean."

"Sorry, but we don't have anything to help babies with daytime sleep. It seems what you need is some time off. Maybe you can get your family or a friend to babysit once or twice a week so you can have some relaxing time for yourself."

It was very fulfilling to help so many people on a daily basis, especially when I believed I knew the answer to their problem. When the results came from the Oregon Boards, I was not surprised. I needed to buckle down and get serious studying for obstetrics and gynecology.

I kept myself busy during the day with my customers' issues and in the evening after studying for the boards, with my internet obsession to find Mr. Perfect.

~ Chapter Ten ~

Blinded by Romance

Besides his short and uncomplicated ad, his picture also caught my eye because it didn't conform to the usual head-shot everyone else used. Dick stood wearing a light tan cowboy hat and matching boots, blue jeans, and a bright red and white plaid flannel shirt. Obviously he was comfortable with his body, even though it showed he could lose a few pounds. Behind him was a bookcase. The picture meant he liked to read and had a flare for western culture. His eyes smiled along with his mouth as if saying, "This is me, and I'm okay!" He did not come across as being particularly handsome, but he was my age of fifty-four, according to the ad. I sent him a short email introducing myself.

Dick responded within ten minutes, also with a short email and his phone number and asked me to call that night. We talked for about an hour. He had a granddaughter. That had to account for some respectability.

"I love the sound of your voice and your accent," he said.

I got a little flustered but then recalled what Ralph had told me time and time again, "Mom, if someone gives you a compliment, just say thank you, and leave it at that. It's not complicated."

"Thank you," I said with difficulty. I had been in America long enough to let go of most of my cultural background shackles, but it was still ingrained in my brain that if someone gives you a compliment, you must do the same. So I had to add, "I like your voice too."

"We seem to have a lot in common," he said.

"Why don't we meet and see if we even like each other," I replied.

"I don't believe in love at first sight, but I wouldn't mind lust at first sight." I liked the way he laughed. He seemed to have a good sense of humor and lots of spunk. I told him where I worked.

After he was done at work at six the next day, he would be stopping by the health store just to say hello.

When I saw a man dressed in a white shirt, tie, and dark suit looking at vitamins, I took him for a customer and approached him with my usual, "May I help you find something?"

"I'm looking for a girlfriend." He laughed playfully. I stared at him.

"I'm Dick," he said, shaking my hand. "I couldn't wait to see you. You're beautiful."

"You showed up an hour early," I said, embarrassed that I didn't recognize him, but in my defense, he looked nothing like his picture on the internet. He was a lot older, with white hair and a receding hairline, and three ugly moles that no one could miss on the left side of his face.

A customer came up to me and asked for help. I excused myself and he said not to worry, as he would wait until we could talk. I purposely took my time taking care of one customer after another, hoping he would get tired of waiting and go away. He lacked any positive physical attributes and I doubted he was my age; he looked more like *sixty*-four. Besides, the moles on his face were repulsive. When I looked at him from across the counter and saw him looking at me and smiling, I knew who he reminded me of. It was the sex pervert who had pinched my little cousin's bottom and then made his way up the steps to the apartment where the prostitutes worked on the first floor of my grandmother's apartment house in Lisbon, Portugal. I was only a child then, and it had happened more than forty-five years ago, but it was still embedded deep in my memory bank.

My mind was racing trying to figure a way out when he approached the counter and said, "Will you be free to have dinner with me Saturday night?"

"Sorry, but I already have plans this weekend to visit family in Seattle."

"How about the weekend after?" he said.

"I'm sure I have plans for that weekend too. Sorry, but I have customers to attend to." I shook his hand and said, "Bye, bye." I turned to take care of another customer.

He left and I took a deep breath of relief. Maybe he had gotten the message. I thought I had given him enough hints not to bother me.

When I got home, I was too embarrassed to share with Ralph that I had met someone from the internet. I felt demoralized by my inadequacy to be more assertive. I skipped dinner and went to bed. After tossing and turning for what felt like hours, I got my courage up and sat at the computer to send a note to Dick canceling all future rendezvous. He had beaten me to it. There was an email message titled, "You've got mail." It was a love poem that he allegedly had written to me as soon as he got home. I answered, "I didn't know you were a poet. Thank you for the lovely poem." Once again my cultural background was to blame; I had to thank him for the poem. Instead of closing the door on him by either ignoring his email or saying what was on my mind, I had just opened my door to him.

Every night when I got home from work, I was guaranteed to find Dick's touching yet philosophical email leading me to opening myself to him. Later in the evening, he would call and his keen sense of humor made me laugh as I tried not to recall what he looked like. "Dear Veronica," he wrote one evening, "I fully understand your thoughts regarding the cutting of flowers. I feel the same way about trees, and actually any of God's gifts here on earth. The fact is that these things are indeed gifts that I believe are here expressly for our benefit and enjoyment. But even though we hate to see the loss of one flower, or one tree, the truth is that that particular flower or tree would eventually be lost anyway. Its real purpose on earth is to benefit and enrich our lives while they are here. All living things must eventually die, but thankfully, are born again to co-exist with other living things and again complete the circle. It is only when mankind abuses other living things, that we endanger their existence. But even then, I believe that God has created a way of compensating for that. It may even be the extinction of mankind, but whatever form evolution takes, the earth will go on. But it is also good that we do at least have the consideration for, and the foresight to be able to recognize the power we have over that evolution."

My goodness, he's so attentive! I thought. *I like the way he addressed all my remarks in the last email I sent him. He reads and listens to what I say, believes in God, and is very thoughtful. So what, he has three ugly moles on his face. What's important is who he is, what he is inside.*

"My particular concern is for endangered animal species," his email went on. "At work, I almost always wear a particular kind of tie with my suit. I don't know if you've seen these ties, but they have pictures of endangered animal species on them. A portion of the proceeds goes to saving these animals. I get lots of comments about my ties and I believe by doing that one small thing, I'm at least able to increase some people's awareness of the problem. My special love of cats is for the "big cats" of the jungle. I've seen them in their natural habitat and have learned to love and respect them for their special role in life. That's why I hate to see them in little cages in the zoo. However, having said that, they are also my favorite exhibits at the zoo. But the reason I enjoy seeing them there is that I believe it may in some way help some people to appreciate their existence and to maybe understand their purpose on earth. I think that perhaps if people weren't able to see them there, they might not take as much notice or have as much concern about saving their lives in the wild. So maybe we do need to "use" these living things to help us appreciate them. I believe the most important thing we can do is to educate ourselves about them so we are able to "use" them without "abusing" them. So I say let's bring in the cats and the flowers if that's what it takes to save them."

Wow, he not only agreed with what I had shared with him on my last email, but he really loves the animal kingdom. He has such a good heart. What more could I ask in a man?

"It's ironic that you should mention dreams." All his emails were lengthy. "I was a bit leery of telling you about mine until now, but maybe it will help you understand my beliefs. Those two nights when I could not sleep was because my mind was on you. In fact, I believe it was only your second letter that made me begin to realize just what a special person you really are. I knew right away that I wanted you to be a part of my life. I have always believed that there must be a woman like you somewhere in the world, but after fifty years, I had almost given up hope of ever meeting her. Now that I know you exist, and know who you are, I just want to be "any" part of your life that you'll accept me as. But I digress; let me get back to the dreams. Also on Thursday night, I dreamed of you. I just remember some of the dream, although it was a long and wonderful dream. The part I remember the most was that we were both having so much fun together. It was a physical and romantic type of fun. We held each other and played together and laughed together and I remember picking you up in my arms and spinning around with you until we fell to the ground in a loving embrace. I also had a dream about you on Friday night. I can't remember that dream as vividly, but the part that sticks in my mind is the "physical-playful" type of fun that we were having together. That is a new feeling for me. Something that I have always dreamed of but never experienced with anyone before. But you seem to have inspired that kind of happiness in me, a sort of childlike enjoyment of life. I guess you could even say a kind of spiritual happiness, or connection with an inner feeling of the love of life and the happiness that another "like soul" can bring."

He was so romantic! I was at a loss for words. But was he pulling my leg or was he for real? Did he cut and paste what he was writing to me to a bunch of other women on the internet? Why was I so hard on him? Was I so desperate that I was willing to forget that he reminded me of the "Portuguese dirty old man"?

"I too, am very spiritual and not so much religious," he went on. "But you must understand that I was raised in an organized Christian religion and was taught that there was only one way that we should believe. I fell away from religion when I was in my late teens because I found that I didn't truly believe the way I was taught I should. I have also tended to keep my spiritual feelings to myself because I had no one that I thought I could share them with, without persecution. In the last couple of years, I have felt a need for a deeper expression of my spirituality, but had no way of developing that, other than to try to get back into the organized religion I had once known. I rejoined the Lutheran Church thinking that might help. But it doesn't seem to be helping. In fact, I fear it is leading me into the wrong direction. It almost turns me away from God, rather than bringing me closer. I long for a spiritual direction and leadership that can bring me into the light I seek. I have spoken to other 'spiritual' people before but no one, so far, has been able to show me the right path."

This was very good. He was not a religious fanatic but he did believe in God and he was not afraid to show his personal fears while looking for answers. He seemed to be an honest to goodness person. It would be funny if he looked into Judaism and found that that was the right path.

There was no end to the email. "It looks like I will be having quite a feast for myself on Christmas day. I went shopping yesterday and bought all the things for a traditional Christmas dinner. I'm going to do a turkey with all the trimmings. It does seem like a bit of a waste to do all that for only myself, but as far as I'm concerned, it's also the mental stability that I'm accomplishing when I do things that I enjoy, even if I'm alone. I really don't mind doing it for myself. I did the same thing on Thanksgiving and spent all morning cooking and all afternoon eating and then sat around all night because I was too full to move."

He cooks! Another good quality; I have a feeling he's inviting me over for Christmas.

"I've heard some rave reviews about the movie *You've Got Mail.* I hope we can see it together," he continued. "Will your schedule allow you to see me soon? I was hoping that we might be able to be together at least one more time before you head up to Seattle for the weekend. How late will you be working tonight? I almost called you, at work, late last night to make sure you were all right and that you had a warm coat because I know it was so cold out last night. I thought about your poor little hands freezing. I was going to come over so you could hold your hands in my pockets while I walked you out to your car. I was wondering if we might at least be able to talk on the telephone tonight? I just love talking to you. Not only for your fascinating and happy conversation, but I just adore your sexy voice. Please let me know if we can talk tonight. Your friend in love and life, Dick."

He was definitely a man of many words. He would make a good friend. I would have to tell him that when he called. I didn't.

Our first official date would be to the McMenamins mansion not far from where I lived. He had never been there and I wanted to show him the wall artwork. I was alone at home when he came to pick me up. I sat at the window waiting and when I saw him getting out of his car I ran downstairs to meet him in our parking lot. When we got close, he handed me a rose but when he was going to kiss me I rapidly moved my face away from him. The idea of kissing him was too much for me. We talked and laughed while walking inside McMenamins and our energy was good together but my goal for the evening was to get the nerve to say, "I just want to be friends." For dinner, he took me to a Chinese restaurant. I had to admit he had a nice smile and the sound of his laughter was catchy, but I was a bit nervous. He reached across the table for one of my hands and said, "I like everything about you. The soft pink nail polish you're using is very sweet." Then with a serious look on his face he added, "I feel a certain chemistry between the two of us."

"I don't feel that way," I responded quickly, pulling my hand away from his.

"I'm very surprised to hear you say that. We've been in tune with each other since our first email to each other and now I can feel it physically too. Can't you feel it?"

"I'm having fun being with you but it doesn't mean I want anything more than being friends."

He became quiet and I felt bad for being so straightforward. I didn't like hurting people's feelings principally when they were so nice but I was proud of myself for finally being assertive and most of all, truthful.

When we got into his car, he was still quiet. Then he turned to me and said, "Can I ask you just one thing? Do you mind if I kiss you?"

"We just went out for the first time. I don't feel that kissing should be included on a first date."

There was sadness in his face. I felt horrible. *What was the big deal,* I thought to myself, *I'll just kiss him and get it over with.* I said, "Okay, just one kiss then."

It was a trap! I had kissed the frog that turned into the prince and I lost the battle once our lips met. I kissed him back. I was starved for affection and kissing was like finding an island after the ship had sunk. It was settled; he would pick me up from work the next evening for our second date.

You've Got Mail was indeed a very appropriate movie since that's how we had found each other, through the internet.

He brought me back to the Washington Square Mall to pick up my car, and we kissed passionately before we parted. Driving over "my bridge" that evening I was "higher" than ever. "My orchestra" was playing in stereo. I was in love!

Before leaving for work the next morning, I checked my email. I had no time to read it. I printed it and took it with me to read during my lunch break. He wrote:

My earliest recollections of "Her" date back to my adolescence. "She" inspired my love of life and offered me completeness of heart.

As I began to develop into manhood, "She" gave me an appreciation for the sheer beauty in woman. I began to settle for others, as means of worshipping "Her."

My continuance into my adult life taught me more about the intellectual stimulant "She" had to offer. I was able to find bits of her mind in some of the different women I met.

As I matured, I discovered the pleasures of her warmth and understanding, within other women's bodies, all the while, longing for the flesh, which surrounds "Her."

I have known and loved "Her" forever, and dreamed of being re-united with "Her" in this lifetime. "She" is a soul that has always been within me.

Finally meeting "You" has connected the circle and brought "Us" back together as "The One" we were meant to be.

Whether "You" are in my life or out of it,

"You" have always been and will always be,
Within my heart and on my mind,
Dick

My goodness gracious, what a beautiful sonnet! I was very moved by it. I told Ralph about Dick's poetry and how romantic he was. Ralph said, "So the guy is good at writing poetry; it doesn't mean anything."

I thought it had a lot to do with who he was. He knew how to express his feelings in a poetic voice; he was sensitive and had a good heart. But I was not completely naïve. I did wonder if the undying love Dick professed for me in his poem was real, since we had only met twice. I was aware of some men being liars and all they wanted was to put another notch on their belt as to how many women they went to bed with. But I was afraid to question it, as it would be the same as to admit defeat and if anything, sabotage his honest intentions. I found myself mesmerized by Dick's personality, and even the way he walked attracted me for some inexplicable reason as he reminded me of a wildcat on the prowl.

I accepted Dick's invitation for Christmas dinner. He'd sworn that no one cooked a better turkey than him. I doubted his turkey or anybody's turkey even came close to my turkey stuffed with chestnuts. My stuffing recipe had been in our family for generations; it was the best stuffing in the world. But the fact was that I was not going to Dick's apartment to find out if he was a good cook. I just wanted to be with him.

The night before I went to see him, Dick ended his email with, "Veronica, obsessive thoughts of your smile occupy my being and the thoughts keep repeating, wearing a most comfortable path, leading to an unknown destiny. But I think I know where the journey ends and I yearn for each day's end, when my monitor screen says, Veronica."

The snowstorm was severe enough to make the stores at the mall close early. I drove directly from work to his apartment in Tualatin, the snow draped over the road like a white blanket. It felt right to me that everything was so white and pure. I stood at his door for a few minutes, combed my fingers through my hair, and brushed away the snowflakes from my coat, before knocking twice. The door opened immediately, like magic. Dick was dressed in a suit and tie as if ready to go out, except he was wearing house slippers. His smile was big and his eyes sparkled with joy. "I was counting the minutes to hold you in my arms," he said as he picked me up by the waist and held me high up in the air for a few seconds and then let me slide slowly down as our bodies remained as one and we kissed, our lips searing the desire we felt for each other. He turned me around and helped me take off my coat. He had put a lot of effort into decorating his apartment. He had a freshly cut Christmas tree and coffee table snacks and there were soft candles strategically set up over the gas-burning fireplace. It was a small, one-bedroom apartment but the kitchen was big enough to fit a small round table and two chairs. The dinner went well and of course the turkey was delicious, but food was the furthest thing from my mind. My stomach felt tight and all I could think about was, what next? He ate with enthusiasm and he expected me to do the same. He added another slice of turkey to my plate. "Please eat some more, you'll need your strength for the night ahead of us." The statement scared me. What was he referring to? Maybe my mother was right when she used to say a honeymoon was very debilitating. I had never found that to be true, but just because I had been married twice and experienced a few flings it didn't mean I knew everything about sex.

After dinner, we sat on the floor's furry carpet by the fireplace and talked for a while and then he said, "Let's move to the couch. I want to hold you up again like the angel I see in you, high above me." He extended a hand to help me up from the floor and then asked me to stand on the couch. He lifted me up as if I were made of feathers just like he had done when I entered his apartment. He looked at me as if I was beyond special and then still holding me up in his arms, he carried me to his bedroom and to his bed.

Merry Christmas

The next morning I woke up to breakfast in bed. On a tray was toast for two, and coffee. Between the butter and jam was a gift box wrapped with red paper and a yellow bow. "Your Christmas present," he said. "I hope you like it."

I opened it carefully, trying not to destroy the wrapping paper. It was a bracelet with little diamonds all around and a gold-shaped heart pendant also with matching diamonds. "These are beautiful; I don't know what to say." Then I added apologetically, "I didn't bring you a Christmas gift. I feel terrible."

"You are my present," he said.

I didn't go home. There was too much snow on the ground and I did not have snow tires.

Winter of 1999

Dick and I began spending weekends at his apartment. During the week, we wrote to each other and at night before I went to sleep, we talked on the phone. When we were together, sex became our priority. I had become addicted to sex with Dick.

Life was good.

Dick had been married three times and had a daughter from the second marriage. She was happily married and had a four-year-old girl. They lived in Ohio. He seemed to have a perfect family. I felt it was about time I settled down with someone more mature than me.

Herb came into the store one morning waving his Naturopathic license. He would be leaving us the end of the month to start his practice. I tried not to even think if I had done well or not when I took the State Boards. I would have an answer in a few months and it didn't do me any good to worry about it.

A week later I was taken by surprise when Herb asked me to follow him into the back room. "I just want you to know that last weekend I worked with the new manager that will be taking over this store when I leave. I believe he was hired because of his credentials as a part-time security guard in this mall, but I don't trust him. I'm warning you, so you be careful."

I felt the reason Herb had said that was because he didn't have a nice word to say about cops of any kind. I thanked him for all he had taught me and we exchanged email addresses.

I felt like the luckiest woman in the world for having worked with Herb. I had learned so much! When I felt the start of a bladder infection, I knew enough to drink Uva Ursi tea and cranberry juice. I no longer needed to see a medical doctor for antibiotics.

Herb was right. Rob, the new manager at the health store, was up to no good. I found it weird how he kept sending me out to take breaks and when I came back, he had a bunch of receipts he wanted me to sign as if I had been present when the customers returned their merchandise. I shared my concerns with Mitch who told me Rob did the same thing to him when I wasn't there, but he wasn't worried because he felt Rob was an okay guy.

Rob was tall and sturdy and he could have easily done the job he requested that Mitch and I do. I figured he was using his title as manager to take advantage of us. We were to climb on a ladder and store some large boxes on the upper shelves of the back room. The boxes were filled with books and were quite heavy. Mitch and I had to struggle to pick them up but there was no way we could climb the ladder together. I suggested for him to stand one step above me and I would be below, and slowly we could carry each box to the top, and then we could slip each box onto the next shelf. All was going fine until I lost my balance. Trying not to fall, I let go of the box and so did he as I grabbed the closest thing to me, his head, which forced his face to dip into my chest. His arms went automatically around my waist and he kept me from falling by keeping his body against mine. I didn't realize how someone so short could be so strong and I hated to say this, but he was well-endowed. He had just saved me from breaking my neck.

"Thanks for holding me up," I said gratefully.

To which he responded while still holding me, "My pleasure."

"Okay, now you can let go of me," I said, moving his head away from my chest. I stepped down carefully while keeping a straight, dignified face and smoothed down my blouse. I went right up front and told Rob I couldn't help Mitch anymore because my back was giving in. The rest of the day Mitch kept staring at me and very uncharacteristically, he did not tell any jokes.

During one of my imposed "breaks" at work, I found a shopping bag on the side of one of the mall benches with two new sweaters in it. I brought the shopping bag to Rob's attention to take to lost and found. At the end of the day, he took the bag home after saying, "My wife will love these sweaters. I'll tell her I bought them for her." Herb had been right; I was working with a dishonest person.

I told Ralph about the incident and he advised me to quit my job immediately. In his opinion, Rob was most likely stealing money from the register and when he got caught, my signature on the receipts would make me his accomplice. I went to work and shared this with Mitch. He said he couldn't afford to stop working and was willing to take a chance.

When I got home, I called the main office and left a message saying, "I can't come to work anymore. Please find someone else to take my place. Sorry about that."

The next morning I received a call from their cooperate office; they were wondering why I had quit so suddenly. According to Joan, their spokesperson, I was a good, reliable employee and they were wondering what was going on. I told her, "I cannot mention names but there is someone working at the health store stealing money and I don't want to be part of it."

"Who is it? I promise you complete confidentiality," she asked.

"Sorry, but I've already said enough. If you really want to know, you need to do some investigating."

Dick asked me to move in with him again. After a few days of considering his reasoning, I agreed.

"Mom, you're rushing into another relationship again." Ralph was clearly annoyed by my decision.

"Maybe you're right, but if it doesn't work, I'll move out, that's all."

"You can do whatever you like. I'm just saying you just met the guy and you should give it some time before making such a major decision."

I answered like a typical woman in love. "We have a lot in common and like he said, we're very happy when we're together, so why live apart from each other?"

Getting to know each other had to be more than jumping into bed on weekends and having sweet talks afterwards. It didn't put into perspective what it would be like if we were living together. I needed to know if he really was the person I would like to spend the rest of my life with, and what better way to find out than sharing the same space?

I left most of my belongings, including the TV and stereo equipment, in Ralph's apartment. I only took my clothes and a few personal items with me. Dick and I would be sharing the rent and utility bills. He offered to pay for the groceries. It was almost like being married, but without the agony of having to suffer if I wasn't happy. I could leave any time I wanted.

A week later, I found a job at a health store in Beaverton, a bit of a drive from where we lived, but it was better than nothing. Every place I went in Oregon was twenty-five minutes away. Martha, the store owner, was thrilled with my working experience at the mall, and hired me on the spot.

The day I moved in with Dick, he opened the hallway closet and pointed to his computer stored on the top shelf. "I want you to see how much you mean to me," he said. "The day I met you, I stopped writing to other women on the internet. I put the computer away so you can see how serious I am about our relationship. I only want you in my life. Veronica, will you marry me?"

"God forbid!" I couldn't help panicking. "After what I went through with Patrick, my second husband," (I had already told him about him), "are you out of your mind? I will never get married again, never, ever."

"I'm not Patrick. I love you and I will always make you happy because I love you."

"I love you too, but marriage is too final. I can't do it," I said, shaking. Then I said more firmly, "Dick, if you really love me, don't ask me again."

He said he understood how I felt and promised not to bring the subject up anymore

For Valentine's Day he only wanted one gift, a glamour photo of myself. I don't like those phony photos making a person look better than what they really are. I only did it because he asked for it. He gave me a ring and a matching gold necklace with blue stones and took me to the mall and bought me a very sexy outfit of tight pants and a low cut blouse at a boutique. Afterwards he insisted on buying me a long black gown. There was a reason for the long black dress. He wanted to film us having sex and the black dress was what I would be wearing before I took it off.

After the shopping spree, the next five days were dedicated to taking videos of me wearing the black gown and lying on our bed surrounded by the half dozen colorful pillows of all sizes that he had bought just for the occasion. It was a bit strange since I never got to take the dress off and all he wanted me to do was to pose for the camera and look sexy. He would take a video of me for about a half hour and then say, "We'll do it again tomorrow."

Perhaps by doing it over and over again, it meant that maybe someday the video would become a classic example of cinematography.

Spring of 1999

The new health store where I worked had a luncheonette attached to it. We served lunch items like soup, salad, and sandwiches. It was a strange place to work. I closed my eyes to everything going on, like the dying cats in the kitchen where Martha, the store owner, nursed them after picking them up from the streets. I had a feeling that sick and dying animals shouldn't be in the kitchen where food was being handled. But I was there to make a paycheck and ask no questions.

One morning a man came into the store, dressed as a woman, and I knew it was a man because of the face shadow and huge feet and hands. I found him in the vitamin aisle looking attentively at the shelves. "Can I be of any assistance?"

"Oh yes, thank you so much." His delicate, soft voice reminded me of that of a child. "Do you have any good vitamins for pregnancy?"

"Is it for you or someone else?" I was being as gentle as possible, just in case he was an ugly woman.

She smiled and lowered her eyelids as if embarrassed. "It's for me. I know it's not showing yet." She cuddled both hands over her abdomen and then said, "I'm pregnant."

I congratulated her and recommended some prenatal vitamins. When Martha, the store owner, saw me ringing the purchases on the register, she waited until the customer left and then hit the roof, yelling from the top of her lungs, "Can't you see that you just sold prenatal vitamins to a man?"

"She said she was pregnant," I said.

"Are you freaking out of your mind? That was a man, how can a man be pregnant?"

"She…he was dressed like a woman," I said sheepishly.

"He has a partner and they both dress as women. I don't want this kind of trash in my store. If either one comes back you are not to acknowledge them. Do you understand?"

"Oh, okay," I said. But I had no intention of not helping the "girls" should they return. What was Martha going to do, fire me? If she did, I would just have to apply for a job at another health store. Besides, my situation wasn't going to remain that way for much longer. I was just waiting to hear from the chiropractic board and then go on with my life. I couldn't wait to be on my own. I hated working for other people. If Martha were a little less prejudiced, I would have tried to explain to her that some people are different but they are not any less human. One of my best teachers at Life University West had been Dr. Mannish who was a woman who had turned into a man after going through several invasive surgeries. Only God knew the physical and emotional distress that Mr. Mannish had suffered all his life. Yet he had no problem talking to us in class about his physical differences and who he used to be. I admired him for his honesty, knowledge, and most of all, his kindness and caring for all the students. He was a great human being.

While living with Dick, our relationship had taken on a new chapter called, "Getting to know him." There were no skeletons in my closet, but Dick had plenty in his. He and his second wife used to be swingers; they had sex with other couples. The first thought to cross my mind was, *Oh my God, I hope he's not carrying some venereal disease!* "Did you and your wife use protection?" I asked diligently.

"You better believe it. Our club had two rules. Everyone was tested and everyone wore the proper gear." He was also a Vietnam veteran and had been subjected to Agent Orange

(HO) chemicals, the reason he had developed a chronic skin rash around his ankles after walking in the sprayed fields. After returning from Vietnam, he did a lot of drugs to cope with what he had seen. It must have been quite horrible, because when Dick and I went with Ralph and his girlfriend to a Vietnamese restaurant in downtown Portland, we had to leave before ordering any food. He was freaking out, saying all he could see were dead Vietnamese around him.

After Vietnam, Dick had managed a porno shop with a prostitution ring on the second floor. He missed those days or at least he liked to reminisce about the "old days" when the girls gave him privileged treatment. But this was all in the past, before we knew each other.

On weekends, Dick liked to go shopping. He had a constant need to buy things. I found shopping to be boring and also a waste of money since his apartment was fully furnished and we already had everything we needed. He suggested we get rid of his old furniture and buy new furniture and I told him, with the money I was making at the health store, it was out of the question for me. Sharing the household bills was more than I could handle. I had worked very hard saving for a sunny day, and I needed the money I had saved to open my office with Ralph. I was against charging and buying things for the sake of self-gratification. Dick reminded me of Al, the way he enjoyed buying whatever was on sale and then just using his credit card to pay for it.

Besides, what if we bought a new toaster together as he wanted to, and then we broke up? Who got to keep the toaster? That trend of thought was what kept me from buying paraphernalia with him. Besides, the toaster he had with four pop-ups worked fine. I rarely made toast.

May 26th Ralph called. "Mom, we haven't had any time together lately. How about if I take you out to dinner, just you and me?"

He drove us to a side of Portland I was not familiar with. I could tell the restaurant had been handpicked. I noticed the white table cloths, the waiters dressed in starched white garb, and the heavy, wood-paneled, dark mahogany walls with clusters of wine bottles. I opened the menu and said, "Great menu choices, but there are no prices showing."

"This is a very special day for you, and it's my treat," he said.

I took it for granted that since we had not seen each other for months, it was his way of saying he loved me. I also wondered what I had done to deserve a son and a friend like Ralph in my life.

My dinner was a delicacy of beet salad with goat cheese, followed by poached salmon stuffed with crabmeat, grilled vegetables, and homemade mashed potatoes. I was about to dig into my yummy chocolate mousse when he handed me an envelope. "Maybe you want to open this first."

It was a letter from the Oregon Board of Chiropractors! I held the sealed envelope to my chest. Ralph was smiling. I used the butter knife to open the envelope slowly and re-moved the one-page letter. I flipped it open and stared at it.

"Oh my God!" I was shocked. "I passed the State Boards! I'm licensed in the State of Oregon!" The only rea-son I acted like an adult and didn't scream out to everyone, "I passed the Boards! I passed the Boards!" was because I didn't want to embarrass my son. "Ralph, you went through a lot of trouble to make reservations at this restaurant. What if I had failed the test?"

"You're my mother, I knew you had passed. I'm very proud of you!"

We had wine and toasted to our future, and it was good that he was driving as the excitement of the evening and the wine had made me very light-headed.

On weekends, Dick enjoyed going with me as I looked in-side malls and strip malls to try to find a place to open my practice with Ralph. But after a couple of weeks, Dick complained that I was too picky. I didn't see the rush and Ralph, who was also looking on his own, felt the same way as I did.

The ten thousand dollars I had to start a practice was basically a zero budget to start any kind of business as business expenses were so high. But I felt confident that when it was the right time, everything would materialize the way it should and always did.

I got a phone call from Joan, the representative spokesperson for the former health store I worked at. "I want to thank you for alerting us about what was going on at our store in the mall. It took a few months to carry out the investigation, but we finally got enough evidence to put Rob behind bars. When Rob was confronted with stealing, he didn't even try to defend himself or apologize. Mitch, the young man working with him, was found guilty for going along with Rob, and was fired for being an accomplice."

"Oh dear, that is very wrong. The reason Mitch stayed on was that he needed the job, but he had nothing to do with stealing."

"We understand that, but our corporation can't take a chance on him, since he knew about the stealing but didn't do anything about it. I also called you to give you the good news that the last month you worked at our store, you were voted as the best employee in the whole mall, for great customer relations, by an anonymous shopper."

"Oh wow, that's great, but I was just doing my job."

"According to the shopper, you were very courteous and your help came across as genuinely caring. You won a five dollar check, a beautiful pen with your name engraved on it, and the mall's once a year best employee certificate award. We would like you to come back and work as manager of our store."

I thanked her for the offer, but told her that I was presently employed at another health store and it was just a question of time before I had to leave to start working full time with my son, a fellow chiropractor.

Living with Dick proved the old adage that a lot of couples, once they're comfortable with each other, drop their act and no longer try to hide their bad habits. This was confirmed when I walked into the living room and Dick was lighting a marijuana pipe. I thought pot smokers were mostly young folks experimenting with drugs, not old men like Dick. I backed away and said, "I didn't know you smoked."

"Do you mind?" he said after a deep inhale.

"You're already smoking, so why are you asking me?"

"If it bothers you I'll smoke it during the week when you're not home."

"You're an adult and this is your apartment. It's not up to me to say if you're allowed to smoke or not, as if you were a child. It's your choice." I went to the bedroom closet, picked up his camcorder and decided to tape all the action. When he saw me, he tried to hide the pipe behind his back, stood up, and was very upset. "Turn that off!" he yelled.

"Oh, okay. I'll do that. Let me see where the stop button is." While "looking" for the "stop button," I kept the recorder going. I was just having fun with the prospect of filming him for posterity.

Seeing him smoke pot decreased my respect for him but I also felt sorry for him. He had an addictive personality. Not that I was better than him, as my addiction was chocolate and I used any excuse I found to eat it even if the consequence was debilitating bone pain. Addiction was not a criminal act, but a personal weakness towards personal pleasure, even at the cost of losing loved ones or destroying one's own life.

Dick wanted me to go with him to visit his mother in Arizona. I was all for it and took it as an opportunity to stop working at the health store and take a well-deserved two-week vacation with him. Once I started practicing as a chiropractor, who knew when my next vacation would be? Dick felt it would be better if we used my car for such a long drive since his car already had too many miles on it.

On Saturday, we got on the road at five in the morning. I wanted to begin our trip at eight, because I knew from experience that lack of sleep was conducive to falling asleep while driving, but he wanted to have an early start and offered to drive. We had barely driven for an hour and hadn't even reached the Gorge when I pushed my seat back and closed my eyes. I fell asleep but in my dream, Dick was driving off the road because he had fallen asleep at the wheel. I opened my eyes to find him driving erratically. "Hey, what are you doing, falling asleep?" I asked, terrified.

"Sorry, I should have told you, but I have a hard time driving on the highways. I get sleepy no matter what time of the day."

Great! I thought. My dream had been an omen so I took over the driving.

Arlene, his mother, welcomed us with open arms. I liked her a lot. She was kind and motherly and in many ways, she reminded me of Patrick's mom. Same white curly hair and a little on the hefty side, but at seventy-one years old, she was as physically active as most people who were much younger than she was.

She lived alone on a huge ranch in the middle of nowhere. The land was dry and the heat outside was too much for me to endure. I really didn't know how she did it, living in the middle of the hot desert. We spent three days with her, almost always inside, where the air conditioner was my best friend. Arlene enjoyed feeding us and even made Dick's favorite handmade noodles that he bragged as being the best in the world.

Dick took his camcorder to show her some videos of the Oregon coast. He connected the recorder to his mother's large television for better viewing and we sat in her living room to watch them. Everything was going fine until it came to the part where I had taped Dick sitting at home smoking pot and he was caught on film trying to hide the pipe. "F***!" came out of his mouth as he sprinted off the couch to turn off the tape.

"Dick," shouted his mother, "you're still smoking that shit?"

"Are you crazy, Mom?" he answered. Then he said, "I was smoking pipe tobacco."

She didn't answer him. She was no fool.

Before we left, Arlene came up to the car window where Dick sat in the passenger seat and said to him, "How about I come to visit you at the end of the year? Maybe I could be with you for New Year's?" Dick didn't answer but I did. "We look forward to seeing you again, right Dick?"

On the way home he protested, "Why did you say she was welcome to come over? That's all I need is for her to come and visit us. She's nothing but a pain in the neck." His dislike for his mother made me wonder why he had told me he wanted a two-bedroom apartment so when his mother came to visit us she had a place to stay and why even bother to visit her if he couldn't stand her? As a mother myself, I took his attitude as a personal offense and felt very sorry for Arlene. I tended to cling to women that were older; they instilled in me a feeling of being with my mother.

It was a long and tedious drive back to Oregon. He slept. I drove. I couldn't wait to see Ralph and get our practice started.

Ralph was able to get a chiropractic mailing list from the Oregon Chiropractic Board. We created a letter inquiring if anyone was interested in selling their practice and we mailed a stack of fifty-five letters. We received a few responses but it was one disappointment after another. The average cost to buy an ongoing practice was $150,000 to $200,000. That meant taking on a major loan. The other choice was to rent a space in a mall at an exorbitant price and build our own rooms. But that was also beyond our means. We had run out of options. We needed a miracle!

Our prayers were answered with a call from a chiropractor with two practices, one in Oregon City and the other in West Linn. Dr. McMahon had just started thinking about selling his West Linn practice when our letter arrived. He was stuck in a four-year rental agreement with the owner of the building. He thought he could run two chiropractic offices, but the doctors he hired to work in West Linn didn't put much effort into their practice and were far from reliable.

We made plans to meet him the next morning. We got there a little earlier than our appointment. The practice in question shared half of the building with a beauty shop next door, but with separate entrances. The gray painted building looked a lot like a ranch house and it faced Hwy 43. "Excellent visibility from the road," I said to Ralph.

"Good size parking lot," Ralph observed.

"Yes," I said, "and the speed limit of 35 mph makes it easier to read the sign by the road."

Dr. McMahon wore a bright smile and spoke with passion for his profession. We looked up to him and bathed in his positive energy as soon as we shook hands. He handed me a key and said kindly, "You go ahead and open the front door." As soon as I walked in, I could feel the walls saying, "Welcome, Dr. Veronica! How are you? Will you stay?" I looked at Ralph and I could read his thoughts; I believed they matched mine.

There were four large adjusting rooms, an old but working X-ray machine in the backroom, and a darkroom for developing film. There were also three old adjusting tables Dr. McMahon was willing to leave for us, including a Toggle adjusting table, which to me was like a present from heaven.

Toggle had always been my preferred way to adjust patients, even more than the Activator Method. I liked the way the headpiece on the Toggle table dropped gently but very effectively when applying the proper trust to the patients' upper cervicals. There was no twisting or cracking of the neck, so it was ideal for patients like me who didn't particularly care for high velocity manipulation but still needed the benefit of spinal adjustments.

Dr. McMahon wanted $10,000—the exact amount I had saved. But we still had to pay the monthly rent for the space in the building, plus utilities, and the usual bills that we expected to come along with running a business. Ralph and I explained our financial situation to Dr. McMahon. He was willing to accept monthly payments and threw us a bonus; we didn't have to start making payments until two months after we moved in. He was doing everything possible to make it happen and he even had the contract handy.

We accepted his offer right then and there. It was our amazing luck that our paths crossed when they did. He became our beloved mentor and was willing to share the patients' intake forms and insurance forms that he used in his Oregon City office so we could get familiarized with the process.

Thanks to Dr. McMahon, our life together as a mother and son team had just become a reality, and we were ready to get started even though we had no patients coming with the practice.

The first two rooms were assigned to me as my adjusting rooms so I could hear the phone ring at the front office or hear or see if someone walked in. Ralph got the other two rooms. Our office hours were to be Monday through Saturday from eight in the morning to seven in the evening.

We made an assessment of our office and what needed to be done to make it more bright and appealing. All the rooms were in dire need of a coat of paint. There were lots of outdated, dark wood cabinets and drawers in the hallway, and the whole place needed an overall "adjustment." The treating rooms were ridiculously large and could be easily divided into two. We would also like to have two bathrooms, one by the waiting room for the patients and another large enough for handicapped patients and ourselves. However, all these changes were now just a dream, something we would have to do in the future. At present, we had to remain focused on working with what we had until we could afford to do any type of remodeling. Like Ralph said, "First things first, we need to order calling cards and patients' forms. We also need to change the name of our clinic, which is currently associated with non-reliable doctors coming and going."

Ralph brought in his computer from home and he set it up at the front desk. He also found a used printer and connected it to the computer. When it came to technology, Ralph was a genius.

I couldn't wait to start working together. It may sound silly to say this, but we had grown up together, and as such I knew him well. He was honest, kind, dependable and always truthful. I couldn't be any happier.

~ Chapter Eleven ~

Mother and Son Team

Summer 1999

We officially opened for business on June 18th. Dr. McMahon left two tall metal filing cabinets for us with a ton of information on office procedures, and he also left business contacts' names so we could order chiropractic supplies.

Ralph and I spent the day going over the examination and intake forms that Dr. McMahon had given us. We went over some of the order books and made a list of the items we needed to order like X-Ray film and toner for the processor, heating pads and a hot water heater for the pads, a small refrigerator, and ice packs. We also looked into the pictures and specs on the latest adjusting tables like the Activator table for me and the Diversified table for Ralph.

Before leaving the office that evening, I wrote a long overdue letter to Lauren, Patrick's daughter. "Dear Lauren, Your dad has asked me to tell you he loves you and that you need to forgive him, because he never meant to do you any harm. Until you forgive him wholeheartedly and go on with your life, he is stuck and can't be at peace. You may wonder how I know to write this, since it's been a long time from the time when he left us. It's easy to explain; he inspired me to use the right words to you and as such, he is writing this letter to you, not me. I hope this letter carries with it the strength and love he had for you. Please keep this letter and anytime you have doubts or feel sad, read it, and hold it close to your heart, and all the hurt will go away. Love you, your step-mom Veronica.

The next day we were thrilled when a middle-aged woman walked into our waiting room in the morning and asked to see the doctor. But when she found out that Dr. Ross no longer worked there and there were two "new" doctors, she started to leave. "Please don't go," I said, getting up from behind the front desk and extending my arms over the counter, not sure if I should jump over it or go around it in order to stop her. "My son and I have bought the practice and we intend to stay. You can count on us being here any time you need care. Will you give us a chance to prove to you that we are reliable and good doctors, too?" I was glad when Ralph offered to see her. I was too nervous about getting started.

Mrs. Robinson left with a smile on her face and made an appointment to see Ralph the following week. Later that same day, a young man came in and became irate when he found out that "his" chiropractor was no longer available. "I'm tired of having to deal with a different doctor every time I come here. What's the matter with this office?"

I was more prepared this time as I walked around to the waiting room and put my hand out to shake his. I smiled courageously and said, "Hi, I'm Dr. Veronica. My son Dr. Ralph and I just bought this practice and we're here to stay. I promise that every time you return for an adjustment we will be here. So, welcome!" He decided to try us out. I gave him to Ralph but I promised myself that I would be the treating doctor for the next patient, even though I was completely stressed out over the idea, which made no sense. Had I not proved to myself that I was a skilled chiropractor by treating patients for a whole year at the chiropractic clinic before I graduated? Yes, but I had constant supervision. This was different, even though Ralph and I had agreed to discuss difficult cases with each other before treating such patients, sooner or later I would have to start making clinical decisions on my own with non-complicating cases, and I couldn't help being scared.

A week later I told Ralph that we were very lucky that we only had two patients. "I don't know what I'd do with insurance billing, co-pays, deductibles, and all kinds of paperwork if we were to get any busier," I said. In back of my mind I was still trying to put off treating any patients on my own, by acting very busy.

"I'm not worried," he said. "I feel very confident that between the two of us, we can handle it." Ralph could not be a better partner; he was my support beam, without him, the internal structure of my confidence would collapse.

Lauren called. "Thank you, Veronica, for taking the time to write to me with my father's words. I do believe my dad inspired you to do that. After reading your letter, I forgave him. I also wanted to share with you that a week ago I was riding on a swing and I fell from it, but when I was falling I had a feeling he held me in the air because I fell softly on the ground. He did love me." I was moved by her insight. She had come to terms with her anger towards her father; it meant she was going to be fine after all. I gave thanks to God for everything

Encouraged by Dr. McMahon, our friend and mentor, Ralph and I began participating at the health fairs and country fairs in West Linn, Oregon City, Canby, and Gladstone. They were usually on a Saturday and/or Sunday, and we found it very beneficial to let the community know what we did and where we practiced. A professional white plastic banner with our office name in blue was hung on the side of our 10 x 10 brand-new, white cloth tent. For those interested, we provided free spinal exams and we had a full sized plastic spine to better explain how the joints moved, even though the kids walking by were only interested in touching the "dinosaur bones." But it did bring the parents and families over and a few signed up to be treated at our office.

Before I moved in with Dick, he had told me how much he enjoyed building a large fish tank in the house where he and his first wife lived. I asked him if he would build one for the office. From the back room where he put several 2 x 4 wood planks to hold the tank into the wall, it wasn't very appealing, but from the front, facing the waiting room, it looked great. The fish tank provided a calming effect to those sitting in the waiting room and I loved the idea that I finally had a fish tank of my own to enjoy every day. Ralph and I would be taking turns cleaning the tank once a month.

Because of the bad rap associated with the old name of our clinic, we had no choice but to change it. After long hours of tossing around ideas for a name, we came up with Gentle Care Chiropractic, LLC. That meant making a new sign for outside, new calling cards, a new letterhead on the stationery, and new patients' forms. We joined the West Linn Chamber of Commerce and planned for an open house. Dick made fun of our new clinic name by going around the apartment saying, "Gentle Dental, Gentle Dental."

Once I treated my first patient, Mrs. O'Hara, a forty-year-old lady with a bad shoulder, I couldn't wait for the next one. Two weeks later, Ralph and I agreed that even though we were not making enough to get a paycheck, chiropractic was the greatest profession in the world. If one of us was to get sick, God forbid, or we needed to take time off, we could cover for each other. Ralph took a loan to cover the same amount of money I had invested in the office, so we were now equal financial partners. It didn't matter who had the most patients when it came to finances as everything was to be divided equally. Ralph was going to stay with the Diversified Manual Technique, which he was still teaching part time at Western States Chiropractic College and I would use the non-manual techniques I had learned at Life West Chiropractic College. Patients would have choices. Some would request manual adjustments and others wouldn't; also some patients would prefer a female doctor and others wouldn't. We were prepared for all scenarios.

Ralph and I had a triple identity in our office. We were the chiropractors, the front desk receptionist, and the insurance billing personnel. I found the insurance agents to be very nice to work with once I told them I was a newbie.

I came home one evening to find dinner ready and a small bouquet of red roses in the center of the table. "You are so sweet." I kissed Dick.

"How are things at the office, seeing more patients?" he asked while chewing on the meat from a spare rib.

"It's good. We are growing slowly but steadily as people get to know us better in the community."

"Veronica, let's not wait anymore, let's get married."

I spit the broccoli to the side of my plate, wiped my mouth with the napkin and said in my harshest tone, "You have been married three times and I have been married twice. That means between the two of us it's a total of five disasters. I already told you, I'm not getting married. We have no kids. There's no reason whatsoever to get married."

"But we're so happy together. Why not make it sanctified in the eyes of God?"

He sounded just like Patrick and that irked me to no end. There was nothing more caustic to my sanity than past experiences connected to my second marriage. I leaned angrily across the table and said without the slightest hesitation, "Marriage makes my skin crawl! To hell with your sanctification!" I put an emphasis on the word *sanctification*, not quite sure if such a word even existed, but it sounded good to me as a concoction of sainthood and satanical beliefs. I removed my plate from the table and scraped the contents into the trash. He continued to eat and didn't say anything more.

Ralph and I took out a loan for $3,000 and ordered an Activator table that worked specifically for the Activator Adjusting Technique. With one foot, I pressed the control pedal on the table and it brought the patient, standing on a small platform, from an upright position to a prone position, exposing the spine for the proper adjustment and showing any discrepancy or inequality in the pelvis or leg length. Once I was done adjusting their spine and extremities, if needed, I stepped on the other pedal and the table slowly brought the patient back into the upright position. The table became a lifesaver with acute patients unable to lie down or stand on their own.

Mr. Farlow, a hefty 250-pound new patient looked at me with a smirk. "And how in the world are you going to adjust me? You're too small!"

I showed him the Activator Instrument, a small hand held device, and explained, "It projects a very quick but light thrust to the subluxated joint and by moving the joint into proper alignment, it decompresses the nerve causing the pain." I followed the explanation with a demonstration on the plastic spine I had in the room for such an occasion.

He was impressed even more when after adjusting his lower back, his pain seemed to dissipate. "This is a miracle!" he said enthusiastically when he stood.

"It's far from a miracle," I said with pride. "It's the science and art of chiropractic at work, nothing more and nothing less."

Over time, little by little, the idyllic passionate nights Dick and I had shared had sizzled down to a level of frustrating conformity.

He liked to watch television in bed. I hated television as much as I hated lying in bed watching him munch on snacks. "I can't sleep unless I watch television first," he said. He kept the sound way up and I had to use an earplug on my good ear if I wanted to go to sleep, since he liked to watch the late shows. These were a few of the things I was learning about him which I would have never known if I had not moved in with him. When we were seeing each other only on weekends, sex was what kept us entertained and also tired enough to go to sleep. He particularly enjoyed watching those television talk shows where everybody is screwing around with each other and once in front of the camera, they try their best to kill each other with fist fights. He found the shows very entertaining but I found them disgraceful and demoralizing.

Dick was still insisting we needed new furniture for our apartment. I had no intention of buying furniture. So what if it was dark mahogany and old, it had character. But I did agree that his coffee table was kind of dumpy and on Sunday we went looking for one.

I found the coffee table of my dreams at a Norwegian furniture store in Beaverton. I insisted on paying for it. The center of the table was inlaid with light brown stone tiles, which made it easy to clean. Dick was used to snacking while watching television in the living room and used the coffee table like a tray where he put his dripping soda, beer cans, and hot dishes. He even put his tools and other heavy items on top of it. But I didn't have to worry about him scratching our new coffee table because it was made of teak wood, which I understood was what ship-makers used for making long-lasting boats.

Once my parents died, I no longer had a reason to write in Portuguese. I had one family member still living in Portugal, my brother, Max-Leão, but he hated writing. With easy access to the internet at my fingertips, I began eagerly looking for Portuguese pen pals. I considered how many amorous Portuguese men were inclined to rapidly fall in love, so I was very clear in my ad, "Looking for a pen pal who enjoys writing since I need to practice Portuguese. If you're looking for romance, I am not interested. Please do not reply unless you are looking for a real pen pal."

Ralph and I took out a much-needed loan to buy a radio wave surgery machine to remove moles, skin tags, and warts, and we also obtained the proper tools to perform the Kinsey method for safely removing hemorrhoids. We put an ad in the yellow pages under proctology. There were only twelve chiropractors in Oregon licensed to do minor surgery and proctology. We felt privileged to be among them.

I offered Dick the opportunity to remove the three moles on his face since we now owned the proper equipment to do it. He was overjoyed with his new flawless skin and so was I.

During my lunch break at work, I checked my emails and there was one from a ninety-nine-year-old man who lived in Lisbon, Portugal. I was impressed that someone so old even knew how to turn on the computer. I sent him an email, "Please respond. I'm looking forward to establishing a correspondence."

A father and his daughter came to our office after being involved in a car accident. The daughter, Miss Wong, wanted to be seen together with her father because he didn't speak English. We put them in the larger room with the two adjusting tables. I told Miss Wong to ask her father to move his head in specific directions as Ralph and I were checking his neck range of motion. She translated to him and he answered her in his native language.

She said, "So sorry, my father cannot move head. Too much pain."

"Who was driving the car?" Ralph asked her.

"My father, driver. Me, passenger."

"Can you ask your father what happened to his head when he got rear-ended?"

Once again she translated the question to him. To our complete shock, he let go of both hands which had been firmly holding his head and whipped his head way back and then just as fast forward adding a twist of his head sideways as if he had just gotten hit.

"Mom," said Ralph. "I need to talk to you in the next room." Then to them, "Excuse us, we'll be right back."

"This has to be the worst-case scenario of a malingerer," Ralph said. I agreed with him. Mr. Wong couldn't have been in too much pain if he was able to move his head to such extremes. We were both sad and devastated by the idea that our first two patients involved in a car collision were faking their symptoms. We decided to continue with the exam and then treat them accordingly.

Ralph took his time explaining to Miss Wong how we were going to adjust their spine and what they were going to experience. He was very informative about the procedure and when he asked her if she understood everything and did she have any questions, she said, "I understand. No questions."

Ralph prompted her to lie down on her back and then proceeded to adjust her neck. However, when he did, her hand swung up and she slapped him hard across his face. Ralph was shocked and she acted very embarrassed by repeating, "So sorry, so sorry, so sorry."

She had been too shy to tell us her English was not good, and the neck adjustment had taken her by surprise. She had acted on impulse. I adjusted Mr. Wong using the Activator Technique and had no retaliation from him. They were to return the next day for further treatment.

The Wong case provided Ralph and me with a very important lesson on how to better understand our patients' needs, principally when their culture dictated their actions. We had been wrong about the Wong family. Mr. Wong was not exaggerating his pain. Neither he nor his daughter were looking for any compensation from the insurance company. He had moved his head in all directions because he wanted to show us what had happened even at the cost of excruciating pain. He felt it was important enough.

Miss Wong recovered completely after two weeks of treatment and Mr. Wong remained under care for three months. Each time he came in, he wore a smelly Chinese herbal patch on the back of his neck to help with pain control. That incident taught us another good lesson. No one was guilty of making believe they got hurt until proven guilty.

I got an email back from the "old" man. "Sorry," he wrote, "but I'm not ninety-nine years old. I'm twelve years old. I was trying to see how many women would answer my ad if I said I'm ninety-nine. António."

I wrote back, "António, it's okay if you're only twelve years old. Can we just keep writing to each other? Like I said, I just want to practice our language."

He didn't write back.

On Saturday, Ralph and I made plans to drive to Seattle, Washington, to visit some of our family. Al's brother Joe and his wife Virginia were flying in from Long Island, and staying with their daughter Laura who lived in Seattle. Ralph and I thought it would be nice to see them again after so many years had gone by. Dick complained, "I'm not going. It's too long of a drive and my lower back can't take it." It was the first time I heard he had a bad back. He wanted to stay home. That bothered me because I went with him all the way to Arizona and didn't whine about the distance I had to drive. "If you're falling apart at your age, what are you going to do when you get older?" I said.

"You'll take care of me, right?" he said bringing his lower lip down like a child.

"Are you kidding? If you don't do this for me why would I take care of you when you get old and sick?" I was joking of course, but he took it seriously and came along.

Laura treated us to an all-day fun trip to one of the islands across the river and we were entertained with a Native American Indian celebration of barbecued salmon with all the trimmings. We had a blast.

We sent birthday cards to all our patients but we weren't sure if that was a good idea since some people didn't celebrate birthdays. It turned out that it was very important that we sent the birthday cards, no matter what. One of my patients came in and hugged me afterwards saying, "Thank you for the birthday card. My mother forgot my birthday, and it was nice to know someone was thinking about me."

Dick made arrangements for a romantic weekend in Lincoln City at a hotel by the beach. Halfway to the shore, we stopped to admire a beautiful sight by a bridge and Dick walked away from me along the river path. I looked at the rocks where he was walking and a déjà vu feeling came over me. If he looked back and came to get me by the hand to walk along with him, it would mean we would always be together. But he didn't, and I took it as a sign that sooner or later we would be taking different paths, very much like what happened between Michael and me, when we lived in New Jersey and Michael had done exactly the same.

When we got to Lincoln City, I wanted to go dancing but he said he couldn't because of his sore ankles. I mentioned going to see a play, but he said he didn't like theatre, he found it boring. We had a steak dinner at his favorite restaurant but upon mentioning a small walk along the beach afterwards, he said his hips wouldn't be able to take the walk on the sand. We retired to our hotel room where he laid in bed watching television and eating chips.

"Since you can't dance, would you like to watch me dance?" I said.

"You know I would."

I went to the bathroom, took a shower, put my hair up with pins and wearing just a bath towel, I began dancing around the bed in what I thought to be a quite provocative way. It did the trick as he got himself all worked up and asked me to remove the towel and lie down next to him. He got on top of me and whispered in my ear how much he loved me when we heard the strangest sounds coming from the next room. It sounded like someone was getting killed, but at the same time there was too much moaning for us to be suspicious of anything else but two people having some kind of rough sex. "Let's go check it out," Dick said as he got up and rushed to put an ear to the door between the rooms. I followed him. There was definitely a male and a female in the other room who were yelling unintelligible words, and furniture was being trashed or knocked onto the floor. When the commotion stopped and it became very quiet, we assumed their love-making had been a juggling act between two very fat people and we could not help laughing our heads off.

The next morning we were coming out of our room when we noticed the room next to us had the door wide open. We saw three very busy cleaning women. There was cake everywhere. It had to be a gigantic cake because even the walls had cake, as did the bed, and also the chaotic furniture that was spread out in different directions. The women were commenting in Spanish about Americans versus "normal" Mexican couples.

I found a Portuguese pen pal but I didn't like his arrogant attitude towards Americans. I was born in Portugal, but politics and innuendos about Americans being stupid, ignorant, or rude, hit me hard. This guy had a lot to learn about his own manners, since he knew I was an American citizen. He signed his email as Ziggy, and then had the audacity of writing, "Tell me Veronica, how come Americans use such stupid nicknames? Just imagine this, a husband introduces his wife, 'This is my wife Pussy, and I'm her Dick.'"

I wrote back, "Isn't Ziggy, short for moron in Portuguese?"

He didn't answer back.

Autumn of 1999

Dick told me his company where he worked as a graphic designer had opened another branch in Sherwood and he wanted to look for an apartment nearby. I believed the reason he wanted to move there was to get away from Joyce, his third ex-wife. Dick was in the bathroom when she knocked at our door.

She was my height, possibly in her late forties, light brown shoulder-length hair, no makeup, and a little on the heavy side. She wore a long black raincoat. "Are you Dick's new girlfriend?" She looked me up and down and without taking her eyes off me, she walked into the apartment and closed the door behind her.

I was afraid to admit anything, whoever she was. I wasn't going to take any chances in case she might be carrying a knife in her coat pocket. Just then Dick walked into the living room, and when he saw her he ran towards her yelling, "What the hell are you doing here, you bitch! You leave right now! You have no business coming into my apartment!" He tried to open the door to send her out but she put her back to the door and blocked it with her body. He grabbed her by the front of her coat and pulled her out of the way, opened the door, and began pushing her out.

She pulled away from him and looking me straight in the face in a way that I took no offense, she blasted out, "I just want to warn you, he cheated on me when we were married, and most likely he's going to do the same to you. You better leave while you can; he's nothing but a bloodsucking bastard." That's when it got very ugly, as Dick grabbed her by the back of her coat and kicked her until he got her out of the apartment. She screamed all kinds of profanities at him and remained outside banging at the door while describing how inhumane he had treated her. She yelled that the main reason Dick wanted a divorce was that she couldn't work anymore after she had been diagnosed with lymphatic cancer. I sat on the couch, shaking.

Dick sat next to me, put his arm around my shoulders, and said, "Veronica, I swear to you that the reason I asked for a divorce wasn't because she had cancer and couldn't work anymore like what she's accusing me of. You have to believe me. I love you, and I'm telling you only the truth. Our marriage fell apart because we had nothing in common and then she gained a lot of weight and I was no longer attracted to her. She came over on purpose to try and destroy our lives together; she's jealous." He held me in his arms, kissing me, and said, "Tell me that you love me. Tell me you'll never leave me and you believe in me."

I didn't like what I heard from both of them. In the pit of my stomach it felt like the truth was on his wife's side, but part of me also said that perhaps she was lying and was just jealous like Dick said. The truth most likely lay in the middle of what they were accusing each other of.

We had a fair amount of patients who suffered from headaches and Ralph was especially good at doing upper neck adjustments which provided immediate relief. Being an adjusting adjunct teacher at Western States College had made him very proficient at the Diversified Technique which was a manual technique. I was able to watch how well it worked when a woman came in with her husband and asked to see the chiropractor because a neck adjustment was the only thing that relieved her headache. I remember looking up from behind the office window and noticed she was lying on the floor of the waiting room, flat on her back, and holding her hands over her eyes to block the light. According to her husband, she had had a brain tumor removed a few years prior, and since then she suffered on and off from debilitating headaches. After the neck adjustment, she walked out smiling and pain free. Afterwards, every time she came to the office, we knew it was headache time, and we got her in immediately.

Some patients loved manual adjustment and others didn't. That's what was so good about working with Ralph. Patients had a choice. We had our own techniques—he did manual and I did the less forceful techniques for those who requested "no popping" as patients referred to the sound of cavitation. My main adjusting techniques were Activator, Sacral Occipital Technique (SOT), Cranial Sacral Technique (CST), Drop Table, and Toggle. As much as we saw amazing results from manual adjustments, we also saw the same results from something as light as CST. My patient Mrs. Hayley swore that that was what kept her from living in the hospital. Her medical doctor called me asking that I please continue taking care of his patient, as each day she got adjusted was one day less that she wasn't at the emergency room suffering from an acute headache.

In the last few months, Dick had been falling apart at the seams. He complained of hip pain, back pain, and indigestion. I tried not to say anything about his burping and farting. Eating, watching television, and shopping on Sundays were the only things registering with him. I took X-rays of his back and nothing out of the ordinary showed. He was getting adjusted and felt better but then complained about other ailments. He had become a hypochondriac. During the week, when I got home from work, I'd find him lying on the couch eating and watching television, and there he remained for the rest of the evening.

I did my best to convince him to take a walk with me after dinner, but he said he didn't like to walk. I bought him some vitamins and tried to get him inspired about working out with me. He was getting further out of shape and lacked the desire for self-improvement.

Al and I still talked on the phone once in a while but I was only being polite as he still got on my nerves with his remarks about minority groups and politics. He didn't even listen, so it was always a one-way conversation. Every time I hung up, I thanked God we were no longer married. Then I thought about Dick and realized my present relationship was not much better. I no longer enjoyed going home.

Ralph and I were making enough money to pay our bills to run the office but that was as far as it went; we still hadn't seen a paycheck. Ralph continued to teach at the chiropractic college and had a few patients that he still treated at their work and at home, so that gave him some personal money. But every month something went awry, such as when the old X-ray processor that came with the practice expired on us, and we had to get a hefty loan for a new one.

Dick was delighted to have found an apartment in Sherwood with two large bedrooms, living room, dining room, kitchen, spacious veranda, and tall windows everywhere. He couldn't wait to show it to me. I had to agree, it was a lot nicer than the place we currently lived. The rooms were very spacious and the large kitchen had brand-new appliances and two skylights.

Our rent climbed to $450 each, plus utilities, but we were living in a palace.

I found two "real" pen pals. Paula was a successful business-woman who lived in the north of Portugal and was looking for a Portuguese pen pal from America because she liked to connect with other women from around the world. And Fernando was a widower who was going through a hard time dealing with his loss and coincidentally also lived in the north of Portugal. I found it peculiar that he said his name was Fernando but he signed the bottom of the email, "Artur."

Ralph and I were very conscious of what we spent. When we went out for lunch, we shared the $5.95 meal at the Thai restaurant a few blocks down the street from our office. Their single portions were large enough to feed three hungry people, which seemed to be the norm at every restaurant we went to. No wonder Americans were getting obese! For some of my patients, I knew they would be a lot healthier if they could lose some weight. When Rosanna, a twenty-five-year-old patient about my height of five foot six inches, but weighing over 250 pounds complained of knee problems, I knew exactly why her knees were wearing out; they could not handle the burden they had to carry. "I love to eat," she told me. "Food is very nurturing when I'm feeling down." She reminded me of my mom who had suffered all her life trying to lose weight. What worked for my mother had been when the cardiologist gave her three months to live. A year later, she returned to the US proud to show me how much weight she had lost. She outlived her three-month death sentence by twenty-six more years.

Sitting at the front desk in the office, I got to welcome the patients as they came in, and Ralph did the same for me when I was treating a patient. Fred, the mailman, and I had developed a chit-chat type of friendship. He was going through a marital crisis. All the other mailmen dropped the mail at the front counter and quickly took off. Fred put his mailbag on the floor and talked to me as if I were his counselor. He had one love in his life, swing dancing, and he was trying to convince me that I should check out the Crystal Ballroom, where he went dancing on Saturday nights. He got my attention when he asked me to step out from behind the front desk to show me a few dance steps. Good thing no one came in, including Ralph.

Dancing with Fred

When I got home, I told Dick about the mailman teaching me some dance steps. "It was so much fun," I said. "How about if we go to the Crystal Ballroom next Saturday and take a swing dance class together?" I sat on his lap, and hugged him trying to get him motivated. "What do you say?"

"I can't dance with my bad hips," he said. He sure could move his hips when we had sex, even though he was not as enthusiastic as he used to be. I had a gut feeling that's what happened with most men. Once the novelty was gone, it became more of a task. "But I don't mind taking a walk around the neighborhood, for half an hour after dinner," he said. I would have rather gone dancing, but walking was better than nothing.

Being in a relationship sure took the enjoyment out of life. If only I could be on my own, then I could do whatever I wanted.

It was pathetic that dancing with the mailman became a lot more exciting than going home. And then, there was Mr. Carson, Ralph's patient, a tall, handsome, blond man who came in earlier than his appointment because he said he liked chatting with me. He made me laugh and a few times he said I was blushing. I looked forward to seeing him. If I truly loved Dick, I wouldn't even take a second look at another man. Well, maybe I would still look, but I wouldn't have sinful thoughts like I experienced every time Mr. Carson leaned over the counter to chat with me.

I was delighted when Dick expressed the desire to learn to play the violin. Maybe once he got good at it, I would play my guitar and we could play some duets. I immediately called Steve to send me a full-size violin since he had a music center in New Jersey and could get instruments at wholesale prices. Dick's birthday was a week before Christmas. Steve didn't charge me for the violin or the case.

In the morning, I always arrived at the office an hour earlier to write to my pen pals. Paula was happily married and had a teenaged son. We wrote about twice a week regarding our daily lives and what each day had brought. Artur and I wrote every day. He wrote super long emails that when printed, could be as much as six pages, and were regarding politics, religion, family values, and lots and lots of philosophy.

Artur's website was essentially dedicated to his deceased wife. A year had gone by but he was still grieving. He wrote, "Having a friend like you to write to is what I needed most in my life. You are most kind to allow me to express my sorrow; you always have the magic words that inspire me to go on. I look forward to your precious emails with your amazing inspirational stories."

Artur stimulated my creative juices. I was enjoying both our philosophical exchanges and sharing some of my personal stories, which he said were very inspiring. The idea that I could help him through my writing made me feel like an accomplished writer. I believed he was a good person, not because he was a Catholic and was always mentioning how much he believed in Jesus, but because the experiences and ideas he shared in his emails showed that he had strong values concerning what was right and what was wrong. I felt like I could trust him. He always added something sweet to his email about his deceased wife, and how much he missed her. He also wrote about how much he appreciated his family and especially his children, and said if it weren't for them, he would have given up living a long time ago. He was definitely a very sweet, sensitive, family man.

I read my responses several times before sending them, to make sure I conveyed to him a positive attitude towards all aspects of life, principally when his email showed a lot of despair about losing his beloved wife. At times like that, I knew the value of having a friend to talk to and I was glad to help.

Dick was focused on winning the $250 Christmas decoration prize for the most creative veranda display in our apartment complex. Sundays were spent buying lots of outrageously colorful outside lights, ornaments, reindeer, and trees.

I found a music school close to where we lived and got Dick a one-month gift certificate for private violin lessons.

He was extremely happy with his birthday present. My goal of getting him off the couch was going to work one way or another.

His mother came to spend Christmas and the New Year celebration with us. While she was visiting us, sex came to a complete halt between Dick and me. He said the first night, "Having my mother in the next room puts a damper on my manhood."

Poor lady, if she only knew her only son couldn't wait for her to leave. The only thing that bothered me about her living with us was her constant burping.

I refused to get "prepared" like everybody else, for the "deadly" arrival of the Year 2000. Dick stocked the kitchen closets with canned food and the freezer had enough meat to feed an army. If it was the end of the world, the food wasn't going to do squat for us. His mom was very quiet and sat all day reading and crocheting. She would shrug her shoulders and give a faint smile when asked if she were worried. I could be wrong, but I believed the reason she came to spend the end of the year with us and didn't leave until January 5th was because like so many, she probably thought it was going to be the end of the world and she wanted to be near her son.

My patient Mr. Stewart owned a restaurant in West Linn and like so many other patients, was worried to death. "What am I going to do? If things go really bad, I won't be able to find meat to serve my customers." I wanted to say, *Come to my house, I have plenty in the freezer.* The whole thing was getting out of hand. If it were going to be the end of the world, I doubted anyone was going to make reservations to eat out. After Mr. Stewart poured his heart out, he would fall asleep on the adjusting table. I let him sleep unless I had another patient right afterwards.

Mr. Stewart had survived a car accident but his restaurant was killing him.

Artur's emails could take one or two pages before he was done making a point on any kind of subject. I thought I was a bit more direct in expressing my thoughts because I had lived most of my life in America where the art of conversation was less important. But I knew I still had the same problem even if to a lesser extent. I had been criticized more than once by some friends and family members that I took too long to get to the end of my story. I didn't do it on purpose. Old habits were hard to break. I bet Artur grew up like me, in the old-fashioned environment of enjoying a conversation, and until the person was done talking, you had nothing to say.

Winter of 2000

When I got home one evening, Dick couldn't wait to show me what he had learned at his violin lesson. I sat next to him listening to him practicing, and had to control myself from grinding my teeth while hearing the bow scratching the strings so harshly. I smiled through the whole five minutes of pure torture and clapped with delight when it was over.

A check came in the mail for two hundred and fifty dollars. Dick had won first place in the Christmas lighting contest. "Now we have enough lights and decorations to fill a whole front yard when someday you and I buy a house," he said.
   God forbid, I told myself.

Artur seemed to love my stories, particularly the last one I sent him where I described a spiritual experience I had as a young girl. He wrote, "You keep saying you don't know how to write poetry, but you write like a poet."

"I write poetically but that doesn't make me a poet," I wrote back, almost apologetically. "The Portuguese language is a Romance language; it is naturally poetic and sweet, yet spicy. One cannot talk or write Portuguese without bringing out such an essence, and that's all I do."

He wrote back, "Look, I say you are a poet and that's all there is to it. As a matter of a fact, very soon I'll have a surprise for you."

I had become used to watching my patients getting better with each treatment; one might even say I expected it from everybody, but Betty, a twenty-four-year-old patient, was showing no signs of improvement. It puzzled me as she had been rear-ended at only 15 mph while waiting at a red light, yet she still presented in acute pain after two months of care. I had call forwarding available from the office to my cell number and many a Sunday when she called me, I would drive to the office to treat her, because she just could not wait until Monday. She got immediate pain relief after the adjustment and was able to move her head easier afterwards, but the adjustments did not seem to hold. Her cervical neck X-rays showed she had suffered whiplash upon impact, but nothing else out of the ordinary. I began considering that I should refer her to Ralph.

January 8th was a date to remember. Ralph and I got our very first paycheck for the week since we opened the office in June of last year. We each got one hundred dollars after paying all our monthly bills at the office! We were both stoked. I told everyone I knew, even Michael, whom I was still in contact with over the internet.

"A hundred dollars?" he wrote. "Did you actually say one hundred dollars? That's a miserable, pathetic paycheck! How can you be so proud of that? You're a doctor for goodness sake! Don't you have any pride, bragging about something like that?" I didn't answer his email. He had no idea what it took to run an office like ours, between our student loans, the loan for the business, the loan for the X-ray processor, the loan for the Activator table, the rent, utilities, office supplies, the building insurance, doctors insurance, and taxes. Let's not forget the taxes. Whatever money came in, it was gone in a blink of an eye. It was a miracle we were making the one hundred dollars a week!

Betty came in and said that whatever I had done to her at the last visit, she had had no pain since. "I had no discomfort for a whole week. This is really amazing," she said, "My dream is to be able to run professionally in marathons. Do you think I can do it?" I didn't feel running was beneficial for her back, but if that was what she wanted to do, I was going to help her to get into shape for it. I loved when wishes came true. I gave her some back and neck exercises to do and encouraged her to start with speed-walking up and down the hills of West Linn.

When I got home one evening, I noticed Dick had set up his computer in our second room. When I asked about it he said, "Oh yeah, I should have told you; I need it for doing specialized work for my job."

But when was he working at the computer? In the middle of the night! We went to bed together but when I got up to go to the bathroom—at the magic hour of three in the morning—there he was, at the computer. When I first moved in with him, I remembered him saying, "Before you came into my life, I used to love writing poetry to women and getting them all excited about meeting me." Hmm, was he back to dating on the internet? Of course I had no proof, so I had to believe he was working in the middle of the night on some graphic job.

That evening we were having dinner when he stopped chewing and said, "You look so much younger! It's not fair!"

It did not sound like a compliment. "It's my jeans," I said.

"I'm thinking about quitting my full-time job and getting a part-time job at Staples or at Home Depot. Would you mind?"

"Why on earth would you want to quit your job which pays a lot more than mine? I don't understand."

"You said you would take care of me and it's just a question of time before you start making a lot of money as a doctor."

There it was again, the rich doctor thing. "You are far from old or disabled. You consider my paycheck of a hundred bucks a fortune?"

"I'm talking about when you start making lots of money in a few more months, not right now!" He sighed and then added, "Ralph really has it made. You put so much work into the practice, but if something happens to you, he gets it all!"

My response was to stand and clear the table. My father used to say, "If you want to know what someone is about, let them talk. What they say will tell you what they're up to." Napoleon had said something close to that, too.

His ludicrous jealousy concerning Ralph's inheritance hurt my feelings. Did he feel entitled to some of it? No wonder he was upset when I didn't accept his marriage proposal—he couldn't count on any capital gains.

His undying love for me was more like blasphemy. I was being used. Still, it wasn't easy for me to say, I want out. I needed what some people might call a valid excuse. That night I prayed to God for some guidance.

January 19th, I got home an hour earlier than usual. Dick had left the house and had forgotten to turn off his computer. I took a look at the screen and was not surprised at the contents. There was an exchange of emails between him and a man promising to send naked photos of his wife having sex with other men. No wonder he had no interest in having sex with me, he was getting it off the internet. I knew it!

He was still using the same email address he used with me. I was going to give him some of his own medicine. I left the room making sure everything was the way he had left it on the computer. Concerned that he might arrive home soon, I quickly went into the kitchen to prepare dinner. When he came in, I hugged and kissed him just the way I always did and said, "I came home earlier just to make your favorite food, spaghetti with meatballs!" I smiled like a professional actress.

"I … I had a violin lesson this evening and left in a hurry. Have you been home long?" He stood rigidly at the doorway and I could tell by his body language that he was not comfortable with the situation.

"Just ten minutes ago, but I've been working hard in the kitchen getting dinner ready." I got busy chopping an onion into the ground meat in a mixing bowl.

"I'll go wash up and be right back," he said.

I watched him out of the corner of my eye as he went to his office first and turned off the computer before he headed to the bathroom.

After dinner, I told him I had a bit of a cold coming on and I needed to go to bed earlier. I lay in bed and didn't fall asleep until I had a script in my mind of what I would be doing the next day. I was a stubborn Taurus but I was also a playful, mischievous Monkey in the Chinese zodiac.

I got to work two hours earlier than usual. I fed the fish so I wouldn't forget them later, and then I sat at the computer, ready to create a new email address and a new identity to go with it. I gave myself the name of "Coral." Her mission was to become Dick's dream girl. I wrote, *Dear Dick, I heard from a friend that you have been writing to on the internet that you are the man I'm looking for. I'm 27 years old and single. I'm also very hot for you right now. If you want me, let me know, I can give you what you want! Coral*

I wrote and re-wrote the email throughout the day and finally saved it so that I could send it exactly at seven, just before I left the office. Also, until the dust settled, I had to put my pen pals on standby.

When I got home, I kept my "happy face" on and went about as if nothing out of the ordinary had happened all day. I even watched television with Dick. Now it was his time to be "sick" because he said he had a slight cold coming on and he felt it was better if he slept on the couch so I wouldn't catch it. "You're so good to me," I said. I stood, turned towards him as I left the room and said, "Good night my love." I went to take a shower and then lay in bed wondering if he was going to answer my email. An hour had gone by. I got up and tiptoed to the hallway corner to see if he was at the computer. Yes he was! I didn't sleep much that night.

When I got to work the next morning, I didn't even turn the lights on inside the rooms. I went directly to my computer. There it was—Dick had fallen for Coral! Like a duck, he had dived headfirst into the water and was waddling all over the place! Yes, he wanted "me." Considering it was his first response, he showed no inhibitions saying what was on his mind. He may have considered *himself* great at writing sexual fantasies, but he hadn't seen anything yet. I wrote back in such a detailed, pornographic manner that when I read it, I came to the conclusion that I had had nothing to do with what was written. The only answer was that while I was typing, I had been taken over by the spirit of some sex pervert. Once again I sent it out exactly at seven, promising to write the next day at noon during my lunch break at the school where I was a gym teacher.

When I got home, I played my part and so did he. He was still having the "sniffles" and felt it was better if he slept on the couch. I bet! After the email I had sent him, I knew he would be up all night!

The next morning three pages of sexual poetry from Dick were waiting for me. He had never written to anyone like me/Coral, he wrote, and couldn't wait to hold me in his arms. He gave me his phone number, asking me to call. He couldn't wait to hear my voice.

I asked my porno ghostwriter to guide my fingers during my lunch break and wrote to Dick in such a way that I could bet my life he was going to go out of his mind. I finished the email with, "Like you I cannot wait any longer. Let's make our fantasies come true. I want to hear your deep moans next to me. Can you get away this Saturday afternoon? I know a hotel downtown that would be perfect for us. I'll send you some more details tomorrow. I'm hungry for your touch, Coral."

I followed up with an email to both my pen pals saying my boyfriend was very sick and as soon as I took care of the problem, I would write again.

I had not even closed the door to our apartment when Dick said, "Oh, honey, I hope you don't mind, but there's a possibility that this Saturday I may be busy helping a friend with his computer and won't be home till late. But I'll let you know tomorrow once I hear from him."

"Really?" I said. "Well, I don't have to work this Saturday. How about if I go with you?"

"Oh, no you can't, honey. He wants to talk to me about some personal things. You know, man to man stuff? When we finish, I'll come home and then we'll go to the movies; how about that?" He gave me a kiss on the forehead.

"Oh, okay then." My mind was not rational enough for me to say anything else except, "It was a long day at work, and I had a late lunch with Ralph. I'm really tired. I think I should go to bed early tonight." I went into the bedroom and didn't look at him, afraid he might see in my face that I was Coral.

"Yeah you go ahead, honey. I'm gonna stay up and watch some TV. I'll be in later. I'll see you in the morning."

Before I left to go to work in the morning, I wondered why he had not left for work. "I don't feel too good today," he said. "I'm taking the day off." Poor man, he sure was sick!

He was sicker than I thought. His email came along with two very explicit, obscene pictures of himself. He wanted to confirm that we would be meeting Saturday because he couldn't wait any longer and was willing to pay any amount of money I wanted. He wrote, "If I can't afford it, I'm willing to sell everything I own just to spend an hour with you."

Not my coffee table, you're not!

I told Ralph what had been going on but I was too embarrassed to show him the pictures Dick had sent Coral as an attachment.

Ralph called Joseph, a friend of his who owned an open pickup, and they were going to help me move out of Dick's apartment the next morning.

At the end of the day, before leaving our office to stay the night with Ralph, I sent what was to be my last email to Dick.

Subject: "You've got mail." I thought the title was very appropriate considering it had been the first movie we had seen together. An exalted feeling of triumph took over; I didn't have to see his face to know exactly how much it was going to hurt him.

Message: I will not be coming home tonight. I will be at your apartment tomorrow at eight in the morning to pick up my personal belongings.

Veronica aka Coral.

Ralph, Joseph, and I were at Dick's apartment exactly at eight in the morning. I opened the door with my key and as we entered, Dick got up from the couch and turned off the television.

"Veronica, you have to give me another chance," he said as he tried to hug me. I stepped back from him and put my hands out indicating he was to stay away from me. "You know that I love you," he supplicated as he followed me to the bedroom. I went into the bedroom closet and began handing my clothes to Ralph and Joseph who put everything into large plastic garbage bags and began carrying them out to the truck. "Please give me another chance." He put his hands together as one would do while praying in church. I left the long black dress that he had bought for me in the closet. I threw the rest of my personal stuff into the empty boxes we had brought along for packing, but I put the jewelry he had given me on top of the kitchen counter. He went on, "I already disconnected the computer. As you can see it's over there, by the front door and I'm throwing it all out in the garbage. You have to give me a second chance. Please don't leave me. I'm sorry. Please forgive me."

I put the house keys next to the jewelry. Even if I wanted to speak, I couldn't. My heart was beating so hard, breathing was difficult.

"How am I going to pay the rent by myself if you're leaving me?" he asked in a demanding tone. His tears had stopped. "You have to give me the money to cover half the rent for the next two years. You owe it to me.

"Mom, do you have anything else you want us to carry out?" Ralph asked.

"Yes, my coffee table over there." I walked out of the apartment followed by Ralph and Joseph carrying the table.

"What a rat," Joseph said to me when we got into his truck. "I had to control myself from punching him. After what he did to you, he still had the nerve to ask you for rent money? I couldn't believe it!"

"Mom, you did very well. I'm proud of the way you handled the situation," Ralph said.

I was pleased too, and most thankful for their support.

I never thought I would be seeing Dick again. But two days later, he showed up at our office. I walked into the waiting room where he was seated and said firmly, "I would like you to leave my office immediately."

"Please, give me a chance to at least explain myself. Can I talk to you privately?" he asked. "Please, it will only take five minutes of your time."

"Okay," I said. He followed me to my first treatment room. He sat on one of the chairs and I stood by the doorway.

"Veronica, I knew it was you writing to me. I was just playing along."

"The nerve to even come up with such a lie is beyond me," I said looking straight at him. "You insult me by thinking I'm that naive." I raised my voice. "You're nothing but a user and a liar. Now get out of here or I'll get Ralph to throw you out."

"Okay, okay, I'll be honest with you. What I did was wrong and I'm sorry if I hurt you." He massaged his neck with one hand as if trying to put himself together to speak and then cried out, "I'm addicted to sex with strangers!"

I remained silent. *Wow! So that's what had happened! Once I moved in, the relationship disintegrated because I was no longer a stranger.*

"After you left me," he said, "that same day I got professional help at my church." He wiped his tears with the back of his hands. "The pastor is going to provide me counseling and I already signed up for a special program they have, to help overcome addictions. Veronica, I swear to you I'm a changed man already. I can't live without you; will you come back to me? Together we can overcome this. I love you and I'll do anything not to lose you."

"For the sake of the next woman in your life, I'm glad you're seeking help. Now if you'll excuse me I have patients to take care of." I walked out of the room and went in the backroom where Ralph was seated at his new computer. I sat at my desk waiting to hear the front door close behind Dick.

He left and I sighed deeply with relief.

~ Chapter Twelve ~

The Birth of Mary Celeste

Spring of 2000

Every morning before starting my day, I looked at Artur's website where he had posted pictures of his paintings, ceramics, and wood carvings. He was a multi-talented person. He was an artist, a published writer, and a poet. I felt very privileged to have someone as talented as Artur interested in what I had to say.

I decided not to tell my pen pals the truth about Dick. I wrote, "We grew apart and as such, things didn't work out."

I was living with Ralph, but he had a roommate, so I was back to sleeping on the futon in the living room, which gave me no privacy if someone went into the kitchen or left the apartment. The good news was that our paychecks had increased to $250 a week. So if I was frugal enough, I could afford to get my own place, preferably close enough to my office so I could walk to work.

Going back and forth to Troutdale put too much wear and tear on my car, and there was the high cost of buying gas every week. I began looking for apartments in West Linn.

Betty had recovered well from her car accident and her case where she was rear-ended had finally been settled. She had also accomplished her dream of becoming a marathon runner and came to be adjusted once a month for maintenance of her spine. One Friday night, Ralph and I were about to close the office when he said, "Mom, do you know you still have a patient in your room?"

"No, that's not possible. My last patient came in at six o'clock and left already."

"Well you better check, because when I went by your first room, I saw some feet on the table. You better make sure."

I did. Betty had been on the table since six o'clock and the moist heated towels were dripping cold! In those days we didn't have digital electrical heating pads.

I was very apologetic but she said in the sweetest tone of voice, "It's fine, Dr. Veronica. I understand how busy you are."

"No, you don't understand. I was going to leave the office and since today is Friday, you would have been on this table until Monday morning!"

She thought it was funny. I laughed too, but I was cringing on the inside, I was so embarrassed.

I couldn't believe my luck! I found a one-bedroom apartment in West Linn, and it was only a few blocks—within walking distance—from my office. The apartment was small, but it had a lot of amenities like a luxurious clubhouse and a gym, and my unit was situated on the highest section of the complex, separated from the other apartments, giving it the feeling of a private cottage. The view from the living room was outstanding. In the evening I would be able to see the surrounding city lights of West Linn, Lake Oswego, Oregon City, Portland, and the magnificent Mount Hood. I couldn't wait for the 4th of July fireworks; the view from my place was well worth the $650 a month for rent.

Once I told Ralph the kind of bed I wished for, he urged me to go ahead and get it. So I used my charge card to buy a queen size bed with a black metal frame with four posts connecting the top at all four corners. I also bought a few yards of see-through white material and decorated the frame by draping the material from the four posts. The night I moved in, I dreamed my bed was an ancient Egyptian sailboat, floating slowly down the River Nile. I woke up in the morning with a smile on my face.

I enjoyed writing to Paula and Artur. Paula kept me up to date on her daily activities, her frozen food business, and her family. Her son, only fourteen years old, had been diagnosed with scoliosis. When I encouraged her to take him swimming, she had a pool built in her backyard. Artur sent me super long emails on philosophy and the meaning of life taken from his past and present experiences. He showed a serious streak of being old-fashioned, which I was sure had come from being Portuguese and only being four years my senior. I did my best to respond to each of my pen pal's diverse interests.

Ralph commented one morning on how fast I typed in Portuguese with just two fingers. When writing every day to my pen pals, I was practically writing without a second thought to grammar.

A month later, Ralph moved to West Linn, into the same apartment complex where I was living. Being close to each other was very nurturing. He bought a new couch and gave me his old one. My nest was complete.

For my birthday, I received several surprises in the mail. Paula sent me three books by the well-known, classic Portuguese authors Eça de Queirós, Fernando Pessoa, and Almeida Garrett. I also got a package from Artur including his published works, *O Mistério de Santa Eulália,* (The Mystery of Saint Eulália) published in 1995, three chapbooks of poetry written respectively in 1993, 1994, and 1996, and a copy of *Felgueiras,* the local town newspaper where he lived, dated April 23, 1999, that included his picture on the front page, and inside, an extended interview with him about his prior involvement with local politics. Artur also enclosed a small book of sonnets by Florbela Espanca, a renowned Portuguese poet whom he admired, and several color photos of him and his family. In all the pictures, Artur wore black pants and a black T-shirt and in the picture where he stood by some Roman ruins, he wore a black jacket over his black ensemble. His white hair in his crewcut along with his white skin produced a drastic disparity with the rest of his body in black attire. It projected the statement of an older man's fashion. He posed in one picture with his grandson Leonardo, a cute little kid of about three, and another with Pedro, his younger son, probably twelve years old with a slight weight problem, but a friendly, beaming smile.

After my experience with Dick, I felt the need to learn everything about Artur, even if he was just my pen pal and most likely we would never meet. But he was still a man. My father used to say, when you look at a picture, look at the eyes. They cannot lie, and they are the pool of the soul, the true image of the owner's character. And so I looked. I scrutinized every detail with my magnifying glass and found all the pictures had three things in common. In each, Artur's eyes behind lightly tinted glasses looked away from the camera as if only his body was present. Also in each, his lips were pressed together with a slight upturn that failed at creating anything more than a faint smile. And lastly, he delivered a lack of warmth in each picture, especially in the picture where he had an arm over his son's shoulders, but kept the other hand in his pocket.

There was one picture he had taken of his home office, where he spent most of his time writing. A large bay window allowed the sun to shine on his desk that held a keyboard, a large computer screen, and two tall speakers that sat on either side of the screen. A wall-to-wall bookcase about three feet tall revealed that its shelves were jammed tight with a variety of dark brown book covers, the kind you see in old libraries. A radio and a cassette tape player sat on the top shelf along with more books, family pictures in small picture frames, and his paintings, which I recognized from seeing on his website. A large portrait of Jesus with a golden halo and wearing a white robe hung in the center of the wall, surrounded by wooden crosses of all sizes, plus more of his original paintings and some carved wood pieces. It was a cluttered room, as I even visualized lots of dust, but he was obviously proud enough of his office that he wanted to share it with me. I was touched by it. Along with the package came a note with three poems. "Since you used to be a guitar teacher and a musician," he had written, "I have no doubt you can easily write the music for my poems. I would be very grateful if you can do that for me."

I wrote back the next day, "I no longer play guitar, but I'll give it my best shot to produce the kind of music you hear in your mind that hopefully will match your poetry."

Betty, my patient, was getting married the next month. I gave her a small crystal bell as a wedding gift. We were both amused as we recalled the day when I forgot she was still lying on the adjusting table and I was about to close the office for the weekend. She and her husband were moving to Arizona after her wedding. She promised to keep me posted on her whereabouts.

A tip from one of my patients led me to check out the Jewish choir at the Presbyterian Church down the road from our office. It sounded like a great social hobby. Mr. Farino, the choir director, tested my voice and I was placed as mezzo-soprano in the second row of singers, versus way in the back and asked to move only my lips, which is what happened when I was in high school.

Once a week on Thursday evenings, we practiced for about an hour in the church's cellar, getting our repertoire ready for the holiday's festivities.

My weekdays were filled with treating my patients from nine to seven. But after dinner, I sat with my guitar on the couch and practiced the music for Artur's poems over and over again. It was my downtime before going to bed. The freedom I felt being on my own was indescribably delicious. I always gave thanks for everything before closing my eyes to sleep.

As strange as it may sound, I had never learned to ride a bicycle as a kid. My mother used to say, "If you fall and cut your face, you'll destroy any chances of ever getting married. Men only like pretty faces." However, when I was dating Patrick, I learned to ride a bike well enough to go around a school track field a few times. True, it was short lived, because we were soon married and then left for Europe, but I was willing to test the theory that once you learn to ride a bike you never forget. The bike had been kept at Ralph's storage and after so many years without being used, I felt it was a good idea to take it to a bike shop to have the tires checked and oil the hardware. I even learned to put the bicycle in and out of the trunk of my car without hurting my back. I planned to ride it during my lunch hour at Mary S. Young State Park, not far from my office.

The timing was perfect; there were no cars to worry about. I rode the bike in small spurts and was prepared not to fall at all costs. Much like the fisherman turning the reel bit by bit until the fish is securely hooked, I rode about five feet, stopped, then ten more feet, then back to five feet. Finally feeling like I had the hang of it, I went on to ride the final twenty feet ahead of me. *I can do it!* I told myself. *I'm going to ride around the lot without stopping.* Suddenly I saw a car coming in my direction and I went for the brakes a bit too hard and went flying into the gravel. I landed with both my hands out and bruised my wrists, my left forearm, and my right shoulder. All skin bruises, nothing serious. But I did take into account the scuffed palms of my hands; I needed them intact. And I had just had my bone density test taken a month ago which showed signs of osteopenia. I could not afford any trauma, particularly a bone fracture. The bicycle was put back into storage.

Over the weekend, I motivated myself to finish reading Artur's book, *The Mystery of Saint Eulália,* for two reasons, in case Artur questioned me about it, and I was curious to see if it would get any better. I reached the last page without a clue as to what the mystery was about. In my humble opinion, Artur was a lot better at writing poetry. With poetry, the poet was entitled to create anything that came into his mind and it didn't even have to rhyme, but with a story, it was like the human body, without legs there was no walking, without hands, there was no grasping, and without hair, well, it could go on and on. Basically, his story lacked working parts and the book cover, oh my goodness, I was shocked! The pages were crudely glued, and the burlap cover held by silver duct tape had air bubbles, or what looked like dirt particles, caught underneath. The title and his name were written with a dark yellow magic marker and the calligraphy was that of a child. I would not be proud to include it with the other books on my bookshelf and I doubted a bookstore would accept such poor workmanship. I did not want to hurt Artur's feelings so I wrote, "I found *The Mystery of Saint Eulália* interesting."

I had learned that from Terry, a friend in New Jersey, who said, "Whenever I see a painting I don't like and the artist insists on hearing my opinion I say, *interesting.*"

Artur's next email caught me by surprise. "I'm writing a new book about *Marie Celeste,* the true story of a ship where the crew and passengers disappear while on route from New York to Genova (Genoa), but I'm stuck as to what direction to go with it. Veronica, my dearest friend, you reveal in your writing so much creativity that I must ask you to help me make this book a reality. How would you feel if I asked you to be co-author with me?"

Helping someone to write a book in my native language sounded like a fun project. I wrote back, "I'm so honored that someone like you, a published author, is asking me to be a co-author. Can you send me what you have written so far? And by the way, soon I'll be done writing the music for your poems."

The internet was like an amazing encyclopedia! I sent an email to Artur, "The name of the ship is *Mary Celeste,* not Marie Celeste. I'm so excited about our collaboration. Between the two of us, I know we'll create a masterpiece!"

But to my disappointment, the more time I spent researching on the internet, the more I was convinced everybody aboard the *Mary Celeste* had been victims of piracy. Most likely they had been thrown overboard by angry pirates who could not find anything of worth onboard except for some barrels of alcohol, and decided to flee when they saw the *Dei Gratia* ship approaching. But I didn't tell that to Artur, I just reminded him once again to send me what he had written and I was looking forward to reading it.

I finally finished the three songs for Artur. It had taken me every evening when I got home from work but I was quite content with the arrangements. I used my tape recorder to record them. I sang and played the guitar. I put the cassette in the mail and kept my fingers crossed that Artur would like them.

I was in dire need of making friends outside the office and becoming more physically active. I recalled the mailman telling me about the Crystal Ballroom in downtown Portland, where he went swing dancing on Saturday nights. Ralph had told me more than once, "Mom, if you want to meet people and make friends, you need to be more proactive." I took his advice to heart.

On Saturday evening, I put on high heels and a dress befitting a social experience at the Crystal Ballroom. I drove to Portland and found a parking spot about two blocks from the address I had downloaded from the internet. I had no idea what to expect. I only knew I was an hour too early. I grabbed a few magazines that I kept in the back seat for moments like these. I also needed the time to unwind and get my nerve up. Forty minutes later I looked at my wristwatch; I was doing well with time. It started to rain lightly, the usual rain associated with Oregon weather, more like a drizzle. Like a sprinkle of sugar to make the medicine go down, or was it, with a spoonful of sugar all the medicine goes down? I knew the tune well, but when it came to the lyrics of any song, I always managed to forget. Even as a child, I was only able to hum a song and when it came to memorizing a poem once for a school project, Mama had to write a note to the teacher saying, "Please excuse Veronica from memorizing poems. Her memory only works with images and hands-on projects. This is the reason she also fails miserably in math; she can't handle anything nonrepresentational." Ten more minutes to go; I had gone through the magazines twice. I checked my lipstick, combed my hair, and stared at the fogged windshield. *What possessed me not to bring a jacket?* I asked myself. I took a quick breath in and let it out and without a second thought, I got out of the car, locked it, and then walked briskly to the building's entrance.

Before I was allowed to enter, I had to buy a ticket at the front ticket booth, which looked a lot like one of those old beat-up theatre box offices made of brick and glass windows all around. I was not surprised by its timeworn look. According to what I had read on the internet, the building had been built in 1914 and since it was classified as a historic building, most likely the proprietor wanted to keep the original look. I expected the foyer to be spacious and brightly decorated, but the dark wood wall panels and the lack of windows made the small lobby gloomy and musty. I prayed I wouldn't go into my usual embarrassing ten steady sneezes with nasty mucus pouring out with each blow, which typically happened when I encountered musty places. I rushed up the dark wood steps but stopped at the next floor to take a quick look at what seemed to be a brewery of some kind. I had never been to one but the large metal tanks were self-explanatory.

I heard the music coming from the next floor and my heart began to beat faster; I was a nervous wreck. I climbed the steps at a slower pace instead of running the rest of the way and stopped against the wall on my right when a group of young women came running down the steps like a horse stampede. "Going to the bathroom?" I asked mockingly to the one who bumped against me. She laughed with the others and kept on going. I was finally facing the famous Crystal Ballroom. The room was big enough to most likely fit a thousand people and it was covered with lively dancers of all ages and shapes. I took in the high ceilings, two impressive chandeliers, and the massive arched windows along the wall on my left, facing the street. A sense of déjà vu came over me as I realized that the ballroom was nothing but a very, very small replica of the dance hall my Aunt Heydee used to take me to in Lisbon. My mother thought it was imperative that I learn to dance the cha-cha, tango, and merengue before getting married to Al. I never mastered those dances as I couldn't learn their specific steps by counting one two three turn, one two turn, move this way, move that way. It made me feel like a robot and constricted my natural disposition to dance freestyle. But it all worked out in the end—Al did not like to dance.

I was surprised when a young man in a yellow and brown plaid oversized wool suit asked me, "Would you like to dance?"

"This is my first time here," I said, feeling like he had made a big mistake. "I don't know how to swing dance." I waited for him to say, "So what are you doing here if you can't dance?" Instead he reached for my hand and said in a most charming tone, "I'll be more than happy to teach you." He carefully guided me to an area less constricted by dancers and we began to dance. He was not wearing the plaid suit for no reason; it was called a zoot suit and it had been made by his sister as a birthday present. Bernard had been dancing for five years and except for when his cousin died and another time when he was bedridden with the flu, he never missed a dancing event. I followed his steps and was surprised at how easy it was. Just keep moving with the music, I told myself. "For someone who doesn't know how to swing dance, you're doing great," he said.

I was not going to tell him about my mailman. When the music stopped I said, "You were very professional at guiding me. I felt like I was dancing on a cloud."

"Thanks," he said, "but I can't take full credit for it. These wood floors were built on rockers and ball bearings; that's why it can feel like you're floating. It's ideal for dancing." We danced once again and he told me about the small stage in the corner. Jimi Hendrix, The Grateful Dead, and Tina Turner, just to mention a few, had performed on that stage. Then someone else asked me to dance and Bernard and I went our separate ways. Except for using the powder room once, I didn't miss a dance for the rest of the evening. I left the ballroom feeling light as a feather. The rain had stopped and the partially translucent moonlight peering between the clouds like a beacon from the heavens smiled gently upon me like a benevolent guide in the quiet of the night. When I got home, I took a hot shower and then went to bed with the satisfied feeling of knowing I had survived on my own. It was about three in the morning when I woke up with muscle cramps in my calves. I don't know how long I jumped up and down in the middle of my bedroom trying to release the muscle cramps, but it felt like forever until the pain finally went away and I fell asleep completely exhausted.

I wasn't going to quit, however. If anything, it confirmed my suspicion that I was out of shape and needed to do something about it. The following Saturday I got to the Crystal Ballroom even earlier as I wanted to sign up for the swing group class. Learning the official steps in a group format gave me a sense of accomplishment when the ballroom opened to the general public afterwards, and I was able to dance with anyone without stepping on their feet.

Ralph had no desire to go dancing. The mailman who introduced me to swing had stopped delivering mail to our clinic. Maybe he had gotten back with his wife and was too happy to go dancing anymore.

I became a devoted Saturday dancer at the Crystal Ballroom. Most dancers were very young, about half my age. But they didn't seem to be affected by it and I never had to go up to someone to ask them to dance with me.

Summer 2000

On Sunday June 4th I received a four-page email from Artur. With it came the attachment of his book that he still called *Marie Celeste.* He started his email by criticizing me for going dancing after I told him my feet were sore the next day. I couldn't help feeling a little irritated because his humor was far from being sophisticated and if anything, it was the epitome of sarcasm with statements like, "I know you want me to feel sorry for you, but you deserve to be in pain after overdoing it on the dance floor. I bet you danced to your heart's content without the wisdom to stop when you should. Well you should know better since you are the specialist, right? So I should say, you know what you are doing."

What was he, my father? But by the end of the first page, he probably felt guilty about being crabby and confessed exercise was important to help people in our age group to remain healthy. He was going to buy a treadmill to use at home and was also going to start taking swimming lessons with his son.

The next two pages were about rebirth. "Even though I don't believe in reincarnation because I am a Catholic, I am open-minded. A good example is the book I'm still writing and hope someday to finish, called *Maka Edom, the Man That Spoke to God.* I feel Jesus is okay with it and wants me to explore the rebirth process so I have written five chapters on that subject but the most significant chapter is yet to be written. The theme of rebirth is very serious and cannot be rushed; I am willing to wait for the right time to put that book together. Oh yeah, I'm happy to know you are working on my poems. I'm sure we will have two successful songs." (He must have forgotten he sent me three poems to write music to, not two. I wondered if the tape had gotten lost.)

He went on, "I can see from the email you sent me you already have some knowledge about the ship and that will help you a lot in the process of writing. You will notice that what I wrote so far is more like a romance and it isn't going to coincide with the actual facts. My intention is to use *Marie Celeste* as an introduction to another story. I want to tell you some of my ideas and later on we can discuss them. We need to create a unique way to have the passengers on board 'transported' to the old world of Atlantis. I imagine such a world must have existed millions of years ago, in the middle of the Atlantic Ocean, but due to some catastrophic event about to happen, the wise men of such a world were able to transport everything in their world to another world very different. Where could it be? Another planet? Another Universe? I still don't know and I have not chosen which. I also don't know how to describe how the transport was achieved but it has to be something very special and different from what we can even imagine. When the entrance doorway was created, it was left open and it pulls in the human beings traveling in such a region. The people on board the *Marie Celeste* would have been taken through such a doorway. I just don't know how. You'll also notice the crew I created is composed of a sailor named James, who is a bit of a rebel, but he is also highly educated and quite smart. I think that should be explored by putting him against the captain as part of the plot and suspense; good idea, hmm? Then there's Luigi, a young Italian man with serious problems, but you'll understand better once you read the manuscript about him; then you can create some drama with it. And there's another guy on board spying on the captain and his wife. I believe I have not identified him yet. But the idea is to create romance, jealousy, and hate towards the captain, etc. Well, from here on, I don't have anything more. This is where I stopped, even though I wrote some small ideas to contribute to the continuation. It's important to give some thought on what happens to them and their way into the other world and to think of what happened to these people after they got taken to the "other" world. I don't believe they are all going to make it. One or two don't make it? Who? The Italian Luigi or James? I don't know. Think about it and let me know. We have time. There's no rush, do you agree? I sent the attachment on "Word 2000." I hope you have it. If not, I'll send it on Word 97. A big hug from your loving friend, Artur."

His book summary had a lot to be desired with only three crew members of whom one was a spy, and nothing significant for the others except lots of question marks. *Relax girl, read the manuscript first,* said the wiser part of me, *then you can make a better evaluation.* I was past the relaxation mode. I downloaded his manuscript and began reading it immediately. I only had an hour left before my first nine o'clock patient arrived. It only took me forty minutes to read the text. *Marie Celeste* was worse than *The Mystery of Saint Eulália.* I felt frustrated. He had told me he wanted me to help him write the end of the book but what he should have said was, "I don't have an answer for any of my ideas. As a matter of fact, you need to write the whole thing." His attachment of forty-two pages was nothing but bunkum; there was no book. He began the manuscript by saying the *Marie Celeste* was rapidly crossing the Atlantic Ocean on its way to Genova in 1872 and Captain Briggs had a crew of experienced sailors except for two Italians, a Napolitano and a Genovese who had offered to work on the boat, (boat?), in exchange for a free trip to their country. (Except for describing their nationalities, they disappear from the plot. Was I supposed to write about them?) Then he mentions James, a highly educated young rebel who had traveled with Briggs three times, but Briggs's wife stopped him from firing James. (Why? What did James do that he should get fired? Briggs's wife knew James?) There was no background history on any of the characters. Then out of nowhere, Captain Briggs befriends Walter Simpson, another crew member, who requests authorization from Briggs to bring a beautiful young woman on board with her eight-year-old son. Their argument goes on for two pages and then they're not speaking to each other after Briggs refuses Walter's request. Briggs was afraid to bring a woman aboard, even if she was a widow and impoverished, because she might get molested by the horny sailors. The next eight and a half pages was about the sailors recounting their visit to a local bar, (Where?), and telling boring, philosophically-tinted stories, sounding more like speeches at a political gathering. Then Artur names Captain Briggs's wife, Marie Celeste. (The same name as the boat? That made no sense to me.) He did offer some background on her; she was the daughter of French immigrants and had been sent on vacation to France when she was younger. (How young?) She was pure, absolutely pure in body and soul.

(Was he kidding?) While in France, she meets a French boy, older than her, who introduces her to the monsters of French literature. (Monsters, wow, that tells me a lot!) Her father orders her to return to America even though her relationship with the French boy was purely friendship. (Yeah, right.) At this point Artur changes Marie Celeste's name to Marice without an explanation. Little by little, Marice forgets the French boy, principally after she meets Captain Briggs and Charlie, one of Briggs's older sailors who upon meeting her, encourages Captain Briggs to ask Marice to marry him and go live on his ship. (I could only guess Charlie and Captain Briggs were buddies and as such, they hang out at Marice's house.) Marice is delighted with the idea of marriage and the opportunity of a lifetime of adventure with her captain who is obviously not concerned about having her travel with him in a boat with horny sailors. (Maybe she is too ugly to worry about since Artur doesn't describe what she looks like.) Marice says, "I have crossed the Atlantic Ocean three times already even though I only remember it twice. I know very well what it's like to live on a ship and I'm not afraid." (Did she sleep throughout one of those trips?) The plot gets worse! Artur goes on to write about the sailors screaming in the middle of the night and the captain tells his wife to stay in bed while he goes to see what happened. An anomalous light in the distance like something never seen or recognized as normal seems to be afflicting the crew who act scared. (How scared were they and what did they do to show they were scared?) The captain's wife disobeys her husband and gets up to see what the fuss is all about. Six pages later of talking out loud to himself, since there's no response from his wife standing next to him or from anyone else on board, he decides the light is nothing but a volcano in the far distance. Meanwhile, there's someone on board spying on the captain and his wife while they embrace lovingly while looking at the ocean below. (What happened to the light? Did they forget all about the light?) Maybe that is the part Artur refers to as romance. Then everyone hears some strange music coming from afar. (Lights, music, hmm, what's next, I wondered. But nothing happens.) The next pages are about the calm sea and some seriously boring talks between Briggs and his wife who supposedly enjoys debating with her husband about the mysteries of life, and of course they debate the Bible, but the way it's written, only the captain has anything to say. Oh yeah, his wife spends her time playing piano, otherwise, she's in the kitchen helping the cook. (That's so Portuguese to write about her hobbies as playing piano and cooking. What does she cook? What does she read? What kind of music does she play? Didn't she have a little girl? There's no mention of their daughter Sophie in his manuscript. Did she fall overboard?) The next pages are ongoing boring philosophy. There's no emotion except for when they say they are concerned with lightning in the distance. Then the last five pages are about the captain being immersed in the memories of meeting Charlie at a bar where he convinced Charlie that he's not too old to become a crew member. (How old is this guy, besides writing that he is old?) The more I read, the more I wanted to cry in desperation. Artur had sent me a puzzle where most of the pieces were missing.

Thank God, when I had something bothering me, I could rely on Ralph's wisdom. I told him about the dilemma and that I was at my wit's end. "Tell him you don't have the time to re-write the whole thing," he said and then added, "Just finish the story and don't worry about what he wrote."

"Finish what? Everything is scrambled up. I can't put an end without a beginning and a middle to connect the dots. Besides, my name will be on it as co-author and the readers will not go beyond the first mind-numbing pages, which means I wasted my time for nothing."

I put the manuscript in one of the drawers in my desk.

As always, Dr. McMahon kept an eagle eye on us and reminded us to participate once again at the local fairs. He even went as far as joining us one morning at the Canby Country Fair to help us pass out some pamphlets about our office and about chiropractic services to passersby.

I did not respond well to extreme heat. The prior summer had been bearable and I had made it without any serious ill effects. But I didn't sweat. Consequently, with high temperatures, I became easily overheated. Then add a bunch of hot flashes to it, and I was ready to keel over. The heatwave on Saturday reached ninety-five degrees and by mid-morning, I started to feel light headed. "Sorry Ralph, but I'm of no use if I drop dead. I have to leave." I got in my car with the air conditioner running at full blast on my face. I barely made it to the office where I lay on the floor next to the air vent with two ice bags, one over my forehead and the other under my neck. As I lay there with a pounding headache for almost two hours, I had enough common sense to realize that that was to be my last summer fair. Our practice was doing well and since Ralph didn't want to do fairs on his own, we sold our tent.

Upon getting Artur's email inquiring if I had received his manuscript, I answered, "Yes, but I have been very busy at work and I have not had a chance to read it."

I really did not know how long I could extend my status quo without telling him the truth. Maybe he would forget all about it.

We hired a front desk person to answer the phone, make appointments, collect fees, and do the office billing with insurance companies. Marcy became our office guardian. At Dr. McMahon's recommendation that we take some time off to recoup from our busy schedule, Ralph and I stopped working on Saturdays. It felt good having two days off. Except for having a sign outside, we didn't need to advertise, for as our patients improved, they referred us to their family and friends.

Usually I had the satisfaction of knowing that most of my patients followed my recommendations. But there were also those who reminded me of a Hollywood movie where the explorers were running away from cannibals but upon reaching a cliff, they had to make a choice—jump and be saved by the river below to carry them to safety, or stay and be boiled in a large cauldron. I never told my patients about this and other vivid scenarios, which made a lot of sense to me. Ralph did his best to remind me that not everyone could be helped and I should respect their choices even if they were the wrong ones. But I could not help myself. When they didn't follow my treatment plan, I felt personally responsible for having done a lousy job explaining the value of chiropractic.

I no longer could live with myself if I continued to ignore my task at hand. Either I grabbed the bull by the horns and put pen to paper on the *Mary Celeste,* or I would tell Artur he expected too much from me and would call it quits. I took the manuscript home and Friday after dinner, I sat on the couch to read the *Mary Celeste* manuscript once again. It didn't work. If anything, it gave me a panicky feeling of dismay and I developed a pounding headache. *What have I gotten myself into?* I asked myself as I got into bed.

The next morning I woke up at six and lay still on my back for a few minutes. *So what, it's a challenge,* I told myself. *Life is a challenge. Now let's see what I can do with the darn thing.* I took the manuscript with me back to the office. I sat at my desk and sent an email to Artur. "I'm sorry to say this but your manuscript needs to be completely rewritten. There are just too many gaps without answers. But before I get started, I need to know if this is okay with you. When I'm done, then you need to go over it and extend it further with your own writing."

In less than an hour, I received an email from Artur. "My dear sweet Veronica, I trust you with my own life. You have my blessings to do whatever you want with it." Having carte blanche from Artur was all I needed to get started.

I made plans to get to my office two hours earlier every morning. Living so close to my office had its advantages and on weekends, I could also spend the mornings there. It would be nice and quiet, except for listening to the voices of the passengers and crew of the *Mary Celeste* who I hoped would guide me to write their true story.

Autumn of 2000

I met someone who was writing a book about regrets and when he asked me if I had any to share with him, I told him I had none.

The next morning I drank a cup of hot milk with toast for breakfast and I remembered Mama sometimes would have only a glass of hot milk for dinner. On the way to my office, I was still thinking about the hot milk and how much Mama had suffered the last years of her life being physically and emotionally abused by the woman taking care of her and my father. I wish I had been able to help my parents. Even though my father would not leave Portugal and my mother would not leave José, my younger brother, or my father to come to America, I felt I had not done enough to save them. I should have forced them to come live with me. I did not tell my writer friend about this regret because it would mean going through a big explanation about my brother José's murder and my parents losing their home and all their possessions while being poisoned by their maid.

When I came to America thirty-eight years ago, Mama had made a seashell necklace for me to give to my cousin Ruth. At that time, I felt embarrassed giving Ruth, my sophisticated American cousin, such a poorly handmade gift. I knew Ruth would never use it so I kept it inside a little box feeling guilty about keeping it, but unable to throw it away.

Over the years, the necklace had grown in meaning. It had been made by my mother, and I relished it. I used it whenever I had a chance, usually in the summertime.

I received a chapbook of poetry and short stories from Artur called *Arts Encounter of 2000,* published in Portuguese, of course. Obviously Artur liked my story about the roses more than I realized. It had been published in the *Arts Encounter of 2000* with the title, "The Wall of Roses," by Artur Barros, August 1st, 2000, dedicated to Dr. Veronica Esagui.

I felt like something was wrong with his "surprise." The story I had written to him a while ago had been put into a poem format and he had put his name as the author. He added a little note, "Now you can see how easy it is to write poetry." It didn't matter what excuse he was using. I felt my writing had been violated no matter what format he used. For a few days I didn't know what to think until I came to the conclusion that I was making a big deal out of nothing. He was just trying to show me how easy it was to turn a story into a poem and even have it published. I sent him an email thanking him for the poetry lesson.

~ *Chapter Thirteen* ~

My Cousin Max

A very disturbing letter from Dr. Shelby, our landlord, arrived one day, during lunch. It felt like a cold shower had dropped over my head. No, let me rephrase that. It felt like I had been hit by a cannon ball, right into the pit of my stomach. Dr. Shelby had donated our office building to Oregon Health & Science University, OHSU. I called Dr. Shelby immediately. We had worked so hard to be established in our community, and now everything was going to go up in smoke.

"Don't worry," said Dr. Shelby in his naturally joyful voice. "Nothing is going to change, just the ownership of the building."

"OHSU is a huge corporation and they will tear down this building or sell it to another medical corporation. We have no place else to go," I cried.

"No, no, my dear, I can assure you they'll not sell it or tear it down, my goodness! OHSU will not sell the building right away and most likely they'll let you stay at least until the end of your lease."

"The end of our lease? It's getting close to the end of our lease now, and we'll lose everything! Please, don't give away your building."

"I'm very sorry but I've been advised by my accountant to donate it rather than pay the taxes I owe. Trust me, everything is going to be fine."

I trusted him as much as I trusted a loaded gun directed at my head. When Ralph came into the office, I handed him the letter. "We can't afford to buy the building," Ralph said.

"I know. But if we don't do something about it, it's going to be the end of our chiropractic office in West Linn."

"Don't worry Mom, at the end of our lease, we can always work something out with OHSU since it would be in their best interest to keep the present tenants they have, thus guaranteeing their monthly income."

"In a perfect world without greed, it could happen." I sank down on my chair next to him. "They're about business. I'm telling you, they'll want to knock down the building and build a medical facility. That's what will happen."

I began thinking about options, but things happened sooner than I had predicted. A week later, we received a letter from OHSU. The building was being put on the market but they were giving us first bid if we wanted to buy it.

I immediately got on the phone calling friends and family. No one had the kind of money we needed. Even if we could borrow $5,000 from one person, we would still need to find four more to make the total of $25,000 just for a deposit, in order to buy the building. A friend from New Jersey said I could borrow $10,000 from him but that was all he could spare. We still needed $15,000 more. The old saying, "God helps those who help themselves," didn't seem to ring true as I had run out of options. Ralph didn't seem to be concerned or at least he didn't show it. We went on with our work but I was profoundly worried.

On October 5th I received an unbelievable email from my cousin Max, in London, in response to the email that I had sent him saying that Ralph and I were apprehensive about our future since the building where we rented space was being sold. I had only met my cousin Max once, when Patrick and I went to London during our honeymoon. Since then I had remained in minimal contact with him, his wife Hilde, and his sister Meta. To be exact, we were only in contact about once or twice a year, during the holidays, when we exchanged good wishes to each other.

"I spoke to Hilde and Meta. We want to help you," Max wrote. "Please let us know how much money you need to make a deposit in order to purchase the building. We also require more information. Could you provide me with a business plan covering the next five years? You should then give an estimate of income and expenditure for the next four years on the basis of your known costs and your mortgage payment when buying the premises. Also, give me details of the lease you mentioned having next door with the hairdresser. This information will show you and us any additional finances needed and the length of time before you can earn adequate reserves. Please do not overlook when working out these figures that an expanding business also requires more working capital. Have you got an up-to-date balance sheet showing your present financial position? How many debtors and creditors do you have at present? Do your patients pay immediately when they come for treatment or do you have to wait for payment from their insurance?

How soon do you need the money?

I await your news.

Love and greetings, Max."

I couldn't stop jumping up and down. I was crying hysterically, thanking God and my cousins. Ralph came out of the back room, most likely wondering if I had lost my mind when I jumped on him with my arms around his neck and began kissing him. I could hardly speak but finally calmed down enough to tell him about Max's email. He smiled in his usual composed way and said, "That sounds good, but let's not celebrate yet until it's definitive. I'll have all the statements downloaded from the computer by the end of today." Sometimes I felt like I never matured as an adult because the festive Brazilian DNA on my mother's side had stunted my emotional development. Maybe the contrast of our behaviors between Ralph and me were due to him having more of his father's DNA. He inherited the cooler, engineering mind, more synchronized and reserved, with relevant facts and conditions influencing the logic and importance of a project.

As such, he possessed the kind of confidence that took away all drama. Whereas I, like a bull, tended to dive straight into a hole without any idea of how deep. Ralph would spend a month or more researching the diving style, what repercussions could be encountered from hitting his head on the bottom, and of course, how deep the hole was.

At seven, after we had seen our last patient and closed the front door, Ralph sat at the computer and about an hour later, he had extracted all the data from QuickBooks, plus a list of creditors, debtors, etc. Before we left our office, I sent an email with all the information Max had asked for and the amount we would like to borrow—$25,000.

Thank God for the internet and how it connected us so rapidly all over the world! If I had been using snail mail to my cousins, I may not have mentioned our situation until New Year's when it would have been too late. I couldn't help wondering if in a few more years, mailing letters would become obsolete, just like cell phones have taken over telephones and answering machines at home.

We received the following response from Max the next morning: "In spite of the further information you sent, I believe that you underestimate the amount of capital needed to finance your business..." He went on and on and then added, "We agree to personally give you a loan of $60,000 for six years. We propose that you start repaying this loan after eighteen months. This means that you make the first payment of $3,000 in eighteen months and then pay $3,000 quarterly. We do not require any security or interest. We can arrange to send you the money at the end of this week by telegraphic transfer to your bank. Please send me your personal bank details. Best wishes. Yours, Max."

Once again, I was reminded about angels living among us. They were human beings with a heart and every time I was in a difficult predicament, all I had to do was let God know I needed help.

Ralph and I applied for a mortgage and soon afterwards became the proud owners of our own building. West Linn had officially become our home and we developed a more profound awareness of our outside surroundings. Behind our office was the West Linn Library, across from it the post office, and right down the street, the grocery store, and the bank. All within walking distance!

Our destiny had been mapped a long time ago. When I first arrived in Oregon from California and had gotten lost, of all the places to get off the highway with my moving truck to ask directions, I picked the place that had a sign that said, "Welcome to West Linn."

~ Chapter Fourteen ~

Nobody Is Perfect

Sometimes I had a feeling Artur was brown-nosing me when he would write that we were a lot alike or he had been moved to tears of joy by my last email. I couldn't help wondering if Artur was like Dick, writing one huge poetic letter to all his female pen pals. Dick had not been the only one to harden my trust in men; Patrick and Michael had also done a great job.

"Did you like the music I wrote?" I asked in one of my emails. I wondered when he was going to let me know. "Did you get the cassette tapes I sent you?" He did not answer.

I really knew how to pick them, that's for sure. Except Al, who in all fairness I had to give credit where credit was due. In the thirty years we were married, he never took me for granted or took advantage of me and even after we were divorced, I could always count on him. Sometimes I wondered what my life would have been like if I had been content with our marriage. Most likely we would still be living in New Jersey. He was eleven years older than me, so now at sixty-six, he would probably be retired. Our grandchildren would visit us during the holidays and most likely he and I would live a sedentary life watching television and getting chubby together.

Artur's website, dedicated to his deceased wife whom he loved more than life itself, had me wondering if he really loved her as much as he had led me to believe. She was the perfect woman, the perfect wife, and no one could compare to her he had written at first, but as the emails kept coming and he opened up more and more with each one, I began to ponder if he was telling the truth. It's a known fact that sometimes one looks at their husband or wife and can't stand the sight of them because of this or that, but when the spouse dies, they suddenly take on the form of a saint. I had an aunt who used to abuse her husband verbally and physically. I remember her telling everyone he was a good-for-nothing and she could not wait to get rid of him. But upon his death from pneumonia, he suddenly became the pinnacle of perfection and she cried copiously over her loss. My instinct proved to be correct when I got an email from Artur confessing that while he was married, he had fallen madly in love with another woman. It had been an idyllic romance lasting quite a few years until she gave him an ultimatum, get a divorce or I leave. He went on to say how serious he was about her, and how far he traveled at the end of the day after leaving his job just to spend a few hours with her, but he was not only married, he was also involved in politics and could not afford a scandal. Even though we were pen pals and friends, I felt his confession had been written on purpose so I could give him some advice on what to do next. Either that or he had been drunk when he wrote to me.

But as Jesus supposedly once said to a group of people ready to punish a sinner, "Let those without sin be the first ones to throw a stone."

I wrote, "This person with whom you had the affair many years ago, is she still single? If so and you love her, why don't you go see her? Perhaps she would be a good person to have back in your life. I'm sure your wife, now that she's dead, would approve of you being happy."

Artur took my advice but things didn't go as he had hoped. He wrote, "She told me to get lost and accused me of abandoning her. But it's okay, I realize now she's not worth my love. Still, I want to thank you because now that I have taken the first step towards a relationship, I can go forward with my life. Veronica, I appreciate your support as a friend. But I must tell you this—you are addicted to romance, that's your weakness."

Artur made me feel very vulnerable with such a statement. But he was right; he had nailed me right where it counted. It was about time I accepted my vulnerability, my Achilles heel. I was emotionally defective. Dick's romancing had swept me off my feet just like it happened with Patrick and Michael. I was easy to take advantage of because I was addicted to love. My mother tried to stop me from reading romance novels while I was growing up; those books on undying love had shaped my personality. Artur had just removed my cover, my protective armor, and there was nothing worse than feeling emotionally naked. I was glad he lived far away and I did not have to face him.

Roy, a married man in his mid-forties, suffered from diabetes and had been advised by his doctor to exercise as much as possible, which was the reason he was a regular at the Crystal Ballroom. I asked him, "Why doesn't your wife come with you?"

He said, "She doesn't like to dance." A nail polish-like odor from his mouth made me want to gag. The only way not to hurt his feelings was to stay busy dancing with someone else. Out of necessity, I lost my anxiety at asking strangers to dance. Roy stood on the side like a watchdog and as soon as he saw I was free, he walked towards me and extended his hand as a motion to dance with him. But I was getting good at avoiding him. I would say things such as, "Sorry, but I'm on the way to the bathroom." Then I would promptly leave and take my time down the steps to the next floor where the bathroom was situated and wait a decent amount of time in the hopes that when I returned, he would be dancing with another victim and leave me alone.

A couple from Mexico came into our office for chiropractic care. Being that I was Portuguese and Nelly, my mother-in-law spoke Spanish at home, it was easy to make myself understood by my Hispanic patients. So I asked Mr. Hernandez to lie down on the table face down, *Por favor, Señor Hernandez echar de boca abajo.*

Mrs. Hernandez stood and said pointing at him, "My husband not a dog!"

"Of course he's not a dog. I'm asking him to lie down on the table. Did I say something wrong?"

"Yes, you did," she said. "'Echar' is a word used when you want a dog to lie down, but to a person you say, 'acostar.'"

I found a Spanish teacher in Wilsonville, but after attending a couple of beginner classes at her house, she felt what I needed was conversational Spanish. She advised me to call Lucia, a friend of hers who ran the Latino Women's Club in Portland.

I was the only Portuguese attending the get-together. The women were from all over South America including places like Mexico, Chile, Argentina, Columbia, Venezuela, and so on. But I really couldn't tell the difference in their dialects, to me it was all Spanish. We met once a month at each other's home for a potluck dinner and Spanish was the only spoken language. They took me under their wing.

After adjusting Julie, a twenty-eight-year-old patient, she sat on the adjusting table hugging her bent knees and said, "I need your opinion." Her voice lowered and she added, "About a personal matter." I made sure the door was closed and waited to hear her speak. She said, "When I go dancing, I feel a sexual release that makes me emotionally and physically satisfied. Is that normal?"

"Of course it's normal," was my no-nonsense answer. "Dancing is a very intimate expression and it is connected with sex, except that you don't have to be in a relationship to enjoy it."

Her face lit up as she said, "I'm so glad you told me that."

Since she was agreeing with my dancing philosophy, I went on, "As humans we are able to express music by movements powered by our souls. It goes back to the primeval days when dancing was sacred for some and entertaining for others, sometimes both!" We laughed as we always did when we had those kinds of personal talks and I confided that even at my age, dancing was one of the most fulfilling things I could do. Before leaving the treatment room, we hugged each other.

Hugging was a heartfelt expression associated with giving thanks, welcoming a new friend, saying good-bye, or comforting someone in need. I hugged most of my patients before they left, just because it felt right.

Roy, the dancer with bad breath, insisted on walking me to my car since he was leaving the Crystal Ballroom at the same time. Outside in the fresh air I would be able to breathe and his face would be away from mine. When we got to my car, I turned towards him and said, "Well Roy, have a good weekend and see you next…" He pulled me towards him with one arm and with the other hand, he grabbed the back of my head, forcing my face forward, and he kissed me right on the mouth. He was very strong because when I pushed him away, he didn't even budge. Out of desperation, I lifted my right foot and stepped hard on his toes, which I knew would hurt since he wore sandals. He let out a cry and moved away from me. When I'm in a situation like that, I never know if I'm going into fight or flight mode. My response was on automatic pilot after I stepped on his foot, and I closed my right fist and punched him on the side of his face. "How dare you! You're a married man, for crying out loud!" I yelled out. "Don't you ever come near me again you smelly creep!" I spit on the ground, wiped my mouth with both my hands and got in my car.

I had no intentions of quitting dancing; if Roy approached me again I was ready to kick him where it really hurt.

When I went back the next Saturday, Roy knew better than to ask me to dance with him.

"Dear Artur," I wrote, "after doing some further research on the internet, I've given some of the crewmen and passengers their actual names except for those whom I had to create as part of the new plot. You mentioned three crewmen, but a ship that big would appear to need at least eight or even nine crewmen. I imagine you're anxious to see what I'm doing but I would like to keep everything undisclosed until I can send you the whole manuscript. Then my friend, you are free to cut and add to it as you like."

Artur wrote back, "Feel free to do your magic. I'm a very lucky man to have found you. I'll wait patiently to see the final product."

Lucia, one of my new friends in the Latino group, turned me on to the International Club. They met on Wednesday nights at a brewery in the Pearl district of Portland.

After my last patient at seven at night, I couldn't wait to drive downtown and meet so many people from all over the world including Portugal, Brazil, Germany, Italy, Holland, China and many other countries. There were also a few Americans at the gathering who felt entitled to join in since they had traveled extensively to foreign countries and enjoyed being part of such an eclectic group. Even though the majority was composed of single people of all ages with some even older than me, it was not a pick-up place; it was more like a get-together between good friends. After just two meetings I had bonded with Julie, an American graphic designer, her partner Carl from Egypt who was a computer nerd with the most amazing sense of humor, Suzette from France, a very successful interior decorator, Dakila from the

Philippines, a prominent chef, and Maria, a chemical engineer from the Portuguese islands of Açores. Maria and I felt a common spiritual bond from the very first time we were introduced to each other. Much like love at first sight, we were drawn to each other by what I believed to be the shared spirit of our distinctive but likeminded culture. When we were together, we only spoke Portuguese.

Friday morning I received a dozen red roses in my office from Phillip, whom I had met on the internet. We had written to each other twice and when I suggested a meeting, he invited me to meet him Saturday evening at Jake's, Grill in downtown Portland.

I asked Ralph for his advice and what he thought of someone who sent roses to a woman he never met. "Be careful," Ralph said. "If I were you, I would ask him if he's married."

Phillip was dressed casually; he had a jovial appearance, was a little taller than me, had dark hair, and was in good shape. He was also quite entertaining while we waited to be seated. But as soon as we sat down, I popped the question, "So Phillip, are you married?"

"Let's not ask personal questions about each other," he said, leaning over the table." "Let's enjoy the moment."

My mind was racing, Ralph was right. He was married and probably figured the roses, the dinner, and his boyish personality would make it difficult for me to resist his amorous advances.

The waiter came to get our order.

"Veronica, do you like fresh oysters?" asked Phillip.

"I like all seafood."

He told the waiter, "We are sharing a dozen oysters, and I would like a very dry Martini for me." He smiled charmingly. "How about you Veronica, what would you like to drink?"

"A club soda with a twist of lemon and no ice, please."
The waiter left and I turned back to the matter in question.
"Phillip, are you married?"

"I like the color of your eyes," he said. "Green is my favorite color."

"Are you married?" I sat back into my chair to show him I was serious.

"Veronica, we just met!"

"That's right, we just met. And, I want to know."

"Okay," he said, "if this is what it's going to be like, then let's get it over with, knowing about each other, that is. Three questions and afterwards we just enjoy each other's company. Is that a deal?"

"Okay, I'll start. Are you married?"

The waiter gave us our drinks and positioned the oysters on a plate between us, adding two small plates to put our empty shells on. We each took an oyster.

"Let's eat the oysters first and have a romantic dinner," he said. "I just want to look at you. You have such beautiful green eyes!" How many times was he going to mention my eyes? I didn't respond and remained motionless as he went on, "Let me ask you, do you like the blues?"

"I love the blues."

"Do you like to dance? I know a very charming blues club very close to here. We can walk there."

"I love to dance, too." I had just answered two of his three questions. One more question and then it was my turn. What a stupid game.

"So you like fresh oysters like me," he said while quickly twirling the tiny fork to loosen the oyster and then slurping it down. I already knew what was coming. He lowered his voice in what he must have believed to sound sexy and asked, "You know what they say about oysters don't you?"

"Yes I do. And that was my third answer to your three questions. Now it's my turn. Are you married?

"This isn't fair. I could lie to you and you wouldn't know the difference."

"Are you a liar?" I grabbed another oyster.

"No, but you're putting a strain on our otherwise pleasant get-together. What if you don't like my answer?"

"I have to tell you, I hate games."

"If I tell you the truth," he said, "you must promise to give me a chance to at least explain my situation. Is that a deal?"

I nodded my head in agreement as I took in another oyster.

"Okay, I am married. But my wife and I are preparing for a divorce which will be finalized at the end of this year. We live in the same house but she lives upstairs and I live downstairs. We don't even see each other. She goes out with other men and I see other women."

"Wow, this is a lot like my ex-husband and me. He called me just this morning and told me he wants to get together tomorrow morning. We're having breakfast and it's possible that we'll be getting together again for the sake of our young children."

"You have children?"

"That would make more than three questions each." I was not going to allow a cheater into my life. I said, "How about us going to the blues club you mentioned earlier?" I had gotten dressed for a fun night with the intention of meeting someone nice. It wasn't my fault that he lacked such an attribute; the least he could do was to be my chaperone.

"It's right down the road. We can walk there," he said, as he finished the last oyster.

The club was about two blocks away. It was a crowded, small, corner, cement-floor-and-walls type of no-frills spot. I was a sucker for blues and the three-piece band put out a good beat with a blues rock style music that put my feet dancing under the table as Phillip guzzled a tall drink and then asked for another. I wasn't going to wait any longer. One of the things I loved about crowded dancing was that I could mingle by myself on the dance floor and no one would even know I was present. Phillip watched me dance and I believe he had finished his second drink when he joined me. From one to ten, he was definitely a ten, the opposite of my usual question to a new patient, "So Mr. Smith, from one to ten, with one feeling good enough to go dancing and ten receiving your last rites at your death bed, where are you, concerning your discomfort?"

We danced to two more tunes. The band was awesome!

"Oh wow, how time flies, it's already midnight. I have to go home," I said after we finished the last dance.

"It's still very early. Why don't we go to another club? There's another one not too far from here."

"I would love to but it's a long drive home and I have to get up very early to meet with my ex-husband for breakfast. As I said before, I must save our marriage for the sake of our children. You understand that, right?"

"I'll walk you to your car then. Maybe you'll change your mind and go home with me instead?" He winked.

I don't know if it was the drinks or the cool breeze of the night but his behavior changed from a pleasant adult to a bizarre child. He began jumping up and down like a bunny while walking along with me. I thought, okay, he feels carefree and comfortable, but this way I'll never get to my car. I began walking at a faster pace. I looked back and saw him pirouetting around and around and of course he would lose his balance and bounce into the buildings. He was either plastered from the two drinks he had at the club or he was crazier than I thought. I kept walking ahead of him as he was laughing at himself and when we crossed the street, he stood in the middle of the road daring the cars to hit him. When we got closer to my car, I was hoping for a miracle of some kind so I could get away safely. He began singing and dancing in the middle of the street as the cars drove around to avoid hitting him. It was my chance to get away as I ran to my car, got in, locked the door, and turned the engine on. When he turned in my direction, I didn't even wave back.

An Internet date

Wednesday night I showed up at the International Club dressed as a gypsy for Halloween. I was ready to play the part when Sal, one of the club members said, "Can you really read palms?"

"I'm a gypsy!" I said, full of it. "Of course I can read palms!"

"Will you read my palm and tell me my future?" He said very seriously. He pointed to a table nearby and said, "Let's sit over there, away from everybody."

"Of course, I'll even tell you your past, if you like." I sat next to him.

He gave me one of his hands and I held it palm up, taking my time to peer at it with a solemn look as if deep in concentration. Then I looked back at him with a face of, *I can see the future,* while trying not to laugh.

A group of people began surrounding our table. From growing up in Portugal, I still remembered the gypsy's style of doing palm readings.

I pointed my index finger at one of the lines on the palm of his right hand and let my finger crisscross the other lines, as if deciding which one to take on, and then said, "You're going to travel across the ocean." I waited a few seconds for added drama, and added reflectively, "In about a month."

"Yes, that's right," said Sal. "I'll be going to visit my family next month and I will be crossing the ocean. How did you know that?"

The people around were just as amazed. Lots of oohs and aahs were heard with their responses. "Ooh, she really can read palms," said one. "Aah, I can't wait to have her read my palm," said another.

"Okay, I'll be convinced of your special powers if you can tell me something that happened to me in the past," said Sal.

Once again I looked at his hand and then looked into his eyes and said exactly word per word what the Portuguese gypsies say after having mentioned the ocean trip. "You have lost someone not too long ago and this person meant a lot to you. I'm so sorry." I made a sad face.

His eyes became teary. "Oh, this is amazing. My father died a few months ago. You can see that?"

"It says right here in the palm of your hand. And I also see something else right here in the corner between these two lines." I closed my eyes, counted to three in my head, sighed as if relieved, and opened my eyes and smiled. "It's good news," I said. "You're about to meet someone very special in your life, but beware of someone who envies you. This person is not to be trusted and is not your friend."

"I know. I know who he is. This is amazing, completely amazing! Can you tell me also if I'll be rich someday?"

"You are destined to get a..." I had to think fast. "A good paying job...soon."

People were lined up to have their palm read, but I had already used all the Portuguese gypsy readings I knew on Sal. I put the back of my right hand on my forehead, rolled my eyes towards the ceiling, and said, "Sorry, but I have to decline any more readings. This reading took all my inner strength."

Zelma, who would not take no for an answer said, "C'mon, Veronica, you have to read my palm, you just did it for Sal. Just look at my hand and tell me when I will find a good man, a rich man."

"Zelma, you're dressed as a vampire, do you drink blood? And does Robert, dressed as an alien, come from outer space?"

"What does that have to do with you being a gypsy?" she asked.

"It's Halloween. None of us are real, okay?" I said, perplexed at how immature adults could act.

Maria came to my rescue by grabbing my arm and taking me with her to the other side of the room. She was from Portugal and she knew all about gypsy palm readings. "You did great," she said. "I almost fell for it, too." We laughed.

My neighbor recommended I check out The Portland Megaband since I liked playing the guitar. I paid them a surprise visit on Saturday morning; they practiced in a church in Beaverton. The church's large cellar seemed to be filled to capacity with about sixty eager volunteer musicians tuning a variety of musical instruments. A harp stood gracefully in one corner of the room being caressed by the slender long fingers of a middle-aged lady wearing her long straight white hair down to her wide waistline. Two others had their small, handheld harps held against their hearts as if cradling a baby. There were an array of stringed instruments including upright basses, cellos, violins, acoustic guitars, and banjos as well as clarinets, flutes, accordions, and drums of all shapes. When the piano player saw me standing at the entryway with my guitar case he waved at me to come in. "C'mon, the more the merrier," said the banjo player close by. Their next gig was going to be at the Northwest Folk Life Festival in Seattle. Rehearsals were always on Saturday mornings—same place, same time. I was in luck since it wouldn't interfere with swing dancing later in the afternoon. I bought one of their recommended books with the collection of their entire contra dance music. I couldn't wait to start practicing at home.

I had not given up dating on the internet. I simply needed extra time in between failures to recover my sense of direction. Robert lived in Clackamas and enjoyed his koi fish in his backyard pond. I thought it would be nice to meet someone who lived close by and liked pets. I suggested we meet Saturday at the Crystal Ballroom.

I recruited Christina, one of my friends who was married but loved dancing, to meet me there. If Robert turned out to be a dud, her mission was to come to my rescue.

Arriving earlier for my first date had its advantages. It gave me a chance to see what I was about to encounter. I remained in my car waiting until it was close to the magic hour when we would meet. I saw a large white car park across the street and a medium-built man in a brown suit and tie come out of it. He held a small piece of paper in his hand and seemed to be looking as to where to go next. It was difficult to tell if it was Robert but my instinct told me it was him. I hurried to get my ticket and ran up the steps to the Crystal Ballroom, which was where we were supposed to meet. Christina was nowhere in sight and I felt flustered, not knowing how to handle the situation, which was ridiculous since by then I could be classified as a professional internet dater. The swing dancing class was about to start as I stood by the doorway of the ballroom. He recognized me from the description of the red dress I was wearing. We shook hands and I had to admit for a man in his late fifties, he was very good looking. But there was something about Robert that made me feel uneasy. Maybe it had something to do with the way his dark brown hair was smoothly combed to the side, or maybe it was his impeccable brown suit just too serious for the occasion, or it could be he was wearing an acid-like cologne. We didn't have time to chat. The dancing instructor quickly encouraged us to join the class that was just starting. The class of about fifty people was geared for beginners with the men standing in a circle as the women changed partners while going around the inner circle. Christine showed up as the class ended. She was a great dancer and didn't need lessons. We sat at a small table but with the loud music, it was hard to hear each other, and it was especially bad for me with my hearing deficit since he sat on my left side.

Even though Christina was married, she did not hide the fact she liked Robert. She asked him to dance and then said to me, "You don't mind do you?"

I watched her flirt with him while they danced. He looked in my direction with the awkward expression, "I thought the date was with you."

I had been wrong to suggest we meet for the first time at a dance class and include a third party person, but since I didn't like him, I was glad it turned out the way it did. When they got back to our table, I told Robert about my ex-husband being back in town, but I could tell he was also disillusioned with our rendezvous. So when Christine asked him for a second dance, he excused himself by looking at his wristwatch. "Oh, dear," he said, "I have to go pick up my kids from the babysitter's house and I'm already late."

I knew I didn't need to send my usual excuse email the next morning, about us never seeing each other again.

While growing up in Portugal, I had eaten flan, a delicate baked caramel custard dessert, just once. They sold it by the slice at the more refined bakeries and restaurants in Lisbon and the price was exorbitant. So when I was at the last Latino gathering of the year celebrating Christmas, my heart fluttered with boundless excitement when I went into the kitchen to help the hostess and there was not one, but two whole flans sitting among an array of other homemade dishes. I was the personification of Pavlov's dogs when with a slightly trembling hand I cut a generous slice. I was not interested in the seafood paella, the empanadas, or the Changua soup. Our hostess, Anna from Argentina asked, "You eat the dessert first?"

I could have said, "I can't take a chance that it might vanish when everybody takes a piece." Instead I replied with a mouthful, "Portuguese are funny that way. But I also would give anything to learn how to make a flan."

"Would you like the recipe?" she asked. I nodded my head up and down repeatedly like one of those car dolls standing on the dashboard when going over a bump. I ran to get a piece of paper and a pen from my purse.

I had always thought a flan was the most time-consuming dessert to make, under the most secretive conditions in a kitchen with bolted doors and under the strict supervision of a chef and his mother. Anna dictated the recipe, "One can of condensed milk, the same amount of milk, and four eggs into a blender. Meanwhile melt a half a cup of sugar inside a flan pan and then pour the blender contents into it. Then put it into the oven inside a water bath for 45 minutes and when a knife inserted into the flan comes out clean, it's done." Before I left, Anna shouted at me from her front porch, "Veronica, I forgot to tell you. Make sure you pre-heat the oven to 375 degrees."

God bless my patients. Sometimes they took everything I said literally. Josephine, a fifty-nine-year-old who saw her plastic surgeon every three years, was a good example. She stopped by our office one afternoon to purchase another bottle of Coenzyme Q10. I had to ask, "Josephine, you bought a bottle a week ago. Is it all gone already?"

"I have been taking ten a day…"

"Ten pills a day?" I interrupted her, dumbfounded. "You're not supposed to have more than one a day!"

"And why not?" She smiled confidently. "You told me it reverses the aging process."

I took her to my treatment room and to her disappointment, I explained it helped reverse aging at a cellular level, not that she was going to be young again.

Joseph, the choir director at the church where I sang, introduced me to Roger, a sixty-five-year-old fellow who was attending the services that evening. Roger had just moved from New York a month ago and didn't know anyone. I told Roger I could always use another friend, and I invited him to go with me to the International Club the following Wednesday where he could make new friends.

Wednesday night Roger met me at my office. There was nothing like taking a twenty-five-minute drive downtown to learn everything about someone. Roger was the epitome of negativity. No wonder his wife asked for a divorce. I could only hope he would find someone else to hang out with soon, because even though I offered him my friendship, there was only so much I could take. He reminded me too much of Al.

Winter of 2001

I got into quite a bit of trouble at the Women's Latino Club. A beautiful woman in her mid-thirties with straight, jet black hair pulled smoothly back into a bun and large, dark, black eyes with thick black eyelashes sat across from me. Possibly because as a chiropractor I can't help noticing when something is out of position, I became distracted by her four millimeter round mole on her forehead. She obviously saw it when she looked in the mirror to put on makeup or combed her hair. And it wasn't that she didn't care about her appearance, because she wore dressy, high-heeled shoes and had a small, matching purse and her two-piece suit and skirt were smartly cut. She smiled at me and when she said she was from Spain I said I was from Portugal and went to sit next to her. She had a charming sense of humor and seemed to be well-educated so I assumed she would take my recommendation with grace and understanding and even a certain amount of joyous relief for finding someone honest enough to address her mole and offer her a way of getting rid of it for good. I used my most delicate tone of voice to say, "By the way, I apologize if I offend you with my suggestion, but that mole on your forehead," I moved slightly away in case she threw me a punch and then went on, "I can remove it easily by using a special technique called radio wave. No cutting or stitching. Imagine no scar. Your skin will be smooth and no one will ever dream you once had that growing on your forehead." I handed her my chiropractic business card and said, "In case you want to make an appointment, here is my number."

I could not believe how Rosalina got so deeply offended. She bit her lips, twisting them to one side, and her face flushed with anger. "My father has the same mole on his forehead. Right here in the same place as me." She acted as if she were wearing a purple medal. "And neither of us is going to remove them; they are part of us, our family." She got up from the couch and walked away.

The next morning I told Ralph what happened. "Mom, you were way off to approach a stranger at a party and talk about their facial moles. The woman was right to be upset." I felt hurt being scolded like a child, I was only thinking how beautiful she could be if her skin were flawless and the truth was that I was a bit excited about removing such a visual "lesion" as Ralph had called it.

It was lunchtime when Rosalina called our office. She had told her husband about my suggestion and he said it was about time she got rid of it. She was calling to make an appointment.

It had felt like forever but *The Mary Celeste* was starting to take form. In the last two months I had been accumulating my scribblings as they came juggling into my brain and then filing them accordingly in the order of events. To the right of my desk I had three shelves created for the purpose of organizing *Mary Celeste's* voyage. On the bottom shelf was one copy of Artur's manuscript. I used it as a draft and I crossed out paragraphs of no use and wrote notes on the borders to remember where to insert my writing later. The next shelf was a compilation of all the research I had been downloading from the internet concerning the true story of *Mary Celeste,* and on the top shelf were my characters pulsating to a vibrant rhythm waiting to be heard. I knew it, I could feel it in my guts that once *Mary Celeste* was fully equipped with the proper crew and passengers, all I had to do was let them loose.

Rosalina came in for her post-surgical check-up. Her skin had healed beautifully. She was very happy with the results and said, "When my father comes to visit in two months I'm going to bring him in and have his mole removed, even if I have to pay for it."

Ralph's beliefs remained unchanged even after Rosalina brought us a box of chocolates as a thank you gesture. "It's not nice to tell people about their skin lesions, you'll only hurt their feelings," he said.

I wasn't forcing anyone, I was simply offering options. If they didn't want to do anything about it, it was their choice. I had a feeling the reason so many people chose not to take care of their skin moles was because they thought it would be painful to take them off and then they would have an ugly scar to boot.

I received a registered letter from the main office where I lived. All the apartments, including mine, were being converted into condominiums. I had one month to move out or buy the one bedroom apartment for an outlandish price. Except for the view, the place wasn't worth half of what they wanted. I asked one of the residents why in the world our apartments were selling at such inflated prices. He said, "Blame those darn people from California. They come up here and gobble up everything, making the taxes go sky-high and affecting our real estate. They're making it impossible for the middle-class, people like us, to live in Oregon. They should go back to California where they belong."

Yes, there were some people in West Linn with huge mansions giving the impression their money grew on their backyard trees, but it was far from the truth. My patients and the people I knew worked hard to pay for their mortgage and their car payment and if anything, they were up to their neck in bills.

To me, a wealthy person was someone who didn't worry about monthly bills or how they were going to pay for their groceries if they lost their job.

I felt heroic concerning the next twenty pages of *Mary Celeste*. The characters kept growing daily, guiding me from one paragraph to the next with their instructive images and their stories. My two fingers had never typed so fast. After so many months of writing daily to my Portuguese pen pals, my Portuguese had returned in its full glory.

After reading about the two faceless characters whom Artur had mentioned but then dropped from the scene, I resuscitated them by giving them two very important roles of Carla, the beautiful young widow and her eight-year-old son, Mauricio. I wanted them on board, they had to be on board, they were vital protagonists of my thought process, and they were needed desperately to unfold the plot about to open, slowly, softly, seductively, like an old rose about to lose its petals gradually to a soft breeze. Carla would board the *Mary Celeste* just before the ship left the New York harbor and would be a companion to Sarah and her daughter. I also added Carlo to the crew so Luigi, who only spoke Italian, could have someone to talk to in his native language. They were close friends and as such, I felt the dynamics between the two of them were important to show the camaraderie that usually develops between sailors.

One evening after dinner, I turned off all the lights in my apartment, stood on the patio, and looked down at the lights of the surrounding cities below and looked out as far as the eye could see. It was a very clear night compared to a few days ago when the heavy grayish-white sky finally burst at the seams and poured out a ton of snow into the earth cradle below. In the distance to the left side of Mount Hood, the moon stood smiling, round and perky as if admiring an anomaly of nature. I went back in, closed the sliding glass door, opened the curtains, and turned on my radio; it was playing one of my favorite tunes by the Rolling Stones. I remained inside by the sliding glass door enjoying the view.

Once I moved out to another apartment, I may never see it again so I wanted to take it all in. A few stars danced above and lights below quivered as if blinking at me. Go ahead, they implied, go ahead and say good-bye to us. There are no next-door neighbors to worry about the music, or any living soul in the distance that can see you standing in the darkness of your living room. I began singing along with Mick Jagger while swaying to the music. I took all my clothes off and danced to my heart's content while facing the outside world. It was a lot like being an astronaut doing all kinds of maneuvers in the darkness of the Universe while the world below rotated on its axis, two distinct identities.

As I had told Julie, my patient, dancing was a divine experience completely powered by our souls; and as I had just discovered, it was also an exuberant celebration of life. I would be moving soon but at least I had said good-bye in a proper manner.

I woke up in the middle of the night with what I thought would be a pretty good reason for Sarah (Captain Briggs's wife's real name) to take Sophie, their two-year-old, on such a long trip and leave their son behind. No mother would do that without a strong motive. Sarah and her little girl had tuberculosis and as such, she wanted to be near her husband when the end came for her and Sophie. In those days, tuberculosis was like a death sentence. According to Artur, when Sarah was single and living in France, she had gotten involved with a young Frenchman who later died from the dreadful disease. He needed an identity and I gave him the name Jean. I was sure there had been more than books between those two. From that relationship, she had become a TB carrier until the birth of her second child, when suddenly she began developing symptoms. So far I had written twenty one pages. I wanted to maintain what Artur had written as much as possible but they needed life, they had to be palpable and human, so to speak.

I found a two-bedroom apartment up Sunset Boulevard, luckily still within walking distance from my office. It didn't have a view like my other apartment. As a matter of fact, it didn't have much of a view at all except for seeing the walls of two rundown apartment houses. But I had hit the jackpot regarding the interior and the price. The place had been gutted due to a fire and was completely renovated so I would be renting this two-bedroom for the unbelievable price of $550 per month. It was the only apartment in the whole complex that was brand-new on the inside. It boasted a kitchen with all new appliances and there were sliding glass doors leading outside to a large, wooden deck that was also new. It had a spacious dining room and living room, two large bedrooms, and a bathroom with a tub big enough to swim in. Once I closed the front door, it would be like living in a luxury apartment. I was ready to move in and make my nest.

Once again, Joseph, Ralph's friend, was kind enough to offer his pickup to help me move my belongings from one place to another. We were driving by a furniture store in Lake Oswego that was having a liquidation sale, and they both encouraged me to take a look and see if there was anything I could use since we had the truck. My eye caught two modern pieces of teakwood interlocking with each other like a puzzle. I visualized the television and stereo on it and the bottom could be used as a bookcase. It had a ticket sale of $150 and matched my coffee table to a tee. They must have meant $1500 but who was I to question their sale.

I loved my new apartment. A hidden gem among the ruins, but to complete it, I needed one important item—a satellite dish so I could watch Portuguese television. A few years back, when I was in Portugal, a taxi driver had asked me if I was from the Islands of Açores. In other words, my true Lisboan's accent had lost the "shhh" sound of the "s's." I wanted it back.

Doug, another older member of the congregation where I sang with the choir, talked to Roger who told him how much fun he had hanging out with me on Wednesday nights. After the last service, Doug introduced himself and said, "Look, I'm married and retired but my life is deadly boring. Do you mind if I join you and Roger on outings and to that place he told me about, some international club? I could use some mental activity in my life."

Doug came with us once. He stood against a wall not talking to anyone and when I approached him to see if he was okay, he remarked with a disdainful look on his face, "I don't have anything in common with these folks. I'm ready to go when you are." I looked for Roger and he was busy talking to a young Russian girl. When I told him we had to leave because Doug wanted to go home he said, "Tell him to get a cab. I'm talking to this lovely lady and I'm in no hurry."

We left an hour later and on the way home, they argued non-stop about which country made the best beer.

The *boys* didn't get along with each other, and everywhere we went I had to put up with two cranky old men trying to outdo each other. When Doug invited us for a hike at his favorite park in Lake Oswego, they got into a heavy argument over the age of the trees.

Finally Roger bought a car and I no longer felt obligated to drive him around, but he wanted Doug and me not only to see his brand-new black Ford Taurus, but to sit inside and listen to his new car stereo. I sat in the back seat because Roger drove badly enough to scare the devil itself. Of all the places to go, he drove us to the parking lot behind Thriftway in West Linn. "Now everyone be quiet," ordered Roger in his typical harsh tone of voice. "Sit back, listen, and appreciate what you are about to experience." He turned on his souped-up stereo system to an extremely loud classical station, pushed his seat slightly back, crisscrossed his arms over his distended abdomen, closed his eyes, and began moving his head side to side as if he were a music conductor. Doug, on the other hand, stared ahead with a straight face but every so often would turn to look at me and shrug his shoulders as if asking, What the hell is this about? I would shrug back at him finding the whole thing very amusing; three adults sitting in a parked car listening to music in the dark, not much different from teenagers. It didn't last long, maybe five minutes into our Mozart "experience," when Roger said, "How much longer do we have to sit here and listen to this crap?"

"Shhhhhh, be silent, and enjoy the music," Roger said without moving or even opening his eyes.

"Don't shush me!" Doug hit the dashboard with a closed fist. "It's ridiculous for us to sit here and not be allowed to even talk because Mr. Roger wants to show off his stereo."

"You say that because you're jealous of my stereo," Roger said, as he brought his seat up to its normal position.

"Big deal, 'your' stereo!" yelled Doug. "I have a stereo at home too, you know."

Once Doug exploded, so did Roger's foul language. They were like two roosters fighting for the hens in a coop.

As I sat quietly listening, since there was no way my voice could be heard over their brouhaha, I came to the realization that I was nothing but a babysitter and if I was going to stop them, I had to treat them like kids.

I leaned over between the two seats and sticking my head between their mouths I yelled at the top of my lungs, "Stop, right now!" They looked surprised. I think they had forgotten I was in the car. "Okay," I said in a more ladylike manner but still sternly, "I've had enough listening to you two battle your differences. Roger, I want to go home."

Doug opened the car door proclaiming he also wanted to go home but was willing to walk rather than to be put through Roger's musical torture.

The next morning Doug came to my office to complain about Roger. I had had it with both of them. Who cared how lonely they were? No matter how I looked at the situation, their friendship was a joke and I saw no reason to put up with them. I told Doug I was too busy to hang out with them anymore. Next, I needed to get rid of Roger; I just had to find the right moment to do it.

And that moment happened on Wednesday while driving back from the International Club. Roger turned to me and out of the blue said, "I feel like grabbing you right now and kissing you on the lips." He moved his face towards mine while I was driving! I pushed him away with my right hand and screamed, "We're friends! Are you crazy? If you do that again I'll kick you out the door and I'm not stopping the car to let you out!"

He moved away saying, "You can't blame me for trying. You're a beautiful woman."

"Yeah, yeah, yeah," I sang in a mocking manner and then I said, "Roger, this is our last trip together."

"But I have night vision. You know I can't drive at night."

"Me too."

Every morning I followed the same protocol of writing more of *The Mary Celeste* before my day became busy with patients. My writing to Artur and Paula had dwindled but they both knew I was busy with writing and working. I kept the romance going strong between Carla and Richardson who began to meet on deck as they had a lot in common besides being attracted to each other. Richardson also got along with Mauricio, Carla's son who looked up to him as the father he could only wish for.

The International Club was still my favorite place to go on Wednesday evenings but it had also flourished into informal potluck gatherings at each other's homes. I was at Brianna's house, one of the club members, when Paul, another club member who was seated next to me, said to the group, "I'm tired of dating, but I'm not going to stop until I find the right woman." Since I was the oldest of the group and consequently I possessed a world of experience in the department of love, I shared with him, "Don't be in a hurry to settle down just for the sake of being with someone. After sleeping with that person, ask yourself, 'Is this the one I really want to wake up next to every morning for the rest of my life?' If the answer is not an excited 'Yeah!' it means you'll be sorry!"

My patients loved the Activator Adjusting Technique and the Activator table, which was wide and comfortable with a slot in the center so my patients had someplace to put their noses while prone. Ray was one of my patients who loved lying on it versus any of the other tables. I had finished adjusting Ray and he was coming off the table when he remarked in a playful manner, "This table reminds me of a James Bond bed, the way it goes up and down."

I liked his analogy. "Yes, and someday when I can afford it, I'll make this room bigger and have a warm Jacuzzi just below the table so when the table brings a patient up they can just slide into the nice warm water." We laughed at the whole idea. On the way out he said, "I could use this table as my bed at home, it's so comfortable."

No matter how frivolous a statement, I had a serious problem with the way my mind absorbed daily occurrences, and at night, everything came into play. That night I had a nightmare that when I arrived at my office the next morning, the Activator table had been stolen. In my dream, I was obsessed by the thought of losing my favorite adjusting table and it felt like this dreadful event had been perpetrated by one of my patients. I immediately went to my filing cabinet and looked through all the patients' files to see who could possibly have done such a felony. To my surprise, it was Ray! It was right there in his file that he had been the last patient I treated and was the one with the spare key to our office. It made sense; he was a tall, well-built body builder and had always taken pleasure in saying to me, "You are so small I could easily lift you up with one hand behind my back." Such a statement made him automatically guilty. Only he could have carried such a heavy table on his shoulders. I woke up all stressed out since I would have to confront him and ask him for the table back. My nightmares were so vivid that sometimes I couldn't differentiate if I was awake or not for at least thirty seconds or so after I opened my eyes.

Zelma was from Germany. We had met at the International Club and started going out together since she was single and lived close to me. She liked to brag about her personality. "I'm a joyful person," she would say with the slight German accent much like my father's. "I'm not at all like my compatriots who are too serious about everything." She laughed louder than anyone else I knew. She was indeed a fun person to talk to and to go on hikes with but she was too blunt about expressing her desire for a man, any man. When she called Friday night inviting me to go to a western dance, I figured since we were friends I could be honest with her.

"Zelma, when a guy walks up to you, do you think you can concentrate at looking at his face instead of his crotch?" I giggled a little so she would not feel like I was being too hard on her.

"Well, they look at my boobs, so what's wrong if I also check them out?" she said with her usual piercing laugh.

"If I were a man, and a woman I just met kept staring at my crotch, I would stay away from her. I think you are intimidating them."

"Maybe you're right." I could almost hear her thinking. Then she said, "I have been wondering why I can't get anyone to ask me out. Do you think that's why they don't ask me out, because I'm intimidating?" She stopped laughing for a moment and then went right back at it.

Momentarily it crossed my mind that her laughter was what drove them away, but I went back to the subject at hand. "It's very possible; I would even go as far as saying you definitely are intimidating them."

"Let's test it out." She laughed. "I'm going to be very proper tonight." She laughed again. Everything sounded funny to her. I also needed to work on the sound of her laughter, but I had a feeling that was going to be a lot more challenging.

Zelma was a sixty-five-year-old woman with the badly wrinkled skin of a ninety-five-year-old. But her skin was the only thing that was worn out, because she had the shape of a slim twenty-year-old and both her stamina and physical health were outstanding. Men her age couldn't possibly keep up with her hiking, canoeing, and skiing and most likely would drop dead while having sex with her.

This morning I woke up thinking about *The Mary Celeste* and couldn't wait to be at my computer. For a touch of softness while traveling on the high seas, I added a scene where the captain, his family, and some of the crew members gather in the evening for a little entertainment, after little Sophie asks her mom to play one of her favorite songs on the piano. The moment is festive and lighthearted as Carla dances with her son Mauricio to the sound of a waltz. Everybody gets involved in the fun including the two Italian sailors who don't mind dancing together. Richardson was another sailor who walked into my plot as I was looking for someone to fall in love with Carla. Richardson asks Carla to dance. I felt we needed to have a real romance going on board and Carla and

Richardson made a good couple. As the music soiree goes on, even old Charlie gets a turn to dance with Carla. But trouble soon begins when James disrupts the joyful scene and violently shoves one of the Italian sailors against the wall so James can grab Carla and have her dance with him. Captain Briggs has to intervene and quickly brings the gathering to an end.

On Monday, Nancy flew in from California. She would be staying with me for two weeks. She drove me to the office every morning and then kept my car to look for treasures at antique shops. Besides Native American straw baskets and pottery, she was also looking for a series of very specific children's books that she and Sean collected. I was not into antiques. When I bought something old, it was because I was attracted to it, not because it would join a personal collection. After work, I took her to all my evening and weekend activities.

Nancy also loved dancing. Saturday evening we went swing dancing at the Crystal Ballroom and on Sunday, I introduced her to tango classes at the Viscount.

Once Nancy returned to California, I went back to cruising the internet searching for my dream mate. Ralph was right; I could not live without someone in my life. Artur was also right; I needed romance. Besides, I didn't want to become a spinster and go from a ripe plum to a dried up prune.

I was not surprised when I found Dick had returned to the internet dating scene. He was still using the same old picture by the fireplace, a definite antithesis of his real character. I had no doubts someone like me would fall for his humble, family man approach. His caption read, "Looking for a Christian woman with good Christian beliefs."

So if the poor woman was a Christian, he would not cheat on her? Another indicator for me not to trust religious men; my list of "the most untrustworthy" was getting longer and longer.

Spring of 2001

Monday morning I added two more people to *The Mary Celeste,* Adrien and Lorenzo, and kept James, who Artur mentioned was a troublemaker. I gave James the job of supervising the loading of alcohol barrels into the ship. At this point I wasn't quite sure where to go with James. I dreamed about him many nights and wondered what it was about the barrels that made me suspicious of his actions. I also moved Captain Briggs's retelling of his meeting with his old buddy Charlie to the start of the book, instead of in the middle during a possible volcano eruption. I was having fun with some of the sailors' stories too, and added Mireilla, who was ready to use a knife to defend her honor.

For the first time since I had been trying to find a soulmate over the internet, there was a good chance I had found the right person. He was an eye doctor and I began to consider our education and mutual backgrounds as the answer to a successful connection. Dr. Marshall was also very anxious to meet me because as he said, "I get a lot of emails daily, but it's very frustrating that these women writing to me don't seem to be reading my posting. You are the only one who obviously read it since you have noted my remarks and answered my questions. I admire that in you. How about us meeting at the coffee shop by Pioneer Courthouse Square on Saturday morning at eleven?

When our rendezvous was over, it crossed my mind that I should write a comedy book about dating. Dr. Marshall was seated on the outside steps of the coffee shop. He was wearing a colorful, flowery Hawaiian shirt, very short striped shorts, and sandals. And it was not that hot of a day. The first thing my eyes noticed were his legs that were covered with large, tortuous varicose veins, followed by his hairpiece, which was a shade darker than his sideburns. I prided myself in saying I was attracted to a man by his intellect more than his physical looks, but in Dr. Marshall's case, I had to admit that I was very disappointed. Also, because I'm a chiropractor, I'd rather hug people instead of shaking hands. Yet when I hugged him, he stiffened up like a statue. I know what Ralph would have said, "Mom, he doesn't know you from beans, what do you expect? You took the poor guy by surprise." Maybe I did. Dr. Marshall asked me if I liked ice cream and of course I said yes. There was a little ice cream parlor across the street. Dr. Marshall had vanilla, I had pistachio, and we took our ice cream cones and sat on a bench overlooking the square. He talked and he talked. His cheery clothes didn't match his negative, angry personality and huge ego. "I attribute my slim physique and youthful looks to eating only one meal a day," he said, looking at me and then at his vanilla ice cream. "This ice cream is it for today." I was thinking, *He's afraid I may want lunch and paying for the ice cream is all he's willing to spend, or he has a weight problem and eating once a day is how he keeps from getting obese, poor man.* He went on, "I can't trust women. All they're looking for is the money I make as a doctor. Except for you, I'm very disillusioned with the women I have been meeting from the internet." I waited to hear what made me special. He went on, "These women wear a ton of makeup and they look like whales. You are a rare find. How do you keep such a nice figure? Do you work out daily?"

I controlled myself from telling him he looked older than his age, the hairpiece needed to go, and if I had his legs, I would never wear shorts. Instead I said, "It's probably a big disappointment to you but I don't take care of myself," I said, "not at all. I attribute my 'skinny' look to my family genes because I eat three meals a day including lots of snacks, and when I get home today, I'll be having lunch and then a big dinner with my ex-husband. For the sake of our small children, I'm seriously thinking about giving my marriage another chance."

Who the heck eats a ball of ice cream and is satisfied for the rest of the day? What a creep! He walked me to the car and we shook hands. Good riddance!

I got into an embarrassing situation when I went to a tango class at the Viscount in downtown Portland. As always, after the one-hour class, just like with swing dancing, I waited for the "professionals" to come in to dance. They were always willing to "show and tell" their craft to a novice like me. With tango there were always more men than women and more than occasionally two men danced together due to a lack of the opposite sex. While everybody sat around the dance floor waiting for the music to start, I was chatting with a man seated to my left.

"That's a big scar you have on your neck!" I pointed to my own neck and moved my finger across it. I asked, "Surgery?"

"Yes, I had a herniated disc."

"Did you see a chiropractor before having surgery?"

"My wife doesn't believe in chiropractic and she felt I was better off with the surgery."

"Well, it's too bad you didn't get a second opinion. Sometimes surgeons are too much in a hurry to use their knives."

"My wife is the one who did the surgery!"

"Oh dear! Wow! I hope she knew what she was doing." I laughed at my own witty comment.

"This is my wife, Helen," he said, introducing me to the woman with a frown seated to his left. "She's an orthopedic surgeon."

"Nice meeting you, Dr. Helen," I said, while wishing I could disappear. But I didn't have to. They both got up and went to sit on the other side of the ballroom.

After my second email exchange with Ross, I wrote, "You sound very nice. How about we meet this weekend downtown?"

After what I went through with Dick, believing his heartfelt emails and then finding out later it was just pretty talk, I preferred to meet my date in person and get to know him face to face instead of through emails.

However, I ended up sending the following email to Ross the next morning after having met him the day before: "Dear Ross, it was wonderful meeting you yesterday but I won't be able to see you again. My ex-husband and I are definitely getting together for the sake of our children. He wants us to try to put our lives together again. I'm sure you can understand that. Sincerely, Veronica."

Oh how I loved computers! It made a messy situation disappear with the click of a mouse. I did like sensitive men but what I encountered with Ross had been beyond sensitivity. We had agreed to meet on Saturday morning at the farmers market in downtown Portland. I would be wearing jeans and a short silver jacket and standing under the bridge at eleven in the morning. I told Ross I was sure I would recognize him from the headshot on his ad. He was better looking than the picture, a very handsome young man with blonde hair and blue eyes. He had to be at least twenty years younger than me. I must have failed to notice his age when I read his ad. He saw me from across the street and without paying attention to the bus driver honking at him, he crossed in front of it and ran towards me. He grabbed my hands and kissed them. Unless I was the Queen of Sheba, I saw no reason to kiss my hands and I could already tell that he was too much of something or another for me. Then he put his right arm over my shoulder as if we knew each other for many years. It was an uncomfortable outburst of familiarity as we walked slowly through the farmers market. When I thought I had better do something to get his arm off me, he stopped, turned towards me with his gorgeous eyes gleaming and said, "You are so beautiful." He immediately proceeded to embrace me and would not let go. I used the rape getaway technique my son Steve had taught me many years ago. I relaxed my body to go limp and let myself slip down from between his arms, and then I quickly stretched my right arm out and used my hand to signal, stop. He laughed and said, "You are so cute when you do that." *Okay, I thought, there are hundreds of people all around us. I'm perfectly safe, and except for kissing my hands, acting all chummy, lying about my looks, and hugging me so strongly, he has not done anything really bad.* He was just too unreal for me.

We were standing by a deli shop and he said joyfully, "C'mon." He grabbed my elbow and led me in. "Let's have lunch," he said. "My treat."

He didn't sit across from me at the small round table. Instead he pulled the chair to my right side and we were so close that I could not keep his long legs and knees from touching mine. But I was glad he sat on my right side versus the left where I was deaf. "Would you like a Reuben sandwich?" he asked assiduously. "They make them really good here; it's their specialty."

"I do love them, but I like mine with extra sauerkraut and no dressing if it's okay."

"Me too," he said, showing a certain amount of emotion in his voice. "I can't believe how much we have in common! How about tea, do you like green tea?"

I nodded my head affirmatively. The waitress walked away with the order and he stared at me with teary eyes. "Do you have allergies?" I asked.

"No," he responded. Then he realized why I had asked him that question and said, "Oh, you mean my eyes. It's from the emotion of meeting you." Then he grabbed my hands and moved his face so close to mine that I looked away, because if I looked at him I would go cross-eyed.

"Tell me about yourself," he said, sitting back somewhat, but not far enough. Then he said, "Tell me everything about yourself. I can feel it here," and he pointed to his heart and added, "right here." He hammered his fist on his chest twice and kept going, "You and I are so much alike; we were made for each other."

I played with the idea of saying, "Let me tell you about my second husband. We grew apart and as such, things didn't work out, and then he died." But I needed some extra time if I was going to finish my Rueben. I was forced to do what my friend Leila once told me not to do on a first date unless I wanted to scare someone away. I pulled my hands away from his, moved my chair back enough not to breath on his face, put on a pensive dramatic look, took a bite of my Rueben, and began telling him bits and pieces about being married to Patrick and all that I had suffered before and after his death. Ross cried and cried and cried. I was proud of the effect of my storytelling. The more tears he poured out, the more memories he brought out of me. People around us were looking in our direction. The waitress brought us more napkins but didn't ask the usual questions, "How is the food? Anything else I can get for you guys?" After taking my last bite, I reached in my purse and put a five-dollar bill on the table. He looked at me, wondering. I said, "I would like to help with the tip." I stood and said, "I really have to go. I'm already late."

"Let's meet tomorrow?" he said.

I told him I would email him the next morning with all the details and just left it at that. When I got into my car, I turned the radio to my favorite classic rock station. The dating scene was a lot of work, but I wasn't ready to give up.

Instead of messing up my Saturday morning like I had done with Ross, I asked Jorge if we could meet on Friday during my lunchbreak at the small ice cream parlor on A Street in Lake Oswego. I sat by the glass window watching for his arrival. He parked his open-top black sports car in front of the ice cream parlor and then struggled a bit to pull his lanky body out of the tiny car seat. He would be better off driving my Toyota RAV4 with extra legroom and higher seats for easier access. His short white hair gave his fifty-five plus years a distinguished look. I had to smile at the thought that a woman his age with white hair would most likely be classified as nice but over the hill. He wore well-creased blue pants and a white sport shirt with a gold stitched insignia over his left chest. But his pleasing appearance became secondary once he began raving about his money, his big corporation, his buildings, and how many more buildings he was going to buy in Lake Oswego. "With the increase of aging folks all over," he said, "the need for more institutions specializing in the care for the aging is an utmost necessity and is an amazing source of money that can be made." His overall hunger for more money made me cringe. I was not meeting him to discuss business or old age homes. Another ten years and he would be a senior; perhaps he was thinking about his own impending future and which institution was most fitting for him. He ordered a burger and fries and I had an ice cream cone. I told him I would be sending him an email later, and once I finished the strawberry ice cream, I left in a hurry saying I was late for my first patient.

The intrigue aboard the *Mary Celeste* continued to thicken as the days went by. James was not only unscrupulous, but he also knew how to manipulate the sailors and create chaos.

Under James's influence, Adrien tried to take advantage of Carla, one evening. When Lorenzo, another sailor, came to her rescue, by pulling Adrien off Carla, Adrien loses his head and in the heat of the moment, stabs Lorenzo. James stood hidden, watching, until Carla cries over the dead sailor, then he shows himself and acts like Adrien's friend. Later in the evening, James pays a visit to Adrien with a cup of hot tea. In the morning, Richardson finds Adrien dead. Sarah's drugs, including the morphine prescribed by her doctor to be used only when Sophie and herself are at their death beds, have disappeared from their cabin's medicine box.

I sent a thank you note to a guy I met over the internet but never met in person. After I responded to his ad and told him my age he answered, "I have to be honest. Even though I'm five years older than you, I'm only attracted to women in their early to mid-twenties. I don't even mind if they have a child but they have to be young." At least he was straightforward and had not wasted my time.

My next date invited me to dinner at a restaurant near Hwy 205. I was fifteen minutes too early and stayed in the car waiting. It was 6:55 when from the corner of my eye I saw a bald, heavyset man entering the restaurant with a basketball in one hand and a bouquet of flowers in the other. It had to be Nathan, because he had told me he would be carrying those items. He didn't even come close to the picture on the internet. I drove off the parking lot but as I was ready to get on the road, I came to the conclusion that since he had lied in his ad, he owed me dinner. I was angry and hungry.

As I walked into the restaurant, Nathan waved. He handed me the flowers and said, "I know I don't look nothing like the picture on my ad. I'm sorry about that. This is the reason I had to tell you I would be carrying a basketball and flowers." He laughed and I felt obliged to laugh too.

His wife had died three years ago and he was still recovering from a nervous breakdown. His medication was making him gain weight. His hobby was collecting radios. We got along great, and he was a really nice guy, but not my type. When the bill came, I told him I felt better if I paid for my own dinner, since my ex-husband was back in town and most likely I was going back to the father of my children. It didn't work.

"I don't expect a woman like you to fall in love with me. You have given me the pleasure of your company this evening and it's been an honor to have dinner with you."

"Thank you. I also enjoyed meeting you," I said honestly.

He walked me to my car. "Would it be okay if I hugged you?" he asked bashfully.

We hugged briefly and then I got into my car. He stood holding the basketball under his left arm. I was sure that sooner or later he would find someone special; he deserved it. If I were fat and bald I would also put an old picture of myself on the internet and take my chances someone would like me for who I was on the inside.

Guys were not the only ones lying about their age or looks. My friend, Zelma, asked my help in putting an ad on one of the dating sites on the internet. I told her she was better off looking through the ads instead, like I did. Not that it was really working out for me. I just didn't want a bunch of emails coming at me like a snowstorm hitting my windshield, splash, splash, splash.

Zelma was sixty-five years old but insisted on entering forty-five years old on her ad. I did everything I could to make her understand that she was being deceitful and besides that, it was going to backfire on her when they saw her. I told her about my own experience with my last date. She responded, "If they don't like the way I look, they don't deserve me and I'm not interested in them, either."

I realized at that moment how similar the sexes were. Women would knock down men for always looking for younger, more attractive females but women did the same, even if not intentionally. In my younger days, I did think intellect was more important than looks. But as I aged, I learned that attraction and intellect went hand in hand, otherwise one might as well just get a roommate.

I made plans to visit my grandchildren in New Jersey. Ralph offered to cover me at the office and treat my patients while I was gone for ten days. New Jersey was far from being home anymore, but I missed my family and my grandchildren, Jacob and Shayna. I was also looking forward to visiting Mr. and Mrs. Ounuma at the Kobe Japanese Restaurant and my friends Fay and Terry.

I had a great time in New Jersey. Steve took a day off from work and we all went to New York City. We voted unanimously to visit the Twin Towers instead of the Empire State Building and we also went to the American Museum of Natural History where Jacob and Shayna enjoyed looking at the dinosaur skeletons. I took the kids to Sandy Hook and pointed to where I used to take their dad and his brother when they were their age, to look for pirate treasures, but now it was closed to the general public. But we did go to the beach and I helped them make sand castles even though it was windy and a bit on the cold side. I saw all my old friends and I felt spoiled by Diane and Steve when I was there.

But when my trip ended, I was glad to be back in Oregon treating my patients and back in my own environment. My heart was split between Oregon, New Jersey, California, and Portugal. I had moved so many times and traveled to so many countries that sometimes my nightmares took me to places where reality was nowhere to be found. I looked straight ahead and saw the ocean and beyond was land, but I couldn't see the land from my bird's eye view. Which side of the world was I standing on, the United States or Portugal? Was I in Oregon or New Jersey? When I flew to California through the magic of my dreams, why was I walking through the rooms of my house in New Jersey, but upon going outside, finding myself in the streets of Lisbon? I called my dreams the shambolic scramble of a time traveler's nightmare!

Summer 2001

They say if someone has one or two really good friends in their life, they are blessed. I felt I had been showered with blessings when I joined the International Club and befriended some awesome people. I had a total of ten good friends, each from another country, except for Maria who was also Portuguese. My friend Gisela, from Germany, had a home in Netarts, just a few yards from the sand, and she invited Maria, Claudia, Odile, Marcy and me to spend the weekend at her house. All we had to do was bring food and drinks. After lunch, we walked along the seashore collecting seashells and talking. Claudia and I exchanged dating horror stories and I learned of her experience growing up in Germany. We were surprised to find out how much we had in common when it came to our childhoods. By the end of our three-hour walk, I came to the conclusion that she was not as rough as she appeared to be. She was a very sensitive, kind, and considerate person, and I realized that she had built a wall to protect herself as her way of dealing with the many downs in her life. I understood that completely.

In the afternoon while running and playing ball on the beach, Odile hit her big toe on a rock. I examined her red blown toe and told her most likely it was broken, but that there was nothing that could be done except to ice it and keep her foot elevated. But just like when someone has a doctor in the family but they'd rather go to someone else for a diagnosis, Odile insisted on having us take her to the hospital. So after waiting over an hour in the ER, they did an

X-ray and told her she had a broken toe and should stay off her feet and use ice. But they did give her a prescription for pain meds.

In the evening, we gathered all the bounty that we had brought. Maria had brought all the ingredients to make a paella to die for and I made pasta with meatballs. Marcy, from England, took care of breakfast the next morning for everyone. Odile had brought some chocolate dessert that was already made, which worked out perfectly. Gisela had provided the accommodations and didn't have much to do except join Odile on the couch to keep her company while we did the cooking.

After dinner I offered to do facials for everyone using my secret skin formula that I had perfected through the years using the purest of ingredients. Before applying my undisclosed formula on everybody's face, including my own, I made my grandmother's original skin cleaning face mask with a couple of egg whites beaten until hard and a few drops of fresh lemon juice. No one could talk or even smile; everyone remained very still so as not to crack their faces as the egg white dried. After we took turns washing our faces with warm water in the bathroom sink, I applied my secret skin formula on everyone.

We all left the next day after Marcy made us pancakes, sausages, and eggs for breakfast. We swore to get together again.

While in chiropractic college, we had been taught how to treat our patients, but we were also told to keep emotionally separated from them. But I couldn't help from getting involved with everyone right on the first visit. I was lucky to work with Ralph as we often conferred with each other if we had a difficult case, but I would still wake up during the night thinking about how I could better help a particular patient. Some patients came in only when measures at home didn't help, so they came to have their pain taken away, but those following through with their treatment plan flourished like flowers in an oasis. We had an office meeting every week and we always brought up a success case to share with each other. My latest flower, my pride and joy, was Mr. Johnson, who was seventy-two years old and used to be an accountant. I bragged about him to everyone, without ever mentioning his real name, of course.

Mr. Johnson had lost his wife to breast cancer three months before he started care at our office a year ago. He had a history of diabetes for which he was taking insulin and he was also suffering from depression. I wasn't surprised to learn he had high cholesterol, too. He ate all his meals, including breakfast, at a fast food restaurant nearby. His life was lifeless. He sat all day watching television. His back and neck gave him constant pain and he told me he would do anything to have a full night's sleep without having to take pain meds. He came to all the appointments but he gave me a hard time about doing anything else, like cooking at home and joining a gym. I began feeling frustrated, so used my mother's tactic, "Mr. Johnson, do you want to live or do you want to die?" This was the way my mother always approached a problem having to do with choices. I told him I had joined the gym down the street from my office and since he lived in West Linn, there was no good reason for him not to be at the gym too. When he said he would think about it, I gave him the "naked truth." "If you stroke out because of your diet and lack of exercise, your wife, excuse my language, is going to be quite pissed off watching you from heaven." He left laughing and I figured I had just lost him as a patient.

I was shocked when I saw him at the gym on Wednesday. He was wearing a brand-new dark blue workout outfit and waved at me while walking on the treadmill. I went up to him and said, "Mr. Johnson, I'm so proud of you!"

"I joined the gym so that I can enjoy looking at all the pretty ladies working out." He was the epitome of happiness and I was thrilled by his new outlook on life.

My next step was his diet. I recalled what he had told me in the gym.

At his next visit, I handed him a cookbook. "I bought you a very special gift. This is a cooking book geared at teaching single people like yourself with diabetes, how to prepare their own delicious meals. Wouldn't it be wonderful if one of those nice ladies at the gym took a fancy to you?" I felt it was important to talk to him with a certain old-fashioned flavor like "fancy" and "nice ladies."

Two months later Mr. Johnson's VA doctor gave him a clean bill of health. He had been taken off insulin.

Mr. Johnson started coming in only once a month for regular maintenance but he was more than happy to share with me all his monthly adventures. He had started doing volunteer work as a bookkeeper at a retirement home in Lincoln City. Once a month he drove over and they let him stay for the weekend.

Jonathan, a West Linn high school teacher, was looking for someone to teach him Portuguese and he called me after one of my patients, who was also a teacher at the high school, told him I was Portuguese. Jonathan hoped to learn the language well enough so he didn't have to hire a translator every time he went to Brazil.

It turned out that Jonathan was a stone smuggler, an Indiana Jones kind of a guy. For the last five years, he had been traveling to Brazil about two times a year to pick up precious stones, which he sold to jewelry stores and private customers all over the world.

We met twice a week at my office and he paid me by the hour, as if he was taking my time as a patient. He knew some Portuguese, and had a basic idea of grammar. In the hour we spent together, we covered the dialogue needed to do his business in Brazil as well as discussing a bit of philosophy. One day he said in a slightly mocking tone, "It must be difficult for you to see how Brazilians have bastardized their mother language."

"Not really. It's kind of fun for me to listen to their accent; it's still Portuguese. The British say Americans have done the same to the English language." I couldn't help going on. "But a language has to change with the times and adapt to different cultures, just like Latin. So many people classify it as a dead language but look what happened. It developed into what is now known as Portuguese, Spanish, Italian, French, and even Romanian."

"Nothing really dies," Jonathan said pensively, and then added, "Latin became a fruit-bearing tree between countries."

I enjoyed talking to him. He was the chemistry teacher at West Linn High School, and a few of his colleagues and students who were also my patients, spoke very highly of him as being a fair teacher open to discussion and feedback from his students. If I had had a teacher like him when I took chemistry, I would have finished my degree in chemistry.

Carla and James had taken over my writing. Their relationship became the focus of mystery throughout the story. I wondered what tied them together? Something was going awry and all I could do was to keep on writing. I wondered if the love Carla felt for Richardson and the Briggs family would be enough to make her have a change of heart concerning whatever was going on between James and her. I did my best not to interfere and to allow the passengers and crewmen of the *Mary Celeste* to guide me with what I wrote. With each scene and dialogue, they were introducing me to several human factors like love, greed, jealousy, grief, romance, and murder. I was heartbroken when Carla's son Mauricio, fell overboard while running away from James. Mauricio had witnessed the murder of one of the sailors. It affected me emotionally to describe such a horrific dark scene as well as when others on board ate the rice pudding for dessert only to find out it had been contaminated with poison. Whether I liked it or not, I had to write as the events unfolded before my eyes. I was glad Artur had not given me a deadline.

I was at the International Club, when I noticed Jeff, who was usually a joyful, energetic person, seated in a corner with his head bowed down between his hands as if he had a headache.

"Are you okay?" I asked. "What's the matter?" I sat next to him.

"It's my birthday next week. I feel terribly depressed." He looked up to me with no tears but the same look a beggar would use to implore for a dime to buy a piece of bread in the streets of Lisbon. "I'll be thirty-nine years old next Saturday! I'm going to be an old man." The corners of his mouth turned down.

"You don't want to be thirty-nine years old?" I asked.

"No," he emphasized keeping his bottom lip down. "I don't want to be thirty-nine years old. I don't want to be old."

"Well, if you kill yourself today, you don't have to worry about being any older." I saw a look of surprise in his face. My mother would have said something like that. Maybe I was more like my mother than I wanted to admit. I tried fixing it. "What I meant to say is the alternative to not getting old is to die young." It did not sound much better but he sat upright and said, "I'd rather get old," he said, and smiled. "I know what you mean and I appreciate it." He hugged me.

"Nothing beats living, that's for sure," I said. "Are you healthy?" Being a chiropractor gave me the right to ask.

"Yes, I am. I really have nothing to complain about."

"Then you should celebrate your birthday. It only comes once a year."

I was invited to his party.

I had been very lucky to have had my Aunt Heydee and Mama in my life while growing up. I had inherited their natural gifts for facing life's ups and downs. Both, in their own way, had taught me how to handle tough situations even though sometimes I did say things that could be misunderstood. I blamed it on English being my second language.

I woke up one morning with a question. Besides alcohol, what kind of cargo was on board the *Mary Celeste?* What was the most precious cargo in the 1800s that could in those days provide enough profit for someone like James? What was his motivation to murder innocent people? The answer had to be something explosive, something for war, something for killing. Dynamite crossed my mind, but I wasn't sure when it had been discovered and had first been used.

I did some investigating on the internet and found the answer concerning what James might have hidden onboard the *Mary Celeste.* In 1867 Alfred Nobel mixed three parts nitroglycerine with one part diatomaceous earth to create dynamite—the most powerful explosive known to man at the time. Diatomaceous earth was a stabilizing component of dynamite, a very precious cargo. When Carla was to confess her involvement with James and the pirates later on, we would learn about the barrels filled with diatomite, which was much in demand in those days. I had to contain myself from writing to Artur about all the twists and turns of events. He was going to be flabbergasted when he read the new arrangement. I wish I could be there to see his face.

~ Chapter Fifteen ~

The Gift

I was entering the Thriftway grocery store in West Linn, just a block away from our office, when a tall woman in her mid-forties wearing a black coat, came running after me. She stopped me at the entrance of the store and called out, "Wait, please wait, this is for you." She was holding a small round ceramic bowl and handed it to me.

"You must be confusing me with someone else." I gave her the bowl back while admiring its earthly brown and gray shades.

"No, I'm not confusing you with anyone else," she said very seriously. "I saw you and I instinctively knew this belongs to you and no one else. By accepting this gift, your wishes will come true. Could even be love, can be anything you are looking for, it will come to you." She handed me the pottery once again.

"Really? Wow!" I was taken by surprise.

"I know it's hard for you to take this from a stranger," her voice took on an imploring tone, "but please, I'm hoping you will accept it. Please, it's yours."

"Thank you. It's really nice of you to give me this gift even though you don't know me." I noticed some dried flowers tied to something odd inside. "Is this an Indian arrowhead tied to a piece of paper?" I held it between my fingers carefully.

"The paper is very fragile. When you read the poem, you'll understand its significance. Thank you for accepting it."

"No, no, thank you for the beautiful pot. I really like it a lot."

She smiled, put both hands together, as if about to pray, bowed her head, and then left the store without looking back.

I bought a salad for lunch and couldn't help feeling special. A stranger had just given me something lovely out of the goodness of her heart. I was not quite sure why she picked me, but I was happy she did. It wasn't just because I loved pottery. The intention was what made it special.

When I got to the office, I showed it to Ralph and together we untied the knot and very carefully unrolled the flimsy little paper which he thought might be papyrus that was inside the pottery. We took turns trying to make sense of its small handwritten words about love never dying and wondered what kind of dried flower had been attached with thin twine to the black arrowhead. We came to the conclusion that the small pottery and its contents were most likely part of some ritual where upon by giving the wish of love to a stranger, love would find its way back to the giver, possibly something to do with Karma.

When I got home, I put the pottery bowl on my coffee table. It would make an interesting conversation piece. I lay in bed thinking about the bowl in the living room and wondered if it was going to work like she had said. I wondered about my destiny and if I was going to sleep alone in my comfortable bed for the rest of my life. Dear God, I prayed, it would be nice to have someone to share my life with. But I really don't want to date on the internet anymore; it's been one fiasco after another. Please dear God, I'd rather meet him naturally, in person. And I would like my soulmate to enjoy intimacy, to be kind, honest, intelligent, and creative, enjoy traveling, love music and the arts, and have a positive attitude about life. And then as I did every night, otherwise I could not fall asleep, I thanked God for all the blessings bestowed on my family and my friends. I always finished my little prayer by asking for peace on earth, which I was aware was a humongous request, but I figured if I asked God for the moon, a little peace on earth would be easier to attain.

Jonathan left for Brazil. He told me he felt confident enough with Portuguese not to hire anyone to translate for him. "When I return, I want to continue to have lessons once a week, so I don't forget what I've learned."

That was a wise decision because if you don't use it you lose it and that went for languages, too.

I was devastated when I received news from England; my cousin Max had been diagnosed with terminal cancer. I had to do something about it. During my lunch break, I bought a professional wooden easel, a small canvas, and a set of watercolor paints.

When I got home, I spent a long time staring at the white canvas, hoping I could get inspired enough to paint a gift of love so strong and magical that upon Max seeing it, the cancer would vanish. The ceramic pot a stranger had given me contained the gift of love. My painting to Max would contain the gift of health by being created from love. I painted the canvas white and then drew a thin gray line across.

Each night I added a different color, not sure of where to go with it except with each stroke of the brush, I prayed for Max to get well.

On Saturday I went to see Ralph and Susie, his girlfriend, parachuting at Skydive Oregon, a first for the two of them. I stood by the fence watching some parachutists landing on their own while others did tandem, as it's called when someone jumps with an instructor attached to their back. All new jumpers like Ralph and Susie were instructed to follow a certain protocol, which they learned in an all-morning class prior to jumping out of the airplane. I noticed everyone made it to the ground safely and I began playing with the idea of trying it myself. Mark, a man about my age waiting for his son to jump, stood next to me by the wood fence and we talked. He was a fire chief and a single dad. He was also very handsome. Before he left to meet with his son, who had landed, he asked me if I would be there the next Saturday. I could tell he liked me and wanted to ask me out but he was too shy. I told him it all depended if Ralph and Susie wanted to return; they had not yet jumped.

Mark left and so did the majority of the people around me. I found a soft grassy spot very close to the fence, and laid flat on my back enjoying the warmth of the sun. A new batch of viewers came by the fence and I joined them to watch the next group jumping. Colorful parachutes were opening in the sky like huge umbrellas, but none had the colors Ralph had told me to look for as the colors he and his girlfriend would have so I could take their pictures. I had not expected their training to take so long, but it made me happy; it meant they were learning the proper way of landing on the ground. I stood by the fence watching the latest parachutists land and then watched them walk by me carrying their gear. Two of them stopped where I was standing. I can't recall who said the first hello, probably me, since I am a scaredy-cat when it comes to getting physically hurt and I was trying to gather as much information as possible to make a wise decision concerning the safety of my possible jump. Our conversation turned into a philosophical exchange mostly between Dan, the younger of the two, and me. I did learn his age, he was younger than my two sons, but in all truthfulness, his youthful look was easily discarded by his mature attitude. In many ways he reminded me of Steven, one of Ralph's younger friends in New Jersey, who always came across as a young boy trapped in an old man's spirit. Dan and I were interrupted by Mike, the other man, who said, "Well, Dan, we better get going. My wife is expecting me about now."

"Nice talking to you both." I waved at them but Dan shook my hand.

I left the side of the fence and sat on one of the wood bleachers with others like me still waiting for their loved ones to jump. I was looking up searching to find Ralph's and his girlfriend's parachutes among some half a dozen others. I was surprised when Dan came back and handed me a little note. "This is my name, my email address, and phone number. Will you consider going out to dinner with me?" he said very politely.

"Oh sure!" I was being facetious. "Thank you for asking."

He left and I turned to two girls seated next to me, "Did you see that? The kid just asked me out. It must be a joke."

"You should take it as a compliment!" said one of them.

Ralph did jump and loved the experience but Susie got cold feet at the last moment and remained in the plane. When we got into the car, I told them about the thirty-four-year-old kid who had asked me out.

"Mom, thirty-four years old is not a kid. That's a man," Ralph said.

"He's too young. I'm not going out with him." In the back of my mind, I recalled what I had gone through with Michael.

"Oh I see, so you're prejudiced against young people," Ralph said.

"I'm not prejudiced."

"Yes you are. Going out with someone should have nothing to do with how old they are."

I was still not convinced and the next morning I called Steve. But he was the wrong person to call for advice. "Mom, a guy that age, he's only going out with you for one reason, sex! Just be careful. You know I love you."

I called my friend Leila in Georgia and told her about Dan. "From what you tell me he sounds wonderful. I think you should go out with him at least once. If you don't want him because he's too young, you can send him over to me." She laughed loudly with her so familiar cheerfulness.

Ujohn, a friend of ours who was building extra rooms in our office advised, "You should give the guy a chance before you make up your mind."

A week had gone by and all signs pointed to the fact that I should go out with Dan. I sent him an email accepting his invitation for dinner.

I got an email from Dan asking if I would like to meet him Friday night at 7:30 at McMenamins in West Linn.

It was a hard decision to pick the right outfit for my first date with Dan. Sylvia, our new massage therapist, advised me to wear the long flowery dress I sometimes wore at the office. "It makes you look professional," she said. I opted instead for the sexy look—a short black skirt, a lacy blue top, and black high-heeled shoes. On Friday I knew I had picked the right outfit, because some of my patients commented I looked very nice and they wanted to know if I was going somewhere special.

Dan was waiting inside the restaurant, seated at a table facing the entrance, most likely picked so he could see me as soon as I walked in. He walked up to greet me with his arm reaching out for a handshake. We sat across from each other. He asked, "Do you mind if I remove my jacket? I'm having a hot flash. I suffer from *men*opause," he said, accenting *men*. And then smiling he added, "No pun intended."

Coming up with a joke about a situation I found to be a curse in my life for the last five years made me laugh in appreciation of its descriptive word, even though men came from the Latin word, month. But I was not there to provide him with Latin facts. He had a very clean look—a starched shirt that was white with thin blue stripes and a dark brown suit, his clean, white shaved face accentuated both his short dirty blond hair and his big blue eyes with their amazing long eyelashes. It was the first time I was truly looking at his features since I was now just listening to him and was face to face. He saw the spine on my key chain that I had laid on the table and asked me about it. I told him I was a chiropractor. He was a machine operator for a cement company. I asked him about his family and he said, "Oh no, I was afraid you would ask me that. I have to be honest with you. I come from a dysfunctional family."

"Who doesn't?" I smiled.

"Oh my goodness," he exhaled loudly. "You can't imagine what a relief it is for me to hear you say that. Most women I've dated, when I tell them, it turns them off. You're an incredible lady."

"Thanks but what you see is what you get. I don't put on airs to impress anyone."

"I appreciate knowing that. I'm the same way."

"Well, then I feel you should also know my age since I'm a lot older than you."

"I don't care how old you are. Age means nothing to me. What's important is who the person is on the inside."

He offered me his coat when I mentioned I was a bit chilly and when his food came, he waited for mine to arrive before starting to eat. He was very polite. I felt protected and a feeling came over me that I could trust him.

We left the restaurant walking side by side to our cars. He stopped, looked up at the moon and sang softly, "When the moon hits your eye like a big pizza pie..."

I sang immediately, "That's Amore!" and kept walking away towards my car.

We laughed.

"Will I see you again?" He had remained in the same spot.

"Yes."

"Is it okay if I give you a hug, then?" he asked.

I didn't give it a second thought. I walked up to him and we hugged. I didn't hug him because I felt sorry for him or had no intention of seeing him again like all the "others."

I drove off smiling.

Dan and I remained in contact by email during the day and by telephone in the evening. I told him I couldn't meet him on Wednesdays because that was the night I went to the International Club. To my surprise, he and his last girlfriend used to be members a few years back. Out of curiosity, I asked a few of my friends at the club if they had ever met Dan, and by my description they remembered him and his girlfriend. Their opinion was very favorable; both were very nice people and they wondered why they had stopped coming.

Every day I learned something from my patients. For years I had wondered why I could not get myself to throw away a tissue after using it to blow my nose just once, and then one morning I saw it as clear as a bell when I watched one of my older patients use his cloth handkerchief, and then tuck it away into his pocket. Like him, I had grown up using a cloth handkerchief, which was supposed to last for at least a day unless you had a cold, and then it became a soggy mess. In those days, I had a collection of at least four or five handkerchiefs. Washing them—as gross as it may sound to us now living in this society of tissues that we immediately throw away after they're used—was something that didn't even enter our minds until the handkerchief was definitely "well used." This realization brought me much joy; I wasn't being cheap or super thrifty. I promised myself to pay more attention and throw away my tissues once I used them once or maybe twice.

I was at the Latino Women's meeting on Saturday morning when my cell phone rang at about noon. I went into the bathroom and closed the door as the music in the living room was making it hard for me to hear. It was Dan.

"Would you like to go to the beach with me today and watch the sunset together?"

"Today? Sure. I'm at a party in Beaverton but I can leave at any time." My heart was beating faster as I experienced a hot flash.

We met at the Home Depot in Beaverton, and I left my car in their parking lot. When I asked him what beach we were going to, he said, "It's going to be somewhere along the seashore; does it matter?"

"Nope, I like the excitement of the unknown. Besides, the whole coast is beautiful."

We talked all the way going and coming back, but I had to turn my head to the left quite a bit to hear him better. I discovered if I cupped the palm of my hand over my right ear as if holding my head up in a discreet way, I was able to hear a lot better. I wondered a few times along the trip if I should tell him I had difficulty hearing him. But I was managing the situation pretty well and I didn't think it was the right time to bring about my physical defects. I was also very careful not to tell him much about my life because as my friend Leila once told me, I had a heck of a life, and it was too overwhelming for anyone to hear about on a date, much less the second date. I let him talk and listened attentively as I was learning more about him. "I have always been attracted to older women," he said. "In my last two serious relationships, Donna was ten years older and Rebecca was twelve years older than me." He had broken off with Donna because they had grown apart and Rebecca had broken off with him because she couldn't see a future between the two of them; their age difference was too much for her to handle. "I gave up trying to find someone to date on the internet and then you and I met," he said.

"I know, and it happened probably because we both stopped looking," I said. Either that or the gift of love given to me by a stranger a few weeks prior, had come into effect proving good wishes always came true. When Dan made a left turn following a sign to a beach, I recognized the area. "We are in Netarts! Oh my goodness, my friend Gisela's house is right over there around the corner."

Except for Patrick, who was domineering to the point of being a bully, every man in my life had been dependent on me to make all the decisions. It was wonderful to finally meet someone who was in control but wasn't pushy. Dan had brought a picnic basket with a bottle of sparkling apple cider and two champagne glasses. He remembered from one of our emails that I didn't drink alcohol. He was so thoughtful! We took our shoes off and walked along the shore. I made sure I stood on his left so I could hear every word he said. He didn't walk ahead of me but walked next to me, and I felt it was right that I should hold his hand. He responded with a smile and said, "Thank you."

We sat on the sand and he opened the bottle of cider and we made a toast to life. As we talked, we would finish each other's sentences as if we had known each other all our lives. We agreed it usually took years of living together for such a thing to happen, so it was a bit weird, it was true, but definitely wonderful. It was late when we got back to Home Depot, but time didn't really matter; we were both happy being together.

On Tuesday night, Dan invited me to see the concrete plant where he worked. It was closed when we arrived but he had the key to open the tall metal gates and took me on a personal tour of the place as if it were his kingdom. Two years ago to be exact, Jim, his friend and co-worker, had come up with the idea of testing the settlement pond for pollution, which was supposed to separate the solid particles from the water. They deposited a dozen gold fish in the pond. The fish not only survived, but they had multiplied into the hundreds and some had grown to over a foot long. Because he loved gardening, Dan had also taken it upon himself to landscape inside the concrete plant by adding shrubs, flowers, and tall grasses, and a waterfall and riverbed along one of the walls of the plant. He undertook the job at no charge to his boss and paid for the shrubberies and flowers out of his own pocket. His work was hard, but he loved it and wouldn't change it for any other job.

We sat on a concrete wall divider listening to the owl family living on a tree not far from where we were and I put my head on his shoulder. His arms came around me and held me for a while and we kissed for the first time. Stars above, owls singing, fish jumping in the settlement pond, and the lights from the stars gracing us from above. When it came to romance, Dan's concrete plant had to be the most romantic place on earth.

I couldn't wait to see Dan again. It wasn't just because when we kissed Tuesday night I could hear fireworks, it went further than that. I had never met anyone like him and I was puzzled by how he had escaped all those years as a single man. I believed I had found a hidden treasure that was meant

Starry, starry night

just for me. I sent him an email and added, "Below the sand way deep in the darkness, the flowers are blooming in the desert garden."

The inspiration had risen from visiting his concrete plant.

Lots of people believe dreams say a lot about the dreamer or possibly what events are about to happen. There's a lot of hypothesis. My dreams tend to go in different directions and are often a concoction of nonsense.

But I would always remember a dream I had one night because it happened in the middle of the week and I wrote about it to Dan. In my dream, which was more like a nightmare, I was running around with a little prehistoric being on my left shoulder. The being looked like the Plecostomus we had in the fish tank in my office, which lived by eating the algae at the bottom and the sides of the tank. He was holding onto my shoulder as if for dear life and was gasping for air as he made fishy kinds of chirping sounds and tears rolled out of his bulging eyes. He was rapidly shrinking in size as I ran up and down streets looking for Ralph to help me. I saw a tall white church on top of a mountain and ran up the mountain, but by the time I got to the church, my legs gave in and I had to crawl up the steps on my hands and knees. At the top of the stairs I found a large bolted metal door. I stood and pounded at it with my closed fists and yelled out, "Open the darn door! We need help!" A priest opened the door and pointed to another priest kneeling by the wooden Jesus on the cross, busily dusting his feet with a feather duster. I cried out, "Please help him," and I pointed to my shoulder where the little being was struggling for air. "It can't breathe; it's going to die." The priest looked at it and waving the feather duster to push me out of his way said, "Sorry, but in my church we can only help Christians. Those things cannot be helped here. Leave." I woke up crying and wondering what that dream was all about.

Thank God when I got to our office Ralph arrived at the same time, because when we went by the back of the fish tank, I almost stepped on our Plecostomus which had obviously jumped out of the fish tank. He was twirling and wriggling on the carpet. I screamed, "Ralph, Ralph, the fish is on the floor! He needs to be put back in the tank!"

"So, put him back into the tank..."

"I can't. I just can't touch a slimy jumping fish. It gives me the creeps. You do it."

Ralph picked up the fish as calmly as pulling a thin thread off someone's shoulder and put him back in the tank. The poor fish was traumatized by the experience as I watched him sit on one of the plastic plants inside the fish tank. I shared my nightmare with Ralph. Was the fish telling me he needed help in my dreams? Could fish have some kind of mental telepathy we were not aware of? They did have a brain; I knew that for a fact, for as a child I used to love to suck on fish heads and the brains were the best part. Ralph said I was being silly to even consider that our fish had sent me a personal SOS message; the whole thing had been co-incidental.

I wondered if fish cried when they got taken out of the water.

On Saturday Dan invited me to dinner at Sweetbriar Inn in Tualatin. The waiter came by our table and inadvertently dropped a jar of cold water all over me. Hot flashes and cold water were a great combination. Dan said, "I admire the way you responded to getting your clothes drenched in water. If it were someone else they would have yelled at the waiter and even try to get him fired."

"Accidents happen," I said. I was glad he appreciated that I was not a stuck up snob.

Dan owned a condo in Sherwood. "I'm remodeling it at present," he said. "I do that when I get home from work in the evenings. When it's finished, I'll show it to you." I had always been turned on by a man who was handy with tools and construction. Like Tarzan, he could easily build us a house on top of a tree and in his strong arms, he could carry me across the forest to our comfortable treehouse.

Dan was in the Air Force reserve and I accepted his in-vitation to go with him the following Saturday to a picnic for soldiers and their families at his base. Dan was a very patient driver and didn't get agitated when other drivers cut him off on the road. I appreciated that attribute after what I had gone through with Patrick. If Dan lost his temper on the road, I would have stopped seeing him immediately. The base was very close to the Portland Airport and after we had hamburgers, potato salad, and corn on the cob, Dan took me inside some of the airplanes on the field. I was very impressed with how much he knew about them. He had an amazing memory for dates and names and anything connected with World War II memorabilia. His hearing was perfect; he could even detect a specific type of airplane engine just from hearing it fly over. I told him he would be fantastic as a history teacher. When he took me home, we made out in the car like teenagers. Then we talked for a while. He had a cat for many years that had been given to him as a kitten. From the picture he showed me, he looked a lot like Snooky. "He loves to play rough," Dan said. "He's like a mini tiger."

I was surprised he had a cat since he told me he suffered from asthma spells on and off. "If you're sensitive to cat dandruff, it can trigger an asthma attack. Did you know that?" I asked.

"What can I do to find out if I'm allergic to my cat?"

"The only thing I can think of except going to an allergy doctor is to put the cat outside for a week and if you have no problems with your lungs, then try it again by having him home, and if you start having problems breathing, then you'll know." I invited him to my apartment for a drink, just like they do in the Hollywood movies, but he said he had to get up early to go to work the next morning.

I still kept in touch through the internet with my friends Rod and Allan from California, but it wasn't the same anymore living all the way in Oregon, so we basically wrote about three or four times a year. The same had happened with my friends from school. Once we graduated we went our own way, and we lost track of each other except for Tom. He had opened a chiropractic office, married a Japanese girl, and had two sons. Every year for Christmas he sent me a picture of his family.

I was still writing at full force every morning at the office. My two hours were sacred; they were dedicated to *Mary Celeste*. For the last month I had been busy describing how everyone on board had been transported to the new world. I went along with them and there was no door like Artur had mentioned. I saw and experienced it as I got to meet "the older and wiser." I believe what helped me in dwelling in such possibilities were my dreams. I dreamed a lot about other worlds and for me to describe a flawless world was something I almost took for granted. All I had to do was pick the world where happiness existed, the one where illness and death were not part of its existence, and as such, little Sophie and her mom could recover their health. I could only presume Captain Briggs loved his family enough to stay with them, for their sake.

Jonathan, my stone smuggler friend, was back from Brazil. He stopped by my office one morning; he was concerned about the severe floods in Minas Gerais, Brazil. That was the region where he bought the precious stones and while staying there, he had bonded with the locals. He was worried about their safety and needs. "Since you speak Portuguese a lot more fluently than me," he said, "would you mind calling Father Rosario, a priest and friend of mine in Minas Gerais, and get a list of the supplies from him that they might need? I want to help them."

I called, but Father Rosario was not in. Maria Joana, the lady I spoke to, told me everyone was safe, but their elementary school had been seriously damaged by the flood. They had lost all their school supplies like books, pens, pencils, paper, and so on. I wrote down the list of items needed and gave it to Jonathan.

On Thursday evening when I finished taking care of my last patient, I rushed out of the office to meet Dan at Shari's at the next exit on Highway 205 in West Linn. When I got there, he was nowhere to be found. I sat on the outside bench waiting. I watched people going in and out and a half an hour later, I was still waiting. I was ready to give up when a man coming out of the restaurant said, "You're still there, huh? I noticed you when I went in."

"Yes, I'm supposed to meet someone. He said he would be at the Shari's in West Linn, but I guess he's not showing up," I said, slightly embarrassed.

"This isn't West Linn, this is Oregon City! If you get back on the highway and get off at the next exit, you make a left and go under the bridge, and that's the only Shari's I know of, even though some people call that area the Willamette, it's considered West Linn."

How fast could I drive? Very, very fast! They didn't call me Roadrunner for nothing when I used to live in New Jersey. Thank God Dan had not given up on me. He was seated at the last booth at the very end of the restaurant. He smiled when I told him what happened. "I had a feeling about that," he said. "That's why I waited. I was afraid that if I went to get you at the next exit, we might miss each other." He had just showed me his common sense and how patient he could be. I also learned why he had picked the furthest booth in the restaurant and why he asked me to sit next to him, versus across the table—he had something private to tell me. "I have to be honest with you," he said. "I hope this isn't a problem for you, but if you want to have more children, my doctor told me I'm not fertile enough, my count is very low."

If that was not lucky for me, I didn't know what was. "That's no problem at all," I said. "As you know, I already have two sons. I don't need or want any more children."

"That's a great relief for me," he said.

He didn't want to know my age, so I couldn't tell him that at fifty-seven my fertility days were over anyway. Actually, they were over when I was in my late twenties and my gynecologist butchered a simple Dilation and Curettage (D&C). But I wasn't quite ready to share my medical history with him just yet.

After dinner we took a walk to a park nearby. Except for the thin sliver of moonlight, it was quite dark when we began kissing. Before I knew it, we were lying on the wet grass making love, right out in the open field. It did cross my mind we could be seen, so I closed my eyes.

We exchanged emails the next morning. I closed my email with, "If you want to know the meaning of life, climb a mountain and take notes."

He wrote back and added at the end, "Even the moon must dream…of the stars."

Jonathan called me at the office. "Veronica, would you mind calling Father Rosario, the priest in Brazil, once again and find out if he received the school supplies and the toiletry items they asked for?"

Father Rosario was in. He said, "Please tell Jonathan we received the care packages and we are all in debt to his kindness, and you, what is your name?" he asked. "You work with him, you are his friend, right?" His happy-go-lucky tone of voice bounced up and down as if any second he would start singing to the beat of the samba.

"My name is Veronica and yes, I'm Jonathan's friend."

"It's a pleasure to speak with you, Veronica. Are you coming over today?" His Brazilian accent was very charming.

"Maybe in the future I can do that. I have never been to Brazil but I would like to someday. My mother was born in Manaus."

"That is nice, I like Manaus, I was there once, very nice. Now you come over today, okay?"

I laughed; he was funny. "I'm sorry," I said. "But Brazil is very far away from the United States. I can't just go today."

"Not too far if you take an airplane now. You can stay with me in my house."

Sounded like a plain and simple request, from a child, maybe.

"Thank you so much for the invitation," I said. "But I really can't leave right now to go to Brazil. I... I have patients to take care of."

"Pleeeease come over now. Pleeeeeease!" He was seriously pleading.

"I'm sorry but I have a regular job and I can't just leave." I felt guilty saying that, as in, what was the matter with me, why couldn't I go?

"Pleeeeease come today, pleeease!" He pleaded again.

"Okay, I have to go now," I said apologetically. "I mean, back to my work, I work, I'm sorry. Bye-bye." I felt horrible hanging up on him. He had to have been a grown man for sure since he was a priest. Maybe he was a very young priest, still a child at heart to even imagine I could just abandon everything, pop onto a plane, and be there in a couple of hours.

Thursday morning, September 6th, Nancy flew in from California to spend two weeks with me. During the day while I was working, she used my car to go antique shopping.

I told Dan about her visit and he was very understanding when I wrote about spending the weekend with Nancy. I invited him to meet her on Monday evening when she and I would be going tango dancing. He said he didn't mind coming as long as he had two drinks prior to dancing. He was so cool and had such a great sense of humor. I knew Nancy was going to like him.

~ *Chapter Nineteen* ~

9/11

September 11th, I was taking my morning shower when I heard Nancy's urgent shouting, "Veronica, hurry up, there's something wrong going on in New York City! I just turned on the television to watch the news and they're showing the Twin Towers collapsing after a plane flew into it. Hurry! Hurry! This is serious!"

I came out wrapped in a towel. "Oh, most likely it's a Hollywood movie," I said. "They did something like that many years ago where they announced on the radio about Martians attacking the earth and everybody fell for it. Try another station."

She did, but all the stations were showing the same video, a plane flying into the Twin Towers and then the building collapsing. Neither one of us could believe our eyes. Was America under attack? I immediately called Steve in New Jersey. They were also in shock with what was happening but thank God they were fine. Just a few months ago when I was visiting them, we had been at the very top of the Twin Towers enjoying the view of New York City.

All flights had been canceled until further notice. Nancy rented a car and drove back to California. Al, who was visiting Ralph for a month and was ready to leave the next morning for New Jersey, could not leave.

Dan came over and stayed the night. He was concerned he might be called back into active duty. A good neighbor of his had shared her nightmare with him that she had seen him being gunned down while holding onto his rifle.

We held each other most of the night counting the blessed time we had together and fearing for the worse.

Since September 11th, there was an increase in patients with complaints of jaw pain and headaches. I had no doubt it was associated with what happened in New York. Even though it was way out on the East Coast, it felt very close to home. Everybody was stressed out and at night, they must have been grinding their teeth.

Our enemies had proven America was no less vulnerable than any other country. On the other hand, some positive events began taking place. Laurie, one of my patients who worked in the courthouse, told me, "Since 9/11 a lot of divorces have been canceled and there has been an increase in marriages."

When I finished writing the last page of *Mary Celeste*, I felt the emotion of the moment as part of me vanished into the ocean along with Carla and Richardson. All the characters visiting me each morning throughout those months, smiled back as they said good-bye. I had been a witness to their existence. I could describe the color of their hair and eyes, and even describe their individual scent.

I gave Ralph a summary of the story. He listened while moving his head slowly up and down in an appreciative manner. "I'm impressed," he said. "It's a very original story with lots of dynamics."

I translated the last few pages into English, word for word. "I really like what you've done with the end. Very original, the whole story is very original. Your writer friend is going to be very impressed, I'm sure."

I also shared the end of the story with Dan. Since we had been dating, I had been sharing with him each new chapter that I wrote. He encouraged me to have *The Mary Celeste* translated into English once it was published in Portuguese. "I can't wait to read it," he said. Knowing that Ralph and Dan liked it was very important to me. I was sure Artur was going to feel the same way when he read the ten chapters I had put together. He didn't want me to send the manuscript as an attachment because he was afraid it would fall into the wrong hands. I sent the floppy disk in the mail. I kept my fingers crossed that as soon as he got it, he would read it, and then start adding his own writing so it could get published next year.

~ *Chapter Twenty* ~

The Loss of Mary Celeste

Autumn 2001

I shared with Paula and Artur, "I have found my true soul-mate." Dan had also been bragging about me, because every time I met one of his friends they said, "So you're the woman Dan talks so much about."

But when Dan told me one morning he was serious about our relationship, I got scared and changed the subject.

I received an email from Paula wishing me the best and that she was very happy to hear I had found someone special in my life, but I didn't hear from Artur.

"I haven't bowled for years," I shared with Dan sitting next to me and with Ralph and Susie, his girlfriend sitting across from us. We were having burgers and fries, something one had to do when at a bowling alley. "Remember Ralph, how I used to take you and your brother Steve to the bowling alley in Lakewood, New Jersey? Let's see, you were about nine and ten years old, and that would make it something like…1973. Wow, how time flies!" At this point of the conversation, Dan found out exactly how old I was. A lot older than he had thought.

He said, "You don't look more than ten years older than me and besides like I told you, I don't care about your age. I love you for who you are."

Dan had been living with me since 9/11. He was still working on his condo after work, which by the way he described it, was a hell hole with the floors being removed and the kitchen being remodeled. I had told him he could continue to live with me while his condo was in such disarray. He really appreciated my offer and a week did not go by without him politely saying, "Thank you," as if to make sure I did not forget he valued my offer. I also noticed when we went out that he never jaywalked and when we went to the movies, he never took advantage of seeing another feature for free; he felt it was utterly dishonest. If he got the wrong change while shopping, even if it was just a penny, he would give it back to the cashier. He really went out of his way to show his honesty in everything he did.

Dan bought a full size washer and dryer set on special at Sears and asked me if I would mind having them in my apartment until his place was finished. Since I didn't own such luxury items, but had the space and even the hook ups available in the kitchen, I was glad not to have to make any more trips to the laundromat on weekends. He was hoping when he was finished remodeling his condo that I would move in with him. I didn't want to move out and I didn't want to think so far into the future. Life was good the way it was.

I had no idea what was going on with Artur. He sent me short, sporadic emails with no mention of *Mary Celeste.* What made it even worse; they were missing the usual enthusiasm that used to be part of his writing. I sent Artur a short email: Please let me know what is going on. Thanks, Veronica PS. Did you get the floppy disk with *Mary Celeste?*

By having Dan living with me, I was learning a lot about him. He had been writing poetry since he was a sophomore in high school. He brought over a collection of handwritten poetry, journals, and photographs; he loved taking pictures. Sometimes I would ask him to read one or two of his poems. He was happy to do it even though he felt bashful about his talent. He seemed to lack selfish thoughts or vanities. He said his favorite color was clear. He was always ready to help and didn't ask anything in return. He was twenty-three years younger than me, but he knew a lot about life and I could even add that he was a lot more mature than me.

Mr. Agar came to our office for the removal of a lump slightly below his armpit. It was a lipoma, a non-cancerous fatty tumor, which for no other reason than it wants to grow, looks like a round welt under the skin. With palpation, a lipoma slip-slides under the fingers, much like in a horror movie where the body snatcher creature moves under the victim's skin. A few months prior, we had removed one from a patient's shoulder that was so big it almost didn't fit into the glass jar we store them in. We stored them as sometimes patients were curious to see what their lipoma looked like. If the skin moles looked suspicious, we sent them out for a biopsy but for lipomas, we never did; they were harmless. Ralph informed Mr. Agar, "If the lipoma doesn't bother you, you're better off leaving it alone, unless you don't mind a scar from the stitches." But Mrs. Agar wanted her husband to get it removed and that was a good enough reason for him to have the procedure. We gave him a local anesthetic and Ralph was pulling the "thing" out and was cutting its thin "tentacles" one by one, very carefully, so as not to leave any behind or it would grow back. Mr. Agar calmly watched the procedure. "Just one more of these to cut out and we will be done," said Ralph, while wiggling one of the "tentacles" under his probe.

"That's funny," said Mr. Agar. "When you do that, it makes my leg move."

Good thing Mr. Agar was awake to give us feedback. Ralph put extra care into removing the lipoma without cutting the nerve that moved Mr. Agar's leg.

I could only imagine what kind of damage was done to the human tissue when a surgical knife cut deep into the body to fix or remove an organ, which wasn't too different than having back or neck surgery.

I received an email from Artur. "I'm so sorry but I'm very busy. Don't worry about me," he wrote. "I'm doing well. I'm just writing to assure you that I liked what you have written." That was it? Short and sweet—he liked it? His response was beyond unnerving. Where was the zest and excitement of finally having the book in his hands? My goodness, we were talking about a whole book, which had taken my heart and soul to create.

Concerning the music tapes I sent him. He gave me a short answer, "I'll let you know if it goes anywhere." He was so melodramatic when asking me to do something, and now he was like a crude, unfamiliar person. It felt as if he was telling me to stop bothering him. I told Ralph about it and he said, "That's not right, what he's doing. Tell him how you feel; be honest."

I wrote, "Artur, you have been a great disappointment by not even letting me know when you received the floppy disk with our book and then waiting this long to acknowledge it. Did you even read it? You could at least show some respect for what I did and the hours I put into writing the music for your poetry. You could at least say what's on your mind. I'm assuming you hated everything I did, but ignoring me is very hurtful after all these years as pen pals." I read it twice and then deleted it.

I got up in the middle of the night to go to the bathroom and instead of leaving the bedroom through the doorway, I walked straight into the bedroom wall. Vertigo! It had happened to me once many, many years ago, when I was still living in New Jersey, and I remember I was taken to the emergency room and given meds that knocked me out for almost a week. And still the symptoms lasted two weeks before the dizziness went away completely.

Dan had to drive me to my office.

"Here I am, one of your patients," I said to Ralph. "Can a chiropractic adjustment help?"

"Let's see what an upper cervical neck adjustment can do," Ralph responded with a confident smile.

He carefully palpated my neck and then he swiftly adjusted it. I felt a puff coming out from my right ear and then an immediate relief from being dizzy. I was able to treat my patients all day without any problems except for getting slightly dizzy at about five in the afternoon. Once again Ralph adjusted my neck, and I went on working until seven without any further issues.

The next morning I felt fine but when I got to the office, I asked Ralph to adjust my neck once again.

I bragged all day to my patients about neck adjustments for the relief of vertigo.

I waited a few days and sent another email reminding Artur to change Carlo's name as it would be too confusing to the reader to have a Carlo and a Carla. I added, "Sorry that I made a mistake when I created that character, but it's an easy fix when you go over the manuscript." It was my way of telling him to get with it, without being pushy.

I guess I had a thing for forenames like Carla, Carlo, and of course, Coral. I had used Coral as my pen name to write to Dick.

Dan took me to see his condo in Sherwood. It was far from finished but he made a pathway between cans of paint and all his tools so I could see the kitchen, the bathroom, and two bedrooms. The three layers of vinyl flooring that Dan had told me kept him so busy trying to peel off had been completely removed except for in the laundry room and part of the kitchen. Holding my hand, he guided me to what used to be his bedroom and was presently being used as a storage space while the living room and kitchen were being painted. When I saw a bed under an array of boxes and saw King Tut standing upright against a wall, I took a deep breath of relief. When we first began dating, he had told me he loved Egyptian history so much that he had a full size sarcophagus of King Tut in his bedroom. In my mind's eye I had visualized him sleeping in it and didn't ask any further questions. Instead I reasoned, so what, he sleeps inside a sarcophagus, maybe he doesn't have a bed. Maybe he bought the sarcophagus so when he dies he already has the type of coffin he likes.

In the second bedroom, I couldn't miss seeing a medium size metal swastika hanging on the wall along with large framed German and American pilots' paintings and pictures. He saw me staring at the swastika and before I could even ask him why he had something associated with the German Nazi Party on his wall he said, "I'm not Jewish so I don't have any personal or emotional feelings towards it. I like collecting all kinds of paraphernalia connected with World War II."

I did not understand his lack of feelings towards a repellent insignia associated with the killing of so many innocent people but it wasn't my house to tell him how to decorate it. I also met his kitty; he was living outside and according to Dan, happy as a clam at high water.

Artur wrote, "I implore you to forgive me but I have been very busy for the last two months." How busy could he be? He was retired and when it came to writing, I was the one doing that for him. How much time could it take to read the manuscript and send me an opinion? I was very disappointed because if it had been me, I would have sat down as soon as possible and read our book. It crossed my mind that he did read it but was too embarrassed to tell me what I had done was trash even though I was very proud of my final product.

Dan and I were attending the International Club and talking to Maureen and Jorge, her boyfriend. We got along great every time we got together. Finally I thought it would be nice to know Maureen a little more in depth.

"So what do you do?" I asked.

"I'm a medical doctor, and you?"

"I'm a chiropractic physician."

Dan added, "Veronica does a great job with fibromyalgia patients." Dan bragged about me every chance he got. She didn't respond.

I went on, "My mother had fibromyalgia and in those days the treatments were sedatives. Her brother was a medical doctor and that's how they kept my mother from complaining about pain. She died from prescription drugs. Because I saw what it did to my mother, I now have a lot more sympathy towards those who are affected."

"Really?" said Maureen. "When I have a patient with fibromyalgia I'll refer them to you. Oh, yes, I did have one patient with fibromyalgia a few months ago. I did give him some pain medication and he's doing great now." She smiled proudly.

"What was the cause of his pain?" Dan asked.

"Who cares? He's not complaining anymore."

"Don't you want to know the cause?" Dan asked.

"I'm not a psychiatrist, I'm a medical doctor. I don't have time for those types of patients. They're all emotionally disturbed."

"My mother was not emotionally disturbed. The pain was very real to her," I said defensively.

Silence fell between us like an ice curtain and our sporadic friendship came to an end.

We no longer sit together at social functions.

I received another email from Artur, "So sorry about my silence, I have been very busy as you know. As soon as I can find the time I'll start working on *The Mary Celeste*." I wasn't going to hold my breath. I was busy too.

In my opinion, Dan's work schedule was beyond human endurance. He complained about the hours and some of the people he worked with. I told him, "If you are so unhappy, quit and do something else." To which he would say, "I get paid well and can't afford to lose such a good paying job. He never knew what time he had to be at the concrete plant until the evening before, because it all depended on when the trucks were called to make the deliveries, which could be any time between two and five in the morning. During the week, nine was officially his bedtime.

I had a choice of staying up, but I chose to be next to Dan so I went to bed early, too. I was getting plenty of sleep; I didn't get up until seven.

Talk about being lucky! My friends Mark and his wife Janice planned on going to England the following month for a two-week vacation. They promised me that when they got to London, they would get in touch with my cousins and give my watercolor painting to Max. I prayed that when he saw the small canvas covered with lots of colorful strokes crossing each other, the positive energy emanating from the painting would cure him. Why not? It was filled with hours and hours of good wishes, and that's what miracles were all about. After all, didn't the pottery filled with love wishes work out for me?

I was the only one who knew the purpose of the painting.

I finally discovered the reason why Artur had been too busy to write. Besides politics and whatnot, he had found someone special. According to him, he had narrowed it down to three women to choose from through his connections on the internet. Supposedly I was his favorite for a long time but when he realized all I wanted was a friend, he gave up on me. "I went to Spain," he wrote, "and met my second choice but she did not fit the criteria I was looking for. I decided then to go to Columbia and visit my third choice. She is a very successful lawyer and has two daughters from a previous marriage. We got along great. I asked for her hand in marriage and we are planning to get married next year. I know you will be happy to know that just like you, I have found the love of my life."

I knew it! I just knew that when he wrote me those really long emails about himself, most likely he was sending copies to other women, as Dick used to. Although I was upset with Artur, I sent my very best to him and his fiancée.

Thursday November 29th Artur wrote me a three-page email. "I received your email a while ago," he wrote, "and I should have responded, but lately as you've noticed, I have not been writing as regularly. But that doesn't mean that I've forgotten you, since you are deep in my heart as a great friend. Even though I don't write to you as often anymore, inside of me I know that even from afar, you are someone I'm connected with by a beautiful feeling of a true and sincere friendship. I must address the past news you've given me, that you found true love, as I cannot go on writing without responding to your news that you have all of a sudden found someone so wonderful. I must tell you how happy I am that you found love and after sharing such an update with me about your new relationship, I can only pray for true happiness and joy in your life. I am overwhelmed by knowing about your newfound happiness and that you are enjoying such a wonderful time in your life. I give thanks to God for all that. Now let me tell you about our book. I read it when I first received it, but it was so long ago, that I had to read it again not once, but twice, to be able to remember what I had originally written."

I was horrified! Except for Carla and her son, he gave me no credit for the other characters I had developed. According to him, he had been the one to come up with all the characters and the whole plot. Even the name of *Marie Celeste,* apparently he had been the one who had decided to change it to *Mary Celeste.* Oh my God, he had forgotten what he had written! Didn't he keep a copy of what he sent me originally? I was amazed at his nerve to write such lies. Either that, or he was going senile since he wrote, "I have been working on *The Mary Celeste* daily. A lot of work, many hours spent typing and I have the first chapter almost done which is about a mysterious old man giving me, the author, the secret documentation to the true story of *Mary Celeste,* which I intend to add to the beginning of our book. I'll be sending this chapter to you soon so that you can put your special touch to it as you have done to some of the stories in our book. About the book, this is it for now." He had been busy writing the first chapter about an old man giving him the story? I had given him the story! He made no sense, nothing made sense. Then he wrote, "I have also been involved in politics these last two months. Very busy indeed as sub-director of the political campaign to help my friend, the president of Felgueiras, to win the election. You won't hear from me for a while as I'm getting prepared for this Christmas to go to Colombia to meet with the lady I'm in love with. Well, this is a long letter but when I open my heart to you this is what happens. A big hug, a very strong hug, and a kiss full of love from your friend, Artur."

A patient asked me, "Will you stop doing chiropractic when you retire?" I was very quick to smile and say, "The day I retire is when I drop dead." I was on a constant spiritual vacation and at the end of the day, I went home smiling, content with my life and feeling privileged to have been of service to others. I shared with Dan my daily encounters and he listened attentively. I believe that was the reason he had become more holistic in his views about health.

Mark, a fifty-two-year-old professional golfer, came in to get adjusted whenever he was in town. He was an interesting case because even after having therapy of moist heat to help relax the muscles, when he got adjusted, his back muscles went into severe spasms. I had another patient who was a sixty-one-year-old woman who swam and did aerobics on a daily basis and ran an apple farm with her twenty-year younger husband. Her response to an adjustment was burping! I had to leave the room right after I adjusted her. Thank God she only came in once a month!

Those two patients had unique responses to having their spine adjusted. Most patients just felt great afterwards.

Even though in many aspects we are all anatomically the same, we are exquisitely different, and I find it interesting how everyone responds differently under the same conditions. A good example would be two patients who had lower back surgery two years ago on the same day and as I found out later, by the same surgeon. Bill was thirty-seven years old and Stephen was fifty-eight years old. Stephen's surgery was successful and he came in for maintenance care once a month for back stiffness. Bill on the other hand, had six unsuccessful back surgeries. He lost his job, and wound up spending most of his time in bed on morphine. When he walked into our office, he used a cane for support and I knew he was hurting bad since he drove all the way from Vernonia. Seeing what had become of Bill was very difficult for me. I helped him get Social Security benefits but in my opinion, his life was over when it came to having a normal existence. Bill and Stephen were the poster adults for surgery of any kind. They were an example that surgery was a 50/50 gamble and it should only be considered if it was a life or death option or if surgery was the only option to possibly having a normal life.

After experiencing flashes of light coming from my right eye, even in the daytime, I went to see an ophthalmologist in Lake Oswego. I was diagnosed with two retinal tears.

Sooner or later there is a point in everybody's life when suddenly one realizes our body parts are far from being indestructible. Surgery was going to be a pain in the neck to put it mildly, since I would have to lie face down for a few weeks. I was also told in some cases that vision could take many months to improve and for some people, it never did. The odds were against me since I didn't do well with gambling or medicine. I needed a miracle.

Ralph and I only saw patients three times a week. We saved Tuesdays, Thursdays and Saturdays for other doctors to rent space in our office and with that in mind, we had two of the larger rooms divided into four treatment rooms. Our practice was growing steadily as we were blessed with three licensed massage therapists, a naturopath and an acupuncturist. I began putting into the Universe the need for us to have a medical doctor to join our holistic practice.

The ad in the Oregonian News worked out great. Dr. Garry Kappel, an optometrist, answered the ad. Jeannette, our front office person, offered to answer the phones, make the appointments, and collect the patients' payments for him as part of her ongoing job. He loved the idea of paying a fixed rental fee and not having to hassle with all the bills attached with running an office. He had all his equipment moved in that weekend and was ready to start seeing patients the following Tuesday.

Joyce, a twenty-seven-year-old mother of two young children, showed me her abdominal hernia. A noticeable bulge under the skin was visible even while lying relaxed on her back with her knees up.

Her insurance would not cover the surgical procedure because they classified it as plastic surgery. She suffered with pain pressure of tissue pushing its way through the weakened region when she was having relations with her husband and also when she wanted to lift her two-year-old and three-year-old. I was going to take matters into my own hands while Joyce was undergoing the fifteen minutes of therapy of moist heat for her neck and upper back. I called her insurance company and asked to speak to her agent, the same one who had told Joyce she was not entitled to plastic surgery.

Some people believe after we die that we keep coming back and that what we learned in a previous life will come in handy in the next visit to our planet. I like to believe that if we pay close attention to what we learn along the way, we can use such knowledge right away and then we don't have to keep coming back like fools over and over again. Why wait to return to do better? If we start using what we learn right away, there's no reason to come back; that's my motto.

Yes, I was half-German, and that part of me made me strong, focused, and some may even call me hardheaded, but when I needed to put on a dramatic performance, I thanked God for being half-Portuguese. I got on the phone with one goal in mind—to convince Ms. Cornelius, the insurance agent, that Joyce needed surgery ASAP. After giving Ms. Cornelius the patient's name, birthdate, and ID number, I added, "If you were twenty-seven years old and your guts were spilling out every time you hugged your children, would you consider fixing such a problem as plastic surgery?"

"What do you mean guts... I didn't..."

"I mean your intestines. I mean your guts pushing through because that's what's happening to my patient. She does not want plastic surgery! She does not care if she gets a scar! She just needs to get her insides held in place by whatever means can be used. Part of her insides can be felt as if trapped. You must have heard of a strangulated hernia and as you know, it can become life threatening, right?" I was only expressing my enhanced emotional state.

"I'm sorry. We didn't know it was that bad. You sound so upset, it must be really awful..."

"You would cry too if you saw her. She's not able to pick up her children in her arms and hug them. It's also affecting her relationship with her husband, if you know what I mean. Pleeease, can you help her? (If anything I had learned something from Father Rosario.) Pleease, she's in my office now, can I tell her that she can go see a surgeon and have her hernia fixed?" I waited silently for a miracle.

"Okay, you go ahead and tell her she can see a surgeon and to give me a call back when she gets a chance. I'm going to accept the claim."

"Thank you Ms. Cornelius, you are an angel!" I ran to the treatment room to give Joyce the good news.

My gloomy future concerning my eyesight was hanging over my head like a dark cloud and then I realized, my goodness, I have an eye doctor right here in my office, Dr. Kappel.

He examined my eyes and confirmed the retinal tears. He did not believe in drugs or surgery, however; he was a holistic doctor. He prescribed OptiVision Forté for me, one of the dietary supplements he had created specifically for patients about to lose their sight and who had other eye problems.

Two weeks later after taking OptiVision, the light flashes disappeared. Just to make sure, I went back to my original eye doctor who said, "I guess sometimes it heals on its own; the tears are gone."

I told him about OptiVision Forté and maybe he should consider prescribing it to his patients. He laughed and said,

"I don't believe vitamins can do anything, you were just lucky."

I considered myself more than lucky, I was blessed to have Dr. Kappel working in my office.

Jonathan was back from another trip to Brazil. "You won't believe what happened to me," he said. "The morning after I arrived in the US, I woke up to my radio alarm and couldn't understand the news. *What's that foreign language?* I asked myself. It was English! Can you imagine? I didn't recognize my own language!" We laughed.

For over a month, he had been submerged in the Portuguese dialect in Brazil and switching the brain waves from one language to another so suddenly was a challenge.

Jonathan handed me a shoebox filled with beautiful precious stones and asked me which one I liked the most. When I picked a blue one, he said he wanted me to have it as a thank you for helping him learn Portuguese.

On Wednesday December 26th an email came from Artur. He wrote, "I wish you a good Wednesday even though this 'holiday' is not part of your religion." He was most likely referring to Christmas but did not say it. His rampage on words had started bothering me more than usual; it was as if he couldn't speak the truth. So much of his text seemed to include a roundabout of words, meaningless words. He went into his usual poetic discourse about how important I was to him. His second large paragraph was about how he had worked for three months now to help a friend to be mayor even though all odds went against her. But she had won and they would be celebrating over dinner with other politicians. I really couldn't care less about politics; all I wanted was to get *The Mary Celeste* finished. He went on, "I want to inform you that I did finish the first chapter as of the 24th but when I got to the end, I changed my mind while writing. In reality it is not complete and I have decided to take the manuscript with me to Columbia where I'll be staying until January 23rd." I thought he had already left for Columbia to spend Christmas with his honey. And I still have no idea what he's talking about when he keeps bringing up this thing about the first chapter. I thought he was working on *The Mary Celeste*, adding some of his writing to it, but he was running around in circles once again it seemed. Finally he came down to telling me the love of his life, the woman lawyer, had offered him a job working with her as an assessor, and he was very interested in the position which supposedly would better him financially since he was retired and living on a meager pension. When he returned to Portugal, he intended to send back the manuscript for me to go over. He finished the email by writing: "Please be patient. Soon you will receive 'our book' to read and please know that it will always serve as a union between the two of us that I never want to lose. God put you in my way with a friendship that was and is precious to me. I want to keep that treasure."

Lots of good wishes, and the usual poetic stuff went on for another whole paragraph. I was tired of him playing with words; it drove me nuts.

Winter 2002

Dan amazed me every day. He called himself a Neanderthal because he had not gone to college and his job had to do with concrete and stones, but he was far from being a Stone Age man, as he could talk to anyone about any subject. He kept saying how much he admired me for what I had accomplished with my life as if I were a superwoman. I told him, "I believe anyone can do what I have done; it's all about mind over matter. When you have a goal in mind and you are passionate about it, nothing is impossible."

Artur's email of Sunday February 24th came with an attachment, Mary Celeste-Final version. I guessed he was back from Columbia. He wanted me to go over the new and improved *Mary Celeste* and make any changes I found necessary. "I am open to any suggestions, please do as you like. I hope you like what I have written, using of course, the ideas you've given me for the final part. I'm sending the text in the attachment."

I gave him ideas for the final part? What was he talking about? I had written the whole story; that was how I had been able to write the final part. The plot was intertwined from beginning to end. I wondered if I should send him a copy of the original manuscript so he could see the difference. After the initial shock of his email, I concluded I needed to remain calm and understand he had just returned from Columbia and must be brain dead. That was, until I printed the manuscript. He had done nothing about *The Mary Celeste!* Instead of expanding on all the text I had written, he introduced Maka Edom, an old man who supposedly had given him the "real" story of *Mary Celeste.* It read like one of Artur's old emails where he went off talking about the meaning of life, politics, and religion, except that in the Maka Edom chapter, Artur was having tea with the old man. That was what he referred to as "writing *The Mary Celeste"?* His Final Version was nothing but the adding of a new chapter describing Maka Edom, the old man, telling the story of the *Mary Celeste.* What I had written came along too but nothing had been modified, he had not done anything with it. One could perhaps say, wow, he really likes your writing that's why he left it untouched. I had a real bad feeling about the whole thing. I cried. And then I went home to cry on Dan's shoulder.

Dan's apartment was officially remodeled and he asked me to go with him to see the final product. There were brand-new kitchen cabinets and counters, wood floors throughout, and freshly painted walls, but I really fell in love with his backyard. It was probably 10 x 20, but what he did with the pond that he built, surrounded by bamboo and wild plants, made it look like a tropical piece of paradise taken directly from the wilderness of the Amazon River. He handed me some food pellets to feed the goldfish in his pond. I felt special being with Dan and I was willing to move anywhere on earth with him. Still, I didn't want to get married again. I was perfectly happy being his girlfriend. I loved the love and friendship we felt for each other. I loved it when he came home and he took a shower, and sometimes when we showered together that was even better. I loved the way he enjoyed all his food, he never left anything on his plate. I cooked and he helped do the dishes and clean up afterwards. I loved that he didn't care for television and would rather sit and talk. I appreciated him.

He asked me to move in with him at the perfect time; my apartment lease would be ending in the spring, in just three weeks.

Dan took me to the Gemini Bar and Grill Club in Lake Oswego where a female blues singer was performing. He also loved the blues. Before the band started to play, I reached in my shoulder purse for my earplugs, or as I called them, my "further" hearing loss prevention plugs. I carried them with me for occasions like this one, when the music or other sounds could get really loud. I showed Dan the earplugs. "Good thing I only need one," I said. Then I offered, "Would you like the other?"

"Don't you need them both?" he asked.

"I'm deaf on the left side. I carry two in case I lose one."

At first he couldn't believe it, but then he recalled how any time we were in a noisy environment I would often say, "What? What did you say?"

All my physical disabilities had now been exposed to Dan. He knew how old I was, that I couldn't have children, and that I had a hearing deficit.

Another email came. Artur wanted to know how much longer before I was done with editing. "I agree the 'old man' needs some work," he wrote. "Go ahead, you can add your own writing to Maka Edom and make him fit." I had no intention of doing any such thing and did the Italian salute which was the same as the Portuguese salute when wanting to seriously offend someone. Ralph was near me and said, "What is that about?"

"Oh, my way of letting out steam when I know someone is trying to use me." I told him about Artur. He said, "He does sound like a smooth operator but it's still up to you to say no. Don't give him any more help and I hate to say this Mom, but since he's co-author, you really don't have much to say if he wants to add whatever he likes even if it makes no sense; he has the right as co-author." He looked at me and saw how sad I was feeling. "I'm so sorry Mom, I know how much this book meant to you and how hard you worked on it. But think of this, now you have enough experience to write your own books."

I could not just let it go; it still hurt, very, very deeply. Then I suddenly had a flash of memory. I went back to reading his emails that I had made copies of and I found one dated Sunday, June 4, 2000. In that email he'd mentioned he had a book he was writing and wanted to finish but hadn't been able to, and the title was *Maka Edom, the Man That Spoke to God*. That was it; he was using the *Mary Celeste* as the vessel of opportunity to include what he had written years ago. One way or another he was going to slip Maka Edom into "my" manuscript. What a joke! That was the epitome of writing laziness. I was at his mercy. I didn't edit Maka Edom. I had no intention of rewriting it for him; I was done writing for him. I sent the attachment back and a one liner, "Maka Edom makes no sense in our book."

I had not seen my patient Mr. Johnson for the last two months. When he came in on Friday, he looked pale and had lost a lot of weight. He told me he felt very weak, was running out of breath even if he took just a few steps, and now that he had moved to King City, he was afraid to drive so far to see me. My first thought was his heart. I checked it, but I couldn't hear any heart murmurs or irregularities, except his blood pressure was deadly low. I asked for his medical doctor's phone number. I felt he needed to be seen immediately. Dr. Wolff was irritated with my call as apparently I was disturbing him from whatever he was doing. I believe that he felt that having the news come from a chiropractor removed the seriousness of my findings. We wound up in an argument when he said it was nothing new about Mr. Johnson having low blood pressure and added, "If he wants to see me he'll have to call my office and make an appointment for next week."

"Next week? Are you joking with me? Don't you have an associate or someone else I can refer him to?"

"There's nothing wrong with him that can't wait."

"I'm sending him to the hospital then."

"You go ahead. I can't stop you."

I hung up and mumbled a few words that were not very professional. I then called Robert, Mr. Johnson's son, to drive his father to the hospital since I was worried he might pass out while driving.

A week later Mr. Johnson and his son came to my office; they wanted to give me the news in person. At the hospital, they had done chest X-rays and found the reason his father was having trouble breathing was because he had lung cancer.

"My father and I feel you may have saved his life by sending him to the hospital when you did. He's going to be on chemotherapy and since it's in the early stages, maybe the cancer will be stopped before it spreads any further," Robert told me.

"I will be here every month for my adjustment and as long as you see me each month you will know I'm still alive," Mr. Johnson said, with a joyful smile. We hugged.

Spring 2002

Dan and I loved Asian, Egyptian, and African culture and between the two of us, we made our "pad" the perfect environment to come home to; we were surrounded by all the things we had collected through the years. He was a data guru when it came to anything even remotely associated with World War II and our second bedroom was dedicated to all his memorabilia. He called it "the war room." "Do you mind if I put the metal swastika back on the wall to go along with the motif?" He was busy hanging his war related posters and pictures.

"I find it very offensive and if you put it up, I'll be very sad," I said, wondering how I'd react if he ignored my feelings and chose to put the swastika back up on the wall. His lack of consideration for those who had died bothered me, especially since he knew more than the average person regarding what had happened during World War II. But he did put it away and I appreciated it.

Dan possessed an amazing memory; he knew just about every singer and songwriter by name and he knew when their hit records were released. He also knew when different movies came out and who their main actors were, and he knew the TV show's hosts and guests and who played what character and when and on which series. He loved watching

TV quiz shows and he was proud of answering most of the questions correctly. He was good enough at sports, politics, and general world events to enter one of those shows and if he could find a way in, I was sure he would easily win.

I no longer played the guitar, sang with the choir, or painted. I stopped going dancing and attending the International Club; I only went to private gatherings with the friends I had made from the Club. Dan had become my world, especially since we had less than two hours together before he had to go to sleep.

It didn't take long for us to throw a potluck party welcoming our family and friends to our new place. Alexandra, our Portuguese friend, sang the *Fado* and I accompanied her on my acoustic guitar. Ralph came over with Cindy, his new girlfriend. We were surrounded by our circle of friends who filled our home with music, laughter, friendship, and lots of good food. Only one thing went wrong—the dining room table, filled only with homemade desserts including my flan and cheesecake, was baptized by the bulb in the ceiling lamp exploding. Minuscule pieces of glass sprayed like rain over every sweet morsel.

Dan and I talked about our world travels and he mentioned how much he would love to go to Italy. We began making plans to visit Italy for his two-week vacation in the middle of September. It seemed to be the idyllic place for two people in love to visit. The idea of going back to Italy, a country I had dreaded while married to Patrick, no longer inflicted me with painful memories. If anything, I looked forward to going back with the man I loved.

While on vacation, my patients would be in good hands, literally, with Ralph. And if he wanted to go paragliding again in Brazil, I would return the favor. We had the perfect coverage arrangement in our office.

I told Dan the hills in Rome were outrageously steep and we needed to start working out if we were going to be in shape for them. We started taking brisk walks up and down the hills by our condo every day after dinner. While I went up at full speed, he would still beat me by speeding up and down twice. "Show off," I would say to him and think, *At his age, he'd better be quicker than me.* Besides Rome, we had plans to visit Naples, Pompeii, and the Island of Capri.

I never thought I would be returning to Italy. My Aunt Heydee's favorite statement, "Never say never. If you ever say I'll never drink from a dirty fountain, beware. When you are thirsty enough, that water fountain may be your only source to quench your thirst."

When I was a child, I listened to all those quotes from our elders but didn't have a real concept of their meaning. Now they all returned like bright beams of wisdom.

I felt I should provide a little more insight about my concerns about the chapter Artur had written so I wrote in my email to him, "I don't see what the new chapter has to do with the story of *Mary Celeste.* It feels like it's been squeezed in. It's out of context and leaves many questions unanswered, like who is this new character you describe as an old man by the name of Maka Edom? What is he talking about while serving you tea? You have him talking for several pages about philosophy and politics, but what does that have to do with *Mary Celeste?* Where did he come from? Maka Edom shows up in the beginning and then disappears completely. What happened to him? I know you want to maintain a certain mystery about the story, but what is the point you're trying to make since you want to call the book *Mary Celeste, the True Story?* I feel it's a deceitful title and I'm very confused about this addition. Our book's genre is historical *fiction,* so why have you added "the True Story," to the title? Sorry if I'm confused, but I need to know."

Two weeks went by and I did not hear from Artur. I began sending him more emails, simply copying and pasting from the last one I had sent him. I kept my fingers crossed that he would come to his senses and remove the Maka Edom chapter since it read more like something written for a political campaign addressing a group of blue-collar workers, or a political study for a class project. I wanted him to write and expand on what I had written, not just add what he wrote years ago.

I believe that our lives are dependent on where we are born; had it been in Germany instead of Portugal in 1944, I would have been dead, my children and grandchildren would have never existed, and my friends and my patients would have gone in a different life direction, including Dan. Who we meet through life and our choices when facing a crossroad—what some may call destiny or others, a chaotic choice—is in my opinion, pure luck. Luck had brought young Paul to our chiropractic office. He enjoyed taking yoga classes, but for the last two months, he had been experiencing lower back pain, which steadily increased to the point where he had to see his medical doctor. After being diagnosed with sprained/strained muscles, he was prescribed pain meds, a muscle relaxant, and an anti-inflammatory. When he didn't get any better, his doctor sent him to a physical therapist three times a week for a month. But he was getting worse, so they took an X-ray of his lower back, which was evaluated as being normal. He complained to a friend, who happened to be one of my patients, and who told him to come see me. He was warned by his doctor not to go to a chiropractor and that he should continue to take the meds because it was just a question of time before he would feel better.

I treated Paul for one week but there was no sign of improvement. I prescribed a massage with our licensed massage therapist (LMT) prior to getting adjusted. Perhaps the massage would help him with the cramping of the lower back muscles. It didn't help. I asked him to bring in the X-rays taken at the hospital. The X-rays had been performed with him lying down. I re-took the same X-ray views but with Paul standing because I find that standing provides a better view of the spinal biomechanics. In the darkroom, I took a rapid look at the X-rays and saw an odd shaped density at L4. I sent the X-rays to a radiologist for a second opinion. The X-ray report stated, "Possible fracture at L4, but not conclusive."

The report bothered me. How could a twenty-one-year-old fracture his back doing yoga? It bothered me even more that the pain was still going on after two weeks of care. When something out of the ordinary happened to one of our patients, Ralph and I conferred with each other as to the best treatment. But Ralph was in Brazil on vacation.

The next morning I woke up thinking about Paul. Medically speaking, except for the pain, he had no neurological symptoms warranting the cost of an MRI. But I was a chiropractor and as such, I needed to know the cause of the symptoms. I decided Paul was going to have an MRI that day.

When I read the fax with the results of two possible malignant tumors in Paul's spinal cord, I could not stand up. I cried. Jeannette gave me a glass of water and tried to console me by saying, "You did a good job, Dr. Veronica." I had not done a good job and I cried even more because I had just been lucky to make the right decision, nothing else. I maintained my composure when I told Paul he needed to see a neurosurgeon. He called his medical doctor who referred him to a surgeon. Two days later, he heard the surgeon was not available to do the procedure. My hypothesis is that the surgeon didn't want to take a chance of cutting so close to the spinal cord and leaving him paralyzed. I immediately called the radiologist I worked with. "If it was your son who needed this type of surgery, who would you recommend?" I asked.

"Dr. Kellogg, I trust him. He is a highly skilled neuro-surgeon."

Dr. Kellogg was on vacation but upon reading the MRI fax report, he made plans to return immediately and do the surgery that week.

Paul's parents flew in from Boston and the night he was operated on, I was at the hospital and met both his family and his surgeon for the first time. The tumor was quite big—the reason it was putting so much pressure on the spinal cord—but there was good news. It was benign.

By Monday April 1st, three weeks had gone by when I received a short email response from Artur concerning my email asking him if he had received my questions about Maka Edom. He wrote, "I already wrote to you confirming that I received everything. It probably went to your son's email address by error." Ralph told me he didn't get anything from Artur. It was April 1st and I did feel like a fool; Artur was still playing with me.

Summer 2002

I got a call from Paul. It had been over a month since the surgery, and he was recovering well at home. He wanted to thank me for what I had done for him. I thanked him for the gift certificate of $150 his family had sent me to use at the Pambiche Cuban Restaurant in downtown Portland. And then I said, "Paul, do me a favor and ask your surgeon for another MRI. You need to make sure the tumor is completely gone." He resisted, saying Dr. Kellogg had also told him to do the same thing, but he was doing great and didn't feel he needed it since he no longer had back pain. But once again my intuition was telling me what to do. Before I hung up, I made him swear he would follow up the request for another MRI.

A week later I got a call from Dr. Kellogg. The MRI showed the tumor was growing back.

"I know how much you care for Paul," he said. "I'm calling you to let you know that Paul's tumor will not return again after I'm finished removing it this time."

The affirmative sound in Dr. Kellogg's voice convinced me the surgery would be a success.

I had a very disturbing experience with a new patient's mother. Mrs. Sager heard neck adjustments could help with headaches and she wanted me to adjust Robert, her nine-year-old, who had suffered from headaches since he was eight.

Upon taking his history, I found out his headaches had started after he began taking meds for his "behavior" in school.

When I was putting together his chart notes so I could give them a report of my findings at the next visit, I found that one of the side effects of the drug he was taking was headaches. I called Mrs. Sager. "There's a good chance that no matter how much I adjust your son's neck, the cause of the headache is not his neck, but the meds he is taking."

"He has to take his medicine! It's the only thing controlling his behavior at school," she said impatiently.

"Before taking this medicine was he doing well at home?"

"Yes, he was fine, but not in school."

"If I may ask, what did he do in school that was so bad?"

"He slapped another boy and made him cry."

"He didn't punch him?" *What eight or nine-year-old boy goes to school and does not get into a fight?* I wondered.

"No, but he slapped him, and that is not acceptable," she said firmly.

"So, he was slapping other kids, too?"

"No, he slapped one kid once and I was called to the school and told he had all the signs of ADHD and needed to be medicated or he wouldn't be allowed back."

"I'm sorry but as long as he takes meds that cause headaches I don't see how I can help him," I said stubbornly. I would regret my decision for the rest of my life. I had closed the door on a little boy whose mother, maybe, just maybe with time, I could have encouraged to cut down her son's medication little by little. But at that moment, I couldn't bear the idea of not addressing the cause of his headaches.

Marcy, our office manager told me the school her son attended received a kickback from certain pharmaceutical companies providing medication to help students with ADHD. A lot of the teachers were being trained by those companies to recognize when students should be referred for "help."

This trend had grown out of proportion compared to when my sons were eight and nine years old. In those days, I remembered they brought home from school a personal little bag of goodies. Someone had come to the school and provided the students with samples of aspirin, cough medicine, and candy. At the time, I thought it was really nice of those companies providing drug samples for the students to take in case they got sick. I guess those companies were now taking a more personal interest in their younger customers and the present sales of their products.

Mrs. Sager, canceled all future chiropractic treatments for her son.

A few years later, I decided once a year for the period of one month that I would offer free chiropractic care to children diagnosed with ADHD as part of my research.

On Saturday June 29th Artur's email came with another attachment, Alterations MC.doc. He wrote, "How time goes by so fast! I just realized how the months have gone by almost without any contact with you. As such I must ask you to forgive me as I must forgive myself that I am guilty as charged and as such I'm the loser." He went on once again on how I was so dear to him and then wrote, "You are right about the character that I put in the beginning making the revelations to me and then it is forgotten through the rest of the book as if it's not important," he wrote. "But I believe it was my enthusiasm over my writing that made me forget completely the character's existence, it's a good thing you caught it. I have made the alterations and added the extra material as you mentioned to do and now send you the file back so you can go over it again and please make all the changes you feel are needed but see if you can hurry up since I want to see if I can publish it in August. Go ahead and make as many suggestions as you like, I will wait for your changes on this matter. And then he went on about his wedding next month and his work as an artist for two more pages. "My errors in writing are due to being distracted or in a hurry," he wrote. "Once the text is approved by both of us I'll give it to a friend who is also a writer to make sure it doesn't need any further editing or corrections." He added he was only going to send me the new stuff he had written so it would be easier for me to open the attachment.

I kept my fingers crossed that he would come to his senses and remove the Maka Edom chapter. To my dismay he had written another chapter about Maka Edom to be inserted further in the book and he wanted me to go over both of them. (As far as I was concerned, he could wait until the cows came home.)

~ *Chapter Sixteen* ~

Sposami

Autumn 2002

We were back from Italy the third week of September. To my great surprise, the unexpected happened while in Rome.

To begin with, the Frommer's book we chose to use as a guide was a great source of accurate and detailed information, from inexpensive to very expensive, where to stay, buses, trains, restaurants, and so on. We found it to be a traveler's bible.

We each took our own roll-on luggage and backpacks. It was a blessing to find our hotel in Rome was only a few blocks away from the train and subway station that connected with every place we wanted to go, including the airport.

Everything was going fine until we got to the hotel. It was eleven thirty in the morning and we were told to come back at one when our room would be available. Dan became frantic and said, "I'm not going to wait until one!" Then his voice became harsh, and his complexion took on a reddish tint as he demanded, "I want the room now. It was supposed to be ready at eleven thirty and I want the room now." It was the first time I had seen Dan getting upset. The concierge kept apologizing over and over again and said, "You can leave your luggage with us, sir. Take a walk around our lovely city and when you come back at one, I promise your room will be ready."

"No, we are not leaving the luggage here," he said. His attitude was too familiar for my comfort. A déjà vu feeling of doom made me quiver as I recalled traveling under the same conditions with Patrick. "We'll have to look for another accommodation somewhere else," he said.

I wasn't going to stand for it. "Well, I'm leaving my luggage and backpack with you guys until the room is ready." I turned to Dan and said softly as if speaking to a naughty child, "You should too."

"I am not," he responded vehemently pulling his luggage closer to him. Maintaining my poise like a mediator about to stop a battle between two countries, I rested my hand on Dan's arm, smiled at him, and then said to the flustered concierge, "We will be back later." I did my best to project a friendly overtone of, "See? We are fine, my boyfriend is not really that mad. We don't mind waiting a few hours; everything is just hunky-dory." I waved at her and Dan followed me carrying his backpack and pulling his heavy, oversize luggage. Outside he took a picture of the façade's building and seemed more relaxed but a certain tension remained between us. I was not saying much; I was trying to remain calm while processing what had just happened. I watched him fearfully as he grumbled a few small curses every time the wheels on his luggage grabbed onto a cobblestone. I experienced a flashback of when I met our next-door neighbor in Sherwood for the first time. She was a vivacious, friendly woman who asked me one morning when I went by her backyard, "How are you two doing there, okay? I've known Dan for a few years now. He sure can carry a lot of rage doesn't he? What a temper, huh?"

"No, I have never seen him lose his temper." I was a bit thrown off by her remark."

"Maybe he's changed for you; love does that to people." And she went on watering her flowers.

My God, his true colors were coming up to the surface like a dead body bloated with water and unable to sink. I pleaded, *Please dear God, don't let this happen to me again. I can't deal with another Patrick.* I tried concentrating on my surroundings but Rome was no different from the old city of

Lisbon where I was with Patrick, with an overabundance of cars and pollution, people and decaying buildings. Trying not to be judgmental, but curious about his behavior, I had to say something. "I don't understand why you didn't leave your stuff with them."

"I don't trust the people in the hotel to keep an eye on my luggage."

"What are they going to do, steal your underwear?" I wasn't laughing. I felt sorry for myself; I had fallen in love with a psychotic, once again.

"I have some important items in the bottom of the luggage and I can't afford to lose them." His voice that was secretively assuring me he was carrying some kind of treasure, concurred with his fear of leaving his luggage unattended at the hotel. *Great,* I thought, *if this gets any worse, I'm leaving on the next airplane even if it costs me double to fly home.*

We did not walk far. Roma Termini railway station was across the street and I suggested we wait there until it was time to go back, since it was difficult to do anything with him carrying his backpack and luggage. There were plenty of restaurants around us, the type one sees at malls. We had a panini type of ham and cheese sandwich and a delicious fresh salad, and Dan seemed to be back to his normal self, being lovable, and making funny comments.

As we had been promised, the room was ready at one. Leaving the luggage in the room seemed to be fine with him, which made me wonder what was the difference between that and leaving it behind the counter with the concierge. I pushed the incident aside as the result of a long flight making him oddly touchy from exhaustion. We were not surprised with the modest accommodations; it matched the modest price but was very clean. It was a small simple room on the third floor, the kind one sees throughout Europe when staying at a pensão, a better motel in the US, but with an old European flair. The room was big enough to fit a wall closet with a full mirror on the door, an ordinary wood chair next to it, and a full size bed. The bathroom with a shower was a few feet down the hallway and it was to be shared with the other guests. I lifted the covers to confirm it had a mattress; it was all I needed. "It will do fine," Dan said. "We'll only be here at the end of the day to go to sleep."

"I hope a little more than just sleep." I winked at him and he took my flirting as an offer to christen the bed. The next days were some of the happiest days of my life, and except for the incident with the luggage, Dan was indeed the man I thought I knew. I could not help but notice the sharp contrast between him and Patrick; it made me feel euphoric. We had a mutual interest in history and took each site in like a honeybee collecting nectar deep from the flower's burrow. I was overjoyed to take in the very essence of the past in the air I breathed and in the ground beneath our feet and saw that Dan was in just as much awe as I was. We walked from morning until night except for eating, which we took advantage of while walking the streets that were filled with bakeries, restaurants, and even pizzerias. At the Roman Forum, Dan took enough pictures to fill several albums. As I stood under the Arch of Septimius Severus while surrounded in all directions with the decay of Ancient Rome, the song "Dust in the Wind," played in my mind's eye. It didn't play as a tune, but as a 3D projection of all the people who had crossed those same streets for hundreds of years, shadows of the past just like the once busy Trajan's Markets with six floors of shops and offices, of which now so little remained. Once we left, Dan and I and all those tourists wondering about the vestiges of the monumental marvels belonged, whether we liked it or not, to the 3D projection, spinning out like dust in the wind.

We thought it was a joke when someone told us that the Italians, the *true* Italians, frowned upon the monument to Victor Emmanuel II, believing it to be an abomination of bad taste so offensive that many good citizens had volunteered to bulldoze it to the ground. Really? We still took pictures.

Not once did Dan or I take any transportation during those first days in Rome. We felt that the city could only be truly savored on our feet but after two days, I thought my hips were going to fall out of their sockets. Surprisingly enough on the third day, as if by magic, I was a "walking machine" and had no problem keeping up with Dan. I felt physically fit enough to walk around the earth if needed. We found a restaurant for dinner that soon became our favorite, tucked away in one of those narrow streets away from tourists even though there weren't many of those. It was mid-September, the kids were back in school, and families were homebound. The nights were invitingly cool as if the air had been brushed with a slight stroke of warmth so we could sit outside "our" restaurant. Our favorite food? Everything! We had one goal in mind; try something new from the menu each night and taste each other's main course so we would not miss anything.

Like children without supervision, we had ice cream for breakfast and late in the evening. There was an ice cream parlor about one block away from our hotel and before retiring for the night, we always stopped there for our midnight snack. We became addicted to it and Dan became concerned that once back in the US we would never find "real" Italian ice cream again.

The Museum and Galleria Borguese took us by surprise, as we automatically slowed down our stroll and used vocal sounds of wonder. There were two floors with rooms filled to capacity with marble, porphyry, and alabaster sculptures and paintings, some as old as three centuries. But the busts displayed in a line in the Emperors Gallery were way too lifelike for me, particularly the bust of Cardinal Scipione Borghese. His eyes were open wide as if caught by surprise with his present situation and his lips were slightly apart as if ready to say, "What am I doing here without my legs?"

The only other time I had been to Italy, Patrick had taken a piece of the Vatican wall to put it into our sand and stone collection but had refused to enter the Vatican under the pretext that the Pope was the devil himself. This time I was going in and Dan was just as excited. Our first encounter was Saint Peter's Basilica. We had just entered the church of all churches, the father of all churches. No other church could ever surpass its opulence and massive interior with its rich domes and splendid chapels. Its corridors held dead popes each entombed in their own space of grandeur and with each newer dead pope trying to outdo the last one's resting place as each was more outlandish than the last. Past the Holy Door—a small portico,—there was an elevator or one could take 320 steps to the roof level. We chose the climb and Dan was gone up the steps before I could even blink an eye. When I thought I was done with the steps, there were 230 more to reach the very top of the cupola. I admired Dan's lung capacity to just keep on going even though he was a lot younger than me. I was very happy that Dan didn't press me to keep up with him, as Patrick used to do. Luckily a few slits strategically set along the climb gave me a chance to take a breather. The top of the dome provided a bird's eye view of St. Peter's Square and the Vatican Gardens or as one might describe it, "the top of the world," from a religious point of view.

The Vatican Palace had us commenting how "they" could have so much gold and precious stones while in so many parts of the world people were dying of hunger. But the Sistine Chapel, particularly those frescoes by Michelangelo, made us forget all about men's greed for trophies and we left with the enlightening feeling of having seen his work, and the rich magnificence of a true genius.

On the way out, Dan left to use the restroom and when he returned he said, "I can't believe it. My back just gave in for no reason and I fell on the steps over there." I figured he had tripped on something from all the excitement because he didn't complain when we climbed the steps to the main dome at Saint Peter's Basilica or the Vatican. But on the way back to the hotel after we crossed the bridge of Sant'Angelo and were in the middle of crossing the street, Dan groaned and went down on his knees.

"What's the matter?" I bent over to him, panic-stricken with the thought he was having a heart attack. I tried to lift him by his arm, but he remained stooped over. Thank God the traffic was at a standstill as other pedestrians surrounded us, inquiring what was going on. They remained by our side as if trying to use their bodies to protect us from the oncoming traffic.

"My back just gave in on me again," Dan said.

I put his backpack on my shoulder and slipped his camera with the strap around my neck, and two men carried him to the sidewalk. He was able to slowly walk to our hotel room and once there, I put him on his side on the bed and adjusted his lower back. He said he felt a lot better afterwards. I told him it was wise if he lightened his backpack during our daily excursions. The next morning I made sure I adjusted his lower back before we took the train to Naples, famous for their pizza and ancient artifacts, even though our main purpose was to take advantage of its proximity to Pompeii by train. As in Rome, we chose a hotel close to the train station so we wouldn't have to go far with our luggage. It turned out to be a very bad idea. We were too close to the station and the night noise was intensified tenfold especially as our hotel room had two windows opening to the street below. At night we were subjected to a cacophony of very Italian vocal arguments, trash cans being thrown to the ground, and blowing horns as well as trying to ignore the bright car lights that also bypassed the old wooden shutters which were too rusted to close properly. Dan was forced to borrow my earplugs. I had to smile at all this. *Gosh, I'm in Italy, the country of beautiful movie stars like Sophia Loren and Gina Lollobrigida and I'm surrounded by dramatic, boisterous Italians. And what makes it all even better is that Dan is my boyfriend and we love each other. So it's noisy, big deal. Thank you God for making me deaf on the left side.* I lay on my right side and silence became blissful except for the car lights blinding us while we were trying to sleep. Dan didn't do as well as me, because he had very acute hearing. Even with earplugs he could hear the cats in heat meowing and the dogs barking and the ongoing cursing of street fights. Like he said the next morning, "Does anybody sleep in Naples?"

We took the train to Pompeii early in the morning. It was only seventeen miles from Naples but we wanted to be there when the gates opened at eight thirty. Once in Pompeii we lost track of time while roving through the ruins, and stayed until the evening when the gates closed at seven thirty. We took it upon ourselves to visit every niche and nook that had been lost for 1700 years. Not once throughout the day did we feel thirsty or hungry. My wish as a child to someday see Pompeii had finally come true, even though we had to wait half an hour in line to get into one of their most famous ruins, the House of Ill Repute, which was jam-packed with two senior tourist groups. Back in Naples, we went to a pizza restaurant for dinner. We loved the pizza and they treated us like royalty but the opposite treatment was directed towards a Chinese couple sitting at the next table to us. We felt very bad for them and decided not to return to the restaurant for that reason. The next day we visited the National Archaeological Museum of Naples and we were not embarrassed to say we easily got lost inside.

The Island of Capri proved to be something from a fairy tale and swimming in the emerald green ocean made me feel so high that even Dan became aware of it and took my picture while in the water. He described me as glowing with happiness.

Dan was proud of my Italian and my expertise in bargaining, and we bought some statues and pottery which were practically given to us. Once they knew I was Portuguese they would say something like, "Oh, you're not an American? You're Portuguese, hmm? What do you want to pay? Okay, it's yours." Dan played bad cop during the harder business deals, saying, "No, no I don't want that, it's nothing but junk. Let's go." And I would say, "My husband hates this marble statue, so what's the best you can do for me?" It worked every time.

Once back in Rome, we settled at the same hotel. Dan gave the blue suit he had been carrying in his luggage to the concierge with a request to have it steamed at a local dry cleaner and then we went out to further discover the city.

We found the Trevi Fountain, and Dan got busy taking pictures. I threw a coin into the fountain to make a wish just like in the movie, *Three Coins in the Fountain,* but I was praying more than wishing. *Dear God, Thank you for bringing Dan into my life. I never thought I was going to find happiness again. I know Dan is a lot younger than me, but for the first time in my life I feel so complete that it feels right. So here I am standing at the Trevi Fountain ready to make a wish but my wish has already come true, so thank you God and...*

"Veronica, there you are! I was looking all over for you!" And we kissed and then sat by the fountain, holding hands. There were no clouds, just perfectly bright blue skies. The sun shined ostentatiously over the fountain as if proclaiming it as its own. A bus full of senior tourists slowed down. We saw them looking from their seated positions through the glass windows, some pointed towards us and others just stared.

We promised each other to see as much of the world as possible before we became those senior citizens inside the bus.

The next two days Dan began acting strange again. He would get up early in the morning and run downstairs, and when I would come down I would find him talking to Bianca, the girl at the front desk. Something was definitely going on, because when I approached them they stopped talking and looked at each other as if they had just been caught doing something secretive. *He has a thing for Bianca. Yes, I'm jealous. He'd rather be talking to Bianca than being in bed, snuggling up with me.* I was sad, even perturbed, but I didn't have the courage to accuse him of anything since all he was doing was talking, even though it was supposed to be *our* time of being together. One night he said, "I gotta go to the bathroom; I'll be right back." He left the room, and I waited and waited and finally I fell asleep. When he returned, I woke up but I gave him the cold shoulder. Obviously he was bored being with me day after day, night after night. That's why he was so eager to talk to lovely, young Bianca. He cuddled up to me and said, "Tomorrow night I want to take you out to dinner to a very special restaurant Bianca highly recommended."

I wanted to say, why don't you take Bianca instead? But I was sad, too sad to respond.

The next day we visited the Pantheon which reminded me of a mosque inside. Considering it had been built around 118 AD, the building, including the dome, was an amazing feat of architecture. According to history, Pope Urban VIII had pillaged the bronze used in the Pantheon's ceiling porch and used it to embellish his own tomb at Saint Peter's Basilica. The rest of the day was spent at the famous Spanish Steps between the Piazza Di Spagna at the bottom and Piazza Trinita dei Monti at the very top. Dan didn't want to do much of anything else, as he already had something special planned for us in the evening. We walked among the street entertainers and checked out the small shops at Piazza Di Spagna and then went back to our hotel to get dressed for dinner. Dan asked me to wear the long black silk skirt and the white brocade shirt embroidered with pearls that he had bought for me a month before we left on our trip. "Take your time getting dressed," he said. "I'll be right back," and he ran out of the room. Darn it! I hated Bianca!

He returned thirty minutes later sporting a radiant smile and carrying his freshly pressed blue suit on a hanger. He took an appreciative look at my attire and said, "You look beautiful." He kissed me on the forehead and then got dressed.

He looked very handsome in his suit, white shirt, and blue tie. On the way out of the hotel, Bianca said, "Have a great night, you two." I caught her winking at Dan. Something is definitely going on between the two of them, I thought once again. Dan must have read my thoughts and said, "Bianca made reservations for us to be at the restaurant at seven, and she recommended we take a taxi."

There were no taxis. We tried to walk to the bus station but there was a loud demonstration going on against the American government and the transit was at a standstill. Three military trucks with Italian soldiers carrying firearms drove by us. We began walking in the opposite direction. "Hey, Dan," I tried reasoning with him, "this doesn't look too good. How about if we have dinner somewhere closer to our hotel?"

"You surprise me," he said. "I never expected you, of all people I know, to lose your sense of adventure." We both stopped walking.

"Me? Lose my sense of adventure?" I asked. "I love adventure; real adventure, not premeditated suicide just to have dinner at some restaurant Bianca likes." I was no longer hiding my resentment.

He laughed. "You are being silly, you know that, right?" Then he put his hands on my shoulders making me face him. He tilted his head slightly to the side, his frowned forehead losing its smooth appearance, and said very seriously, "Veronica, I love you." His big blue eyes with super long eyelashes started to blink in unison like those dolls that can open and close their eyes as fast as one can rock their heads back and forth. Then he stared at me while concentrating to keep his eyes wide open. I bust out laughing. We kissed and then I said, "I love you too. Okay, let's go to the restaurant at the end of the Universe." It wasn't too far from the truth; according to his map, the restaurant was on the other side of Rome. There were no taxis and no buses; our legs were the only transportation available. One of the things we noticed which made us very aware of what clothing did for appearances was that people walking towards us would move out of the way so we could pass. We looked affluent, which was quite contrary to a few days prior when we were dressed like tourists and upon walking into a men's clothing store, the owner threw us out because he assumed we had no money. At the time, Dan was seriously looking to buy a pair of pants and a shirt for himself and took the insult personally. He went to another men's clothing store across the street and bought two pair of pants and three shirts.

We kept our walk at a steady pace. I was wearing high heels but thank God I had the smarts to bring the pair with thicker heels. The cobblestone streets and walkways with their cracks and crevices here and there were no different from the ones in Portugal. It also helped that we walked arm in arm as it provided me with more balance. The farther we walked away from all the turmoil, the calmer and more lethargic the city became, as if a lullaby had been playing in the silent evening long enough to sway the beasts into submission. Then we saw a taxi, one lonely taxi, laboring around a plaza as if lost, much like an ant looking desperately for his coworkers. Lucky for us the taxi driver dropped us off in front of the restaurant exactly at seven. The entrance to the restaurant was a small glass door opening into a large reddish foyer covered with a variety of oil paintings, mostly of naked cupids holding their bow and arrow and looking very mischievous while others were busy flirting with a couple of naked nymphs bathing in a lake. Two white marble columns stood on each side of a wall-to-wall painting of a countryside lake with white swans and several naked girls. The maître d' asked for the name on the reservation and after bowing to us ceremoniously, asked us to follow him upstairs to a table with a sign that said, RESERVED. Dan left to go to the bathroom and I took a good look around the room. Everybody was dressed up and I was glad we were, too. Several mirrors with thick gold-encrusted frames adorned the white walls and long red silk drapes hung on the side of the two balcony's windows. The waiters wore long white starched coats that harmonized with the impeccable tablecloths, decorations, exquisite mirrors, and arrangements of fresh flowers.

Dinner had been pre-ordered it seemed, as there was no menu. They brought us a small basket of little, hot crusty breads and cute butter pieces shaped like tiny hearts although like me, Dan never used butter on bread. From a terrine, our waiter used a ladle to fill our small bowls with soup. "Minestrone," he said, putting a singing accent to the last "e" vowel, sounding a lot like Portuguese. We had just finished the soup, when one of the waiters came to the table and said, "Per voi, Madam." He handed me a dozen red roses.

"Per me? For me?" I asked the waiter, while looking around the room. I saw Dan's straight face and I figured they were not from him. "Da chi? From whom?"

"È da lui," said the waiter pointing to Dan who maintained the same pokerfaced expression towards the waiter. "No, sei sicuro? Are you sure?" I asked the waiter. The waiter rolled his eyes up impatiently and repeated, "È da lui."

"Dan? They're from you?" I said, completely taken by surprise since there was no emotion coming from him. If anything, he was far from joyful. "What's the matter?" I asked him.

"The waiter was supposed to bring you a red rose every ten minutes," he said apologetically. "I guess something got lost in the translation between Bianca and the restaurant staff."

"Oh, so that's what was going on between…" I was so relieved I had to control myself from becoming too emotional. "My goodness Dan, the flowers are beautiful, the restaurant and the food are perfect. Honey, I love everything you've done to surprise me. It's a perfect evening and I really, really appreciate everything. Thank you, Dan." We kissed and then rapidly parted to welcome the waiter serving us what he called Arancini, fried rice balls stuffed with tomato sauce, mozzarella, and peas. I took a bite just to taste it and then gave it to Dan who had no issues eating fried food. The next dish was Ossobuco alla Milanese, tender veal shanks cooked in white wine with a side of brightly colored steamed vegetables. Dan watched me as I scooped out and relished the creamy marrow from the bones and then he did the same. "It's delicious!" Dan said.

We ate, talked, and looked into each other's eyes with each bite we took. The dessert was odd: for him, a piece of chocolate cake, which looked a lot like a shrunken brownie, and mine was a ten-inch oval platter piled high with fresh fruit stuffed with sherbet. "I have never seen anything so spectacular," I said to him. "How come you are only having a little piece of chocolate cake?"

"I thought it was going to be a lot bigger from the way Bianca had described it to me." We laughed.

"Well, there's no way in heaven that I can eat all this fruit and sherbet too. How about you helping me with it?" Gosh, how I hated wasting food. But once again, he was edgy about something and kept saying, "I wonder where the waiter is? I need some more water; I'll be right back." The waiter followed him back and when Dan sat down and looked up at him, the waiter, wearing a noncommittal look, just stared at the large fruit platter. I figured the waiter expected us to finish it, much like the chef who had an emotional breakdown when Al and I were served Crepes Suzette at a restaurant in Estoril, Portugal, and after one bite, Al spit the food out of his mouth and sent the crepes back to the kitchen.

We tried to eat as much as we could, and Dan helped me with several pieces. I ate a mini banana, a plum, and a nectarine, each stuffed with sherbet, but there were still mounds of fruit left. The waiter stood by our table staring at Dan, and Dan was staring at the waiter who kept moving his chin towards the fruit.

"I wonder what that is?" Dan said, pointing to the center of the fruit filled platter where a small, black something seemed to be peeping out between a stuffed mini orange, a stuffed fig, and a stuffed lemon.

"Dan, it's either a decoration piece or it contains some kind of sauce to pour over the fruit. I really can't eat another morsel." My reasoning didn't stop him. He reached over the table and began feverishly burrowing his fingers into my dessert trying to pull out the dark object from deep within the center of the fruit compilation. He reminded me of a nervous squirrel trying to dig up his buried nuts. My goodness, people were now looking in our direction. "I really can't eat another morsel," I announced once again, pushing away the small dessert plate in front of me with the half-stuffed plum. I smiled back at the people staring at us, an apologetic yet condescending smile, as if trying to say, *You see my boyfriend is very young, and as such, he is very curious. And like all kids, he's doing what any normal kid would do, he wants the little toy inside the dessert platter.*

He had finally been able to retract the dark object covered with thick plastic wrap and began fumbling under the tablecloth trying to remove the sticky wrapping. What was his problem? Why was he embarrassing me? Couldn't he see the conspicuous looks from the other diners? I used the small dessert fork to play with my half-stuffed plum, since I didn't know what else to do.

Toy boy

He uncovered the object; it was a small black velour box. "Would you like to look inside?" He put the box in my hands. I nodded and held my breath in anticipation as I tried opening it. The box was frozen shut.

"I'll open it for you." He used the butter knife to wedge it open and then holding the box open in his right hand, he kneeled in front of me. There it was, glistening in all its glory, a gold engagement ring with ten diamonds staring brightly from inside the black velour box.

"Veronica, will you marry me?" I didn't have to look. I knew everyone at all the other tables were watching our every move.

"Oh my God, oh my God, I don't know what to say," I said.

"Does that mean yes? Will you marry me?"

"Yes, I will marry you. Oh my goodness, this is amazing. I never expected this to happen. I must be dreaming."

Everybody in the room clapped as he slipped the ring on my finger and we kissed.

He had not expected the box to be wrapped in Saran Wrap, which was also the reason he didn't know it was hidden under the fruit. They were supposed to put the box on top of the fruit platter, not at the bottom!

The maître d' offered to call us a cab to take us back to the hotel, but we were too overjoyed to sit. We both needed to walk and let out our energy.

Prior to us leaving the US, Dan had asked Ralph for my hand in marriage, out of respect for being my son, he said. I thought that was really sweet and I wondered what he would have done if Ralph had said he did not approve. Even our good neighbor at the apartment complex where we lived, whom we affectionately called Cousin Jodi, had been in on it. They had gone shopping for the ring together and Dan had even "stolen" one of my rings to get the right size. No wonder he didn't want to let go of his luggage when we arrived in Rome! The ring was hidden between his clothes. I had to admit the whole thing had been well planned. I had imagined the worst and suffered for nothing thinking he was almost as crazy as Patrick and that he was deceiving me with Bianca. I felt like such a fool.

Before we left Rome, I hugged lovely Bianca and thanked her for helping Dan with the arrangements at the restaurant.

On the way back to the US, Dan, who had blue eyes and blonde hair got pulled off to the side by the airport security guards and searched before entering the plane. No one bothered with me, even though I have a foreign accent, dark hair, and an olive skin complexion.

I took X-rays of Dan's lower back and upon doing a physical, I diagnosed him with a herniated disc at L5-S1, most likely protruding to the left side.

He was going to need ongoing chiropractic care for the rest of his life because his back had become weak and more susceptible to flare ups due to the kind of job he did as a laborer and heavy equipment operator. Since we were back from Italy, he began seeing Ralph once a week for a manual adjustment of his lower back and that helped him a lot.

Dan became very chiropractic oriented. Whenever he met someone with back problems, he immediately recommended they come to see me or Ralph and he always shared his personal story with them. "They x-rayed my back at Kaiser, then they sent me for an MRI, and then I was seen by a neurologist who did a nerve conduction test, which should be described as needle torture. Finally, after all those tests, they told me I had a herniation at L5-S1. Veronica gave me the same diagnosis simply by running two fingers on the sides of my legs and feet! So why didn't they just do that?" He always followed with a description of the meeting with his medical doctor:

"Mr. Larson, I'm going to prescribe some pain medicine for you."

"Pain medicine? Do you mean narcotics, like Vicodin?"

"Yes, Vicodin or I can prescribe you Oxycodone. It will help you with the pain."

"But doctor, I'm a heavy equipment machine operator. How am I going to do that under the influence of pain drugs? Can you give me something else?"

"Very well, I can prescribe you some anti-inflammatory meds."

"Doctor, isn't it true that one of the side effects of anti-inflammatory drugs is a possible bleeding stomach?"

"If you follow the instructions and take your medicine after eating, you should be alright."

"I already have stomach problems. Can you give me something else to help me with the pain?"

"I can give you a prescription for muscle relaxants."

"Muscle relaxants? My fiancée is a chiropractor and she told me that muscle relaxants could affect the iris of the eyes and mess up my vision. Am I supposed to stop working?"

"I guess I can't do anything to help you with your problem if you are not going to take the medicine you need."

"I was just wondering if there was any medicine that won't affect my job or my health."

"The only thing left to recommend is physical therapy."

"You mean, doing exercises?"

Even though the story was basically true, it seemed to be getting funnier each time I heard it.

Mr. Johnson had lost all his hair from the chemotherapy, but he had not lost his sense of humor. On the way out of our office, last August he put his baseball cap on and said joyfully, "This is the reason hats were invented! See you next month!"

When Mr. Johnson did not show up the following month, I asked Jeannette, our front desk person, not to call. As long as I did not know for sure about Mr. Johnson, he would live forever, in my heart.

Dan borrowed my stethoscope and Ralph's white coat, and I wore my grandmother Rica's long evening dress from the mid 1920's, to go to a Halloween party at David's huge mansion in Portland. David was a member of The International Club. His parties were known for being the "it" place to attend. One room had disco music going and another had an opera singer accompanied by a pianist. The food was catered and as always, there was someone overseeing the food and someone else making sure no one went thirsty. Every room in the house was occupied with wall-to-wall guests. With so many people around, Dan and I lost track of each other. I found him in the hallway against the wall with a Princess on one side and a French Maid on the other. When I approached him, he pulled me close to his side and put his arm around my waist. "I would like to introduce to you my fiancée, Veronica," he announced with a certain disdain towards them.

They smiled and then excused themselves.

"Veronica, you won't believe what this costume is doing for me," he said. "I have never had women coming up to me like this. By looking like a doctor, I'm like a magnet."

"Dan, this is a costume party. They know you're not a 'real' doctor."

"They like what I represent. I've been to many, many parties in my life and I've never been approached like this. Without this doctor's jacket, I'd be invisible."

"That's silly," I said, not quite convinced since he was so obstinate about his previous experiences.

"Remember what happened to us in Rome," he said. "When we got dressed up, people on the sidewalk moved out of our way so we had more space to go by. It's the same here. Society has been taught to respond to what we look like, instead of who we are."

I pointed to Elizabeth dressed as a hooker. "What do you think of her?"

"Well, look at all the guys hanging around her."

I had just learned another lesson in life and I was delighted to pass it on to Joanna, one of my patients, who had been looking for a job without success. She had three interviews on Friday and even though she had lots of experience with computers, she was starting to give up. "Joanna," I asked. "What are you wearing when you go for your job interviews?"

"What I'm wearing now, why?"

I told her what happened to Dan at the Halloween party and emphasized the way she presented herself was going to be the main factor if she got hired. "For a professional job, you must be professionally dressed. If you don't have a styled suit, you need to go shopping today for one."

It was agreed she would go shopping at my favorite thrift shop and get something nice. The whole idea was to make money, not spend it.

On Monday, Joanna called with a dilemma. She wanted to thank me as all three companies had called back and now she had to decide which one she wanted to work for! I told Dan about Joanna and he was very happy for her, but he was still stewing about his experience at the Halloween party.

We had Thanksgiving at our beautiful condo with Dan's friend Richard, Ralph, and Susie, his girlfriend. Dan enjoyed cooking as much as I did and he made his special mashed potatoes with sour cream, fresh garlic, and butter, and I prepared the turkey and stuffed it with chestnuts. I also made roasted peppers and tomatoes which are murder on the fingertips when they need to be peeled still hot from the oven. Dan peeled them for me and even volunteered to cut the carrots for the Moroccan salad, which by now he was addicted to.

Winter 2003

My friend John, who had directed a very successful play for me when I used to produce theatre in New Jersey and who had performed as an actor in several of my productions, was also a lawyer. I called him to ask, "If a parent smokes inside the house without regard for his or her children's health, isn't that considered child abuse?" I gave him a condensed version of a fourteen-year-old who had come to our office for a sports physical. I had done my usual routine exam and when I listened to the boy's chest, his lungs were not clear. I asked him if he smoked or was around smokers in school, because I was concerned it would affect his lungs and his chances to be an athlete. He pointed to his father sitting in the corner of the exam room, reading a magazine, "I don't smoke...but my dad does."

"You smoke, but not inside the house, right?" I said to his father.

He looked up from his magazine and after staring defiantly he said, "My wife and I both smoke, and yes we smoke inside the house."

The boy said softly, "I wish my parents didn't smoke. I really don't want to ruin my lungs."

I felt bad about the situation. "Look," I said to the boy loud enough so his father would hear too. "I'm sure your parents love you, but the truth is that cigarette addiction is very hard to overcome, so until they quit, you have to be understanding and need to stay away from the room where they are smoking. Use your bedroom to escape the secondhand smoke. Close the door, and open the windows if you can, or even better, take a walk outside. In order for you to be a runner, you'll need your lungs at full capacity."

Then I turned to his father, who was still engrossed in whatever it was he was reading, and told him very gently, if he ever wanted to try to quit smoking, I would do my best to help him and his wife. He showed no interest.

John told me there was nothing legal I could do to help that kid or any others. If I were to do anything, I would have lots of parents angry at me. As someone else told me, "What are you trying to do, break families apart?"

That was not my intent. I was simply frustrated at how an adult could negatively affect a child's health and not be held accountable just because they were the parents. But like Nancy's husband, Sean once told me, "Gorillas have babies, but that doesn't make them parents."

Dan and I were busy getting ready for our Jimmy Buffett-style wedding on Saturday, July 12th in Netarts. Our honeymoon trip to Portugal and England would follow in September when Dan could once again take two weeks off from work.

I was still writing to Paula and Artur but our correspondence had slowed down to a grind once again. Paula and her husband were expanding their frozen food business in Europe and when it came to Artur he wasn't writing much, he was too busy getting ready to get married. I had given up on him and *The Mary Celeste,* but since Dan and I would be in Portugal the second week of September, I sent an email to Paula and Artur suggesting we all get together since they lived in the north of Portugal. It had been three years since we started writing to each other, and I looked forward to meeting them. In my heart I was also hoping that once Artur and I got together perhaps we could come to an understanding concerning the truth about the *Mary Celeste.*

We were also planning to visit my family in London, even though my Cousin Max had passed on and I wouldn't be hugging him until it was my turn to join him.

Spring 2003

It was lunchtime and I was alone in the office going over some of my patients' files when a woman came in with a young girl of about eighteen years of age. The woman approached the front desk where I was seated and said in a bit of a pushy manner, "We need to see the doctor. My daughter needs to have her back adjusted immediately."

"I'm the doctor and I can adjust her, but first I'll have to do a physical exam."

"Why do you need to do an exam?"

"I've never seen your daughter before. It's in her best interest I examine her before I decide if I can treat her." I handed the daughter the intake paperwork, but her mother took it from her hand and disregarded most of the questions.

In the exam room, I gave the daughter, Elizabeth, a gown. Her mother took the gown from my hands and said, "What does she need a gown for?"

"I need to look at her back. I'll be back when she's ready." I left the room and closed the door behind me.

I waited about five minutes before I returned. Elizabeth's back from mid thoracic to her waist was seriously bruised.

"What happened to your back?" I asked Elizabeth, who stared at her mother, standing over her.

"Nothing happened. She woke up that way," her mother answered.

She must have thought that I was an idiot to believe such a story. "It looks like someone hit your back with a stick," I said directly to the girl. She began crying.

I left the treatment room and went to get an ice pack.

"No, please, I can't take anymore ice. I've had ice on my back all night already." Elizabeth cried even more.

"So, you did not wake up like this. I'm not going any further with your physical exam. I can hardly touch you; you're in so much pain. I need to take X-rays."

"No!" said her mother. "There's no reason for taking X-rays. She does not need X-rays. What she needs is for you to adjust her back. That's all she needs."

"Your daughter got a beating. Of that I'm sure, and I'm not touching her back until I do X-rays to rule out a fracture."

The argument went on for a while and finally her mother said, "If you're not going to treat her, we're leaving!"

I wrote my home phone number on a piece of paper and slipped it into Elizabeth's hand before they left.

The next morning I called Elizabeth. No answer. I left a message in the answering machine for her to call me if she was in trouble. Then I called the Oregon Chiropractic Board to find out with whom I could get in touch to get help for Elizabeth. I was told that since the girl was eighteen she was considered an adult and nothing could be done unless she sought help on her own.

Thursday, May 8th I received a short email from Artur. "It is late and I will have to write more another day. I just want to give you your birthday present:

THE MARY CELESTE IS BEING PUBLISHED THIS SUMMER. I'll write again to talk to you about that, and your trip to Portugal."

I couldn't help myself from reading it over and over again. An initial feeling of joy came over me upon facing its publication, and then an overbearing trepidation took over my senses and I began to cry. Our book was getting published and soon I would have it in my hands, but Artur had made it clear in his emails that he was adding the Maka Edom story and was sticking with it. I turned to Ralph seated by the office's computer next to mine. He reminded me once again that Artur was also the co-author and as such he had the right to add anything he wanted to it even if he was lying about the story being given to him by Maka-Edom.

Mrs. Haylee, my patient, had been taken to the hospital for a stomach problem, but after three days, she developed one of her migraine headaches. Her husband called the office to see if I would consider coming to the hospital to adjust his wife's neck. I went to see her during my lunch break. When I arrived, her family was expecting me. We waited for the nurse to leave the room and then Mr. Haylee stood outside by the closed door to her private room to make sure nobody would come in. We figured the staff at the hospital would flip out if they saw me adjusting one of their patients.

I got a call from Mrs. Haylee the next morning. Since her headache was gone, and her stomach was no longer hurting, she discharged herself from the hospital the night before.

Mary, my seventy-nine-year-old patient whom I had been treating for a little more than a year, presented to my office one morning with serious apprehension. "My doctor told my husband I'm developing signs of Alzheimer's. But I'm fine, I feel fine. This is horrible to tell me such a thing. I'm so scared."

I guided her to a chair, put her seeing-eye cane against the wall and sat next to her. I held her hands. "Mary, the doctor is the one with Alzheimer's; you have lost your eyesight and that's all that's wrong." She smiled and we hugged each other and then I guided her to the adjusting table to adjust her spine. She had lost most of her eyesight about the time her daughter had been murdered by her son-in-law, ten years ago. He was still in jail, but that didn't bring her daughter back. Before leaving the room she said, "I'm afraid John might listen to the doctors and they'll put me in a home. You're the only friend I have. Please don't let them take me away."

"I promise to look out for you the best I can." I gave her my cell number and put it in her hand. "This is my number. Have someone call me, if they try to take you away."

Why did some people have to suffer so much through their lives? She always came in with a smile and she had such a positive attitude. But I knew in my heart that when she was home she had to be depressed. Losing her child, and then having to live in the dark for the rest of her life would put anyone way down. John took me to one side and told me he was worried about her. They were the nicest couple I knew and it broke my heart to see them at such a horrible crossroads in their lives.

I was a bit surprised to find a lot of my patients had scoliosis. Some had no symptoms; others where the curvature had increased severely over a short time were suffering from an array of health issues like chronic pain, difficulty breathing, and muscle spasms. After my experience with someone I met at a health fair where she had done nothing proactive to help with her curvature and then had to have back surgery at the age of fifteen, I decided it was my obligation not to sit back and watch my own patients go through the same ordeal. No patient of mine was going to come to my office and not get motivated to do specific exercises for the spine, learn about other options of treatment, and try to reverse their curvature with chiropractic adjustments.

The first time I had Breyers ice cream it felt like a religious experience. It tasted just like the old-fashioned ice cream I loved as a child. Even though Dan and I loved pistachio ice cream, when it came to Breyers, I always had the strawberry flavor and Dan went for vanilla and chocolate. Most of the time we ate it plain, but sometimes I liked to add fresh chopped almonds and poured Portuguese Port wine over it. Dan felt Port wine was best enjoyed in its own merit and sipped slowly. "Serving Port wine over ice cream is sacrilegious," he would say. But when we had guests for dinner that's the dessert I served most of the time. "Wow, this is the best ice cream I ever ate," said Richard, Dan's friend. "What did you put on it besides the almonds?"

"Portuguese secret recipe!" I said, and winked at Dan.

I had a lot of Hispanic patients because of Mario, a patient I had treated a year ago. If he knew someone who had been in a car accident, he immediately referred them to my office. The reason I could tell he referred them to me was because they always said, "Doctor, please take an X-ray of my neck and make sure it's not broken like it happened to Mario."

Mario had been stopped at a stop sign when he got rear-ended by another car, which according to him, was most likely going at about 45 mph.

After the accident, Mario was taken to the hospital but they sent him home after diagnosing him with sprained neck muscles and prescribing meds for pain.

Three days later, his neck pain got worse and he went back to the hospital. They took X-rays of his neck and confirmed he was suffering from muscle sprain and should continue to take the meds for pain. On the advice of one of his friends who happened to be one of my patients, he came to see me. I told Mario I needed to look at the X-rays taken at the hospital before I could treat him. He said he would be right back and left. He returned two hours later with the films. I looked at the X-rays on the view box and left the treatment room to call the radiologist I worked with.

"I could be mistaken," I told the radiologist but I'm looking at an anterior to posterior open mouth cervical view of a patient rear-ended about a week ago and it shows a serious large gap on one side in comparison with the other, as if nothing is holding the top vertebra in place. Any advice?"

"Take two more anterior to posterior open mouth views," said the radiologist, "one with lateral flexion to the left and the other view to the right side. That should show you if there is any serious instability of the neck."

I did the X-rays as I was told. There was no question in my mind, I fitted Mario with a neck brace and sent him to an orthopedic surgeon.

It was confirmed with an MRI that same evening that he needed neck fusion to save his life. The next day he had neck surgery.

I didn't say anything, but I wondered if Mario as an American would have won a suit against the hospital for misdiagnosing his condition. It was also too bad that he didn't see a lawyer, as the insurance company only gave him $30,000.

Summer 2003

Thursday June 26th Artur wrote me a five-page email. After writing back and forth with him for so many years I was very aware of his style when he was getting ready to say something he could not say unless he went around and around first. He discussed philosophical statements about life and the meaning of religion and his unselfish acts for others less fortunate. Of course he talked of his newest sacrifice for his new wife whom he had married by proxy, but for whom he was going beyond the limits of hardship, staying up nights trying to solve the issues at hand and traveling by train back and forth from Felgueiras to Lisbon. Then he went on and on regarding his feelings for me with the purest friendship that had ever existed in his life. Weird, but suddenly he reminded me of a certain theatre director who had worked for me in New Jersey and who would go into lengthy melodramatic behavior just to get his way. I skipped the next paragraphs of his usual blah blah blah and finally found the word *Mary Celeste,* as it was all I was interested in. He knew Dan and I were going to Portugal in September and that I was looking forward to launch the book with him but he didn't seem to want me to be part of the book launching. "I don't know if you are still interested in coming over," he wrote, "since the book launching will not be where I live and besides the book will be ready next week and is being launched at the Felgueiras library, July 18th, as it will coincide with the celebration of Felgueiras becoming a city and the new president has requested the book be launched on such an occasion. I know you told me you're getting married July 12th so I can send you a copy of our book and then you can have it as proof of our friendship and my gratitude for being in my life in a time that was very difficult for me." Then he jumped off the subject to, "I have horrible news to give you, mostly for me. My friend, the one I told you about who took on a prominent position in the counsel of the Municipal Chamber of Felgueiras, was caught appropriating funds from the government. Myself as a municipal counselor for six years, I know that in order to do what's right sometimes one has to deviate away from the law. This is something that is perfectly normal in the government, everyone does it, and I felt terrible she had to run away to Brazil so she would not be prosecuted in Portugal." Then he shared the news about another book he had written called *Os Olhos de Lidia Jorge* (The Eyes of Lidia Jorge) and he would like to send me the manuscript so I could make some suggestions.

One book had been more than enough for me. I was not sorry I had written *The Mary Celeste*. If anything, it had brought me up to par with my language, it provided me a creative outlet, and it promoted my interest in pursuing my writing career. Dan and others convinced me to translate my Portuguese diaries to English since they found some of my stories funny and sometimes moving. Also because they had been following my writing process with *The Mary Celeste*, they couldn't wait to read it in English.

I agreed with them wholeheartedly about *The Mary Celeste*. Once Artur published it in Portuguese, it was my intention to surprise him by doing the translation, and after taking out the Maka-Edom chapters, because as a co-author I had the same rights as him, I would add more to the story and send it to an American publishing company.

Dan and I were invited to a friend's birthday party. Jan's house was full of guests, mostly people from the International Club. While standing by the living room entrance, I was talking to three other single women and the subject at hand was romance.

"I like to believe in love at first sight even though I have never experienced it myself," said Leslie.

"Oh that stuff doesn't exist. It's only in Hollywood movies," Dayna remarked.

"I'm like Leslie," said Linda. "I would give anything to see a handsome man across the room looking at me." She closed her eyes momentarily as if envisioning the scene. "Our eyes meet and we fall madly in love with each other." We all giggled except Dayna who said, "You girls are living in a dream world!"

Across the room I saw Dan talking to Jan and her husband. On behalf of love, I had to intervene.

"Okay, here's the proof. Love lives when eyes meet. You see Dan over there talking to our hosts? Watch what he does when our eyes meet across the room. We don't need words to communicate." I was taking a big chance.

With the three women standing behind me chuckling like schoolgirls, I waited until Dan looked in our direction. Then I perked up my lips, slightly cocked my head to the left side, and batted my eyelashes at him. His response was far from amorous; he shrugged his shoulders at me and shook his head twice as in, "What's wrong?" I had just remembered he absolutely hated when women batted their eyelashes at him; he had told me that a few times. I immediately changed the expression I was trying to project to being just me. I looked at him and smiled. His face took on a question mark reinforced by turning his palms up in the air as if saying, "Yeah? What do you want?" It looked like he excused himself, and then walked up to us. "Did you want something, honey?" he said inquisitively.

I didn't have the courage to tell him I was playing with the myths of passion. "Oh, I was just looking at you and wondering if you tried the potato salad, it's delicious."

"Oh, okay, I'll do that. Thanks for letting me know." And he left to chat with the same couple. The girls stared at me and I felt an obligation to apologize for my excessive expectation. "I confess, I made a fool of myself," I told them. "Dan and I have a great relationship and sometimes I take too much for granted." I sighed while thinking what to say next. "This may sound old-fashioned," I said, perfectly convinced I had found the answer. "A lot of women are now changing their roles in society, but the truth is men are still hunters by nature, and once they catch what they want, they no longer have the need to pursue what's already theirs. If you want a passionate encounter, you need to look for a one-night stand. Otherwise you need to count your blessings and be happy with what you have." They laughed with me.

July 12th came around quickly. Our invitations read: *Potluck to follow immediately after ceremony, live entertainment, beach bonfire, barbecue, and dancing are planned.* **Suggestion tips:** *Bring your favorite potluck, swim trunks, sandals, suntan lotion, shades to protect from the blushing bride, and your own beach chair.* **No presents are being accepted.**

Our wedding list was extensive and we encouraged everyone to sleep over, all ninety-seven guests. There were plenty of tents available at the beach, two story houses were being rented for those willing to share rooms and who weren't as excited about sleeping on the sand, my friend Gisela's house just one block away was also open for grabs—there was plenty of space for everyone. The list included my son Ralph and his girlfriend Susie, and from New Jersey, my son Steve, his wife Diane, and my grandchildren Jacob and Shayna, and my friend John Fraraccio. From California came Nancy, Sean, and Lauren and her boyfriend Mark, and Rod my old buddy and roommate. Rod had become Cousin Jodi's new beau after I introduced them through the internet. From Michigan came Dan's mom, his two sisters, and their whole families. Some of his family drove and others, like his mom, flew in. A few of Dan's coworkers and their families came and so did all our close friends from the International Club, and the Latino Club, my office staff and their families, our naturopath physician, the acupuncturist and his family, and my very special patient Mary who had recently been diagnosed with Alzheimer's, and John, her husband who said they wouldn't miss it for the world. Later on I found out they couldn't find a parking spot and had to drive to the next beach and then walked along the seashore all the way to our gathering; it had taken them two hours. The wedding ceremony was performed on the beach and we were lucky to find a judge willing to travel to Netarts.

Keeping up with the Jimmy Buffett theme, I wore a blue and white flowery sarong that Dan had bought me a year ago at one of the beach shops in Cannon Beach, and a lacy, sleeveless white top I found at a thrift shop in Sherwood. My good luck, I came across some slip-on sandals that just happened to have little blue stones matching the same color blue in my sarong. Brandy, one of my patients who was a seamstress, offered to cut part of my long sarong and use it to make a vest for Dan. And so his vest matched my skirt. He wore white shorts and sandals.

No gifts were accepted unless someone wanted to make us something special. Our neighbor Cousin Jodi made my bridal veil, and decorated it with tiny seashells. Dan's friend Nancy made me a white and pink rose bridal bouquet and a matching lapel pin for Dan. My friend Izildinha, from Brazil, insisted on making the wedding cake—a seven-layer, healthy, carrot cake. In case we ran out of cake, she made two. Our friend Paul filled the back of his pickup with enough wood to create an amazingly huge beach bonfire, which went on through the night. The plan was for everyone to sit around the fire wrapped in blankets or snugging close with their loved ones or both, while roasting s'mores, with the chocolate, marshmallows, and graham crackers provided by the happy bride and groom. Dan's best friend, Kyle, who lived in Washington, brought a bunch of illegal fireworks which lit up the skies as far as the eye could see, making one of our guests from Serbia go into a panic attack and had to be taken away into the house by a friend until all the fireworks had been exhausted. Later in the evening Rodrigo from Brazil said to me, "Don't expect much loving tonight." And then at Dan, "After all is done, believe me man, tonight all you'll want to do is go to sleep." His wife Sara nodded her head up and down, saying, "Yep, Yep!"

I thought that was kind of crude but later on, close to two in the morning when we went to bed, Dan and I fell asleep instantaneously.

The next day everyone who had stayed overnight was served a French breakfast of crepes with cheese, crepes with veggies, crepes with sausages, or crepes with ice cream. There were about six volunteers in the kitchen under Elisa's guidance. Elisa was French. And of course we had more guiltless, wedding carrot cake.

Two weeks later, I received a very distressing call from John, Mary's husband. He had to put Mary in an assisted living facility dedicated to the treatment of people with Alzheimer's. I asked for the address and made plans to visit her on Saturday morning. In the back of my mind, I wanted to believe that Mary was fine and if at all possible, I was ready to take her out of there and bring her home back to her husband. Dan offered to go with me.

Upon entering the residence facility where Mary was being looked after, I recognized the same greasy stagnant-like scent I found when visiting nursing homes. I believe the chemicals they used to clean the floors on a regular basis added a certain astringent effect and my response was a sneeze attack that went on and on until Dan got tired of saying God bless you, and said with one of his cute smiles, "Let me know when you are finished, so I can give you my final blessing."

We were taken to the family room, and we were to wait until a nurse could bring Mary to meet us. An old pine dining room table in the center of the room with old pine chairs all around were all the furnishings present. The walls were naked of any artwork or even someone's picture, the window shades were down, and on both sides hung a brown-looking curtain as if waiting to be donated to Goodwill. There were no flowers, not even the plastic kind. Mary was wheeled in in a wheelchair wearing a safety belt across her chest. "Here we go," said the girl putting on the brakes. "When you're done visiting her," she said, "just stop by the front desk and I'll come and get her."

"You mean Mary?" I asked sarcastically.

Dan remained seated and so did I, staring at Mary. For a few seconds none of us spoke. She had aged, and her long dark hair had been cut short, very short. She looked straight at me, with a blank expression. Her hands, clasped together on her lap, shook ever so slightly; the only sign I took that Mary was alive inside the sitting corpse. I got up and put my hand on one of her shoulders, "Mary, how are you?" She did not answer. Stupid me, how was she supposed to know who was talking to her? I bent down and put my arms around her and spoke into her ear, "I'm Veronica, your chiropractor, remember me?" She remained expressionless. I tried her other ear, "Hi Mary, I'm Dr. Veronica, your chiropractor. I am here to see how you are doing." I kissed her face on both cheeks and then said, "I miss you." I stroked her hair gently. She moved her head forward and put it on my chest, but her hands remained on her lap. We stood like that for a while. She did not speak. I moved away and said, "Is there anything I can do for you? Is there anything you need?" She did not speak, only stared; she stared straight ahead with the same blank expression.

"I don't think she knew I was there," I said, trying to contain my tears when I got into the car.

"You're wrong," Dan said. "She knew very well it was you. Why do you think she laid her head on your chest?"

"She was saying good-bye?" It was not a question. I cried louder.

~ Chapter Seventeen ~

Artur's Deception

Tuesday, August 19th I received an email from Artur. He wrote, "You won't believe how busy I've been, just want to let you know the book launching was a huge success. Many of my political friends attended the event. I already sent you the book by mail but it looks like you have not received it. In relation to the book, I had told you a long time ago I intended to use our names (yours and mine) as authors, but I found out it can't be done due to taxes. Since you are not a resident of Portugal, it would be very complicated. I would have to register you as contributor and as such you would be obliged to make yearly declarations of moneys received and that would be complicated and embarrassing. Therefore I had to opt to put my name only, but inside I made an author's notification which clarifies the participation and the help you gave me to finish *The Mary Celeste*." Then, he followed with one and a half pages on how to get to his house when Dan and I came to Portugal on our honeymoon and he was looking forward to meeting Dan and me on September 4th.

I read and re-read his email completely dumbstruck. But in all fairness I had to find out if what he was saying was true, and I immediately sent a copy of Artur's email to my friend Paula, who told me she would show it to a Portuguese lawyer. Meanwhile, she advised me to call the Portuguese Society of Authors in Lisbon, Portugal, and see what they had to say.

I spoke directly to the director of the Portuguese Authors Society and read Artur's last email of August 19th to Mrs. Sousa. She said what he had written to me was not true. I was devastated with the news and told her I had copies of the emails Artur had written asking me to write *The Mary Celeste* with him as co-authors. She said what he had done was called plagiarism and as such they would like to know his name and go after him for fraud. They felt very strongly about it. I told them I would call back with his name, address, and phone number, and copies of his emails would be faxed to the Authors Society so they could read them and then help me to proceed charges against him.

August 25th, I received a fax from Paula. She had spoken to a lawyer and it was confirmed, Artur was a liar. There was no reason for him not to put my name as co-author except to take full credit for what I had written. The lawyer she knew had told her he could help me to proceed charges against Artur and we could meet at his office when Dan and I went to Portugal in September. Paula invited us to stay at her house and said the lawyer's office was not too far from where she lived. She was told since I had copies of Artur's emails, and the original manuscripts, I had a good case to legally have his name removed as the author, because it was a clear case of fraud.

Mary Celeste arrived in the mail a week later. I was trembling when the mailman handed me the thick envelope. Nancy and Sean were visiting me from California. They sat on the coach next to me. I opened the envelope slowly and pulled out a blue covered book with a sketch of a ship. Below it I read, Mary Celeste the True Story by Artur Barros. Next page, Author, Artur Barros. Editor, Artur Barros. Next page was a handwritten dedication, *To Veronica, with my love and a kiss, Artur Barros 2003-08-12.* Next page, Author's Note, "I wanted this book to be my first one but due to several problems I encountered along the way, I had to finish it as my third book. Also due to spending a serious amount of investigation into the facts and realizing the intricate work of the story, I was forced to put it aside while waiting for a conclusion. In reference to that, it is my dear friend Veronica Esagui an American/Portuguese doctor, a true woman in arms, multifaceted, wonderful person that came along as a friend to give me some of her support and effort to the final part of my book. The fact that I decided to publish this work before any others should be interpreted as a homage absolutely prioritized and sincere to such a great friend, owner of a great heart as big as the Universe."

"What a kiss ass!" I said to Nancy and Sean. "The thought of him putting my name in his Author's Note as his friend makes my skin crawl." He was nothing but a disgraceful crook who masterminded the whole thing and who used me right from the beginning of our "relationship." How could he even sleep at night knowing he had stolen my work?

Suddenly everything was coming at me from all directions, like his involvement in politics, and defending the woman who had been caught stealing funds but in his judgment it was okay since in order to achieve what one needs to do, it is okay to stray a little from the law. Those had been his words, the words of a man without ethics.

"Basically all those years he was doing the same to me, using me to his benefit," I said. "I believed I was working with someone I could trust. I'm so confused. I don't know what to do. Part of me says let it be, it's ruining my health and making me a nervous wreck. Look, look at my hands shaking! I haven't been sleeping well either. Then part of me says, sue the crook and take him for everything he has but then that other part says, screw it, it's not worth it. What do you think?" I stared at Sean.

Sean was studying to be a psychologist but he had a natural gift for giving advice. "Veronica you must follow what feels right to you," he said. "You need to evaluate what's most important to you."

I thought about it for about two minutes and that was enough for me. The next morning when I got to my office I sent an email to Artur stating he had lied to appropriate my work. Since the book was more important to him than our friendship, everything was over between us including my intention of translating our book to English, which had been my intention. I finished with, "Our friendship is over, forever."

I received an email from Artur the next day. He was sorry about what he had done and was also guilty of doing the same to others that had meant so much in his life and then to his regret lost them forever. He said he had been the one that had published the book and as such he promised to remove the other few copies he still owned from the market. He finished the email by apologizing once again in his melodramatic tone so typical of him and begging me to remain his friend.

I had no intention of ever answering his email.

~ *Chapter Eighteen* ~

My Redemption

When Dan came home from work, he felt that while we were in Portugal, we should hire the Portuguese lawyer and sue Artur to the full extent of the law. But I didn't want to mar our honeymoon with stress and anxiety. He finally agreed to let bygones be bygones and move on with our lives in a more positive manner. Once we returned from our honeymoon trip, I would start translating my diaries to English and Dan and I would continue to live happily ever after just like in the romance stories I had read when I was a teenager growing up in Portugal.

Artur had been a manipulator and a deceiver of the worse kind but he had given me a very precious gift, the confidence to write in either Portuguese or in English. I also realized that life with its multiple ups and downs and diversified experiences is what gives us the fulfillment and courage to recognize the growing changes within ourselves, and once we open our hearts and allow such changes, we become complete. I promised myself to carry on and try my best to share such knowledge with my patients, my family, and my friends.

I took the clay pot gift from the coffee table at home and put it where it should be, next to my computer on my desk at Gentle Care Chiropractic.

Then I prayed that the lady in the black coat who shared her gift of love with me had found what she was seeking and that her life was as happy as mine.

Happily ever after

Books by Dr. Veronica Esagui

The Scoliosis Self-Help Resource Book — Includes the illustrated step-by-step approach to TESP (The Esagui Scoliosis Protocol), a very specific group of exercises for the spine. With this book, a person with scoliosis will discover that there are other alternatives besides drugs or surgery. As Dr. Esagui says, "If I can shed some light onto scoliosis management that is more proactive than waiting under observation, then patients will understand their options and I will have done my best as a chiropractor and educator."

Veronica's Diary Series:
Veronica's Diary — The Journey of Innocence (1944-1962)
Describes in the most candid manner the first eighteen years of Veronica's life growing up in Portugal, until a pre-arranged marriage with her cousin brings her to the USA in 1962.

Veronica's Diary II — Braving the New World (1962-1988)
Follows her Americanization and trail blazing accomplishments as a music teacher, performer, news reporter, owner of three music centers, playwright, theatre director, producer and owner of the only American dinner theatre in the world in a Japanese restaurant.

Veronica's Diary III — Awakening the Woman Within (1988-1994)
Her children are now grown. Her ex-husband is still her friend, but her lovers don't fit the model of the romance novels she read as a young girl.

Veronica's Diary IV — Angels Among Us (1994-1996)
Experiencing the darkest days of her life, Veronica is thankful for the angels along her path, some of whom were still exorcising their ghostly past as they strived to earn their wings.

Veronica's Diary V — The Gift (1996-2003)
A stranger follows Veronica into a supermarket and hands her a small piece of pottery, insisting the gift is meant only for her. She accepts it. Veronica's rich life experiences as a time traveler have finally taught her to recognize that her quest for happiness has been granted.

Other works:
Aged to Perfection, a comedy play written by Dr. Veronica Esagui and Linda Kuhlmann, was sponsored by Fertile Ground and performed at Lakewood Center for the Arts, 2014.

Mary Celeste: The True Story (2003)
This book is only available in Portuguese. Even though it was written in collaboration with Artur Barros and published in Portugal, her collaborator took full credit for writing the entire book. A detail of his plagiarism and pilfering scheme is addressed in *Veronica's Diary V — The Gift.*

For information on upcoming events, book clubs, interview requests, and comments please visit the author at:
www.veronicaesagui.net or email to Handson13@hotmail.com

CPSIA information can be obtained
at www.ICGtesting.com
Printed in the USA
FSOW01n1822270317
32230FS